ULTIMATE BIBLE GUIDE

THE BIBLE

A BOOK-BY-BOOK OVERVIEW

KENDELL H. EASLEY

REFERENCE

NASHVILLE TENNESSEE

Ultimate Bible Guide
© 2018 by Holman Bible Publishers
Nashville, Tennessee
All rights reserved

Maps © 1998 by Holman Bible Publishers
Nashville, Tennessee
All rights reserved

ISBN 978-1-4627-7663-4

Dewey Decimal Classification: 220.07
Subject Heading: BIBLE—STUDY

Unless otherwise indicated, all Scripture passages are taken from the Christian
Standard Bible® (CSB)
© Copyright 2017 by B&H Publishing Group. All rights reserved.

Typesetting and design by 2/K DENMARK, Højbjerg, Denmark

Printed in China

5 6 7 8 9 10 • 24 23 22 21 20

INTRODUCTION

The Bible is both a book—the world's best-selling book—and a library of 66 books. The impact of the Bible on Western civilization is enough to spark anyone's curiosity about its content.

Victor Hugo, author of *Les Misérables*, observed, "England has two books, the Bible and Shakespeare. England made Shakespeare, but the Bible made England."

Immanuel Kant, one of the world's most influential philosophers, said, "The Bible is the greatest benefit which the human race has ever experienced. . . . A single line in the Bible has consoled me more than all the books I ever read besides."

President John Quincy Adams treated the Bible as the key educational resource in the lives of his children: "So great is my veneration for the Bible that the earlier my children begin to read it, the more confident will be my hope that they will prove useful citizens to their country and respectable members of society."

A number of years ago, 1,200 university presidents and 1,000 CEOs were asked to name the book that had most affected their lives. The Bible was by far the most influential book in this survey of leaders. One in four listed the Bible as the most important book in their lives. The second book on the list—Charles Dickens's *A Tale of Two Cities*—was named as the most influential book by one in twenty-five.

In their classic *How to Read a Book*, Mortimer Adler and Charles Van Doren noted, "It would be true to say that, in the European tradition at least, the Bible is the book in more sense than one. It has been not only the most widely read, but also the most carefully read, book of all."

The *Ultimate Bible Guide* is designed for those just beginning their study of this amazing book. The Bible is daunting just because of its size. More than that, it was written in times and cultures very different from our own. We are all like the Ethiopian official, riding along in his chariot reading the prophet Isaiah.

Philip approached him and asked, "Do you understand what you're reading?" He replied, "How can I . . . unless someone guides me?" (Acts 8:30-31).

This *Ultimate Bible Guide* walks with you through the Bible—book by book—and provides a concise overview of each book beginning with

- **Key Text**: a verse that gives a clue to the meaning of the book
- **Key Term**: summarizes the book in one word
- **One-Sentence Summary**: shows how this particular book relates to God's story. Fuller explanation of this summary is found in the section **GOD'S STORY**

The *Ultimate Bible Guide* then looks at how that particular book of the Bible contributes to and shapes a Christian's worldview. Twelve themes that make up a *Christian worldview* are as follows:

God; creation; sovereignty and providence; faith and reason; revelation and authority; humanity; rebellion and sin; covenant and redemption; community and church; discipleship; ethics and morality; and time and eternity.

For each book, the *Ultimate Bible Guide* indicates which of those themes are present in significant ways. It then

- God
- Creation
- Sovereignty and Providence
- Faith and Reason
- Revelation and Authority
- Humanity
- Rebellion and Sin
- Covenant and Redemption
- Community and Church
- Discipleship
- Ethics and Morality
- Time and Eternity

addresses the questions of *Author and Date of Writing, First Audience and Destination,* and the *Occasion* that prompted its being written.

The 66 books of the Bible are made up of numerous genres. Knowing the type of literature of a particular text is an important step in interpreting the Bible. The *Ultimate Bible Guide* addresses the *Literary Features* of each book.

The great reformer Martin Luther found Christ in the Scriptures, first in Romans and then in Psalms. As a result, he came to the view that the center of all Scripture is Christ. "The Scriptures begin very gently, and lead us on to Christ as a man, and then to one who is Lord over all creatures, and after that to one who is God. So do I enter delightfully and learn to know God." Following Luther's cue, each chapter in the *Ultimate Bible Guide* has a feature called:

✝ CHRIST IN . . .

While the *Ultimate Bible Guide* is designed for those who are just beginning their journey with the Bible, it will serve well those who have considerable experience with this book. Pastors and experienced Bible teachers will be acquainted with much of the material in this book, but the way the material is configured may provide new perspectives as they teach and preach.

At the beginning of our journey with the Bible, it's helpful to summarize, to compress a lot of information into some bite-size statements. In fact, we can summarize the entire Bible in the following sentence:

> *The Lord God through his Christ*
> *is graciously building a kingdom of redeemed people*
> *for their joy and for his own glory.*

Notice that there is one subject (*the Lord God*—it's his story) and one agent (*Christ*—the one actively bringing about God's story). There is one major activity (*building a kingdom*, the main theme of Scripture) and one object of that activity (*redeemed people*, the center of God's mighty acts in both Testaments). There are also specific goals for God's story (*their joy*—the human goal; *his own glory*—the ultimate divine end for everything). When we keep this central truth before us, everything in Scripture falls into place as a development of this single concept. This is not just a story that you read about and put the book down. It's a story in which you are a participant. That's exciting!

Think of the biblical narrative as something like a modern novel. There is a *prologue*, giving background information that helps make sense of the plot. Then there is the plot development in a number of chapters. In the biblical narrative, the story develops in *six chapters* that take the account from beginning to culmination. Then finally at the end is an *epilogue*, telling what happens after the main story has ended.

PROLOGUE: THE NEED FOR REDEMPTION
(Genesis 1–11)

It all begins by explaining why the story must be told. God is building a kingdom of redeemed people because human beings are rebels who cannot save themselves. Other religions begin by assuming that people can do enough good works or perform enough religious deeds to earn a place in heaven. The Bible starts by telling the opposite story. Genesis 1–11 belongs to real human history, but the events are almost impossible to date. The main thing about the prologue is that it describes events involving the entire human race and shows that humanity has rebelled against God from the beginning.

CHAPTER 1: GOD BUILDS HIS NATION
Israel Chosen as the People of Promise, ca. 2000–931 B.C.
(Genesis 12–1 Kings 11; 2 Chronicles 9)

The first chapter in God's plan to build an everlasting kingdom was to build an earthly nation in a particular time and place. This chapter carries the plot from the first family he called to his covenant (Abraham and Sarah) to the full splendor of the Israelite nation at its grandest expression (under David and Solomon).

CHAPTER 2: GOD EDUCATES HIS NATION
Disobedient Israel Disciplined, ca. 931–586 B.C.
(1 Kings 12–2 Kings 25; 2 Chronicles 10:1–36:21;
Some Prophets)

The second chapter in God's plan was to educate Israel about the consequences of sin. The Israelites compromised by worshiping other gods during the entire time they were in the land. God raised his prophets to urge people to repent of idolatry and injustice, to warn of the coming "day of the LORD" in judgment. They also predicted the coming of the Messiah. Their message was largely ignored. This chapter carries the plot from the division of the nation (because of sin) to its destruction (because of sin).

CHAPTER 3: GOD KEEPS A FAITHFUL REMNANT
Messiah's Space and Time Prepared, ca. 586–6 B.C.
(Ezra through Esther; Some Prophets)

Chapter 3 in God's story is the "quiet chapter." Outwardly, it appeared that God was doing nothing for more than five centuries. For those who read the story carefully, however, he was doing two important things. On one hand, God was keeping the Jews together as a nation. They had their own land, laws, and temple, even though the kingship and national independence had disappeared. God was preparing to send his Son at just the right time (Gal. 4:4). On the other hand, God scattered most Jews throughout the nations to be testimonies to his name. By building synagogues to preserve their religious and ethnic identity, these Jews were often the starting point for proclaiming the message that the promised Messiah had come. This chapter carries the plot from the Babylonian captivity until the birth of the Messiah.

CHAPTER 4: GOD PURCHASES REDEMPTION AND BEGINS THE KINGDOM
Jesus the Messiah, 6 B.C.–A.D. 30
(Matthew, Mark, Luke, and John)

The fourth chapter in God's plan to build an everlasting kingdom of redeemed people is the most important one of all—the four Gospels. It shows how God's unconditional covenant promises—first to Abraham, then to David—were fulfilled by the new covenant of Jesus. This chapter carries the plot from the birth of the Messiah to his resurrection and exaltation.

CHAPTER 5: GOD SPREADS THE KINGDOM THROUGH THE CHURCH
The Current Age, A.D. 30–?
(Acts and the Epistles)

With chapter 5 in God's story, we come to our own part of the story. We belong here. This is the period of the Great Commission, when God's plan no longer focuses on people of one ethnic group in one place (Israel). He is now redeeming people out of every ethnic group in every place. Wherever God's people are, they meet as churches, worshiping communities of the new covenant. From Pentecost until the end-time scenario unfolds, God is about the business of spreading the message of the kingdom through the church.

CHAPTER 6: GOD CONSUMMATES REDEMPTION AND CONFIRMS HIS ETERNAL KINGDOM
(Revelation 1–20; Other Scriptures)

In chapter 6, God's plan to build an everlasting kingdom of redeemed people through his Christ for their joy and for his own glory is fully realized. Although students often disagree in interpreting the details of this chapter, the main points are clear. There will be violent hostility against God's people in the end times. Yet God will prevail through the personal, bodily, glorious return of Jesus. When he returns, the world's kingdoms will become the kingdom of Christ forever under his visible rule. This chapter carries the plot from the opening of "the day of the LORD" to the final judgment.

EPILOGUE: NEW HEAVEN AND NEW EARTH
(Revelation 21–22)

The kingdom of God will last forever. God's people will be filled with everlasting joy. God's glory will be magnified as his redeemed people fully enjoy him forever, without any taint of evil. This is visualized in the last two chapters of Revelation that describe a new heaven and new earth. The people of God are compared to a great and glorious city, as well as to a wonderful bride. God's servants will reign with him forever and ever, and they will serve him gladly, clearly beholding his face. The epilogue to God's story shows a brief glimpse of the glory that will be. The end of the story in time is only the beginning of the story in eternity, for *the Lord God through his Christ has graciously built a kingdom of redeemed people for their joy and for his own glory.*

May this book provide a growing understanding of the Bible and help you experience the abundant Life it reveals.

CONTENTS

GENESIS
THE FIRST BOOK OF MOSES

The English title is based on the name given by the Greek translators of this book in the second century B.C. The name could be translated "source" or "generation." The original Hebrew title is simply the first word of the book, *Bereshith*, "In the Beginning."

○ KEY TEXTS: 1:1 AND 12:3

"In the beginning God created the heavens and the earth."

"I will bless those who bless you, I will curse anyone who treats you with contempt, and all the peoples on earth will be blessed through you."

○ KEY TERM: "BEGINNING"

This book tells the beginning of many things: the creation of the world, the origin of the human race and marriage, the rise of sin and death. The book also shows the beginning of God's glorious plan to build a kingdom of redeemed people.

○ ONE-SENTENCE SUMMARY

The God who created humankind and punished disobedience with death began his great plan of redemption with his covenant to Abraham, whose descendants arrived in Egypt as God's cherished people.

A reconstruction of the ark Noah built. The dimensions of the ark made it eminently seaworthy. The vessel in the *Epic of Gilgamesh*, a Mesopotamian account of the flood that has some parallel to Noah's, is a cube. Such a vessel would have rolled over at the slightest disturbance.

GOD'S MESSAGE IN THE BOOK

Purpose

Genesis lays the historical and theological foundation for the rest of the Bible. If the Bible is the story of God's redemption of his people, Gen. 1–11 tells why redemption is necessary: humans are rebels, unable to redeem themselves. Further, Gen. 12–50 shows the steps God initiated to establish a redeemed people and to make a way for the Redeemer to come. He did this through his unconditional covenant with Abraham, Isaac, and Jacob and with his providential care through Joseph's life. God's people who study Genesis today should view it with this original purpose in mind.

Christian Worldview Elements

Genesis deals particularly with the worldview categories of *God*; *creation*; *humanity*; *rebellion and sin*; and *covenant and redemption*. No Bible book more fully teaches God as Creator and humanity as sinners who cannot save themselves.

- o **God**
- o **Creation**
  - Sovereignty and Providence
  - Faith and Reason
  - Revelation and Authority
- o **Humanity**
- o **Rebellion and Sin**
- o **Covenant and Redemption**
  - Community and Church
  - Discipleship
  - Ethics and Morality
  - Time and Eternity

Teachings about God

Genesis reveals God first as Creator. He is righteous in his commands, and he judges when humankind disobeys him. Genesis further reveals God as the One who makes his covenant with undeserving people (see Gen. 15). The first promise of Christ is given in Gen. 3:15; the Spirit of God is mentioned in Gen. 1:2 and 6:3.

Teachings about Humanity

Genesis shows the glory of humanity by emphasizing that mankind alone of all creation was made in "the image of God." On the other hand, Genesis shows the shame of humanity by recounting three incidents involving the whole race: the fall, the flood, and Babel. All three events portray humans as sinners in need of a Savior.

Teachings about Salvation

Genesis introduces critical truths about salvation developed in later parts of Scripture. In particular, the incident of the death of a ram instead of Isaac points to a substitutionary understanding of sacrifice. Further, the New Testament makes much of Abraham as a pattern of salvation for all the redeemed: "Abram believed the LORD, and he credited it to him as righteousness" (15:6). Genesis 12–50 shows the beginning of God's covenant people.

 CHRIST IN GENESIS

Creation is the first theme of Genesis and Christ is the agent of creation. "For everything was created by him" (Col. 1:16). Christ as Redeemer is first promised in Gen. 3:15. When God commanded Abraham to offer Isaac as a sacrifice, he provided a substitute for Isaac (22:8) in the same way he provided Christ as our substitute through his sacrificial death. Through Abraham's seed, Jesus Christ, all families of the earth will be blessed.

GOD'S STORY

When the Events of This Book Happened:
From creation until Joseph's death (ca. 1805 B.C.)

There is insufficient information to date the events of Gen. 1–11. Using the traditional early date for the exodus, Abraham's birth in Ur was ca. 2166 B.C. and Joseph's death in Egypt was ca. 1805 B.C., an amazing total of some 360 years for four generations. (This was the time of the First Dynasty of Babylon in Mesopotamia and of the Middle Kingdom in Egypt. The Bronze Age had developed by the end of Genesis.)

2166 B.C.	2066	2006	1915	1805
Abraham born	Isaac born	Jacob & Esau born	Joseph born	Joseph dies

How Genesis Fits into God's "Story"

Genesis shows why redemption is needed and presents the first steps in God's bringing a people into right relationship with him. The beginning of God's plan is to bless all nations through the covenant he began with Abraham. Initially that plan focused on Abraham's biological descendants, reaching its geographical zenith during the kingdom of David and Solomon. The greatest descendant of Abraham is Jesus, who inaugurated the kingdom of God at his first coming and will consummate it at his second coming.

ORIGINAL HISTORICAL SETTING

Author and Date of Writing:
Moses, perhaps ca. 1445 B.C.

The book is technically anonymous. On the other hand, according to uniform Jewish and early Christian belief, the first five books of the Bible were written by Moses. Collectively these five books are called the Torah (Hebrew), the

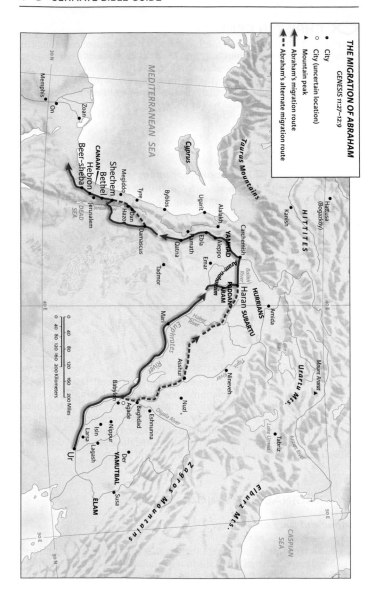

THE MIGRATION OF ABRAHAM
GENESIS 11:27–12:9

- ● City
- ○ City (uncertain location)
- ▲ Mountain peak
- Abraham's migration route
- Abraham's alternate migration route

Pentateuch (Greek), or the Law (English). Both Jesus and Paul affirmed that Moses wrote the Law (John 7:19; Rom. 10:19). Scholars who accept the testimony of Scripture at face value continue to affirm that Moses wrote Genesis.

During the 1800s, most critical scholars abandoned the belief that Moses wrote these books. The influential German scholar Julius Wellhausen presented evidence for a documentary theory (often called "JEDP") for the composition of the Law. This theory argued that the Torah evolved over several centuries and was finally compiled during the time of Israel's kings. Although Wellhausen's theory has been modified over the years, it still dominates scholarly discussions of the origin of the Pentateuch.

The time of Moses's life has been interpreted two ways. Because 1 Kgs. 6:1 notes the time between the exodus and Solomon, the exodus has been dated traditionally ca. 1446 B.C. Others, however, date the exodus ca. 1290 B.C., based on the word "Raamses" (or Rameses) in Exod. 1:11, and the first known occurrence of that name applied to a pharaoh. (See *Exodus* for more information.) Assuming an early date for the exodus and that Moses wrote while Israel camped at Mount Sinai, Genesis was written in the middle of the fifteenth century B.C.

First Audience and Destination:
The Israelites at Mount Sinai
The original hearers and destination are not stated but are believed from tradition. The first audience was the Israelite nation in the wilderness on their way to Canaan.

Occasion

Genesis does not tell what prompted it to be written. Its events occurred centuries before the writer's birth. Although some historical records from the dawn of humanity may have survived for Moses to use as sources, this does not appear likely. If one believes that Moses received the Ten Commandments by divine revelation, then one can just as readily believe that God also revealed to Moses the content of Genesis.

 ## LITERARY FEATURES

Genre and Literary Style:
A historical narrative written in excellent Hebrew
Although Genesis was the First Book of the Law, it recorded relatively few divine commands, some of which are 2:17 and 9:7. Genesis has preserved two historical narratives. Chapters 1–11 contain a selective history of the entire human race. (Other religions have their stories about creation and beginnings, with which Genesis shares certain features. The Babylonian *Gilgamesh Epic*, e.g., contains parallels to the flood narrative.) Chapters 12–50 tell the story of the direct ancestors of the Israelites. Genesis also contains a few passages of

poetry (see 3:14-19) and important genealogies (see chap. 5). The Hebrew style of Genesis is like that of the rest of the Pentateuch. The writer composed his account carefully.

Themes:

Creation, death, flood, covenant, providence

The account of the creation of the world and of humankind in God's image provides the theological basis for the Bible's insistence on human account-

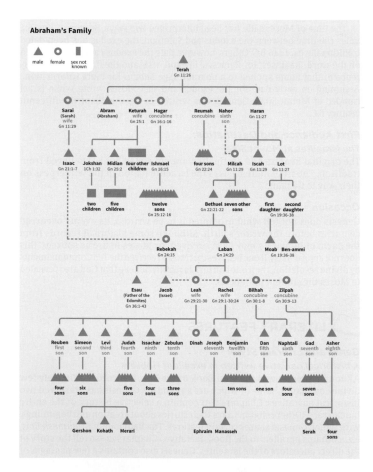

ability to the Creator. The words "and he died," repeated with depressing regularity, show that the fall indeed had the effect God warned about. The flood narrative shows how God judged the race he had created. In God's covenants with Noah and then with Abraham, he reached out in mercy to his fallen human creatures. The last half of the book, notably the story of Joseph, emphasizes God's providential care over his covenant people (see 50:20).

Book Features and Structure

Genesis introduces themes that the rest of Scripture develops. Genesis is necessary to make sense of the rest of the Bible. The author organized chapters 1–11 around four great events: creation, fall, flood, and Babel. Genesis 12–50 has preserved the story of four great men: Abraham, Isaac, Jacob, and Joseph.

The geographical focus shifts from section to section. Chapters 1–11 happened generally in the Fertile Crescent. The action for Abraham, Isaac, and Jacob shifts between Haran and Canaan, while the Joseph story alternates between Canaan and Egypt. Ten times the author uses the Hebrew word *toledot*, translated "records" or "family records." Many scholars view this as a clue to the structure of the book.

The Great Sphinx and the Great Pyramid at Giza, Egypt. Both of these architectural wonders were several hundred years old by the time Jacob and his family moved to Egypt during a time of famine in the Ancient Near East.

EXODUS
THE SECOND BOOK OF MOSES

In the Hebrew text, the book's first two words are its title, *We'elleh Shemot*, "These Are the Names." The English title is the name first used by the book's Greek translators (second century B.C.). *Exodus* could be rendered "going out" or "departure."

⊙ KEY TEXT: 14:30-31

"That day the LORD saved Israel from the power of the Egyptians, and Israel saw the Egyptians dead on the seashore. When Israel saw the great power that the LORD used against the Egyptians, the people feared the LORD and believed in him and in his servant Moses."

⊙ KEY TERM: "REDEEM"

Exodus shows how the Lord for his name's sake redeemed his people Israel by buying them out of slavery through payment of a price, the death of the Passover lambs (see 12:13). Further, it records God's commands to those redeemed people.

⊙ ONE-SENTENCE SUMMARY

When God redeemed his chosen people Israel through his servant Moses, he entered a covenant relationship with them and instituted his dwelling with them, the tabernacle.

Jebel Musa: a traditional site of Mount Sinai where Moses received the law

GOD'S MESSAGE IN THE BOOK

Purpose

Exodus is double pronged. First, it narrates God's greatest redemptive act of the Old Testament, Israel's exodus from Egypt. Second, it recorded many of the laws by which those redeemed people were to live. If the overall Bible tells the story of God's kingdom, then Exodus tells how the first phase of that kingdom came into being by God's mighty power. Moses, of course, is the central human figure as God's agent of salvation. God's people who read and study Exodus today should also view it in light of the ultimate Redeemer who purchased people by his own death (John 1:17).

Christian Worldview Elements

Exodus provides insight on the worldview categories of *sovereignty and providence*; *revelation and authority*; *covenant and redemption*; and *ethics and morality*. No Old Testament book more fully portrays that humans cannot know God unless God reveals himself or that humans must depend wholly on God for their redemption.

> God
> Creation
> ○ **Sovereignty and Providence**
> Faith and Reason
> ○ **Revelation and Authority**
> Humanity
> Rebellion and Sin
> ○ **Covenant and Redemption**
> Community and Church
> Discipleship
> ○ **Ethics and Morality**
> Time and Eternity

Teachings about God

Exodus reveals the Lord as Redeemer. Because of his love and for his name's sake, he takes the initiative to save his people from bondage. Exodus further reveals him as the One who expects his redeemed people to live according to the provisions of the covenant made at Sinai. Christ is prefigured both by Moses and by the Passover lambs. Exodus 31:3 and 35:31 mention the Spirit as empowering a person for special service.

Teachings about Humanity

Exodus highlights the universality of human evil by showing rebellion against God in a variety of ways. Pharaoh's wickedness (chaps. 4–14) and redeemed Israel's shameful idolatry in the golden calf incident (chap. 32) are perhaps the clearest examples. On the other hand, Exodus shows the great value God puts on humanity through the high price paid at the time of Israel's deliverance from Egypt.

Teachings about Salvation

Until Christ's coming and his death on the cross, the exodus was the greatest divine redemptive act. God taught explicitly the substitutionary meaning of the Passover lamb's death: "When I see the blood, I will pass over you" (12:13). This, however, only prefigured the coming One, "the Lamb of God, who takes away the sin of the world" (John 1:29).

 CHRIST IN EXODUS

Exodus is a book of redemption. God's freeing his people from Egyptian slavery is a picture of Christ's delivering sinners from their sin and its consequences. Christ was with Israel as the rock that followed them through their journey from slavery to the promised land (1 Cor. 10:4; Exod. 17:6). The Passover lambs are a picture of Christ's death for sinners (John 1:29,36) and his providing access to God.

 GOD'S STORY

When the Events of This Book Happened:
From Joseph's death through the completion of the tabernacle (ca. 1805–1445 B.C.)

Based on the data in 1 Kgs. 6:1, the date of the exodus has been figured to the middle of the fifteenth century B.C., ca. 1446. This is the traditional and early date for the exodus. Based on this view, the pharaoh who oppressed Israel was Thutmose I, and his son Amenhotep II was the one whom Moses challenged. (This was the time of the New Kingdom, the Eighteenth Dynasty in Egypt.)

Critical scholars understand the data differently, using the name "Raamses" (or Rameses) in Exod. 1:11 as a clue that the Israelites must have been building the new Egyptian capital of that title, named for Rameses I (ruled in the early 1300s). On this view, the pharaoh of the oppression was Sethos I, and Moses challenged his son Rameses II. In this view, the exodus occurred ca. 1290 B.C. (This was the time of Egypt's Nineteenth Dynasty.) The critical view has been widely disseminated in popular culture through influential movies and television. The traditional date, however, remains credible and takes the wording of 1 Kgs. 6:1 (and Acts 13:20) to be reliable.

How Exodus Fits into God's "Story"

In bringing people into a right relationship with him, God determined to make the descendants of Abraham into a true nation. Exodus shows how this happened, beginning with a multitude of disheartened, enslaved Israelites. The book ends with a national identity established through a divinely called leader (Moses) and divinely given laws. The establishment of Israel as a nation prefigures God's great fulfillment of the eternal kingdom over which Jesus reigns forever.

1805 B.C.	1526	1486	1446	1446	1445
Joseph dies	Moses born	Moses flees Egypt	God calls Moses	The exodus	Ten Commandments

ORIGINAL HISTORICAL SETTING

Author and Date of Writing:
Moses, perhaps ca. 1445 B.C.
The book is anonymous. Because Moses is the central character, however, everything in the book is compatible with the traditional belief that he was its author. The book refers to Moses as physically writing down some of God's commands (24:4; see also 34:27). Scholars who accept the testimony of Scripture at face value continue to affirm that Moses wrote Exodus. (See *Genesis* for comments about the critical theory that Exodus was written during the times of Israel's kings.) Assuming an early date for the exodus and that Moses wrote while Israel camped at Mount Sinai, this book was written in the middle of the fifteenth century B.C.

First Audience and Destination:
The Israelite people at Mount Sinai
The original hearers were the children of Israel living in the wilderness on their way to the promised land.

Occasion
Although the book does not say so, the need for Israel to have a permanent historical record of the events that brought it into existence as a nation surely is what prompted the composition. If one believes that Moses received the Ten Commandments by divine revelation, then one can just as readily believe that God also prompted him to write down everything recorded in Exodus.

▶ **CHRONOLOGY FOR EXODUS**

1900	1800	1700	1600	1500	1400	1300
Israel to Egypt			slavery in Egypt		exodus, conquest	

1876   1446

(430 years in Egypt, Exodus 12:41)

 ## LITERARY FEATURES

Genre and Literary Style:
Historical narrative, with some laws, composed in Hebrew
Although Exodus was the Second Book of the Law, it preserved more historical narrative than law. Most of chapter 15, "Israel's Song," is poetry rather than prose and the first extensive poetry in Scripture. The Hebrew style of Exodus is like that of the rest of the Pentateuch.

Themes:
The Lord, plagues, redemption, covenant, Ten Commandments, tabernacle

God's revelation of himself to Moses as the Lord (Yahweh) stands as one of the most profound passages in all Scripture. The famous account of the plagues demonstrates the power of the Lord over the gods of Egypt. The Ten Commandments remain unsurpassed as God's wise rules for living life to the fullest. The importance of the tabernacle is seen in God's solemn pledge about it: "I will dwell among the Israelites and be their God. And they will know that I am the LORD their God, who brought them out of the land of Egypt" (29:45-46).

Book Features and Structure

People of the ancient Near East understood the idea of a covenant agreement between a god and a king (or his people). They also grasped the related notion of a peace treaty between human parties. Many features of the covenant/treaty that God made with Israel at Sinai parallel ancient covenants/treaties discovered by archaeologists. The Sinaitic covenant began with the manifestation of God (chap. 19) and ended with confirmation by blood (chap. 24), with the "Book of the Covenant" stated in chapters 20–23. This was a suzerain-vassal covenant in which the master (suzerain) promised to protect and bless the subjects

Splitting the Sea by Dr. Lidia Kozenitzky (Exod. 14:21-22)

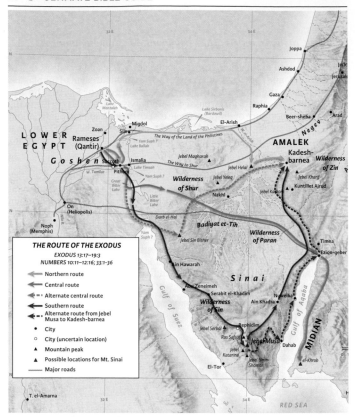

THE ROUTE OF THE EXODUS
EXODUS 13:17–19:3
NUMBERS 10:11–12:16; 33:1–36

← Northern route
← Central route
←-- Alternate central route
← Southern route
←-- Alternate route from Jebel Musa to Kadesh-barnea
• City
○ City (uncertain location)
▲ Mountain peak
▲ Possible locations for Mt. Sinai
— Major roads

(vassals) as long as they obeyed and submitted to him. This contrasted with the "royal grant" unconditional covenant, such as the one in which God categorically promised to make Abraham into a worldwide blessing (Gen. 12; 15).

The life and travels of Moses provide the organizing principle for the book. The action occurs wherever Moses is present. The first half is mainly narrative, chapters 1–18 (Israel's deliverance from Egypt and journey to Sinai) as is the last fourth, chapters 32–40 (Israel's violation of the covenant, the restoration, and the building of the tabernacle). Sandwiched between the historical sections are law chapters 19–24 (the covenant at Sinai) and 25–31 (rules concerning the tabernacle and the priesthood).

LEVITICUS
THE THIRD BOOK OF MOSES

The English title is based on the name given by the Greek translators of this book in the second century B.C. The name could be translated "pertaining to Levites." The original Hebrew title is the first word of the book, *Wayyiqra'*, "And He Called."

○ KEY TEXT: 11:45

"For I am the LORD, who brought you up from the land of Egypt to be your God, so you must be holy because I am holy."

○ KEY TERM: "HOLINESS"

Holiness throughout Scripture, but especially in Leviticus, is first an attribute of God. It refers to his glorious moral perfections as the One who is the standard of ethical purity. Second, holiness is commanded by God to his redeemed people. This holiness includes both moral living (submitting gladly to God's laws) and being separated from common use (intentionally set apart to God and his service).

○ ONE-SENTENCE SUMMARY

God forgives sin and makes people holy through blood sacrifice; further, he then expects his people to live in fellowship with him by following his regulations concerning separated living.

GOD'S MESSAGE IN THE BOOK

Purpose

Leviticus was God's word to Israel to teach two essential truths about how people can sustain a right relationship with God. First, people enter a relationship with God based on forgiveness of sins, obtained by offering the right sacrifices the right way by the right priest. Second, forgiven people maintain fellowship with God by living according to his regulations. This means that his people are separate (and therefore different) from others. The specific laws in Leviticus are both precise and peculiar.

Of all the books of the Old Testament, Leviticus is the most challenging for Christians to apply. First, the New Testament, especially Hebrews, teaches that the right sacrifice offered the right way by the right priest has been truly fulfilled in Jesus, thus rendering Lev. 1–10 obsolete. Second, the entire thrust of the New Testament is that fellowship with God is no longer based on external matters such as circumcision, keeping dietary laws, or following Israel's holy days. Today fellowship with God and holy living are essentially internal. God's people who read and study Leviticus today should remember that its two essential principles are certainly still true, but that God intended its particular rules to be in effect only until Christ came (Gal. 4:24-25).

Plate of pure gold
with inscription:
"HOLY TO THE LORD."
Exod. 28:36

Turban or mitre
Exod. 28:36-38

The shoulder straps for
the breastplate capped
with two onyx stones
bearing the names of
Israel's twelve sons, six on
each, in order of their birth
Exod. 28:9-10

Twelve gemstones,
each bearing a name of
one of the twelve tribes
Exod. 28:17-21

Sash
Exod. 28:4,39,40

Ephod, woven and
reflecting the colors of
the sanctuary
Exod. 28:5-15,31

Fringe composed of
alternating pomegranates
and gold bells; the pomegranates
are woven from blue, purple,
and scarlet yarn
Exod. 28:33-35

Artist's rendition of the high priest's garments (Exod. 28:1-38). Aaron
and his descendants of the tribe of Levi served in the tabernacle and
temple as priests. Their holy garments are prescribed in detail, and their
consecration ritual is given in Exod. 28–29.

Christian Worldview Elements

Leviticus presents the worldview categories of *God*; *covenant and redemption*; *community*; and *ethics and morality*. This book proclaims that God is holy and that his people must live holy lives.

God
Creation
Sovereignty and Providence
Faith and Reason
Revelation and Authority
Humanity
Rebellion and Sin
○ **Covenant and Redemption**
○ **Community** and Church
Discipleship
○ **Ethics and Morality**
Time and eternity

Teachings about God

Leviticus teaches that in his holiness God has the absolute right to instruct his people in what holiness demands, down to the minute details of life. Sinful people may approach him for forgiveness only through the sacrifices he has ordained. The specific sacrifices described suggest the multiple aspects of Christ's atoning sacrifice. The chapters on the priesthood foreshadow Christ's perfections as the ultimate high priest.

Teachings about Humanity

God has made complete provision for forgiving the sins and failures of people, if only they make use of his means. Further, humans can enjoy full fellowship with God, but only if they live according to the way he has revealed. Leviticus teaches that following the commands of a holy God is not only possible as a way of living, but the true way to lasting fulfillment: "Keep my statutes and ordinances; a person will live if he does them. I am the LORD" (18:5). Leviticus also shows how God expected his people to live in community with each other during that era.

Teachings about Salvation

"Blood" occurs more than 60 times in Leviticus. Readers are overwhelmed with the truth that in God's design, blood outpoured through ritual sacrifice is the key to atoning for sins (17:11). This is critical for understanding the necessity of Christ's violent death as the atoning sacrifice for the sins of people. The death of sacrificial animals in ancient Israel may be compared to the modern practice of using credit cards. When Israelites sacrificed an animal, they were truly forgiven—just as when people today use a credit card, they truly receive the merchandise. But, in both instances, a future price is to be paid: on one hand, the credit card bill comes due; on the other hand, the true cost of sin came due and was paid in full through the crucifixion of Jesus.

SACRIFICIAL SYSTEM

NAME	REFERENCE	ELEMENTS	SIGNIFICANCE
Burnt Offering	Lev. 1; 6:8-13	Bull, ram, male goat, male dove, or young pigeon without blemish. (Always male animals, but species of animal varied according to individual's economic status.)	Voluntary. Signifies propitiation for sin and complete surrender, devotion, and commitment to God.
Grain Offering Also called Meal, or Tribute, Offering	Lev. 2; 6:14-23	Flour, bread, or grain made with olive oil and salt (always unleavened); or incense.	Voluntary. Signifies thanksgiving for firstfruits.
Fellowship Offering Also called Peace Offering; includes (1) Thank Offering, (2) Vow Offering, and (3) Freewill Offering	(1) Lev. 3; 7:11-36; 22:17-30; 27	Any animal without blemish. (Species of animal varied according to individual's economic status.) (1) Can be grain offering.	Voluntary. Symbolizes fellowship with God. (1) Signifies thankfulness for a specific blessing; (2) offers a ritual expression of a vow; and (3) symbolizes general thankfulness (to be brought to one of three required religious services).
Sin Offering	Lev. 4:1-5:13; 6:24-30; 12:6-8	Male or female animal without blemish—as follows: bull for high priest on congregation; male goat for king; female goat or lamb for common person; dove or pigeon for slightly poor; tenth of an ephah of flour for the very poor.	Mandatory. Made by one who had sinned unintentionally or was unclean in order to attain purification.
Guilt Offering	Lev. 5:14-6:7, 7:1-6; 14:12-18	Ram or lamb without blemish	Mandatory. Made by a person who had either deprived another of his rights or had desecrated something holy. Made by lepers for purification

CHRIST IN LEVITICUS

The specific sacrifices described in Leviticus (e.g., chap. 16) suggest the multiple aspects of Christ's atoning sacrifice. The chapters on the priesthood (21–22) foreshadow Christ's perfections as the ultimate high priest.

 GOD'S STORY

When the Events of This Book Happened: ca. 1445 B.C.

The only historical events recorded in this book are the consecration of Aaron and his sons as priests and what happened to them next (chaps. 8–10). This all occurred while Israel was still camped at Mount Sinai in the year after their exodus from Egypt.

How Leviticus Fits into God's "Story"

Leviticus continues God's story that began in Exodus: God builds his nation (Israel chosen as the people of promise). It shows that God expected citizens of the earthly nation Israel to live holy lives. How much more does he desire citizens of his heavenly kingdom today to live in holiness. Sanctification is not optional for God's people. The New Testament equivalent is to "live worthy of the calling you have received" (Eph. 4:1).

 ORIGINAL HISTORICAL SETTING

Author and Date of Writing:
Moses, ca. 1445 B.C.

The book is anonymous. But the exact words "the LORD spoke to Moses" occur 27 times in the CSB text. This is one basis for the belief that Moses wrote Leviticus. (See *Genesis* for comments about the critical theory that Leviticus was written during the times of Israel's kings.) Assuming an early date for the exodus and that Moses wrote while Israel camped at Mount Sinai, this book was written in the middle of the fifteenth century B.C. (See *Exodus* for comments about a later possible date for the life of Moses.)

First Audience and Destination:
The Israelite people at Mount Sinai

The first hearers were the Israelites camped around Mount Sinai.

Occasion

Apparently what prompted Leviticus to be written was the need to preserve permanently for Israel the oral commands that God gave to Moses. Even the brief narrative sections deal with the application of God's laws concerning the priesthood.

JEWISH FEASTS AND FESTIVALS

NAME	MONTH: DATE	REFERENCE	SIGNIFICANCE
Passover	Nisan (Mar./Apr.): 14	Exod. 12:2-20; Lev. 23:5	Commemorates God's deliverance of Israel out of Egypt.
Festival of Unleavened Bread	Nisan (Mar./Apr.): 15-21	Lev. 23:6-8	Commemorates God's deliverance of Israel out of Egypt. Includes a Day of Firstfruits for the barley harvest.
Festival of Weeks, or Harvest (Pentecost)	Sivan (May/June): 6 (seven weeks after Passover)	Exod. 23:16; 34:22; Lev. 23:15-21	Commemorates the giving of the law at Mount Sinai. Includes a Day of Firstfruits for the wheat harvest.
Festival of Trumpets (Rosh Hashanah)	Tishri (Sept./Oct.): 1	Lev. 23:23-25; Num. 29:1-6	Day of the blowing of the trumpets to signal the beginning of the civil new year.
Day of Atonement (Yom Kippur)	Tishri (Sept./Oct.): 10	Lev. 23:26-33; Exod. 30:10	On this day the high priest makes atonement for the nation's sin. Also a day of fasting.
Festival of Shelters, or Tabernacles (Sukkot)	Tishri (Sept./Oct.): 15-21	Lev. 23:33-43; Num. 29:12-39; Deut. 16:13	Commemorates the forty years of wilderness wandering.
Festival of Dedication, or Festival of Lights (Hanukkah)	Kislev (Nov./Dec.): 25—Tebeth (Dec./Jan.) 2 or 3	John 10:22	Commemorates the purification of the temple by Judas Maccabaeus in 164 BC.
Festival of Purim, or Esther	Adar (Feb./Mar.): 14	Esth. 9	Commemorates the deliverance of the Jewish people in the days of Esther.

LITERARY FEATURES

Genre and Literary Style:
Ancient laws, with a little narrative, composed in Hebrew

The laws in Leviticus were stated in two forms. First was command law (or apodictic law), often introduced with the formula "you are to . . ." (positive) or "you are not to . . ." (negative). This parallels modern constitutional law or legislative acts. Second was case law (or casuistic law), often using the formula "if a man . . . ." or "if and man and woman . . ." These introduced examples or situations parallel to modern verdicts of judges that become the basis for later judicial rulings. The Hebrew is like that of the rest of the Pentateuch.

Themes:
Holiness, blood, atonement, priesthood, uncleanness, feasts, rules

This chapter has already discussed the first four themes. The issue of "clean or unclean" was not a matter of healthful or unhealthful but rather fit for God's presence or unfit for God's presence. Because God is holy, he has the absolute right to declare what pleases him. The same was true concerning the feasts, whether weekly (such as the Sabbath) or yearly (such as the Festival of Shelters). Many rules in Leviticus had a social dimension, telling how to live in fellowship with fellow human beings. According to Jesus, Leviticus contained the second greatest commandment, "love your neighbor as yourself" (19:18; see Mark 12:31).

Book Features and Structure

Many scholars designate Lev. 17–26 the "Holiness Code" based on the words, "I, the LORD who sets you apart, am holy" (21:8). In Christian theology, some scholars have attempted to divide the laws of Leviticus (and other commands in the Pentateuch) into the categories moral, civil, and ceremonial. Evidence does not support that the people of Israel made these distinctions. The law was a complete entity that stood together, and Leviticus makes the best sense when read in this way.

Leviticus 1–10 recorded laws concerning sacrifices and the priesthood.

Leviticus 11–16 focused on uncleanness in a variety of ways.

Leviticus 17–26 presented laws concerning holy living for the Israelites, ending with a magnificent chapter (26) proclaiming blessings for obedience.

Leviticus 27 originated as an appendix dealing with paying vows and tithes.

"When they came to the Valley of Eshcol, they cut down a branch with a single cluster of grapes, which was carried on a pole by two men. They also took some pomegranates and figs. That place was called the Valley of Eshcol because of the cluster of grapes the Israelites cut there" (Num. 13:23-24).

NUMBERS
THE FOURTH BOOK OF MOSES

The English title is based on the lists of numbers in the book and is the name given by its Greek translators in the second century B.C. The Hebrew title is more apt, *Bemidbar*, "In the Wilderness," a word taken from the opening verse.

○ KEY TEXT: 9:17

"Whenever the cloud was lifted up above the tent, the Israelites would set out; at the place where the cloud stopped, there the Israelites camped."

○ KEY TERM: "WILDERNESS"

This book explains what happened to the Israelites during the 38 years they traveled through the wilderness from Mount Sinai to the border of Canaan. The term "wilderness" appears more than 40 times.

○ ONE-SENTENCE SUMMARY

God used Moses to lead Israel from Sinai to Kadesh, but even after they rejected God there, resulting in the wilderness years, he remained faithful to them and led a new generation to the edge of the promised land.

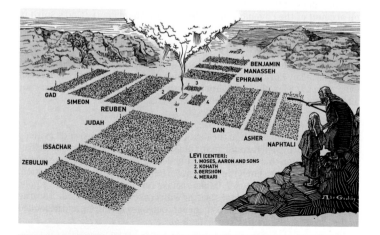

The Lord prescribed a specific arrangement for the Israelites to camp in the wilderness around the tent of meeting (Num. 2).

GOD'S MESSAGE IN THE BOOK

Purpose

Numbers mainly answers the following questions: how did Israel get from Mount Sinai to the border of Canaan? and, why did the journey take so long? The book contrasts God's faithfulness with Israel's disobedience. Ultimately, however, Numbers shows the progress of God's people in moving toward the goals he had promised. Because God accomplished this despite his people's waywardness, he received all the glory. Those studying Numbers today should view it with this original purpose in mind.

Christian Worldview Elements

Numbers deals particularly with the worldview categories of *sovereignty and providence*; *rebellion and sin*; and *covenant and redemption*. This book clearly demonstrates God's sovereign power to accomplish his purposes. He even used a talking donkey.

God
Creation
○ **Sovereignty and Providence**
Faith and Reason
Revelation and Authority
Humanity
○ **Rebellion and Sin**
○ **Covenant and Redemption**
Community and Church
Discipleship
Ethics and Morality
Time and Eternity

Teachings about God

Numbers emphasizes two attributes of God: his sovereign power and his covenant faithfulness. He is faithful to Israel on account of the covenant he made with Abraham (32:11). God's Spirit is present as the One enabling service and inspiring true prophecy (11:25-26; 24:2).

Teachings about Humanity

This book shows how painfully sinful and flawed all humans are. The rebellion at Kadesh led by Korah and the story of Balaam demonstrate this. Moreover, even Moses the lawgiver, to whom God spoke directly, sinned and was not allowed to enter Canaan. Without divine mercy all perish.

Teachings about Salvation

Exodus (redemption through the death of the Passover lambs) and Leviticus (forgiveness provided through many blood sacrifices) teach more extensively about salvation than Numbers. The incident concerning the brass serpent on the pole, however, shows the centrality of faith in receiving God's provision: "Then the LORD said to Moses, 'Make a snake image and mount it on a pole. When anyone who is bitten looks at it, he will recover.' So Moses made a bronze snake and mounted it on a pole. Whenever someone was bitten, and he looked at the bronze snake, he recovered" (21:8-9).

CHRIST **IN NUMBERS**

Christ is foreseen both as the water-giving rock (1 Cor. 10:4) and as the bronze snake that gives life to those who look (John 3:14-15). He is foretold as a star that will come out of Jacob and a scepter out of Israel. The first fulfillment of this prophecy is in David, who brought down a wicked nation (Moab). The perfect fulfillment of this prophecy is in David's Son, Jesus Christ, who will subdue all the enemies of God.

 GOD'S STORY

When the Events of This Book Happened:
From Israel's encampment at Sinai to its encampment by the Jordan River near Jericho (ca. 1445–1407 B.C.)

The events covered by Numbers took almost 39 years, from the second month of the second year after the exodus to the eleventh month of the fortieth year (Num. 10:11; Deut. 1:3). The years noted above assume the early date for the exodus.

How Numbers Fits into God's "Story"

Numbers continues God's story: God builds his nation (Israel chosen as the people of promise). God's plan to bless his people despite their unworthiness magnifies his mercy. Numbers shows that the progress of God's kingdom depends on him and not on sinful people. The odd story of Balaam and his prophecies shows that no force can stop God's kingdom purposes. In fact, Balaam even predicted the coming of Jesus, the true King over God's kingdom (24:19).

Silver amulet scroll containing the blessing Moses gave to Aaron and his sons to use in blessing Israel: "May the Lord bless you and protect you; may the Lord make his face shine on you and be gracious to you; may the Lord look with favor on you and give you peace" (Num. 6:24-26). This artifact contains the oldest known copy of Scripture portions, dating to the late seventh or early sixth centuries B.C. The silver scroll was found August 4, 1979, by Judith Hadley who was then an archaeology student at Wheaton College working as part of an excavation led by Israeli archaeologist Gabriel Barkay. Dr. Hadley is now associate professor of theology and religious studies, Villanova University.

ORIGINAL HISTORICAL SETTING

Author and Date of Writing: Moses, ca. 1407 B.C.

The book is anonymous, but, as in Exodus and Leviticus, Moses is the central human character. Further, 33:2 notes that Moses kept a journal of the Israelite travels. Numbers indicates the Lord spoke more than 50 times to Moses. There are many good reasons to affirm that Moses wrote Numbers.

The book may have been slightly edited after Moses's death. For example, 21:14-15 seems to insert a citation from an otherwise unknown "Book of the LORD's Wars." Further, many Bible students believe that if Moses himself penned comment about his humility (12:3), it would disprove the point. Under divine inspiration, the end product of Numbers is entirely true and exactly what God intended it to be. (See *Genesis* for the critical view of authorship of the Pentateuch. See *Exodus* for the view of a later date for Moses's life.)

First Audience and Destination:
The Israelite people, camped at the Jordan River

The original hearers and destination are not stated directly but were apparently the Israelite nation camped on the plains of Moab shortly before they crossed the Jordan River into the promised land.

Occasion

Although the book does not say so, Israel needed a permanent historical record of the events that continued their national existence from the time of the covenant ratification at Sinai to the edge of the promised land. If one believes that Moses received the divine commands recorded in this book, then one can just as readily believe that God also prompted him to write down everything recorded in Numbers.

LITERARY FEATURES

Genre and Literary Style:
Narrative and laws (written in Hebrew prose) with some prophecies (written in Hebrew poetry)

The narrative portions of Numbers continue along the lines of the narrative of Exodus and Leviticus. As the Fourth Book of the Law, its laws are also similar to those previously recorded. One new feature is the prophetic oracle, given by Balaam (chaps. 23–24), written in the poetic parallelism so familiar in books such as Isaiah and Jeremiah. The Hebrew style of Numbers is like that of the rest of the Pentateuch.

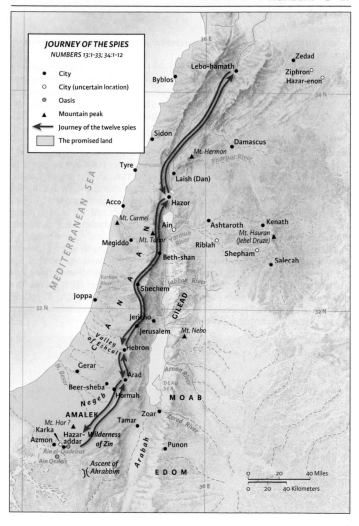

JOURNEY OF THE SPIES
NUMBERS 13:1-33; 34:1-12

● City
○ City (uncertain location)
◉ Oasis
▲ Mountain peak
← Journey of the twelve spies
▢ The promised land

Themes:
God's faithfulness, human waywardness, wilderness sojourn, number-ing the people.

The contrast between God's covenant faithfulness and the waywardness of his people has already been noted. Numbers develops this historically by tell-ing why Israel had to sojourn in the wilderness for so long and what happened to them there. The censuses at the beginning (chaps. 1–4) and the end (chap. 26) of the wilderness era figure prominently in the book.

Book Features and Structure

One feature that challenges Bible interpreters is the record of huge numbers of Israelite adult men (those of military age). An army of 600,000 suggests an overall population of at least 2 million (2:32; 26:51). This raises many questions: How could the 70 who went with Joseph into Egypt multiply to such a host in a few generations? How could so many be managed? Is an organized camp of 2 million really possible? How could the massive herds and flocks of so many survive in the desert? Why aren't there archaeological remains if such a great migration actually occurred?

There have been several "solutions" to account for these large numbers. Many scholars dismiss them as simply wrong. Others have argued that the Hebrew words translated "thousand" and "hundred" may mean something else (such as "clan"). Some see the numbers as symbolic rather than literal. The problem of the large numbers has not been satisfactorily resolved, yet the numbers in Numbers demonstrate the greatness of God's providence and his miraculous supply during his people's time in the wilderness.

Travellers at the Tomb of Aaron on the Summit of Mount Hor by David Roberts (Num. 20:22-29)

DEUTERONOMY
THE FIFTH BOOK OF MOSES

The Hebrew title is *'Elleh Haddebarim,* "These Are the Words," or more succinctly *Debarim,* "Words," from the opening of the book. The English title reflects the Greek word *Deuteronomion,* meaning "Second Law."

○ KEY TEXT: 6:4-5

"Listen, Israel: The LORD our God, the LORD is one. Love the LORD your God with all your heart, with all your soul, and with all your strength."

○ KEY TERM: "COMMANDMENTS"

Keeping the commandments of God (out of love for him) lies at the heart of his covenant with Israel, seen especially by the repetition of the Ten Commandments. Forms of the noun or verb "command" occur almost a hundred times in the book.

○ ONE-SENTENCE SUMMARY

Through Moses's great speeches near the end of his life, God reminded Israel on the verge of entering the promised land about his mighty acts, his covenant, and his many commands.

 GOD'S MESSAGE IN THE BOOK

Purpose

According to its own testimony, Deuteronomy originated as farewell messages from Moses to a new generation of Israelites. He pleaded passionately for them to keep God at the center of their national life once they settled in the land. The book is essentially a covenant-renewal document. The large central section largely repeats laws found earlier in the Pentateuch. So important was Deuteronomy to early Christians that the New Testament writers cited it more than 50 times.

Christian Worldview Elements

Deuteronomy deals especially with the worldview categories of *revelation and authority; covenant and redemption;* and *ethics and morality.* No Old Testament book more clearly teaches that God's love for his people means that he asks for their love in return, which gladly expresses itself in obeying his commands.

Teachings about God

Deuteronomy emphasizes the unity of God in the famous *Shema,* "Listen!" (See *Key Text,* above.) God's love as the basis for his covenant, his acts on Israel's behalf, and his commands are also prominent. On the other hand,

A Jewish man praying at the Western Wall in Jerusalem. He wears phy-lacteries that come from a Jewish tradition dating to the second century B.C. A black phylactery, or frontlet, is a small black leather or parchment case containing four Scriptures. It is attached to a long, single leather strap by a loop, forming two long straps on either side of the loop. In Moses's second address he reminded Israel of the greatest command-ment: "Love the Lord your God with all your heart, with all your soul, and with all your strength" (Deut. 6:5). The people of Israel were to talk about the Lord's commands through the course of the day and repeat them to their children: "Bind them as a sign on your hand and let them be a symbol on your forehead. Write them on the doorposts of your house and on your city gates" (Deut. 6:8-9).

idolatry or apostasy is so serious an affront to God's glory that the book commands the most severe penalties against those who insult God by turning away from him.

Teachings about Humanity

Deuteronomy faithfully records Israel's failures and gives solemn warnings of divine curse on disobedient and rebellious people. Yet the tenor of the book is that living according God's commands is a true delight and that obedience is no drudgery but the response of love and faith—an easy yoke. "But the message is very near you, in your mouth and in your heart, so that you may follow it" (30:14; see Matt. 11:29).

Teachings about Salvation

Deuteronomy emphasizes that salvation is entirely God's provision. He sets his covenant love on people sheerly out of his love. The remarkable text in Deut. 7:1-10 denies that God's redemption of Israel from Egypt was based on any quality in Israel but only "because the LORD loved you" (7:8)—his sovereign choice. This book also shows that redeemed people demonstrate their love and faith by their obedience.

◁✕ CHRIST IN DEUTERONOMY

Moses tells of a prophet like him whom God will raise up from among Israel (18:15-22). Christ is seen as a fulfillment of that prophecy (Acts 3:22; 7:37). The law states that whoever is hung on a tree is under God's curse (Deut. 21:23). Christ has redeemed us from the curse of the law by himself becoming a curse for us (Gal. 3:13).

GOD'S STORY

When the Events of This Book Happened:
In the last days of Moses (ca. 1406 B.C.)
Using the traditional early date for the exodus, Israel crossed the Jordan River and began the conquest of the promised land ca. 1406 B.C. The events recorded in Deuteronomy occurred just before this. (Critical scholars who date the exodus much later put Israel's entrance into Canaan ca. 1250 B.C.)

How Deuteronomy Fits into God's "Story"

Deuteronomy continues God's story: God builds his nation (Israel chosen as the people of promise). Deuteronomy looks forward to the time when Israel will be settled in the land, at peace with her enemies, under the rule of a righteous king (17:14-20). The king must "write a copy of this instruction for himself on a scroll in the presence of the Levitical priests. It is to remain with him, and he is to read from it all the days of his life, so that he may learn to fear the LORD his God, to observe all the words of this instruction, and to do these statutes" (17:18-19).

 ## ORIGINAL HISTORICAL SETTING

Author and Date of Writing:
Moses, ca. 1406 B.C.

The book refers to Moses's involvement in writing it (1:5; 31:9,22,24). Later Scripture refers to Mosaic authorship (1 Kgs. 2:3; 8:53; 2 Kgs. 14:6; 18:12). Both Jesus and Paul believed Moses wrote Deuteronomy (Mark 10:3-5; John 5:46-47; Rom. 10:19). The book's formal prologue (1:1-5) and the epilogue about Moses's death (chap. 34) were perhaps added by Joshua to round out the book.

Many modern critical scholars believe that Deuteronomy (or at least chaps. 12–26) first came into being as a pious fraud composed by scribes during the 600s B.C. at the time of King Josiah. These scribes subsequently "discovered" the book and claimed it came from the time of Moses (2 Kgs. 22–23). This belief became the keystone of the famous Documentary Hypothesis, sometimes called "JEDP." Two centuries of modern critical study, however, have not proven that anything in the book could not have occurred from the time of Moses.

First Audience and Destination:
The Israelite people on the plains of Moab

Of all the books of the Pentateuch, Deuteronomy is the one that most clearly began as oral communication by a human speaker. Later he put it in written permanent form. The first audience was the new generation of Israelites listening to their beloved leader of 40 years as they faced the prospect of entering Canaan without him. (Without doubt the religious reforms instituted during the time of King Josiah were an application of the teachings of Deuteronomy for a new audience in another situation.)

Occasion

Deuteronomy alone of the books of Moses states its precise occasion: "When Moses had finished writing down on a scroll every single word of this law, he commanded the Levites who carried the ark of the LORD's covenant, 'Take

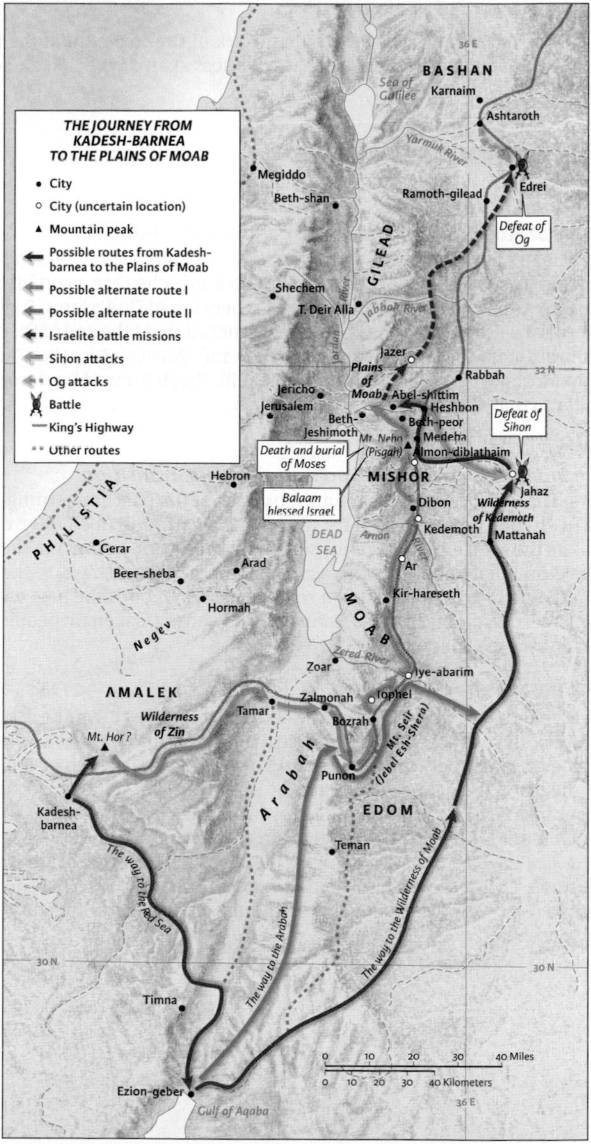

THE JOURNEY FROM KADESH-BARNEA TO THE PLAINS OF MOAB
City
City (uncertain location)
Mountain peak
Possible routes from Kadesh-barnea to the Plains of Moab
Possible alternate route I
Possible alternate route II
Israelite battle missions
Sihon attacks
Og attacks
Battle
King's Highway
Other routes
BASHAN
Sea of Galilee
Karnaim
Ashtaroth
Yarmuk River
Edrei
Ramoth-gilead
Defeat of Og
Megiddo
Beth-shan
GILEAD
Shechem
T. Deir Alla
Jabbok River
Jordan River
Jazer
Plains of Moab
Rabbah
Jericho
Jerusalem
Abel-shittim
Heshbon
Beth-peor
Beth-Jeshimoth
Mt. Nebo (Pisgah)
Medeba
Almon-diblathaim
Defeat of Sihon
Death and burial of Moses
Balaam blessed Israel
Hebron
MISHOR
Jahaz
Dibon
Wilderness of Kedemoth
Kedemoth
Mattanah
PHILISTIA
DEAD SEA
Arnon River
Gerar
Arad
Ar
Beer-sheba
Hormah
Kir-hareseth
MOAB
Negev
Zered River
Zoar
Iye-abarim
AMALEK
Zalmonah
Iophel
Tamar
Wilderness of Zin
Bozrah
Mt. Seir (Jebel Esh-Shera)
Mt. Hor ?
Arabah
Punon
Kadesh-barnea
EDOM
Teman
The way to the Red Sea
The way to the Arabah
The way to the Wilderness of Moab
Timna
Ezion-geber
Gulf of Aqaba
36 E
32 N
30 N
0 10 20 30 40 Miles
0 10 20 30 40 Kilometers

this book of the law and place it beside the ark of the covenant of the LORD your God so that it may remain there as a witness against you'" (31:24-26).

 ## LITERARY FEATURES

Genre and Literary Style:
A record of Moses's final speeches, composed in Hebrew
Many scholars have noted the sermonic style of Deuteronomy, which sets it apart from the other books of Moses. The three speeches are a combination of narrative (reminders of God's acts) and repetition of God's laws. Together they serve to renew the covenant for a new generation. At the end of the book, the extraordinary "Song of Moses" (chap. 32) and "Moses's Blessings" (chap. 33) show Moses to be a poet of considerable skill. The Hebrew of Deuteronomy is similar to that of the rest of the Pentateuch.

Themes:
Commandments, covenant, God's mighty acts, transition
The first 11 chapters of Deuteronomy look back at the past concerning what God had already accomplished for his people. Beginning in chapter 12, the focus is on the future. Deuteronomy serves as a transition book from the time of Israel's national founding (with a charismatic leader and laws) to the time of its settlement (with a land and a royal dynasty). In both the past and the future, Israel must remember its status as God's chosen, covenant people who owe him supreme allegiance.

Book Features and Structure
There is general agreement that three sermons of Moses form the essential structure of the book. Scholars disagree whether chapters 12–26 were originally the astonishingly long conclusion of the second speech or whether Moses inserted the catalogue of laws at this point when he converted his speeches into writing. The topic changes from speech to speech.

Deut. 1:1–4:43—Speech 1 reviews the mighty acts of the Lord.

Deut. 4:44–28:68—Speech 2 presents the wonderful laws of the Lord.

Deut. 29:1–30:20—Speech 3 proposes covenant renewal with the Lord.

Deut. 31–34—These chapters describe the change of leadership from Moses to Joshua.

JOSHUA

The English (and Hebrew) title is based on the name of the central character. Moses changed his original name *Hoshea* ("Salvation") to *Yehoshua* ("The Lord Is Salvation"), traditionally spelled "Joshua" in English. The Greek equivalent is Jesus.

O KEY TEXT: 21:44-45

"The LORD gave them rest on every side according to all he had sworn to their fathers. None of their enemies were able to stand against them, for the LORD handed over all their enemies to them. None of the good promises the LORD had made to the house of Israel failed. Everything was fulfilled."

O KEY TERM: "CONQUEST"

This is a book of victory and conquest. It shows God's people on the march throughout Canaan, subduing their enemies and claiming their promised possession.

O ONE-SENTENCE SUMMARY

God fulfilled his promises to Israel to give them a land through the conquest of Canaan and through the allocation of the land among the tribes, all under the leadership of Joshua.

GOD'S MESSAGE IN THE BOOK

Purpose

The covenant God made with Abraham included a promise that his descendants would take possession of Canaan (Gen. 12:7). For long ages the promise lay unfulfilled. The book of Joshua shows how God—in his time and way—fulfilled the land promised in the Abrahamic covenant. Yet the New Testament book of Hebrews speaks of a greater Joshua who gives his people ultimate rest (Heb. 4:8-9). God's people who read and study the book today should view it with both Joshuas in mind: the Israelite general and the King of kings.

Christian Worldview Elements

Joshua draws attention to the following worldview categories: *sovereignty and providence*; *covenant and redemption*; *ethics and morality*; and *community*. This book shows God as the righteous Judge who will not forever tolerate those who insult him, such as the Canaanites.

Teachings about God

The two attributes of God most on display in Joshua are his faithfulness to fulfill his promises and his ultimate judgment on evil. If the promise made to

Joshua Passing the River Jordan with the Ark of the Covenant by Benjamin West (Josh. 3:14-17)

Abraham concerning land for Israel was kept only after many centuries, then today's believers should not be surprised if the promise he made concerning the return of Christ is kept after many centuries.

Teachings about Humanity

Although the book is careful to report Israel's occasional failures during the conquest, it is optimistic in its view that God's people can live in victory as they trust in him. For this reason, Joshua has been popular in Christian pulpits with the positive principles it contains.

God
Creation
○ **Sovereignty and Providence**
Faith and Reason
Revelation and Authority
Humanity
Rebellion and Sin
○ **Covenant and Redemption**
○ **Community** and Church
Discipleship
○ **Ethics and Morality**
Time and Eternity

Teachings about Salvation

The account of Rahab the harlot (chaps. 2 and 6) profoundly illustrates salvation by "grace through faith." So thoroughly was she converted that she was considered an Israelite and became a biological ancestor of Jesus (Josh. 6:25; Matt. 1:5; Heb. 11:31). Although most of the victories in Joshua are military, the entire tenor of the book is that salvation—of whatever kind—comes only from God's hand.

 ## CHRIST IN JOSHUA

The very name "Joshua" is a variation of "Jesus." Joshua's leadership of God's people in taking possession of the promised land is a foreshadowing of Christ's leading the people of God to their eternal inheritance. Joshua is one of only a few Old Testament heroes pictured without major character flaws or sins. The "commander of the LORD's army" (5:14-15) who spoke with Joshua was doubtless Christ in preincarnate form.

 ## GOD'S STORY

When the Events of This Book Happened:
From Israel's entry into Canaan until Joshua's death (ca. 1406–1380 B.C.)

Archaeologists of the ancient Near East call the period of 1550–1200 B.C. the Late Bronze Age. Many Canaanite ruins from this era have been excavated, revealing an advanced but idolatrous civilization. The archaeological data support either an early date for the destruction of Jericho (ca. 1406 B.C.) or a late date (ca. 1250 B.C.). The late date, however, does not allow the premonarchy period to last at least 300 years (Judg. 11:26). The earlier, more traditional, date is preferred. (See also 1 Kgs. 6:1 and *Exodus*.)

How Joshua Fits into God's "Story"

Joshua continues God's story: God builds his nation (Israel chosen as the people of promise). Joshua describes how God's kingdom triumphed at a time when nations were viewed as the creation of local deities and the proof of that deity's power. The Lord's victories over the Canaanites demonstrated that Israel's God is the one true God. It looks forward to the climax of all human history when God will triumph over all the world's kingdoms through his anointed King.

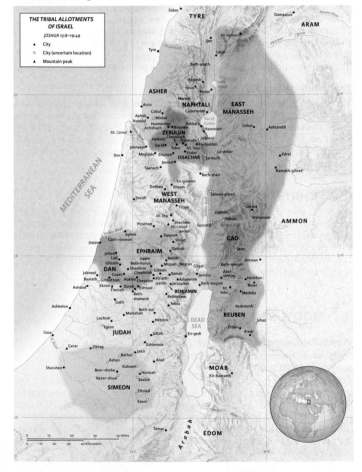

THE TRIBAL ALLOTMENTS OF ISRAEL
JOSHUA 13:8–19:49
- • City
- ○ City (uncertain location)
- ▲ Mountain peak

ORIGINAL HISTORICAL SETTING

Author and Date of Writing:
Possibly Joshua, ca. 1380 B.C., or Samuel, ca. 1050 B.C.

The book is anonymous. Because Joshua is the central character, Jewish tradition held him to be the author. Joshua's writing activity is mentioned twice in the book (8:32; 24:26). Everything in the book could have been written by Joshua, except for the last few verses that tell of his death. On the other hand, many students believe that several instances of the word "today" (e.g., 4:9; 5:9) point to a time after Joshua's lifetime. The reference to the "Book of Jashar" (10:13; see also 2 Sam. 1:18) may also suggest a later date. If the book was not written by Joshua, then the next likely candidate is Samuel, who would have used sources that were passed on to him from the time of Joshua.

Nablus by David Roberts. Nablus (Shechem) was located between Mount Ebal and Mount Gerazim. Some archaeologists believe this may be the site where Joshua led the people of Israel in renewing their covenant with God and their commitment to the law of Moses. (Josh. 24:1,25). Here the Israelites buried the bones of Joseph that they had brought up from Egypt (Josh. 24:32).

First Audience and Destination:
Israelite people after they settled in Canaan, before kingship was established
The first audience was the Israelite nation living in its own land. No doubt the book—which first existed in scroll form, as did all the biblical books—was deposited with the five books of Moses at the tabernacle (24:26).

Occasion
The book does not tell what prompted it to be written. If Joshua was the primary author, then he was continuing the pattern established by Moses. He put into written form the mighty acts God accomplished through his leadership. If the author was Samuel or some writer living shortly before kingship was established, the need was to give Israel a permanent account of its early days of triumph in the land.

 LITERARY FEATURES

Genre and Literary Style:
A historical narrative composed in Hebrew
Joshua is mainly a report of the military conquest and settling of Canaan, recounted with a great deal of skill. The dialogues and the farewell speech of Joshua add vividness and excitement. In the Hebrew Scriptures, this book is positioned as the first of the four Former Prophets. (The others are Judges, Samuel, and Kings.) Together these books describe the 800-year period from Israel's entry into Canaan (ca. 1406 B.C.) through the destruction of the temple and Jerusalem and the exile to Babylon (ca. 586 B.C.). (See comments on *Genre and Literary Style* in *2 Kings* for further material about the possible literary relationship of the Former Prophets.)

Themes:
Conquest, God's promises, "holy war"
The notions of conquest and fulfillment of God's long-standing promises are cherished by all devout students of Scripture. However, the idea of "holy war" is more challenging. The destruction of all remnants of the pagan culture of Canaan must be understood as the sovereign God's judgment on human sin in his time and manner. It was strictly limited to that time and place, so the book cannot be used today to justify military or civil violence for the purpose of advancing God's kingdom. (The notion of a "just war" is a different matter.) The book does show, however, that those who oppose God will not stand forever. During the present (Christian) era, the only weapon Christians are to wield as Christians is "the sword of the Spirit—which is the word of God" (Eph. 6:17). One day, the "second Joshua" will strike all evil with his powerful sword (Rev. 19:15).

Book Features and Structure

Perhaps the most interesting feature of the book is its realistic presentation of Joshua's military strategy, a divide-and-conquer approach. After the victory over Jericho, the Israelite army drove west to take Ai and then neutralized Gibeon, breaking the backbone of opposition. Then they conquered the southern cities (chap. 10) and later the northern cities (chap. 11).

The Hebrew term *cherem*, translated "accursed" in the KJV (6:17-18; 7:11-15), deserves mention. It carried the idea of religious taboo or ban (NASB). *Cherem* referred to people or things that were so devoted (NIV) to God that they were totally given up to him, even to the extent of destroying (CSB, ESV, NLT) them so that they could not be used in ordinary life.

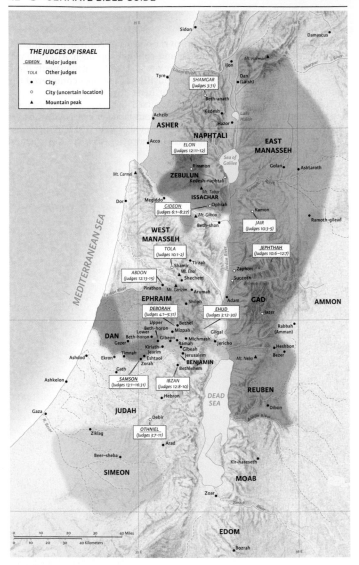

THE JUDGES OF ISRAEL

GIDEON	Major judges
TOLA	Other judges
•	City
○	City (uncertain location)
▲	Mountain peak

Sidon

Damascus

35 E

Ijon

Mt. Hermon ▲

Tyre

Dan (Laish)

Pharpar River

SHAMGAR
(Judges 3:31)

Beth-anath

Litani River

Kedesh

Lake Huleh

Achzib

Hazor

ASHER

NAPHTALI

EAST MANASSEH

Acco

ELON
(Judges 12:11-12)

Golan

Ashtaroth

Rimmon

Sea of Galilee

Mt. Carmel ▲

ZEBULUN

Kedesh-naphtali

Dor

Mt. Tabor ▲

ISSACHAR

Ophrah

Kamon

Megiddo

GIDEON
(Judges 6:1–8:27)

Mt. Gilboa ▲

Ramoth-gilead

JAIR
(Judges 10:3-5)

Beth-shan

Yarmuk River

WEST MANASSEH

TOLA
(Judges 10:1-2)

JEPHTHAH
(Judges 10:6–12:7)

Tirzah

Shamir

Mt. Ebal ▲

Zaphon

ABDON
(Judges 12:13-15)

Shechem

Succoth

Jabbok River

Pirathon

Mt. Gerizim ▲

Arumah

GAD

AMMON

MEDITERRANEAN SEA

EPHRAIM

Shiloh

Adam

DEBORAH
(Judges 4:1–5:31)

Bethel

EHUD
(Judges 3:12-30)

Jazer

Upper Beth-horon

Mizpah

Jordan River

Rabbah (Amman)

DAN

Lower Beth-horon

Gibeon

Gilgal

Michmash

Jericho

Heshbon

Gezer

Ramah

Bezer

Kiriath-jearim

Gibeah

Mt. Nebo ▲

Timnah

Eshtaol

Jerusalem

Ashdod

Ekron

Zorah

BENJAMIN

Cath

Bethlehem

SAMSON
(Judges 13:1-16:31)

IBZAN
(Judges 12:8-10)

REUBEN

Ashkelon

Hebron

DEAD SEA

Gaza

Debir

Dibon

N. Besor

JUDAH

Arnon River

OTHNIEL
(Judges 3:7-11)

Ziklag

Arad

Kir-hareseth

Beer-sheba

SIMEON

MOAB

Zoar

Zered River

0   10   20   30   40 Miles
0 10 20 30   40 Kilometers

EDOM

35 E

36 E

Bozrah

JUDGES

The name translates the Hebrew title, *Shofetim*, which could also be rendered "Leaders" or "Chieftains." It refers to the style of government in Israel from Joshua's death to Saul's kingship. The judges did not preside over courts as the English term might suggest.

○ KEY TEXT: 21:25

"In those days there was no king in Israel; everyone did whatever seemed right to him."

○ KEY TERM: "SAVE"

Judges tells the repeated cycle of how the Israelites fell into apostasy, so God handed them over to their political enemies. Then after they cried out to God, he raised up a leader who saved them from their oppressors. In both situations, God was the agent of discipline and rescue because he is the ultimate Judge (11:27).

Mount Tabor. "Then Deborah said to Barak, 'Go! This is the day the LORD has handed Sisera over to you. Hasn't the LORD gone before you?' So Barak came down from Mount Tabor with ten thousand men following him. The LORD threw Sisera, all his charioteers, and all his army into a panic before Barak's assault. Sisera left his chariot and fled on foot. Barak pursued the chariots and the army as far as Harosheth of the Nations, and the whole army of Sisera fell by the sword; not a single man was left" (Judg. 4:14-16).

O ONE-SENTENCE SUMMARY

Israel experienced the repeated cycle of apostasy, oppression, repentance, and restoration by divinely appointed judges throughout the long period following Joshua's death.

GOD'S MESSAGE IN THE BOOK

Purpose

Judges serves two main purposes. Historically it sketches the dark period in Israel's history from the exciting days of Moses and Joshua to the promising time of Samuel and Saul. Sadly there were only fleeting times when Israel truly fulfilled its role as God's people. Theologically it tells with tedious repetition that when God's people sin, he punishes them, but that when they repent, he forgives and restores. With its negative understanding of how easily God's people may turn away from him, Judges balances the positive picture of inevitable conquest shown in the book of Joshua. God's people who interpret Judges today should view it with its original purposes in mind.

Christian Worldview Elements

Judges emphasizes two complementary pairs of worldview elements: *rebellion and sin* (the people's readiness to forsake God) and *covenant and redemption* (God's gracious restoration of the people because of his covenant). As clearly as any book in Scripture, Judges shows the close connection between people's commitment to God and his dealings with them.

God
Creation
Sovereignty and Providence
Faith and Reason
Revelation and Authority
Humanity
o **Rebellion and Sin**
o **Covenant and Redemption**
Community and Church
Discipleship
Ethics and Morality
Time and Eternity

Teachings about God

Judges shows the severity of God, who does not lightly ignore it when people claiming his name forsake his ways (2:11-15). It also shows the mercy of God, who is moved with pity when his children cry out to him, even when their troubles are caused by their own sins (2:16-18). The Spirit's power in enabling certain judges to perform mighty works is noteworthy in the book.

Teachings about Humanity

This book paints an embarrassing picture of human fickleness. Israel was seemingly ready to turn away from God to serve idols at the drop of a hat. The shameful incident of the Levite's concubine (chap. 19) demonstrates how degraded the times of the judges were. Even the three most memorable judges (Gideon, Jephthah, and Samson) were seriously flawed heroes.

Ein Harod—the Springs of Harod at the foot of the Gilboa Mountain Range. Here Gideon tested his men to identify those qualified to fight against the Midianites (Judg. 7:4-8).

Teachings about Salvation

Judges teaches that salvation involves more than just an individual's forgiveness from sin. Sin has consequences that are social and can affect an entire society. Therefore, when God brings salvation, he may dramatically change societies and nations as well as individuals. Further, this book teaches that salvation—deliverance—is always from the Lord and never because someone (or some group) deserves it.

✂ CHRIST IN JUDGES

The judges were God's agents for delivering his people from a variety of enemies. In a much greater way, Christ confronts and defeats Satan and his forces, thereby delivering the people of God from their enemies. This theme is seen in Matthew, Mark, and Luke, in Paul's letter to the Ephesians, and in Revelation.

GOD'S STORY

When the Events of This Book Happened:
From Joshua's death until Samson's death, almost three centuries (ca. 1380–1060 B.C.)
While archaeologists debate the date of Israel's conquest of Canaan (see *Joshua*), there is general agreement that Saul's kingship began ca. 1050. Jephthah's reference to 300 years (11:26) is evidence for a very long period for the judges. Archaeologists consider this period remarkable for two reasons. First, the ancient Near East advanced technologically from the Bronze Age to the Iron Age. According to Judg. 1:19, the Israelites lagged behind in this development. Second was the increasing Philistine challenge. Mentioned in the record of the patriarchs and the exodus, they were evidently a serious military threat to Israel only in the days of Samson and later (at the end of the period of judges and the beginning of the monarchy). The Philistines were probably "Sea Peoples" who arrived at the southern coast of Canaan in boats from their original homeland in Caphtor (Crete).

How Judges Fits into God's "Story"
Judges continues God's story: God builds his nation (Israel chosen as the people of promise). Judges functions negatively in the story of God's kingdom. After the exhilarating days of victory under Joshua, it stands to warn God's people not to be careless in their relationship with him. After three centuries of judges, Israel was worse off at the end of the period than at the beginning. Their darkest hour, however, was just before a wonderful new day. David's birth (ca. 1040 B.C.) came only a few years after the tragic death of Samson and the seeming triumph of the Philistines (ca. 1060 B.C.).

ORIGINAL HISTORICAL SETTING

Author and Date of Writing:
Unknown, perhaps Samuel, ca. 1050 B.C.

The book is anonymous. It could hardly have been completed until after all its events, and the repeated refrain "in those days there was no king in Israel" (17:6; 18:1; 19:1; 21:25) suggests the author wrote at a time when there was a king. Jewish tradition identified Samuel as the author. There is no reason Samuel could not have written from the early days of Saul's kingship, in which case this is his companion to the book of Joshua. The author used ancient sources, such as "Deborah's Song" (chap. 5).

First Audience and Destination:
Israelite people after they settled in Canaan, after kingship was established

The first audience was the Israelite nation living in its own land. No doubt the book—which first existed in a scroll form, as did all the biblical books— was deposited with the growing canon of Hebrew Scripture at the tabernacle in Shiloh.

Occasion

Judges captured for a later generation the story of earlier national failure. It was perhaps prompted by the need to give a long historical explanation to the question first asked by Gideon: "Please, my lord, if the LORD is with us, why has all this happened?" (6:13). Some scholars believe Judges originated as a long prophetic sermon.

 LITERARY FEATURES

Genre and Literary Style:
A narrative with a long prologue and epilogue, composed in Hebrew

Judges is essentially narrative, but "Deborah's Song" (chap. 5) is a superb example of early Hebrew poetry. In the Hebrew Scriptures, this book is positioned as the second of the four Former Prophets. (The others are Joshua, Samuel, and Kings.) Judges (like Kings) tells the story of several centuries with only a few episodes given any detail. (Joshua and Samuel lavish attention on central characters: Joshua, Samuel, Saul, and David.) (See comments on *Genre and Literary Style* in *2 Kings* for further material about the possible literary relationship of the Former Prophets.) The book of Judges is composed in good Hebrew style, with chapters 3–16 noted for the repetitive language describing the cycles of oppression and deliverance.

Themes:

Apostasy, oppression, repentance, and restoration

These four theme words make up the cycle described six times in the book. The following exact phrases are repeated often: (1) "The Israelites did what was evil in the LORD's sight"; (2) "[God] handed them over (or sold them into the hand of) _____"; (3) "The Israelites cried out to the LORD"; (4) "He judged Israel _____ years."

The oppressor kingdom and the major divine deliverer associated with restoration are as follows: (1) Aram-naharaim defeated by Othniel; (2) Moab defeated by Ehud; (3) Canaan defeated by Deborah; (4) Midian defeated by Gideon; (5) Ammon defeated by Jephthah; (6) Philistia defeated by Samson.

Book Features and Structure

The cyclical nature of the book is its most unusual literary feature. Judges is also noted for its long explanatory prologue, which lays the foundation for the repeated cycles that follow. Also of note is the long epilogue, which gives two horrible examples of how morally degenerate life was in the days of the judges.

When the six major judges are added with the six minor judges, the total of 12 matches the total number of tribes. That one of these judges was female (Deborah) is striking confirmation of God's sovereignty in raising up leaders whom he chooses in any era. The structure of the book is clear:

Judg. 1:1–3:6—Prologue
Judg. 3:7–16:3—Cycles of oppression and deliverance
Judg. 17:1–21:25—Epilogue

The English title is the name of the heroine of the story. The title carries over from the Hebrew Bible.

⊙ KEY TEXT: 4:14

"The women said to Naomi, 'Blessed be the LORD, who has not left you without a family redeemer today. May his name become well known in Israel.'"

⊙ KEY TERM: "KINSMAN"

Boaz willingly fulfilled the responsibility of the *go'el*, "kinsman" or "family redeemer," for Ruth (as well as for Naomi). As such, he beautifully illustrates God, who gladly redeems his people. Ruth and Boaz became ancestors of Jesus, the ultimate Redeemer.

⊙ ONE-SENTENCE SUMMARY

Ruth, a Moabite widow, found love and fulfillment through Boaz, a rich Israelite who redeemed the land and the name of Ruth's deceased husband, thereby restoring Naomi, Ruth's mother-in-law, from emptiness to fullness.

The Field of Boaz is east of Bethlehem.

GOD'S MESSAGE IN THE BOOK

Purpose

Biblical scholars have debated the original purpose of this book, for there are a number of lessons the author may have been teaching, for example, the need for a society to take care of its childless widows or the importance of racial tolerance. More obvious than these, however, is its portrayal of God's providential care of people committed to him in the midst of overwhelming challenges to their faith. This charming account of faith in God contrasts sharply with the faithlessness displayed in Judges, the other biblical book that tells of the same time period. God's people who read and study Ruth today should enjoy it for its own sake in its Old Testament setting.

Christian Worldview Elements

The book of Ruth focuses attention on the worldview category of God's *sovereignty and providence* like few other passages in the Scriptures. Ruth the foreigner came to Israel and to Israel's God and then became an ancestor of King David. This reflects the worldview category *community*.

God
Creation
○ **Sovereignty and Providence**
Faith and Reason
Revelation and Authority
Humanity
Rebellion and Sin
Covenant and Redemption
○ **Community** and Church
Discipleship
Ethics and Morality
Time and Eternity

Teachings about God

The sovereign hand of God in all circumstances is prominent throughout Ruth. The famine and the deaths of three husbands at the beginning of the book were not random acts that "just happened." They were the divinely arranged circumstances for Ruth's incorporation into God's family and to bring her to joy. God's bringing about Naomi's journey from emptiness to fullness parallels the way he brings all his people in the end to eternal fullness of joy. Many scholars recognize Boaz's role of family redeemer as a prefiguring of Jesus Christ.

Teachings about Humanity

One of the virtues held up throughout the Old Testament is *chesed*, "loving kindness" or "act of loyal friendship." Ruth, Boaz, and Naomi all did memorable deeds based on *chesed*. Further, although human life inevitably includes pain and loss, it becomes purposeful when people see themselves living under God's protective care. Also, people find great blessing when they live according to God's commands, illustrated by Boaz's blessing because he followed both the law of gleaning and the law concerning levirate marriage. (See *Book Features below.*)

Teachings about Salvation

In this story, the most unlikely person was reached by God's grace and gained full membership in the community of God's people. This shows that, even in the Old Testament, God's grace was not limited only to the descendants of Jacob. Further, Ruth's famous declaration of loyalty to Naomi (1:16-17) includes the concept that conversion and commitment to the Lord is a way of life, not just a point of decision.

CHRIST IN RUTH

Boaz's role as family redeemer is fulfilled in greater measure by Christ who is both our brother and our redeemer. Ruth is in the genealogy of Christ. She is the great-grandmother of Israel's messiah figure, King David.

GOD'S STORY

When the Events of This Book Happened:
Late during the period of the judges (ca. 1140 B.C.)
This love story is about King David's great-grandparents. David's birth is dated ca. 1040, but there is no data for the length of each generation. A reasonable

Ruth in the Field of Boaz by Julius Schnorr von Carolsfeld opinion is that about a century passed from the time of Ruth's marriage to Boaz until David—youngest son of their grandson Jesse—was born. (For more information about this era in general, see *Judges*.)

How Ruth Fits into God's "Story"

Ruth tells part of "chapter 1" of God's story: God builds his nation (Israel chosen as the people of promise). This book shows that even in the Old Testament era the family of God was not limited only to people of one ethnic group. God chose people from nations other than Israel as well. Second, Ruth tells the beautiful story of some of King David's ancestors—in fact, the ancestors of Jesus Christ, even though they could not have known this.

 ## ORIGINAL HISTORICAL SETTING

Author and Date of Writing:
Unknown, anytime from 1000 to 500 B.C.
The book does not leave any personal traces of the author. It was written after David's rise to power, but beyond that, little is certain. The author's skill in writing is matchless in the Old Testament, but who this was cannot be established.

First Audience and Destination:
Israelites living sometime after David came to power
The golden age of Israelite culture during the days of Solomon would serve admirably as the original setting for the book's composition. It is, however, strikingly different from the Song of Songs, the other Old Testament book that tells an individual love story.

Occasion
The beauty of a story told well is sufficient reason to bring it into being. Because nothing is known about its original author or audience, no one knows what first prompted it to be written.

 ## LITERARY FEATURES

Genre and Literary Style:
A compact narrative written in excellent Hebrew
Many call Ruth a short story, and it may be called this with the understanding that its events really happened. In the Hebrew Scriptures, it was placed in the third section, the Writings or *Kethuvim* (the other two sections are the Law and the Prophets). Among the Writings it was one of the Five Scrolls. Each of these Five Scrolls became associated with one of the Israelite festivals and

was read publicly during that festival. Ruth was identified with *Shavuoth* ("Weeks" or "Pentecost"), which celebrated the end of the barley harvest and the beginning of the wheat harvest. Its Hebrew is so carefully polished that Ruth has been likened to a precious jewel.

Themes:
Loyalty, redeemer, contrast

The concepts of loyalty (*chesed*) and redeemer (*go'el*) have already been noted in this chapter. The contrasts in the book are part of its literary attractiveness: pleasant versus bitter; full versus empty; living versus dead. The greatest contrast is between Ruth (the poor foreigner) and Boaz (the rich Israelite), who come together in delightful resolution. Both of these central characters acted according to loyalty (*chesed*) but were related to minor characters who did not show loyalty.

Book Features and Structure

The book is noteworthy because it includes four cultural expressions that appear exceptionally odd to modern readers. First, gleaning was a kind of early welfare provision that allowed the poor to reap the edges of grain fields (2:2). Second was the symbolism of Ruth's claiming Boaz's protection by urging him to cover her with his cloak (3:9). Third is the real estate transaction made legal by exchanging sandals, which had to be explained even for the first readers (4:7). Most important of all, however, the entire story makes sense only in light of the law of levirate marriage, stated in Deut. 25:5-6. The law guaranteed ongoing family lines and decentralized the control of farmland. It required that when a married man died childless, his brother or next of kin had to marry the widow. Their firstborn would then receive the name and inheritance of the deceased.

The story is framed by a historical prologue of Naomi's emptying (1:1-5) and a forward-looking epilogue of Naomi's filling (4:13-22). Between these are four deftly drawn scenes: Naomi's journey home (chap. 1); Ruth's gleaning (chap. 2); Ruth's visit to Boaz (chap. 3); and Boaz's redemption of Ruth (chap. 4).

David's Family

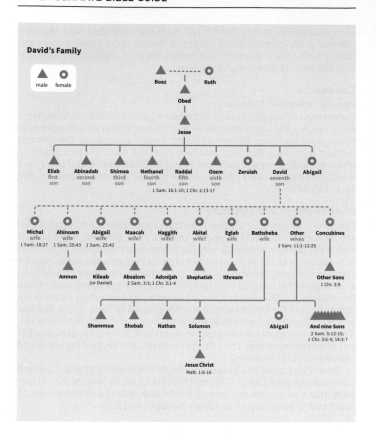

▲ male   ○ female

Boaz ---- Ruth

Obed

Jesse

| Eliab first son | Abinadab second son | Shimea third son | Nethanel fourth son | Raddai fifth son | Ozem sixth son | Zeruiah | David seventh son | Abigail |

1 Sam. 16:1-10; 1 Chr. 2:13-17

| Michal wife 1 Sam. 18:27 | Ahinoam wife 1 Sam. 25:43 | Abigail wife 1 Sam. 25:42 | Maacah wife? | Haggith wife? | Abital wife? | Eglah wife | Bathsheba wife 2 Sam. 11:1-12:25 | Other wives | Concubines |

Amnon   Kileab (or Daniel)   Absalom   Adonijah   Shephatiah   Ithream   Other Sons 1 Chr. 3:9

2 Sam. 3:3; 1 Chr. 3:1-4

Shammua   Shobab   Nathan   Solomon   Abigail   And nine Sons
2 Sam. 5:13-15;
1 Chr. 3:6-9; 14:3-7

Jesus Christ
Matt. 1:6-16

1 SAMUEL
THE FIRST BOOK OF KINGDOMS

The book is named for Samuel, the judge who anointed Saul and David, the first two kings of Israel, of whom 1 and 2 Samuel tell the story. In the Hebrew Bible, 1 and 2 Samuel were originally one book. The Greek translators (second century B.C.), who divided the book, used the titles 1 and 2 Kingdoms.

O KEY TEXT: 18:7

"As they danced, the women sang: 'Saul has killed his thousands, but David his tens of thousands.'"

O KEY TERM: "MONARCHY"

This book describes the beginning of the monarchy in Israel. The first king, Saul, was a failure; the second king, David, succeeded, even though he struggled to survive Saul's bitter jealousy.

O ONE-SENTENCE SUMMARY

After Samuel's leadership as judge, the people of Israel turned to Saul as their first king, whom God rejected and instead chose David, who had many adventures as a renegade from Saul's court.

The Valley of Elah, where David defeated Goliath (1 Sam. 17:48-52)

GOD'S MESSAGE IN THE BOOK

Purpose

Since this book was originally the first half of a single composition, the purpose for the books now called 1 and 2 Samuel must be considered together. This work answered important questions for Israelites (probably living in the days of Solomon) about the true nature of the Davidic dynasty. If the people had been wrong to ask for a king and if God had rejected Saul as king, then why should they now suppose that the monarchs of the Davidic line would continue? The work is filled with narrative tension between the dangers of a king (1 Sam. 8) and the hope for an enduring dynasty (2 Sam. 7). The answer is that despite human evil God worked to bring about his plan for an everlasting kingdom with an everlasting King (2 Sam. 7:16). God's people who study the books of Samuel today should view it with this original purpose in mind.

Christian Worldview Elements

First Samuel brings into sharp focus the worldview categories of *rebellion and sin* (demonstrated in the life of Saul especially) and *ethics and morality* (demonstrated especially in the life of David, who was treated unfairly and had to respond righteously).

God
Creation
Sovereignty and Providence
Faith and Reason
Revelation and Authority
Humanity
○ **Rebellion and Sin**
Covenant and Redemption
Community and Church
Discipleship
○ **Ethics and Morality**
Time and Eternity

Teachings about God

God of Israel was responsible for shaping Israel's destiny. He allowed Israel's choice of Saul to stand, but he judged Saul for his disobedience. He chose David, who by the end of 1 Samuel was not yet secure in his position as king. The Spirit of God is seen as the divine enabler: he came upon both Saul and David to empower their service.

Teachings about Humanity

This book teaches about humanity through telling the stories of three heroes: Samuel, Saul, and David. Samuel was a dedicated servant of God who nevertheless failed as a parent. Saul was a handsome, talented leader who failed in his primary task: glad obedience to God's revealed will. David's life (in 1 Sam.) demonstrates that those whom God chooses may come as a surprise (to other humans), and that they may face great difficulties and yet serve him wholeheartedly.

Teachings about Salvation

This book shows that a right relationship with God inevitably brings with it obedience from the heart and that God values heart obedience much more than external conformity to religious rituals: "Then Samuel said: 'Does the

LORD take pleasure in burnt offerings and sacrifices as much as in obeying the LORD? Look: to obey is better than sacrifice, to pay attention is better than the fat of rams'" (15:22).

✝ CHRIST IN 1 SAMUEL

First Samuel presents Israel's first two kings, Saul and David. These kings of Israel foreshadow Israel's true King, Jesus Christ. Jesus is in the lineage of David and is called Son of David, a term that is equivalent to Messiah. Samuel's model of priest, prophet, and political leader foreshadows Jesus's role as prophet, priest, and king. First Samuel includes the first mention of a person being called the anointed of Yahweh. This is significant, because the word "Messiah" means "anointed one."

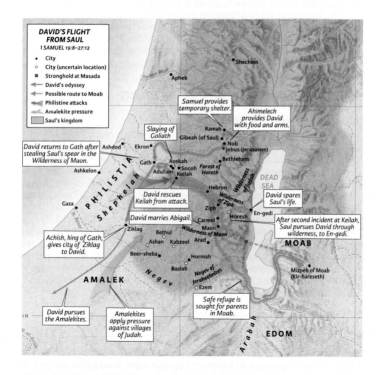

DAVID'S FLIGHT FROM SAUL
1 SAMUEL 19:8–27:12

- City
- ○ City (uncertain location)
- ■ Stronghold at Masada
- ◄ David's odyssey
- ◄--- Possible route to Moab
- Philistine attacks
- Amalekite pressure
- Saul's kingdom

Samuel provides temporary shelter.

Ahimelech provides David with food and arms.

Slaying of Goliath

David returns to Gath after stealing Saul's spear in the Wilderness of Maon.

David rescues Keilah from attack.

David marries Abigail.

Achish, king of Gath, gives city of Ziklag to David.

David spares Saul's life.

After second incident at Keilah, Saul pursues David through wilderness, to En-gedi.

David pursues the Amalekites.

Amalekites apply pressure against villages of Judah.

Safe refuge is sought for parents in Moab.

Shechem · Aphek · Ramah · Gibeah (of Saul) · Nob · Jebus (Jerusalem) · Bethlehem · Ekron · Ashdod · Gath · Azekah · Socoh · Adullam · Keilah · Forest of Hereth · Hebron · Ashkelon · Ziph · Horesh · Carmel · Maon · En-gedi · Gaza · Ziklag · Bethul · Ashan · Kabzeel · Arad · Beer-sheba · Hormah · Baalah · Ezem · Mizpeh of Moab (Kir-hareseth)

PHILISTIA · Shephelah · Wilderness of Judah · DEAD SEA · Wilderness of Ziph · Wilderness of Maon · MOAB · AMALEK · Negev · Negev of Jerahmeelites · EDOM · Arabah

GOD'S STORY

When the Events of This Book Happened:
From Samuel's birth until Saul's death (ca. 1105–1010 B.C.)

This is the first biblical book for which scholars generally agree concerning the dates. Although not all the events for 1 Samuel can be dated with certainty, there is a general consensus that David's reign over Judah began ca. 1010 B.C. This dates the beginning of Saul's kingship ca. 1050 B.C. and the birth of David about 10 years later. (The Iron Age had fully developed in Israel by the time of David.)

How 1 Samuel Fits into God's "Story"

First Samuel continues God's story: God builds his nation (Israel chosen as the people of promise). Throughout the period of the judges, the people of Israel had stagnated. In 1 Samuel, the story of God's kingdom leaps ahead dramatically. Just as Moses came as a powerful God-sent leader to bring change after centuries of little progress, so now Samuel came as a powerful God-sent leader. Just as Moses led Israel to receive the law, so Samuel led the people of his day to receive the king of God's choice. This book tells the rise of that king: "The LORD has found a man after his own heart" (13:14).

ORIGINAL HISTORICAL SETTING

Author and Date of Writing:
Unknown, perhaps ca. 950 B.C. (during Solomon's reign)

The book (1 and 2 Samuel together) was composed by someone who used sources, for none of the characters in it could have been an eyewitness to all the events mentioned. Some scholars think a clue to authorship is found in 1 Chr. 29:29: "As for the events of King David's reign, from beginning to end, note that they are written in the Events of the Seer Samuel, the Events of the Prophet Nathan, and the Events of the Seer Gad."

    The author's use of the phrase "still continues today" (see 1 Sam. 30:25) suggests a time of composition somewhat removed from when the events occurred. If the purpose of the composition was to answer questions about the legitimacy of Israel's kingship (see *Purpose,* above), then a date during Solomon's reign but before the divided monarchy fits. Other scholars suggest that the historical note in 1 Sam. 27:6 requires a date after the monarchy divided, but this could be an editorial comment added later.

First Audience and Destination:
Israelites living in their land during the monarchy

The book does not state its original audience or destination. The deduction noted above is surely true. Perhaps the original Scroll of Samuel was deposited in a book depository in Solomon's temple when it was first completed. There it would have joined the growing collection of Israel's sacred Scriptures.

Occasion

Since the authorship and date of composition are unknown, the occasion cannot be surmised. Because of its ultimate position in the Hebrew canon of Scripture as the third of the Former Prophets, 1 and 2 Samuel may have been prompted by the author's desire to continue the story of God's people Israel begun in the books of Joshua and Judges. Some scholars believe that the author was propelled by discovering long passages, originally composed by someone else, that stood on their own. These include the Ark Narrative (1 Sam. 4:1–7:1), David's Rise to Power (1 Sam. 16:14–2 Sam. 5:10), and Absalom's Revolt (2 Sam. 13–20).

 ## LITERARY FEATURES

Genre and Literary Style:
A historical account written in Hebrew

First Samuel tells the story of the rise of monarchy in Israel by giving the biographies of three men: Samuel, Saul, and David. When secondary characters such as Hannah and Jonathan enter the story, they are important only as they relate to the major characters. Although the Hebrew writing style is acceptable, the hand-copied Hebrew manuscripts of 1 and 2 Samuel have occasional defects in which words are missing, for example, Saul's age and length of reign in 1 Sam. 13:1. (Compare CSB with the KJV at this point.) In these cases, scholars rely on other ancient versions of the book. In the Hebrew canon, this was included in the Former Prophets. (See comments on *Genre and Literary Style* in *2 Kings* for further material about the possible literary relationship of the Former Prophets.)

Themes:
Kingship and covenant, the ark of the covenant, David's exploits

These three concepts dominate the book. Explaining the relationship between Israel's desire for a king and the national covenant with the Lord was the central concern of the writer. The writer's focus on the ark of the covenant is significant for two reasons. First, it looked back to the time of the ark's origin (Exodus). Second, it looked forward to the permanent home for the ark that David longed to build but Solomon finally constructed (1 Kgs.). The ark theme is thus one of continuity. The writer's pleasure in preserving David's ventures has given us some of the most memorable stories in Scripture, for example, his encounters with Goliath, Jonathan, and Abigail.

Book Features and Structure

David's career anticipates what his descendant Jesus later experienced. Both were identified by a prophet (Samuel and John the Baptist); empowered by the Spirit (16:13); and found refuge in a foreign land (Philistia and Egypt). Other parallels could be found.

Everything in this book happened in Israel or Philistia. Hannah's song (chap. 2) is a devotional high point of the Old Testament. The book is organized around three great men and tells their stories successively: Samuel and his ministry (chaps. 1–7); Saul's selection and rejection (chaps. 8–15); David's selection and exploits while Saul falls (chaps. 16–31).

2 SAMUEL
THE SECOND BOOK OF KINGDOMS

The book is named for Samuel, the judge who anointed Saul and David, the first two kings of Israel, of whom 1 and 2 Samuel tell the story. In the Hebrew Bible, 1 and 2 Samuel were originally one book. The Greek translators (second century B.C.), who divided the book, used the titles 1 and 2 Kingdoms.

⭕ KEY TEXT: 7:16

"Your house and kingdom will endure before me forever, and your throne will be established forever."

⭕ KEY TERM: "DAVID"

The name "David" appears more than 200 times in this book. It focuses entirely on the time that he was king of Israel.

⭕ ONE-SENTENCE SUMMARY

David's reign over Israel included times of elation, such as his conquest of Jerusalem and the Lord's promise of an everlasting dynasty, as well as times of failure, such as his adultery with Bathsheba and the treason of his son Absalom.

GOD'S MESSAGE IN THE BOOK

Purpose

Because 1 and 2 Samuel first existed as a single composition, see the discussion in the *Purpose* section for *1 Samuel*.

Christian Worldview Elements

Second Samuel touches on a number of worldview elements. However, above all it draws attention to the category *covenant and redemption*. God's covenant promise to David that he was the first king of an everlasting dynasty marked a major advance in the progress of divine revelation.

God
Creation
Sovereignty and Providence
Faith and Reason
Revelation and Authority
Humanity
Rebellion and Sin
⭕ **Covenant and Redemption**
Community and Church
Discipleship
Ethics and Morality
Time and Eternity

Teachings about God

God is sovereign in carrying out his kingdom plans. His unconditional covenant with undeserving David (chap. 7) is as magnificent as his covenant with Abraham. This book also says a great deal about approaching God in worship. He desires the worship of his people, but only in the ways he has revealed, as the material about the ark of the covenant emphasizes.

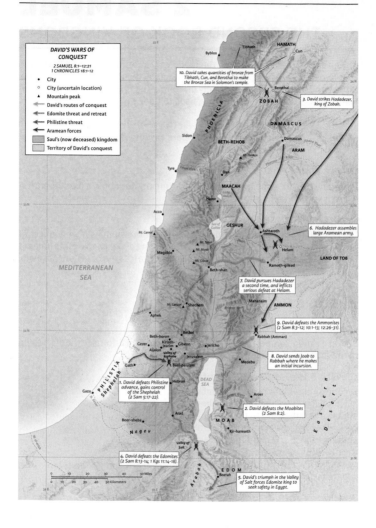

DAVID'S WARS OF CONQUEST

2 SAMUEL 8:1–12:21
1 CHRONICLES 18:1-12

- • City
- ○ City (uncertain location)
- ▲ Mountain peak
- ← David's routes of conquest
- ← Edomite threat and retreat
- ← Philistine threat
- ← Aramean forces
- ▨ Saul's (now deceased) kingdom
- ▨ Territory of David's conquest

10. David takes quantities of bronze from Tibhath, Cun, and Berothai to make the Bronze Sea in Solomon's temple.

3. David strikes Hadadezer, king of Zobah.

6. Hadadezer assembles large Aramean army.

7. David pursues Hadadezer a second time, and inflicts serious defeat at Helam.

9. David defeats the Ammonites (2 Sam 8:3-12; 10:1-13; 12:26-31).

8. David sends Joab to Rabbah where he makes an initial incursion.

1. David defeats Philistine advance, gains control of the Shephelah (2 Sam 5:17-22).

2. David defeats the Moabites (2 Sam 8:2).

4. David defeats the Edomites (2 Sam 8:13-14; 1 Kgs 11:14-18).

5. David's triumph in the Valley of Salt forces Edomite king to seek safety in Egypt.

MEDITERRANEAN SEA

DEAD SEA

HAMATH
Byblos
Tibhath
Cun
Berothai
ZOBAH
DAMASCUS
Damascus
ARAM
PHOENICIA
Sidon
BETH-REHOB
Mt. Hermon
Tyre
Dan
MAACAH
Hazor
Acco
GESHUR
Sea of Galilee
Ashtaroth
Helam
LAND OF TOB
Mt. Carmel
Mt. Tabor
Mt. Moreh
Mt. Gilboa
Megiddo
Beth-shan
Ramoth-gilead
Mt. Gerizim
Shechem
Mahanaim
AMMON
Aphek
Rabbah (Amman)
Bethel
Beth-horon
Gezer
Kiriath-jearim
Gibeon
Jericho
Aijalon
Valley of Rephaim
Jerusalem
Gath
Baal-perazim
Medeba
PHILISTIA
Shephelah
Hebron
Gaza
Aroer
Beer-sheba
Arad
MOAB
Ki-hareseth
Negev
Valley of Salt
EDOM
Bozrah
Eastern Desert
Arabah

0   10   20   30   40   50 Miles
0   10   20   30   40   50 Kilometers

Teachings about Humanity

Second Samuel throws the spotlight on one individual, David, who modeled magnificently that humans can accomplish great tasks for God when their heart is passionately turned to pleasing him. On the other hand, David's sins and failures show that redeemed humans still must deal with the effects of the fall in their lives.

Teachings about Salvation

The account of David's adultery, Nathan's confrontation with the king, and David's subsequent repentance and restoration stand as a profound paradigm of salvation. The following exchange distills the message of redemption even today: "David responded to Nathan, 'I have sinned against the LORD.' Then Nathan replied to David, 'And the LORD has taken away your sin; you will not die'" (12:13). David's reflection on this experience, Ps. 51, stands unsurpassed in Scripture on the relationship between confession of sin and divine forgiveness.

The Prophet Nathan Rebukes David by Eugène Siberdt (2 Sam. 12:1-14)

CHRIST IN 2 SAMUEL

As founder of the dynasty of which Jesus ("Son of David") is the eternal King, David illustrates Christ's kingship in many ways. His compassion and loyalty to Mephibosheth was one example of the undeserved love we receive from God.

GOD'S STORY

When the Events of This Book Happened:
From Saul's death to David's death (ca. 1110–970 B.C.)
The 40-year reign of David saw the beginning of the flowering of Israelite culture. Although scholars have a general consensus about the years of David's rule, there is insufficient evidence to date some of the prominent events of his reign, such as the birth of Solomon or the rebellion of Absalom.

How 2 Samuel Fits into God's "Story"
The book of 2 Samuel brings almost to a climax the beginning of God's story: God builds his nation (Israel chosen as the people of promise). This book tells, in more detail than for any other Israelite king, the story of the dynastic founder. It was critical to show that David, the man after God's heart (1 Sam. 13:14), had valued wholehearted obedience to God above all else in the way he went about establishing his kingship. Despite his flaws, David was the model king to whom the later kings looked for inspiration. Jesus, the greatest descendant of David, established the kingdom of God at his first coming and will consummate it at his second coming.

ORIGINAL HISTORICAL SETTING

Because 1 and 2 Samuel first existed as a single composition, see the discussion in the *Original Historical Setting* section in *1 Samuel*.

Author and Date of Writing:
Unknown, perhaps ca. 950 B.C. (during Solomon's reign)

First Audience and Destination:
Israelites living in the land of Israel during the monarchy

Occasion:
Unknown, but see *Occasion* for *1 Samuel*.

LITERARY FEATURES

Genre and Literary Style:

A historical narrative written in Hebrew, with a few passages of poetry

The narrative of 2 Samuel focuses on David's exploits as king. His relationship to God, Israel's true King, also receives attention. The writer portrayed him realistically and was careful not to gloss over David's faults. The memorable poetic sections were David's compositions: "The Song of the Bow" (1:19-27); "Song of Thanksgiving" (22:1-51, which is also Ps. 18); and "David's Last Words" (23:1-7). Second Samuel in the Hebrew canon was part of the Former Prophets. (See comments on *Genre and Literary Style* in *2 Kings* for further material about the possible literary relationship of the Former Prophets.)

Themes:

Kingship and covenant, the ark of the covenant, David's exploits

Because 1 and 2 Samuel first existed as a single composition, see the discussion in the *Themes* section of *1 Samuel*.

Book Features and Structure

The central theological feature of 2 Samuel is the unconditional promise of an unending dynasty that God made to David. In the overall understanding of God's redemptive purposes, it stands with and is an extension of the "royal grant" covenant that God initiated with Abraham (Gen. 12; 15). God promised that Abraham would be the father of nations; he promised that David would be the first king of an unending dynasty of kings that would rule forever. Jesus Christ fulfills these promises: "The kingdom of the world has become the kingdom of our Lord and of his Christ, and he will reign forever and ever" (Rev. 11:15).

The narrative of David's rule is developed in three stages: David's kingdom secured (chaps. 1–4); David's capital, covenant, and conquests (chaps. 5–10); David's faults (chaps. 11–20). Chapters 21–24 are an epilogue, perhaps compiled from a variety of materials about David's reign.

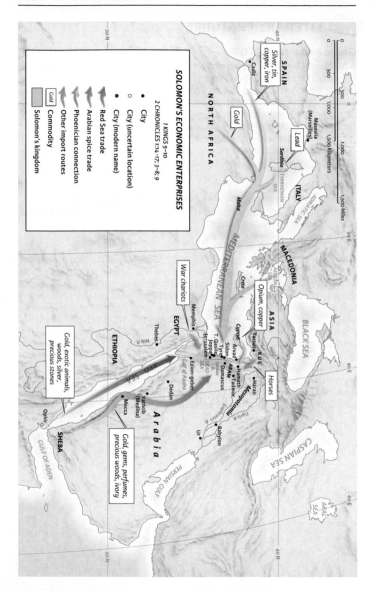

SOLOMON'S ECONOMIC ENTERPRISES

1 KINGS 5–10
2 CHRONICLES 1:14–17; 3–8; 9

- • City
- ○ City (uncertain location)
- • City (modern name)
- ➤ Red Sea trade
- ➤ Arabian spice trade
- ➤ Phoenician connection
- ➤ Other import routes
- ▨ Solomon's kingdom
- *Gold* Commodity

SPAIN
Silver, tin, copper, iron
Cadiz •
NORTH AFRICA
Gold
Massalia (Marseilles) •
Lead
Sardinia
Malta
ITALY
TYRRHENIAN SEA
ADRIATIC SEA
MEDITERRANEAN SEA
MACEDONIA
Crete
AEGEAN SEA
ASIA
Opium, copper
BLACK SEA
Cyprus •
Tarsus •
KUE
Horses
Arvad •
Sidon •
Tyre •
T. Qasile •
Joppa •
Jerusalem •
GILEAD
Hamath •
Damascus •
Tadmor •
ARAM
Hiran •
Euphrates R.
Mesopotamia
Tigris R.
Babylon •
Ur •
PERSIAN GULF
CASPIAN SEA
ARAL SEA
War chariots
EGYPT
Memphis •
Thebes •
Nile R.
ETHIOPIA
RED SEA
Gulf of Aqaba
Ezion-geber •
Dedan •
Mecca •
Yathrib (Medina) •
Arabia
Gold, gems, perfumes, precious woods, ivory
Gold, exotic animals, woods, silver, precious stones
SHEBA
Ophir ○
GULF OF ADEN

0   500   1,000   1,500 Kilometers
0   500   1,000   1,500 Miles

20 N   40 N   20 E   40 E   60 E

1 KINGS
THE THIRD BOOK OF KINGDOMS

Melakim, the Hebrew title, means "Kings." Originally a single work, 1 and 2 Kings was first divided into two books by the Greek translators (second century B.C.), and English Bibles follow this pattern. The Greek version used the titles 3 and 4 Kingdoms.

○ KEY TEXT: 11:35-36

"I will take ten tribes of the kingdom from his son and give them to you. I will give one tribe to his son, so that my servant David will always have a lamp before me in Jerusalem, the city I chose for myself to put my name there."

○ KEY TERM: "DIVISION"

This book describes the division of the Israelites into two competing kingdoms. The kings of Israel, the northern kingdom, were invariably idolatrous, while the kings of Judah, the southern kingdom, were sometimes good and sometimes evil.

○ ONE-SENTENCE SUMMARY

After Solomon's splendid rule, culminating in the dedication of the temple in Jerusalem, the kingdom divided, and God raised up prophets to confront idolatry, notably Elijah, who opposed the evil Ahab.

GOD'S MESSAGE IN THE BOOK

Purpose

Since this book was originally the first half of a single composition, the purpose for the books now called 1 and 2 Kings must be considered together. This work answered important questions for Israelites (probably living in the years of exile in Babylon) about the period of the kings from God's perspective. If they were now in exile, why had this happened, especially since Solomon's rule had been so splendid? Had the later kings failed militarily? Politically? Economically? The answer was that the kings (and the people under them) had all in all failed religiously. They had abandoned the Lord, their true King, and he had sent three painful lessons to teach them the importance of staying true to him. First, he divided Israel into two kingdoms (1 Kgs. 12, ca. 931 B.C.); second, he sent the idolatrous northern kingdom into permanent captivity through the Assyrians (2 Kgs. 17, ca. 722 B.C.); third, he sent the idolatrous southern kingdom into (temporary) exile through the Babylonians (2 Kgs. 25, ca. 586 B.C.).

So the author wrote a highly selective account of the kings, evaluating each one as to whether he did right or evil in the eyes of the Lord. The author's religious perspective is also seen in that about a third of the narrative focuses on the prophetic ministries of Elijah and Elisha. God's people who study the books of Kings today should do so with this original purpose in mind.

The Anointing of Solomon by Cornelis de Vos (1 Kgs. 1:39)

Christian Worldview Elements

Because 1 Kings covers more than 120 years in so brief a narrative, it brings into sharp focus the worldview category of *time and eternity* (that history moves forward according to God's plan). It also adds insight into the categories of *covenant and redemption* (demonstrated in the wonderful achievements of Solomon, especially the temple) and *rebellion and sin* (shown particularly in the conflict between Ahab and Elijah).

God
Creation
Sovereignty and Providence
Faith and Reason
Revelation and Authority
Humanity
○ **Rebellion and Sin**
○ **Covenant and Redemption**
Community and Church
Discipleship
Ethics and Morality
○ **Time and Eternity**

Teachings about God

First Kings emphasizes "one God, one temple." Because Israel's God is the one true Lord of all, then he can be worshiped properly at the one place that he has designated: the temple in Jerusalem. He will not tolerate the worship of rival deities (such as Baal). He will not long endure being worshiped in rival sites (such as at the shrines of the golden calves in Dan and Bethel or on the "high places"). The Spirit is present to inspire God's prophets.

Teachings about Humanity

This book looks at humanity by evaluating the kings' lives. The only thing that really mattered was whether a king did "right in the LORD's sight" (15:5,11; 22:43) or whether he did "evil in the LORD's sight" (11:6; this phrase occurs eight times in the text).

Teachings about Salvation

On one hand, 1 Kings emphasizes that salvation is entirely due to God's sovereign work. Solomon's temple dedication prayer emphasized this: "For you, Lord GOD, have set them apart as your inheritance from all peoples of the earth" (8:53). On the other hand, his people were expected to live in loyalty to the covenant, and both kings and people are evaluated according to the terms of the covenant established at Mount Sinai.

 CHRIST IN 1 KINGS

Solomon, David's son and Israel's third king, is prominent in 1 Kings. Solomon's wisdom and splendor were known far beyond Israel. This shining hour in Israel's history points to the wisdom and glory of Christ. Jesus reminded one of his audiences that the Queen of Sheba made a long journey to hear Solomon and One greater than Solomon is now among them (Luke 11:31).

 GOD'S STORY

When the Events of This Book Happened:

From David's death through Jehoshaphat's death (ca. 970–848 B.C.)
During the first 40 years covered by this book, the Israelite nation reached its splendid apex. After Solomon's death ca. 931 B.C., the Davidic dynasty was restricted to the southern kingdom of Judah. First Kings describes the rule of the next four Davidic monarchs. In the northern kingdom during the same era, political instability was the norm, with dynasties coming and going. The most important northern kings politically were Jeroboam I (who established the northern kingdom and set up golden calves); Omri (who established Samaria as his capital); and Ahab (who forged a foreign alliance by marrying a pagan princess, Jezebel, daughter of Ethbaal, king of Tyre and Sidon).

How 1 Kings Fits into God's "Story"

First Kings completes "chapter 1" of God's story: God builds his nation (Israel chosen as the people of promise). It begins "chapter 2" of the story: God educates

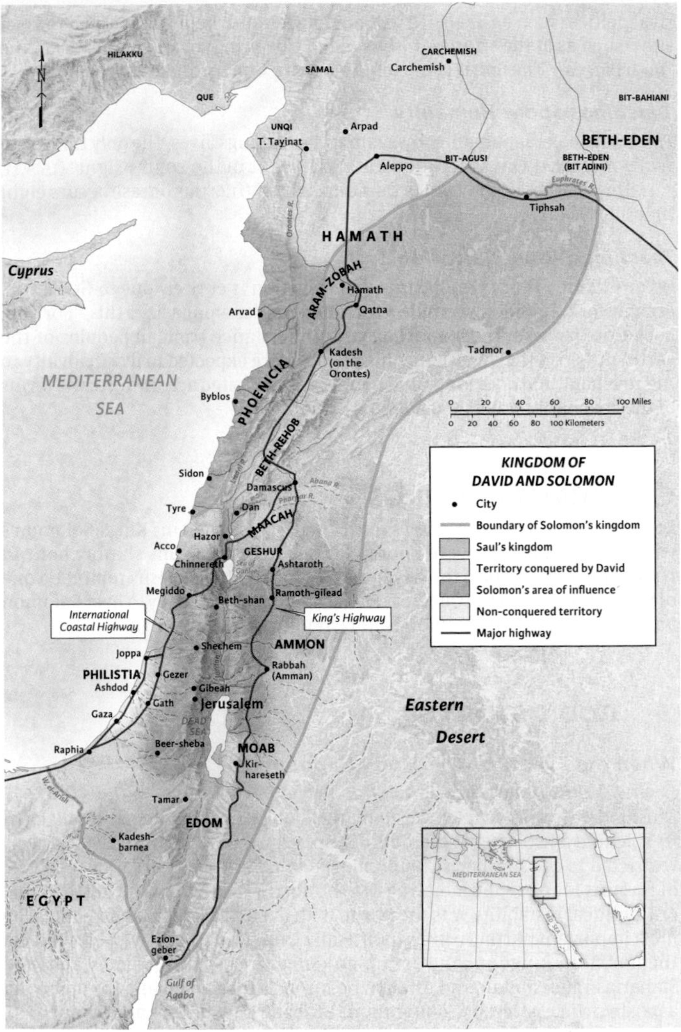

KINGDOM OF DAVID AND SOLOMON
City
Boundary of Solomon's kingdom
Saul's kingdom
Territory conquered by David
Solomon's area of influence
Non-conquered territory
Major highway
HILAKKU
QUE
SAMAL
UNQI
T. Tayinat
Arpad
CARCHEMISH
Carchemish
BIT-BAHIANI
BETH-EDEN
BIT-AGUSI
Aleppo
BETH-EDEN (BIT ADINI)
Euphrates R.
Tiphsah
HAMATH
ARAM-ZOBAH
Hamath
Qatna
Cyprus
Arvad
Kadesh (on the Orontes)
Tadmor
MEDITERRANEAN SEA
PHOENICIA
Byblos
BETH-REHOB
Sidon
Damascus
Tyre
Dan
MAACAH
Hazor
Acco
GESHUR
Chinnereth
Ashtaroth
Megiddo
Ramoth-gilead
Beth-shan
International Coastal Highway
King's Highway
Joppa
Shechem
AMMON
PHILISTIA
Gezer
Rabbah (Amman)
Ashdod
Gibeah
Gath
Jerusalem
Gaza
Eastern Desert
Raphia
Beer-sheba
MOAB
Kir-hareseth
Tamar
EDOM
Kadesh-barnea
EGYPT
Ezion-geber
Gulf of Aqaba
0 20 40 60 80 100 Miles
0 20 40 60 80 100 Kilometers
MEDITERRANEAN SEA

his nation (disobedient Israel disciplined). It depicts the earthly nation of Israel at its grandest and most glorious during the rule of Solomon. Jerusalem was truly splendid as a wealthy, walled capital city whose king was legendary for his wisdom and to whom other nations brought tribute. Although this was a blip in the history of the ancient Near East, it stood forever in the hearts of Israelites as a time that could be regained. Strikingly, the portrait of the eternal state in Rev. 21–22 is like Solomon's Jerusalem, but infinitely more glorious.

ORIGINAL HISTORICAL SETTING

Author and Date of Writing:
Unknown, perhaps Jeremiah ca. 560 B.C.

First Kings and 2 Kings are anonymous, but Jewish tradition named Jeremiah, who was also credited with the books of Jeremiah and Lamentations. Most modern scholars discount the traditional view. Whoever the author was cannot now be known. The perspective is that of the exile in Babylon. The writer, however, used sources from an earlier time, incorporating their phrase "still there today" (e.g., 1 Kgs. 8:8; 2 Kgs. 8:22) for matters that did not exist during the exile.

Elijah and the widow at Zarephath (1 Kgs. 17:17-24)

First Audience and Destination:
Probably the Israelites living in Babylonian exile
The original audience is not stated but is judged from reading the book. (See the discussion above on *Purpose* for an explanation of how 1 and 2 Kings met the needs of Israelites living after the destruction of Jerusalem and the temple.)

Occasion
Some official court records from the monarchy were evidently preserved and transported to Babylon. These included "the Book of Solomon's Events" (1 Kgs. 11:41); "the Historical Record of Israel's Kings" (1 Kgs. 14:19 and 17 other references); and "the Historical Record of Judah's Kings" (1 Kgs. 14:29 and 14 other references). The writer selected materials from these records to interpret the era of Solomon and the divided monarchy for people of his day.

 ## LITERARY FEATURES

Genre and Literary Style:
An extremely selective account written in Hebrew
First Kings focuses on the days of Solomon and then tells of the reigns of most other kings with broad strokes. Then when he comes to Ahab, the author provides a number of details once again, in particular describing the role of Elijah as the prophet of the Lord. First Kings in the Hebrew Scriptures was one of the Former Prophets. (See comments on *Genre and Literary Style* in *2 Kings* for further material about the possible literary relationship of the Former Prophets.)

Themes:
The temple, kingship and covenant, the rise of the prophets
The completion of the temple brought the Israelite people to their finest hour. After Solomon's death, the unending challenge was to keep Israel and its kings true to the Lord and true to worshiping him at the temple. Thus monarchs are evaluated as righteous or evil in this light. God raised up the prophet Elijah (and his successors) to call Israel back to God.

Book Features and Structure
The author was interested in chronological data. He noted that the temple was built 480 years after the exodus (6:1). For the period of the divided monarchy, he maintained a cross reference system between the kings of Israel and Judah, which has the effect of showing that both kingdoms were still God's people. The typical formula the author used was, "in the ____year of ____ son of ____, ____became king over Judah [or Israel], and he reigned ____years" (see, e.g.,15:1).

Everything in this book happened in either Israel or Judah, with the exception of Elijah's travels outside the land. The book has three sections: Solomon and his splendid reign (chaps. 1–11); the early period of the divided monarchy (chaps. 12–16); and Elijah and the events surrounding his ministry (chaps. 17–22).

2 KINGS
THE FOURTH BOOK OF KINGDOMS

Melakim, the Hebrew title, means "Kings." Originally a single work, 1 and 2 Kings was first divided into two books by the Greek translators (second century B.C.), and English Bibles follow this pattern. The Greek version used the titles 3 and 4 Kingdoms.

○ KEY TEXT: 17:22-23

"The Israelites persisted in all the sins that Jeroboam committed and did not turn away from them. Finally, the LORD removed Israel from his presence just as he had declared through all his servants the prophets. So Israel has been exiled to Assyria from their homeland to this very day."

○ KEY TERM: "DISPERSION"

This book tells the ongoing story of the Israelites in two competing kingdoms with its sad conclusion. The northern kingdom fell to Assyria and was dispersed forever. Then the southern kingdom fell to the Babylonians and likewise went into dispersion.

○ ONE-SENTENCE SUMMARY

Even after Elisha's ministry, Israel persisted in idolatry and so went into permanent captivity; yet Judah, despite the prophets and a few righteous kings, continued to be so wicked that God sent Babylon to remove the people into exile.

GOD'S MESSAGE IN THE BOOK

Purpose

Because 1 and 2 Kings first existed as a single composition, see the discussion in the *Purpose* section of *1 Kings*.

Christian Worldview Elements

Second Kings covers nearly three centuries, so it brings into sharp focus the worldview category of *time and eternity* (that history moves forward according to God's plan). It also adds insight into the category of *rebellion and sin*, demonstrated in the ongoing idolatry of Israel and Judah culminating in their destruction.

God
Creation
Sovereignty and Providence
Faith and Reason
Revelation and Authority
Humanity
○ **Rebellion and Sin**
Covenant and Redemption
Community and Church
Discipleship
Ethics and Morality
○ **Time and Eternity**

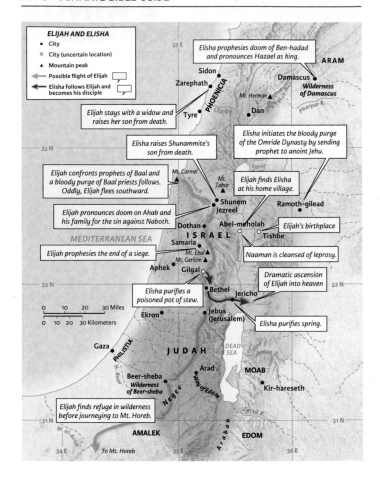

ELIJAH AND ELISHA

- • City
- ○ City (uncertain location)
- ▲ Mountain peak
- ← Possible flight of Elijah
- ← Elisha follows Elijah and becomes his disciple

Elisha prophesies doom of Ben-hadad and pronounces Hazael as king.

Elijah stays with a widow and raises her son from death.

Elisha raises Shunammite's son from death.

Elijah confronts prophets of Baal and a bloody purge of Baal priests follows. Oddly, Elijah flees southward.

Elisha initiates the bloody purge of the Omride Dynasty by sending prophet to anoint Jehu.

Elijah finds Elisha at his home village.

Elijah pronounces doom on Ahab and his family for the sin against Naboth.

Elijah's birthplace

Elijah prophesies the end of a siege.

Naaman is cleansed of leprosy.

Dramatic ascension of Elijah into heaven.

Elisha purifies a poisoned pot of stew.

Elisha purifies spring.

Elijah finds refuge in wilderness before journeying to Mt. Horeb.

ARAM
Sidon
Zarephath
PHOENICIA
Damascus
Wilderness of Damascus
Mt. Hermon ▲
Pharpar R.
Tyre
Dan
Litani R.
Sea of
Mt. Carmel ▲
Kishon R.
Mt. Tabor ▲
Shunem
Jezreel
Ramoth-gilead
Dothan
Abel-meholah
Tishbe
MEDITERRANEAN SEA
ISRAEL
Samaria
Mt. Ebal ▲
Mt. Gerizim ▲
Jordan R.
Aphek
Gilgal
Bethel
Jericho
Jebus (Jebus)
(Jerusalem)
Ekron
Gaza
PHILISTIA
JUDAH
DEAD SEA
Arnon R.
Arad
MOAB
Kir-hareseth
Beer-sheba
Wilderness of Beer-sheba
Way of Edom
Negev
Zered R.
N. Besor
Arabah
AMALEK
EDOM
W. el-Arish
To Mt. Horeb

0   10   20   30 Miles
0   10   20   30 Kilometers

35 E
33 N
32 N   32 N
31 N   31 N
34 E   35 E   36 E

Teachings about God

Like Judges and 2 Chronicles, 2 Kings shows the severity of God in judging those who rebel against him. Deuteronomy had promised divine condemnation on those who were unfaithful to the Lord. The story of 2 Kings is largely one of disloyalty, and God's "educational program" meant teaching his people that he values faithfulness to him above all else, even if that means exiling them. The book ends with a ray of hope: God's promises about an everlasting Davidic dynasty are intact, for the king is still alive.

Teachings about Humanity

Like 1 Kings, this book evaluates people by just one criterion: did they do "right in the LORD's sight" or not? Tragically, for the most part, both kings and people did not. (See *Key Text above.*) The author reached the following verdict about the last king of Judah: "Zedekiah did what was evil in the LORD's sight just as Jehoiakim had done. Because of the LORD's anger, it came to the point in Jerusalem and Judah that he finally banished them from his presence" (24:19-20).

Teachings about Salvation

God's prophets in 2 Kings (Elijah, Elisha, Jonah, Huldah, and Isaiah are named) called people to repent for their religious apostasy and to worship the Lord alone. Hezekiah is the model of trust in the Lord for salvation (18:5-6). Turning from the sin of idolatry, when accompanied by a desire for God's glory to be displayed, may even bring salvation from military threats (see Hezekiah's prayer and God's response in 19:15-37).

 CHRIST IN 2 KINGS

Second Kings presents the ministries of Elijah and Elisha, prophets through whom God performed mighty acts. In the Gospels, Jesus is described as "a prophet powerful in action and speech before God and all the people" (Luke 24:19). God preserved Israel's monarch as long as he did because of his promises to David (8:19). Israel may even count on God to preserve a lamp for David forever (Rev. 21:23).

 GOD'S STORY

When the Events of This Book Happened:
From Ahab's death through the thirty-seventh year of King Jehoiachin's exile in Babylon (ca. 853–561 B.C.)

During the early years of the divided kingdom, the enemies of Israel and Judah were the surrounding petty kingdoms, for example, Aram to the north (called Syria in the KJV), with its capital in Damascus. About 900 B.C., the Mesopotamian power Assyria, with Nineveh as its capital, entered a period of aggressive expansion. In the 730s under Tiglath-Pileser III (also called Pul), most of the eastern Mediterranean came under Assyrian domination. Shalmaneser V laid siege to Samaria, and his successor, Sargon II, took Samaria and the northern kingdom captive in 722 B.C. His successor, Sennacherib, invaded Judah ca. 701, but God protected King Hezekiah and the temple.

The ancient Babylonian Empire experienced new power and came to dominate the ancient Near East (626–536 B.C.), conquering Nineveh in 612. Scholars refer to this as the neo-Babylonian or the Chaldean period. Their most important

The Taylor Prism contains an account of Sennacherib's campaign in Judah that included the siege of Jerusalem. Second Kings 18:13–19:37 provides a parallel account. Sennacherib's account doesn't mention the fact that he was unable to take Jerusalem. The prism was discovered in Nineveh and purchased in 1830 by Col. Robert Taylor, British Consul General.

king was Nebuchadnezzar, who invaded Judah more than once. He was responsible for burning the temple and Jerusalem in 586 B.C. and for carrying the people of Judah into captivity.

How 2 Kings Fits into God's "Story"

Second Kings completes "chapter 2" of the story: God educates his nation (disobedient Israel disciplined). It depicts Israel in spiritual disgrace and shame. Despite the ministry of Elisha, the northern kingdom never had a righteous king—all worshiped idols—and, true to his word, God sent its people into permanent dispersion. The southern kingdom had a few righteous moments, particularly in the reigns of Hezekiah and Josiah. Ultimately, however, God sent the southern kingdom into exile. Yet God's kingdom plan was never in jeopardy. The royal Davidic line lived on, even though a temporal kingdom and temple were not the goal.

 ORIGINAL HISTORICAL SETTING

Because 1 and 2 Kings first existed as a single composition, see the discussion in the *Original Historical Setting* section in *1 Kings*.

Author and Date of Writing:
Unknown, perhaps Jeremiah ca. 560 B.C.

First Audience and Destination:
Probably the Israelites living in Babylonian exile

Occasion
Unknown, but see *Occasion* for *1 Kings*.

 LITERARY FEATURES

Genre and Literary Style:
An extremely selective account written in Hebrew
In describing the period of the divided monarchy, the writer alternated between the kings of Israel and the kings of Judah. He gave attention only to Jehu, the founder of yet another dynasty in Israel, and Joash, the boy king of Judah. After describing the fall of the northern kingdom, the author focused only on two righteous kings, Hezekiah and Josiah. His interpretation of the reason Israel fell (chap. 17) and then Judah (chap. 25) was entirely theological, rather than military, political, or economic.

In the Hebrew Scriptures, the single composition 1 and 2 Kings was placed as the last of the four Former Prophets. Beginning with Joshua and Judges, and then moving on to Samuel (collectively) and Kings (collectively), these books described the 800-year period from Israel's entry into Canaan (ca. 1406 B.C.) through the destruction of the temple and Jerusalem and the exile to Babylon (ca. 586 B.C.). Their common theme is that sin brings divine punishment, but obedience brings blessing and peace (in line with the teachings of Deuteronomy, especially chaps. 27–28).

This interpretation is commonly called Deuteronomic History. Critical scholars have argued that this view arose quite late in the Israelite monarchy, perhaps at the time of Josiah, yet it is much more believable that Moses himself by divine revelation originated this perspective, as Deuteronomy plainly claims. Then the later historians more or less uniformly used the interpretive lens of Deuteronomy to write their respective parts of Israel's history. Finally, the books reflecting this perspective were gathered into Israel's canon as the first section of the Prophets.

Themes:
The temple, kingship and covenant, the rise of the prophets
Because 1 and 2 Kings first existed as a single composition, see the discussion in the *Themes* section in *1 Kings*.

Book Features and Structure
The writer was especially interested in the ministry of Elisha (chaps. 2–8), for which he may have borrowed from an existing source. He also emphasized two major sieges of Jerusalem. The first by Sennacherib of Assyria, ca. 701 B.C., was thwarted by divine intervention (chap. 19). The second by Nebuchadnezzar of Babylon, ca. 586 B.C., destroyed the city and Solomon's temple (chap. 25).

Second Kings has three sections: Elisha's ministry (chaps. 1–8); the later period of the divided monarchy (chaps. 9–17); and the period of Judah alone (chaps. 18–25).

1 CHRONICLES

First divided by the Greek translators (second century B.C.), 1 and 2 Chronicles were originally one book, *Dibre Hayyamim*, "Events of the Days," in the Hebrew Bible. The English title comes from *Chronicon*, the name given by the Latin translator Jerome.

○ KEY TEXT: 28:4

"Yet the LORD God of Israel chose me out of all my father's family to be king over Israel forever. For he chose Judah as leader, and from the house of Judah, my father's family, and from my father's sons, he was pleased to make me king over all Israel."

○ KEY TERM: "DYNASTY"

First Chronicles focuses on how God established the everlasting dynasty of David, describing David's positive achievements, both religiously and militarily.

○ ONE-SENTENCE SUMMARY

After extensive introductory genealogies, the author tells how David ruled for 40 years under the blessing of God, particularly as he lavished attention on Jerusalem, the priesthood, and preparation for building the temple.

 GOD'S MESSAGE IN THE BOOK

Purpose

Since this book was originally the first half of a single composition, the purpose for the books now called 1 and 2 Chronicles must be considered together. This work answered important questions for Israelites who had returned after years of exile in Babylon. Their times were difficult and disappointing. Did they still fit into God's plan? Were the promises of God still applicable to them? Further, what religious and political institutions were important? Finally, what lessons from the past could they learn to keep from making the same mistakes?

The author answered these questions by compiling a highly selective religious history. The covenant God made with David concerning an eternal dynasty was still in effect. Even with no Davidic king on the throne, they were still God's people and could still wait in hope for restoration of the monarchy. While waiting, they could do the things God required, such as offer the right sacrifices with the right priests at the right place. Finally, although David and Solomon are presented as ideal kings, the apostasy of later kings is noted as the cause of Babylonian exile (2 Chr. 36:16). God's people who study the books of Chronicles today should do so with the author's original purposes in mind.

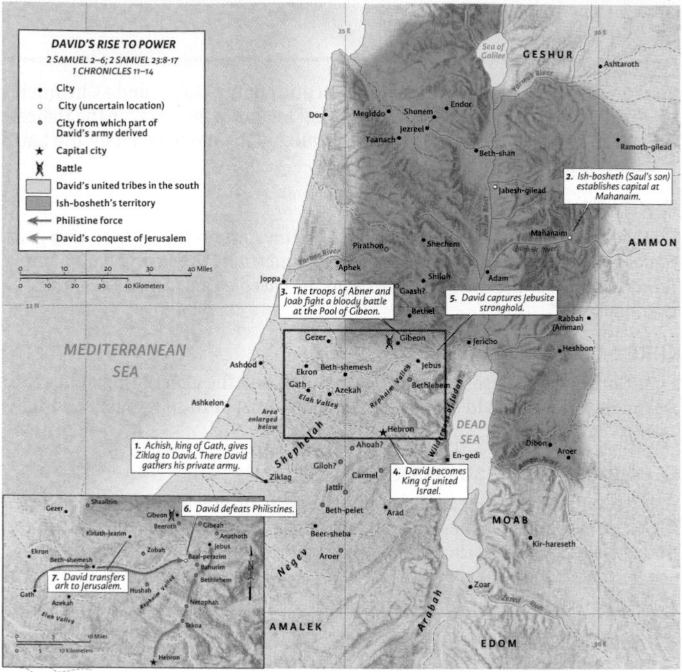

DAVID'S RISE TO POWER
2 SAMUEL 2–6; 2 SAMUEL 23:8-17
1 CHRONICLES 11–14

- City
- ○ City (uncertain location)
- ● City from which part of David's army derived
- ★ Capital city
- ✗ Battle
- David's united tribes in the south
- Ish-bosheth's territory
- ← Philistine force
- ← David's conquest of Jerusalem

1. Achish, king of Gath, gives Ziklag to David. There David gathers his private army.
2. Ish-bosheth (Saul's son) establishes capital at Mahanaim.
3. The troops of Abner and Joab fight a bloody battle at the Pool of Gibeon.
4. David becomes King of united Israel.
5. David captures Jebusite stronghold.
6. David defeats Philistines.
7. David transfers ark to Jerusalem.

Christian Worldview Elements

First Chronicles touches on a number of worldview elements. However, above all, it draws attention to the category *covenant and redemption*. God's covenant promise to David that he was the first king of an everlasting dynasty marked a major advance in the progress of divine revelation.

God
Creation
Sovereignty and Providence
Faith and Reason
Revelation and Authority
Humanity
Rebellion and Sin
○ Covenant and Redemption
Community and Church
Discipleship
Ethics and Morality
Time and Eternity

Teachings about God

God is sovereign in carrying out his kingdom plans. His unconditional covenant with undeserving David (chap. 17) is as magnificent as his covenant with Abraham. He desires the worship of his people in the ways he has revealed. (See 28:11-12 for the Holy Spirit's work in revealing the plans for temple construction.) David's concern for the ark, his preparation for building the temple, and the elaborate material on organizing the priests and Levites properly all shows this.

Teachings about Humanity

The long genealogies at the beginning of 1 Chronicles show that God cares for people as individuals. Each one has worth as created in the image of God. If a historian took the trouble to discover and preserve these lists that may seem tedious, how much more does God care for the "little people" who can appear to be insignificant? Moreover David modeled magnificently that humans can accomplish great tasks for God when their hearts are passionately turned to pleasing him.

Teachings about Salvation

The book's clearest teaching on salvation as the gift of God is David's psalm of thanksgiving when the ark of the covenant was finally moved into a tent (chap. 16). The conclusion especially demonstrates that the purpose of salvation is to bring glory to God:

"Give thanks to the LORD, for he is good; his faithful love endures forever. And say: 'Save us, God of our salvation; gather us and rescue us from the nations so that we may give thanks to your holy name and rejoice in your praise. Blessed be the LORD God of Israel from everlasting to everlasting'" (16:34-36).

 CHRIST IN 1 CHRONICLES

The messianic promise of a son of David to rule over Israel occupies the center of 1 Chronicles (chap. 17). The family lines of Israel's kings are traced (chap. 3), showing God has been faithful to maintain a son of David to lead Israel even in the face of exile. This son of David is described as the eternally loved son of God (17:13; Luke 1:32-33; Heb. 1:5). David's prayer of praise (29:10-13) is applied to Jesus (Rev. 5:12-13).

 GOD'S STORY

When the Events of This Book Happened:
During David's reign (ca. 1010–970 B.C.)
The genealogies at the beginning of 1 Chronicles cover the generations from Adam until sometime after the return from Babylonian exile, perhaps around 450 B.C. The 40-year reign of David saw the beginning of the flowering of Israelite culture. Although scholars have a general consensus about the years of David's rule, there is insufficient evidence to date some of the prominent events of his reign, such as the conquest of Jerusalem or the purchase of the land on which to build the temple.

How 1 Chronicles Fits into God's "Story"

First Chronicles tells part of "chapter 1" of God's story: God builds his nation (Israel chosen as the people of promise). David desired to build a house (temple) for God. God promised instead to build an everlasting house (dynasty) for David (17:1-15). Although temple and kingship go together throughout Chronicles, neither existed by the end of the book. This was, however, only temporary. God intended for his people to become his temple (1 Cor. 3:16; Eph. 2:21). Further, Jesus, the greatest descendant of David, fulfills the promise of everlasting kingship. Thus Chronicles tells the initial space-and-time fulfillment of a reality that will come to joyful fruition throughout eternity.

 ## ORIGINAL HISTORICAL SETTING

Author and Date of Writing:
Unknown, possibly Ezra ca. 450 B.C.

Scholars refer to the anonymous author of 1 and 2 Chronicles as the Chronicler. According to Jewish tradition, Ezra was the composer, but this cannot be either proved or disproved. The work was written after the return of the exiles from Babylon. Some scholars date the book in the 300s, but on the whole an earlier date seems more likely.

First Audience and Destination:
Israelites in Jerusalem after they returned from exile

The book does not state its original audience or destination, but see the earlier discussion on the book's purpose. Perhaps the original manuscript was placed in a book depository in the rebuilt temple. There it would have joined the growing collection of Israel's sacred Scriptures.

Occasion

Because the authorship and date are uncertain, no one knows what prompted Chronicles to be written. The author used many sources, including the biblical books of Samuel and Kings. The author mentioned official court documents, called "the Book of the Kings of Israel (or "Judah and Israel") (1 Chr. 9:1; 2 Chr. 16:11). He also had access to material written by certain prophets, such as "the Events of the Seer Samuel, the Events of the Prophet Nathan, and the Events of the Seer Gad" (1 Chr. 29:29); "the Events of Jehu son of Hanani" (2 Chr. 20:34); and "the Visions of the Prophet Isaiah" (2 Chr. 32:32). Other sources, such as old genealogies and temple lists, appear likely.

LITERARY FEATURES

Genre and Literary Style:
Genealogical tables, narrative history, and some poetry, all composed in Hebrew

The genealogical material is the most extensive found in Scripture. The account of David's kingship is focused differently from the account in 2 Samuel. Neither his adultery with Bathsheba nor the treason of Absalom is considered. David is almost perfect in 1 Chronicles; even his taking a census of Israel is attributed to Satan and resulted in the royal discovery of the proper site for the temple (chap. 21). The brief poetic sections preserve prayers of David (chaps. 16; 29). (See comments on *Genre and Literary Style* in *Nehemiah* for further material about the possible literary relationship of Chronicles, Ezra, and Nehemiah.)

Themes:
Davidic dynasty, temple, blessing of obedience and punishment of disobedience

The author focused only on the Davidic kings. The rising and falling fortunes of Solomon's temple are another great theme. In 1 Chronicles (unlike 2 Samuel), David is shown making grand preparations to build the temple. In 2 Chronicles, the temple is built and dedicated—and restored more than once—before being destroyed. The Chronicler also demonstrated that obeying the laws of Moses and proper worship in the temple resulted in divine blessing, while unfaithfulness brought disaster.

Book Features and Structure

By repeating often the phrase "all Israel," especially in reference to the exiles (9:1), the author emphasized to his initial audience that they were God's people. Perhaps the most striking feature of 1 Chronicles is the variety of name lists. Chapters 1–9 are genealogical lists. Other lists include "David's Warriors" (chap. 11); "Divisions of the Levites" (chap. 23); "Divisions of the Priests" (chap. 24); "The Levitical Musicians" (chap. 25); "The Levitical Gatekeepers" (chap. 26); and "David's Secular Officials" (chap. 27). First Chronicles has two major sections: genealogies (chaps. 1–9) and David's reign (chaps. 10–29).

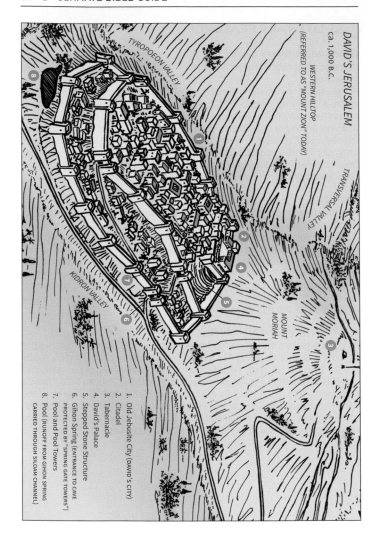

DAVID'S JERUSALEM
ca. 1,000 B.C.

WESTERN HILLTOP
(REFERRED TO AS "MOUNT ZION" TODAY)

TYROPOEON VALLEY

TRANSVERSAL VALLEY

KIDRON VALLEY

MOUNT MORIAH

1. Old Jebusite City (DAVID'S CITY)
2. Citadel
3. Tabernacle
4. David's Palace
5. Stepped Stone Structure
6. Gihon Spring (ENTRANCE TO CAVE PROTECTED BY "SPRING GATE TOWERS")
7. Pool and Pool Towers
8. Pool (RUNOFF FROM GIHON SPRING CARRIED THROUGH SILOAM CHANNEL)

2 CHRONICLES

First divided by the Greek translators (second century B.C.), 1 and 2 Chronicles were originally one book, *Dibre Hayyamin*, "Events of the Days," in the Hebrew Bible. The English title comes from *Chronicon*, the name given by the Latin translator Jerome.

O KEY TEXTS: 7:1 AND 36:19

"When Solomon finished praying, fire descended from heaven and consumed the burnt offering and the sacrifices, and the glory of the LORD filled the temple."

"Then the Chaldeans burned God's temple. They tore down Jerusalem's wall, burned all its palaces, and destroyed all its valuable articles."

O KEY TERM: "TEMPLE"

The book begins with Solomon's plans to build the temple in Jerusalem and ends with its destruction. Between dedication and destruction (ca. 384 years, from 959 to 586 B.C.), the temple was sometimes neglected and sometimes refurbished, but it was always the most important building in Israel.

O ONE-SENTENCE SUMMARY

After Solomon's glorious reign, which culminated in the dedication of the temple, kings of the Davidic dynasty—some righteous and some evil—continued ruling in Jerusalem, ending in the destruction of the temple and the exile.

GOD'S MESSAGE IN THE BOOK

Purpose

Because 1 and 2 Chronicles first existed as a single composition, see the discussion in the *Purpose* section of *1 Chronicles*.

Christian Worldview Elements

Second Chronicles covers more than four centuries, so it brings into sharp focus the worldview category of *time and eternity* (that history moves forward according to God's plan). The category of *community* is also important, demonstrated in the ongoing use of the phrase "all Israel."

Teachings about God

Second Chronicles shows that God blesses faithfulness to him and punishes his people when they turn away from him. God's "educational program" meant teaching his people that he values allegiance to him above all else. The book ends with a note of hope: the Israelite exiles have been permitted to return

SOLOMON'S TEMPLE, Exterior View (LOOKING WEST)

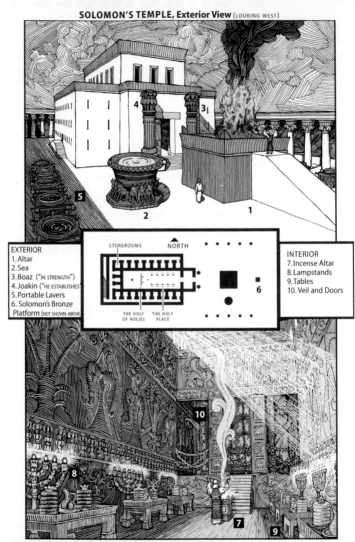

EXTERIOR
1. Altar
2. Sea
3. Boaz ("IN STRENGTH")
4. Joakin ("HE ESTABLISHES")
5. Portable Lavers
6. Solomon's Bronze
   Platform (NOT SHOWN ABOVE)

STOREROOMS   NORTH

THE HOLY   THE HOLY
OF HOLIES   PLACE

INTERIOR
7. Incense Altar
8. Lampstands
9. Tables
10. Veil and Doors

SOLOMON'S TEMPLE, Interior View (LOOKING WEST)

home in order to rebuild their temple. God's Spirit is noted as inspiring certain priests and prophets.

Teachings about Humanity

Second Chronicles focuses at length on Solomon, whose splendid rule in Jerusalem was a preview of Christ's everlasting reign in the New Jerusalem (Matt. 12:42; Rev. 21–22). As in 2 Kings, the worth of the kings is determined only by whether they did right or evil in the sight of the Lord. (This terminology occurs 17 times in 2 Chronicles.)

God
Creation
Sovereignty and Providence
Faith and Reason
Revelation and Authority
Humanity
Rebellion and Sin
Covenant and Redemption
○ **Community** and Church
Discipleship
Ethics and Morality
○ **Time and Eternity**

Teachings about Salvation

As in 2 Kings, God's prophets in 2 Chronicles called both king and people to repent for religious apostasy and to worship the Lord alone. (Shemaiah, Oded, Micaiah, Eliezer, and Huldah are less familiar; Isaiah and Jeremiah are known from their writings.) Four kings led Judah to turn from sin, repair the temple, and recommit to wholehearted worship of the Lord (Asa, Joash, Hezekiah, and Josiah).

✦ CHRIST IN 2 CHRONICLES

Solomon's glorious reign as third king of Israel is a picture of Christ's eternal reign in the New Jerusalem (Rev. 21–22).

GOD'S STORY

When the Events of This Book Happened:
From the beginning of Solomon's reign until the first year that Cyrus, king of Persia, ruled over Babylon (more than 430 years, ca. 970–538 B.C.)

The military superpowers of the ancient Near East were weak and not aggressive during the time of Solomon, allowing his kingdom to expand to Israel's greatest geographical size. Later, three successive Mesopotamian superpowers took their turn at world dominion. First was Assyria, which fell in 612 B.C. (after conquering the northern kingdom of Israel in 722). Next was Babylon (or Chaldea), which fell in 538 B.C. (after conquering the southern kingdom of Judah in 586). Third was Persia, which allowed the Israelite exiles to return and endured throughout the rest of the Old Testament period, falling to Alexander the Great and the Greeks in 331 B.C.

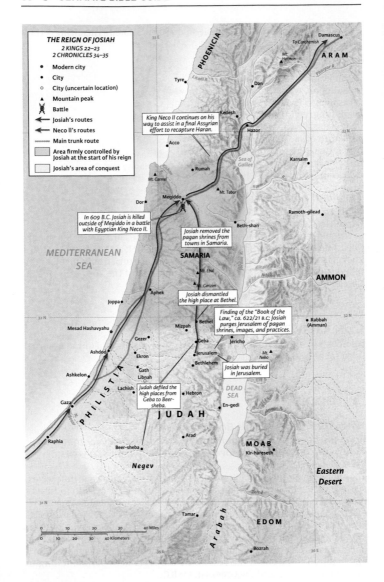

THE REIGN OF JOSIAH
2 KINGS 22–23
2 CHRONICLES 34–35

- Modern city
- City
- City (uncertain location)
- ▲ Mountain peak
- ✕ Battle
- Josiah's routes
- Neco II's routes
- Main trunk route
- Area firmly controlled by Josiah at the start of his reign
- Josiah's area of conquest

King Neco II continues on his way to assist in a final Assyrian effort to recapture Haran.

In 609 B.C. Josiah is killed outside of Megiddo in a battle with Egyptian King Neco II.

Josiah removed the pagan shrines from towns in Samaria.

Josiah dismantled the high place at Bethel.

Finding of the "Book of the Law," ca. 622/21 B.C.; Josiah purges Jerusalem of pagan shrines, images, and practices.

Josiah was buried in Jerusalem.

Judah defiled the high places from Geba to Beer-sheba.

How 2 Chronicles Fits into God's "Story"

Second Chronicles concludes "chapter 1" of God's story: God builds his nation (Israel chosen as the people of promise). It also describes the entire period of "chapter 2" of the story: God educates his nation (disobedient Israel disciplined).

Second Chronicles tells the story of David's royal successors who ruled from Jerusalem. They succeeded when they honored God and worshiped at his temple. By the book's end, there was neither reigning king nor temple. Yet God's long-term kingdom plans were never in jeopardy. A temporal kingdom and temple were not the goal. God was preparing the way for the birth of the eternal King who will rule as Son of David forever. The everlasting temple is the people of God, indwelt by his Spirit (Eph. 2:20-21).

 ## ORIGINAL HISTORICAL SETTING

Because 1 and 2 Chronicles first existed as a single composition, see the discussion in the *Original Historical Setting* section for *1 Chronicles*.

Author and Date of Writing:
Unknown, possibly Ezra ca. 450 B.C.

First Audience and Destination:
Israelites in Jerusalem after they returned from exile

Occasion
Unknown, but see *Occasion* for *1 Chronicles*.

 ## LITERARY FEATURES

Genre and Literary Style:
An extremely selective account written in Hebrew

Although 2 Chronicles describes the same time period as 1 and 2 Kings, its approach is distinctive, concentrating only on the kings of Judah. The author's perspective on the northern kingdom is plain: "Israel is in rebellion against the house of David until today" (10:19). Thus King Hezekiah (who ruled in Judah both before and after the fall of the northern kingdom) invited people from "all Israel and Judah" to his great Passover, and many people came (30:1,6,10). Consequently, from Hezekiah's time until the final destruction of Jerusalem, the Davidic king in Jerusalem ruled "all Israel" (31:1; 35:3). The Chronicler was concerned mainly with the state of the temple and whether the Davidic king was devoutly following the Lord.

In the Hebrew Bible, Chronicles was placed in the third section, the Writings (*Kethuvim*), rather than in the Law or the Prophets. In fact, it was the last book of the Hebrew Scriptures. So, just as modern Christians use the phrase "Genesis to Revelation" to mean the entire canon, Christians living in the first century thought in terms of "Genesis to Chronicles." (See comments on *Genre and Literary Style* in *Nehemiah* for further material about the possible literary relationship of Chronicles, Ezra, and Nehemiah.)

Themes:
Davidic dynasty, temple, blessing of obedience and punishment of disobedience
Because 1 and 2 Chronicles first existed as a single composition, see the discussion in the *Themes* section for *1 Chronicles*.

Book Features and Structure
The most striking feature of 2 Chronicles is the way the author connected the temple and the kingship by noting the kings who initiated repairs to the temple and thus initiated religious reform and renewal. The history of Solomon's temple can thus be outlined as follows:

Event	King	Text	Approx. Year
Temple dedication	Solomon	5:1	959
First repair and reform	Asa	15:8	895
Second repair and reform	Joash	24:13	830
Third repair and reform	Hezekiah	29:3	715
Fourth repair and reform	Josiah	34:8	622
Temple destruction	Zedekiah	36:19	586

Second Chronicles has three major sections: Solomon's reign (chaps. 1–9); the divided kingdom (chaps. 10–28); and the reunited kingdom (chaps. 29–36).

EZRA
THE FIRST BOOK OF EZRA

The book is named for Ezra, the leading character. In the Hebrew Bible, Ezra and Nehemiah were initially one book. English Bibles follow the Latin translator Jerome, who named the two parts Ezra and Nehemiah. Others have used the titles 1 and 2 Ezra.

⊙ KEY TEXT: 6:16

"Then the Israelites, including the priests, the Levites, and the rest of the exiles, celebrated the dedication of the house of God with joy."

⊙ KEY TERM: "RESTORATION"

The book describes two restorations from Babylonian captivity. First, more than 40,000 Israelites returned under Sheshbazzar (530s B.C.). Second, a smaller group accompanied Ezra, whose goal was to teach the people the law of Moses (ca. 458 B.C.).

The Cyrus Cylinder, written in cuneiform, was discovered in 1879 in Nineveh, Iraq, by Hormuzd Rassam. It is now in the British Museum. The cylinder contains inscriptions in which Cyrus gives credit to the Babylonian god Marduk for choosing him and enabling him to conquer Babylon. The inscriptions express Cyrus's policy of allowing captive peoples, such as the Jews, to return to their homelands. The biblical writers saw God's hand in these world events (2 Chr. 36:22-23; Ezra 1:2-4; Isa. 44:24-28; 45:1).

○ ONE-SENTENCE SUMMARY

The first group of returning exiles restored worship of the Lord, culminating in a rebuilt temple, but Ezra, who led the second group, reestablished Israelite community under Mosaic law.

GOD'S MESSAGE IN THE BOOK

Purpose

Since this book was originally the first half of a single composition, the purpose for the books now called Ezra and Nehemiah must be considered together. This work continued the history of Israel at the point that 2 Chronicles ended. It showed Israelites, who had come back to their land, that they were still God's people, despite the years of exile and the difficulties they had experienced since their return. God was at work through pagan kings such as Cyrus and Artaxerxes (1:1; 7:27) to bring about the return from exile and the rebuilding of the temple. God had worked to bring devout teachers (7:9-10) and strong governors (Neh. 2:12) to help the people of God. From an even broader perspective, the second temple, the Jewish community, and a stable Jerusalem were important circumstances for the coming of Jesus more than four centuries later. God's people who read and study Ezra and Nehemiah today should keep the author's purpose in mind.

Christian Worldview Elements

Ezra deals particularly with the world-view categories of *sovereignty and providence*; *community*; and *ethics and morality*. The notion of the people of God working together to accomplish his objectives is especially prominent.

God
Creation
○ **Sovereignty and Providence**
Faith and Reason
Revelation and Authority
Humanity
Rebellion and Sin
Covenant and Redemption
○ **Community** and Church
Discipleship
○ **Ethics and Morality**
Time and Eternity

Teachings about God

Because God is righteous, he acts on behalf of his people. This includes working through pagan kings (who issue decrees) and godly teachers (who teach his word to his people). Further, as the last two chapters show, God may require his people to forsake family ties for the sake of following his will.

Teachings about Humanity

As with 1 Chronicles, Ezra has many name lists. Although such lists may seem tedious today, they show the importance of each individual in God's purposes. If the author made the effort to preserve all these names and numbers, then how much more does God care about individuals! This perspective is strengthened by observing that the work of restoring worship (altar and temple) was a community task. The work accomplished for God was done by people working together more than by a great leader.

Teachings about Salvation

The people who returned from exile were cured of the idolatry that had taken their ancestors into captivity. Ezra revives an emphasis found in Mosaic law: without the shedding of blood, there is no forgiveness (Lev. 17:11). So the first concern of the returning Israelites was to reinstate an altar on which to offer the appointed sacrifices (3:1-6). Only secondarily were they concerned with the temple (6:13-18). As throughout the Old Testament era, personal trust in God is expressed through participation in the right sacrifices and through obeying God's law.

◯ CHRIST IN EZRA

Ezra was a priest who played an important role in leading God's people from captivity in Babylon back to Judea. In a sermon at the synagogue in Nazareth, Jesus announced his agenda, part of which was "to proclaim release to the captives" (Luke 4:18).

The Euphrates River. The difficult journey from exile back to Judah was approximately a thousand miles and likely proceeded along the trade route that ran parallel to the Euphrates River from Mesopotamia to Aleppo. Sheshbazzar led the first groups between 537 and 522 B.C. and Ezra the second group, 458 B.C.

GOD'S STORY

When the Events of This Book Happened:
From Cyrus's decree permitting the return through Ezra's initial ministry (more than 80 years, ca. 538–457 B.C.)

The emperor Cyrus the Great ruled Persia from ca. 559. The Persians defeated the Chaldean Empire and the city of Babylon in 539, then initiated the policy of allowing exiles of all ethnic groups to return to their homeland. The first Israelite return under Sheshbazzar occurred during Cyrus's rule. The second temple was dedicated in 516, exactly 70 years after Solomon's temple was destroyed (2 Chr. 36:21). The next return of exiles (with Ezra the priest) occurred in 458, during the time of Artaxerxes I, some 80 years later than the first return.

How Ezra Fits into God's "Story"

Ezra begins "chapter 3" of God's story: God keeps a faithful remnant (Messiah's space and time prepared). It is an important historical link in the story of God's rule. Although there was no Davidic king, that did not keep God's people from worshiping properly or doing what they were able to do. Although the second temple was only a pale replica of Solomon's temple, it would prove to be more important. Jesus, the Son of God and Son of David, was presented in this temple and ended his public ministry by teaching there. The book of Ezra shows how such a temple came into being.

ORIGINAL HISTORICAL SETTING

Author and Date of Writing:
Unknown, perhaps Ezra ca. 430 B.C.

Jewish tradition held that Ezra the priest composed the single work Ezra-Nehemiah. There is no reason he could not have done so, particularly since he was a "scribe skilled in the law of Moses" (7:6). In 7:28–9:15, Ezra is referred to in the first person ("I," "me," "my"). If Ezra was not the composer, then a later composer directly copied his memoirs. (The book of Nehemiah included similar first-person memoirs of Nehemiah.)

First Audience and Destination:
Israelites in Jerusalem after they returned from exile

The book was a permanent record of the events that reestablished Israel's national identity. Perhaps the original "Scroll of Ezra-Nehemiah" was placed in a book depository in the rebuilt temple when it was first completed. There it would have joined the growing collection of Israel's sacred Scriptures.

Occasion

What originally prompted the writing of this book is not clear. The author could not have been an eyewitness to all the events of Ezra-Nehemiah since

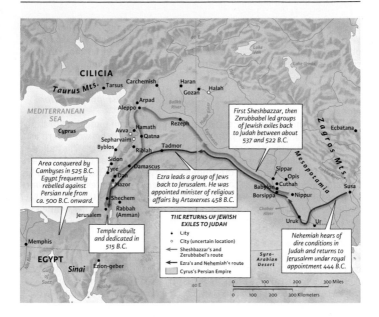

First Sheshbazzar, then Zerubbabel led groups of Jewish exiles back to Judah between about 537 and 522 B.C.

Area conquered by Cambyses in 525 B.C. Egypt frequently rebelled against Persian rule from ca. 500 B.C. onward.

Ezra leads a group of Jews back to Jerusalem. He was appointed minister of religious affairs by Artaxerxes 458 B.C.

Temple rebuilt and dedicated in 515 B.C.

Nehemiah hears of dire conditions in Judah and returns to Jerusalem under royal appointment 444 B.C.

THE RETURNS OF JEWISH EXILES TO JUDAH

● City
○ City (uncertain location)
→ Sheshbazzar's and Zerubbabel's route
→ Ezra's and Nehemiah's route
▭ Cyrus's Persian Empire

they cover about a century. He could, however, have seen all events of both Ezra's and Nehemiah's ministries. The author skillfully knitted his sources into a powerful account of God's provision and protection of his people.

 LITERARY FEATURES

Genre and Literary Style:
Court documents, lists, and narratives written in Hebrew, with some Aramaic sections

The author had access to many sources, including official Persian documents, lists, and memoirs. The lists are similar to the lists in Chronicles and may indicate the same historian at work (Ezra?). The Hebrew vocabulary and style is considered "late Hebrew," as is fitting for a postexilic composition.

One striking element of Ezra is the presence of documents untranslated from their original Aramaic form. (Aramaic was the international trade language of the ancient Near East under the Persians.) The Aramaic parts of Ezra are 4:8–6:18; 7:12-26.

In the Hebrew Bible, Ezra-Nehemiah was placed in the third section, the Writings (*Kethuvim*), rather than in the Law or the Prophets. (See comments on *Genre and Literary Style* in *Nehemiah* for further material about the possible literary relationship of Chronicles, Ezra, and Nehemiah.)

Themes:
Return from exile, rebuilding the temple, reestablishing life under Mosaic law

These three themes are specific displays of the overall motif "restoration" (see *Key Term*). A secondary theme is the relationship between Ezra as a qualified interpreter of Scripture and the response of his hearers. The italicized verbs in the following verses show the connection between devout teachers and a heartfelt response by the students: "Now Ezra had *determined* in his heart to *study* the law of the LORD, *obey* it, and *teach* its statutes and ordinances in Israel" (7:10). "Everyone who *trembled* at the words of the God of Israel gathered around me, because of the unfaithfulness of the exiles, while I sat devastated until the evening offering" (9:4).

Book Features and Structure

Ezra has preserved seven official documents and letters similar to nonbiblical Persian records that have survived. These are the "Decree of Cyrus" (1:2-4); "Letter of Rehum to Artaxerxes" (4:8-16); "Artaxerxes's Reply to Rehum" (4:17-22); "Letter of Tattenai to Darius" (5:6-17); "Memorandum Concerning Cyrus's Decree" (6:1-5); "Darius's Letter to Tattenai" (6:6-12); "Letter of Artaxerxes to Ezra" (7:11-26). All are preserved in Aramaic except for the first, which was copied from the end of 2 Chronicles.

The book of Ezra has two sections. The first describes the first return of exiles and the rebuilding of the temple (chaps. 1–6); the second describes the return of Ezra and his ministry (chaps. 7–10).

NEHEMIAH
THE SECOND BOOK OF EZRA

The book is named for Nehemiah, the leading character. In the Hebrew Bible, Ezra and Nehemiah were initially one book. English Bibles follow the Latin translator Jerome, who named the two parts Ezra and Nehemiah. Others have used the titles 1 and 2 Ezra.

○ KEY TEXT: 6:15
"The wall was completed in fifty-two days, on the twenty-fifth day of the month Elul."

○ KEY TERM: "WALLS"
In the ancient world, a city without walls was helpless before its enemies. For Jerusalem once more to have its walls complete was evidence of divine favor and meant that the inhabitants could carry on life with a measure of security.

○ ONE-SENTENCE SUMMARY
Through Nehemiah's leadership, God enabled the Israelites to rebuild and dedicate Jerusalem's walls as well as to renew their commitment to God as his covenant people.

GOD'S MESSAGE IN THE BOOK

Purpose
Because Nehemiah and Ezra first existed as a single composition, see the discussion in the *Purpose* section for *Ezra*.

Christian Worldview Elements
Nehemiah focuses on the worldview categories of *sovereignty and providence*; *community*; and *covenant and redemption*. The notion of God's people working together to accomplish his objectives is particularly noticeable.

God
Creation
○ **Sovereignty and Providence**
Faith and Reason
Revelation and Authority
Humanity
Rebellion and Sin
○ **Covenant and Redemption**
○ **Community** and Church
Discipleship
Ethics and Morality
Time and Eternity

Teachings about God
God works on behalf of his people to enable them to accomplish his purposes. He works through kings; he sends good leaders (such as Ezra and Nehemiah). Further, God does not change, even though the circumstances of his people change. The same God who had graciously revealed himself at

Mount Sinai as the covenant-making God a thousand years before (ca. 1446 B.C.) still wanted Israel to be in a covenant relationship with him (10:29).

Teachings about Humanity

Nehemiah shows that there are really only two kinds of people: those who oppose God and his purposes and those who identify with God and his pur-

Nehemiah Views the Ruins of Jerusalem's Walls by Gustave Doré

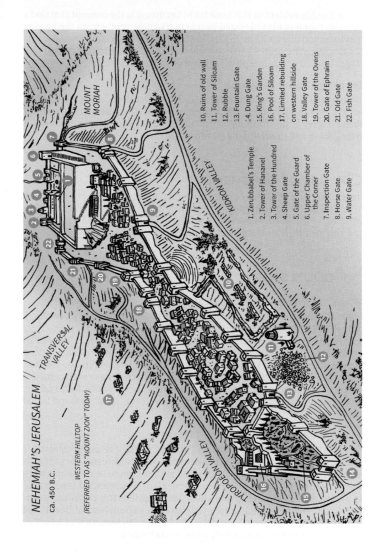

NEHEMIAH'S JERUSALEM

Ca. 450 B.C.

WESTERN HILLTOP
(REFERRED TO AS "MOUNT ZION" TODAY)

TRANSVERSAL VALLEY

MOUNT MORIAH

KIDRON VALLEY

TYROPOEON VALLEY

1. Zerubbabel's Temple
2. Tower of Hananel
3. Tower of the Hundred
4. Sheep Gate
5. Gate of the Guard
6. Upper Chamber of the Corner
7. Inspection Gate
8. Horse Gate
9. Water Gate
10. Ruins of old wall
11. Tower of Siloam
12. Rubble
13. Fountain Gate
14. Dung Gate
15. King's Garden
16. Pool of Siloam
17. Limited rebuilding on western hillside
18. Valley Gate
19. Tower of the Ovens
20. Gate of Ephraim
21. Old Gate
22. Fish Gate

poses. Equally evident in this book (as in Leviticus) is the concept that God's holiness requires his redeemed people to live differently from the pagans that surround them. Although Ezra and Nehemiah fulfilled different personal roles, each illustrates someone who was wholly committed to God and whom God used to accomplish kingdom purposes.

Teachings about Salvation

Nehemiah teaches the doctrine of salvation as clearly as any Old Testament book. It contains no more profound confession of sin at the community level than chapter 9: salvation means acknowledging and turning away from wrongdoing and then clinging steadfastly to God.

 ## CHRIST IN NEHEMIAH

Nehemiah was a key leader in the restoration of God's people from Babylon to Jerusalem. He called for undivided loyalty to the work at hand in the same way that Jesus did when he said, "Anyone who is not with me is against me, and anyone who does not gather with me scatters" (Luke 11:23).

 ## GOD'S STORY

When the Events of This Book Happened:
From Nehemiah's prayer for Israel until his second term as governor (ca. 446–430 B.C.)

Artaxerxes I ruled Persia 465–424 B.C. The events of the book of Nehemiah occurred during his reign. Nehemiah's first term as governor of Judah lasted 12 years (the twentieth to the thirty-second year of Artaxerxes, 445–433 B.C., Neh. 5:14). There is insufficient information to date the length of Nehemiah's absence from Judah when he returned to Artaxerxes's service, Neh. 13:6. His second term as governor possibly began ca. 431 ("only later," 13:6) and lasted an unknown length of time.

How Nehemiah Fits into God's "Story"

Nehemiah continues God's story: God keeps a faithful remnant (Messiah's space and time prepared). It continues the historical link in the story of God's kingdom that Ezra began. With the second temple complete, the people were able to turn their attention to making Jerusalem secure and to functioning as a covenant community. In God's plan, Jesus came to this community centuries later and presented himself to Jerusalem as both "Son of David" and "King of Israel" (Matt. 21:9; John 12:13). The book of Nehemiah tells how this city and this covenant community were reestablished.

Ruins of the palace of Artaxerxes I at Persepolis (Neh. 2:1; 5:14; 13:6)

ORIGINAL HISTORICAL SETTING

Because Ezra-Nehemiah first existed as a single composition, see the discussion in the *Original Historical Setting* section for *Ezra*.

Author and Date of Writing:
Unknown, probably Ezra ca. 430 B.C.

First Audience and Destination:
Israelites in Jerusalem after they returned from exile

Occasion
Unknown, but see *Occasion* for *Ezra*.

LITERARY FEATURES

Genre and Literary Style:
Mainly Nehemiah's first-person memoirs and official lists, written in Hebrew

The book of Nehemiah has the longest first-person sections (where the writer uses "I," "my," and "me") of any narrative book in Scripture. Chapters 1–7 and 12:27–13:30 appear to be copied from the "Memoirs of Nehemiah" (except for the lists noted in *Book Features and Structure* below). The material in chapters 8–10 tells about Ezra's preaching, which is further eyewitness material if Ezra in fact wrote this work.

In the Hebrew Bible, Ezra-Nehemiah was placed in the third section, the Writings (*Kethuvim*), rather than in the Law or the Prophets. Many Bible scholars believe that 1 and 2 Chronicles (originally one book) and Ezra-Nehemiah were composed by a single author, designated the Chronicler, perhaps Ezra himself. The books all have a common postexilic perspective, share a fondness for lists, like to describe Israelite feasts, and focus extensively on the temple and the temple workers (priests and Levites). They also share unusual vocabulary features, such as calling the temple "the house of God" (more than 60 times in these books) and the reference to "gatekeepers" (or "porters," more than 30 times). Further, the end of Chronicles is the same as the beginning of Ezra.

Themes:
Rebuilding the walls of Jerusalem, reestablishing life under Mosaic law
Because Ezra-Nehemiah first existed as a single composition, see the discussion in the *Themes* section for *Ezra*. In Nehemiah, the focus is on rebuilding the walls instead of rebuilding the temple.

Book Features and Structure
Ezra-Nehemiah includes striking lists: "Temple Articles Returned" (Ezra 1:9-11); "Exiles Who Returned" (Ezra 2 and Neh. 7); "Ezra's Genealogy" (Ezra 7:1-5); "Heads of Families Returning with Ezra" (Ezra 8:1-14); "Descendants of Priests Married to Foreign Wives" (Ezra 10:18-43); "Wall Builders" (Neh. 3); "Covenant Signers" (Neh. 10:1-27); "Citizens of Jerusalem and Other Towns" (Neh. 11); and "Priests and Levites" (Neh. 12:1-26).

The book of Nehemiah has three sections. The first describes the first return of Nehemiah and the rebuilding of the walls (chaps. 1–7); the second describes the ministry of Ezra and the covenant renewal (chaps. 8–10); the third describes the dedication of the walls and then Nehemiah's second term as governor (chaps. 11–13).

The English title is the name of the heroine of the story. The title carries over from the Hebrew Bible.

○ KEY TEXT: 4:14

"Who knows, perhaps you have come to your royal position for such a time as this."

○ KEY TERM: "PROVIDENCE"

This book is famous because it does not directly mention God. Yet one cannot understand the story apart from God's remarkable presence and providence with his people—however invisible he may seem to be at times.

○ ONE-SENTENCE SUMMARY

Esther, a Jewish beauty selected by Persian king Ahasuerus to become his new queen, saved the Jews from Haman's wicked plot, so her relative Mordecai established the yearly Jewish feast of Purim.

Haman and Mordecai by Paul Alexandre Alfred Leroy (Esth. 3:5-6)

GOD'S MESSAGE IN THE BOOK

Purpose

Esther primarily preserves the historical origins of the Jewish festival of Purim. Secondarily it portrays God's providential care of people committed to him in the midst of overwhelming challenges to their faith. In this sense, Esther functions similarly to Ruth, the only other biblical book named for a woman. The characters Esther and Ruth, however, are a study in contrasts: the one was a powerful and wealthy Jew who always lived outside the promised land and became the bride of a pagan king; the other was a humble and impoverished Gentile who moved to the promised land and became an ancestor of Israelite kings. People who read and study Esther today should enjoy it for its own sake in its Old Testament setting.

Christian Worldview Elements

The book of Esther presents the worldview category of God's *sovereignty and providence* in a tangential way, for God is not directly mentioned or visible. Further, Esther's risky work in preserving the Jewish people reflects the worldview category *ethics and morality*.

God
Creation
○ Sovereignty and Providence
Faith and Reason
Revelation and Authority
Humanity
Rebellion and Sin
Covenant and Redemption
Community and Church
Discipleship
○ Ethics and Morality
Time and EternitY

Teachings about God

The book reveals the providence of God in caring for his covenant people. Although many evils—including satanic opposition—may come against God's people, nothing ever happens beyond God's ability to work all things "together for the good of those who love God, who are called according to his purpose" (Rom. 8:28).

Teachings about Humanity

The villainy of Haman demonstrates human depravity at its worst; the integrity of Mordecai shows the enormous good that one person can do. Esther's story (like Joseph's in Genesis) demonstrates that when God's people face difficult circumstances they are to act courageously and risk themselves for a righteous cause rather than give in to "fate" or "being unlucky."

Teachings about Salvation

God will accomplish his redemptive purposes. If Haman's edict to destroy the Jews had succeeded, the coming of the Jews' ultimate deliverer, Jesus the Messiah-King, would have been imperiled. God's plan to save cannot be thwarted, and he has always taken the initiative to bring about salvation.

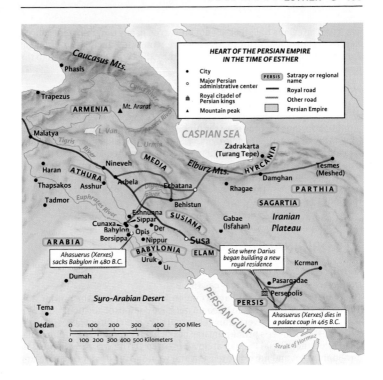

✝ CHRIST **IN ESTHER**

Although the name of God is not mentioned in Esther, nowhere in Scripture is the care of God for his people more evident. Prior to his arrest, Jesus prayed, "While I was with them, I was protecting them by your name that you have given me. I guarded them and not one of them is lost, except the son of destruction, so that the Scripture may be fulfilled" (John 17:12).

🕊 **GOD'S STORY**

When the Events of This Book Happened:
During the reign of Xerxes I of Persia (ruled 486–465 B.C.)

Bible scholars have generally agreed that the king called "Ahasuerus" in Esther was known to the Persians as Xerxes I, who ruled a huge empire at the height of its powers. Esther became queen in Xerxes's seventh year (Esth. 2:16; ca.

478 B.C.). The events of Esther are not preserved in any other ancient source. Xerxes I reigned just prior to Artaxerxes I, who ruled during the time that Ezra and Nehemiah were leaders among the exiles who had returned to the land of Israel.

How Esther Fits into God's "Story"

Esther continues God's story: God keeps a faithful remnant (Messiah's space and time prepared). First, it shows how God preserved the Jewish people from annihilation, thus keeping alive the promise and hope of a future everlasting King to come from the Davidic dynasty. Second, Esther illustrates that many Israelites who had been scattered in the exile remained faithful to the one true God. These Jews later came to preserve their identity through the synagogue. The synagogues became the beginning point for spreading the good news of Jesus Christ throughout the Roman Empire in the first century (as the book of Acts shows).

 ## ORIGINAL HISTORICAL SETTING

Author and Date of Writing:
Unknown, perhaps Mordecai ca. 465 B.C.
The book is anonymous, but according to Jewish tradition the author was Mordecai. There is no reason he could not have composed the book, since he was an eyewitness to everything that occurred (or had direct access to eyewitnesses). As Xerxes's prime minister, he is a likely candidate for adding this incident to the official Persian archives (9:32; 10:2). The writer was gifted in developing plot and narrative tension and wrote with considerable literary skill.

First Audience and Destination:
Jewish exiles living in Persia
The first ones to hear the book of Esther were Jews in Persia, sometime after the feast of Purim had become an established custom. By this time, the postexilic people of Israel had adopted the name "Jew," for the term "Jew(s)" occurs more often in the book of Esther than in the rest of the Old Testament combined.

Occasion

The book of Esther was prompted in general by the desire to preserve the origins of the feast of Purim. Since the author is not known, the specific occasion is unclear.

LITERARY FEATURES

Genre and Literary Style:
A historical narrative written in excellent Hebrew

Esther is a carefully crafted short story, but its events really happened. In English Bibles, it is positioned as the last of the historical books of the Old Testament. In the Hebrew Scriptures, it was placed in the third section, the Writings or *Kethuvim* (the other two sections are the Law and the Prophets). Among the Writings, it was one of the Five Scrolls. Each of these Five Scrolls became associated with one of the Israelite festivals and was read publicly during that festival. Esther was, of course, identified with Purim, a late winter festival that originated in the fifth century B.C. and which is still celebrated annually by Jewish people as a minor holiday.

The Hebrew of Esther is carefully polished, but the Greek translators (second century B.C.) were apparently troubled by the lack of reference to God. Therefore, when they translated Esther from Hebrew to Greek, they inserted more than a hundred verses that frequently refer to God. Protestants, however, have accepted as Old Testament Scripture only texts that had a Hebrew original.

The Feast of Esther by Jan Lievens (Est. 7:1-10)

Themes:
Providence, accomplishments of a woman of integrity, rest from enemies

God's providential care has already been discussed in this introduction. The narrative of Esther, more than any other Old Testament book, highlights what one woman did for good. The importance of God's people finding rest from their enemies is noted in several Old Testament books: Josh. 21:44; 1 Chr. 23:25; 2 Chr. 14:6; Esth. 9:22 are important examples. Ultimately rest for God's people is found only in Jesus Christ (Heb. 4:8-11).

Book Features and Structure

Particularly interesting is the author's use of paired elements. There are twin banquets of Ahasuerus (1:3-4,5-8) twin banquets of Esther (5:4-8; 7:1-10), and twin festivals of Purim (9:17-19). There are also two lists of royal servants (1:10,14), two references to Esther's hiding her ethnic identity (2:10,20), two fasts (4:3,16), two royal decrees (3:12-15; 8:9-13), and two letters establishing Purim (9:20-32). Other repeated elements add a certain stylized feel to the book: the size of Ahasuerus's kingdom (1:1; 8:9; 9:30), the king's promise to give up to half his kingdom to Esther (5:3,6; 7:2), and Esther's repeated reception of the king's favor (2:9,17; 5:2,8; 7:3; 8:5). The eunuchs (chamberlains) always come on the scene at just the right time to move the story along (1:10,15; 2:3,14,15; 4:4,5; 6:14; 7:9). Another striking literary element may be called "reversal of fortune." Vashti and Esther, as well as Haman and Mordecai, dramatically exchange positions by the end of the story.

JOB

The English title is the name of the central character in the narrative and the chief speaker in the poetic dialogues. The title carries over from the Hebrew Bible.

○ KEY TEXT: 1:21

"Naked I came from my mother's womb, and naked I will leave this life. The LORD gives, and the LORD takes away. Blessed be the name of the LORD."

○ KEY TERM: "SUFFERING"

The book of Job explores the issue of human suffering despite God's goodness and power. The question of why people suffer and why evil continues has been the focus of intense thought throughout the ages. Job is the main biblical treatment of this issue.

○ ONE-SENTENCE SUMMARY

After the upright Job suddenly lost family, health, and possessions, he and his friends dialogued at length about the reasons for his sufferings, but God alone had the final word and ultimately restored Job's losses.

Job Rebuked by His Friends by William Blake (Job 16:2)

GOD'S MESSAGE IN THE BOOK

Purpose

Job is the fullest development in Scripture of what theologians and philosophers refer to as "the problem of evil" or "theodicy." Simply put, the matter is this: since humans, especially the seemingly innocent, suffer pain and evil, then what kind of God must there be? Logic suggests one of three answers: (1) God is righteous, but he is not powerful enough to prevent suffering; (2) God is all-powerful, but he is not truly good and has elements of evil in his nature; or (3) all pain and evil is in fact deserved by the sufferer and sent by God (in other words, the truly innocent do not suffer).

The biblical view finds these answers unacceptable, and the book of Job wrestles with the alternative. Job reveals a wider arena than humanity can observe. The conflict of the ages between God and Satan must in the end demonstrate both the righteousness and supremacy of God. He lets the innocent suffer to demonstrate that in his sovereignty he receives glory even when his people suffer and persevere in faith without understanding why. From a merely human point of view, the answer is that there is no answer given to the problem of evil. From a divine perspective, the answer is that God's glory is served even when evil is permitted. (Christ's death is God's ultimate answer to the problem of evil.) Those who study Job today should interpret it in view of its original purpose.

Christian Worldview Elements

Job focuses attention particularly with the worldview categories of God; *sovereignty and providence*; and *ethics and morality*. No Bible book more fully teaches that human beings who live uprightly before God may experience suffering that they will never understand in this life.

○ **God**
  Creation
○ **Sovereignty and Providence**
  Faith and Reason
  Revelation and Authority
  Humanity
  Rebellion and Sin
  Covenant and Redemption
  Community and Church
  Discipleship
○ **Ethics and Morality**
  Time and Eternity

Teachings about God

Job reveals God in his heavenly court (Isa. 6 and Ezek. 1 may be compared). The book shows that God permits an adversary (Satan) to challenge his sovereign righteousness, but that God's glory is served in the end. Job's expectation of a coming Redeemer (19:25) was fulfilled in Jesus Christ. The creative work of God's Spirit is evident in texts such as Job 33:4.

Teachings about Humanity

The prose sections of Job (chaps. 1–2, 42) show that human behavior is on display before supernatural powers. The poetic sections (chaps. 3–41) show that, however logical it appears, human reasoning alone can never penetrate to the mind of God. Job and his counselors reached only partial truth about suffering; only when God revealed himself did the inadequacy of human wisdom become evident.

Teachings about Salvation

Job 1 is consistent with Genesis in showing a family head offering sacrifices for the sins of his own family members. Job's personal confession of faith anticipated both the coming of Christ and the resurrection (19:25-26).

 CHRIST IN JOB

In his great losses and suffering, Job cries out for a mediator to stand between him and God. Christ is the answer to that heart cry. "For there is one God and one mediator between God and humanity, the man Christ Jesus" (1 Tim. 2:5).

 GOD'S STORY

When the Events of This Book Happened:
Unknown, but probably in the time of the patriarchs (sometime between 2000 and 1500 B.C.)

There is insufficient information to date the events of Job. Job's long life (42:16), the measurement of wealth in livestock, and the fact that Job acted as personal priest for his family points to the time of Abraham, Isaac, and Jacob. Further, Job and his friends (in poetic sections) prefer to refer to the Creator as "God" (*Elohim*) or "the Almighty" (*Shaddai*) instead of by the Israelite covenant name, the Lord (*Yahweh*), suggesting a time before the exodus.

"Who set the wild donkey free?" (Job 39:5-8)

How Job Fits into God's "Story"

Job does not fit into the narrative of the story of the kingdom. Rather, it offers timeless insights for those already committed to the King of the kingdom of God. The wisdom teachings of this book are directly applicable to kingdom citizens, whether Israelites living in premodern tenth century B.C. or North Americans living in a postmodern twenty-first century A.D. It shows how to live in submission to what God permits, even when his purposes are unknown and when suffering and evil appear to fall unfairly. Job does not tell how to get into the kingdom of God; rather, it tells those already in the kingdom one important aspect of living in right relationship to God in this lifetime. If Job (and later Jesus) suffered evil triumphantly and thereby served the purposes of God, then God's people today can do the same. (The only New Testament reference to Job commends his perseverance or endurance; he wasn't really all that patient; see Jas. 5:11 in contemporary translations.)

 ## ORIGINAL HISTORICAL SETTING

Author and Date of Writing:
Unknown, perhaps during Solomon's rule (ca. 950 B.C.)
The book is anonymous. The author's frequent use of "the LORD" (*Yahweh*) in the prose sections suggests that he wrote from an Israelite national perspective. It may have been penned anytime in the millennium between Moses and the end of the Old Testament period (1400–400 B.C.). The flowering of Hebrew culture under Solomon, particularly in light of Solomon's association with wisdom literature, suggests a date during or shortly after Solomon.

First Audience and Destination:
The Israelite people
The original hearers are not stated and can be only generally suggested.

Occasion
The book does not tell what prompted it to be written. Its events evidently occurred centuries before the writer's birth. Although some records of the various speeches may have survived for the author to use as sources, the material in chapters 1–2 could be known only by divine revelation.

LITERARY FEATURES

Genre and Literary Style:

Wisdom literature, emphasizing dialogues in poetry, framed by a narrative prologue and epilogue, written in difficult Hebrew

The book of Job belongs to the literary type called "speculative wisdom," which explored the great questions of human existence. A number of other ancient Near Eastern texts have parallels to Job, for example, the Egyptian "Admonitions of Ipuwer" or the Mesopotamian "I Will Praise the Lord of Wisdom." Israelite wisdom, however, based on the fear of the Lord, surpassed that of other nations. Job was placed in the third section, the Writings (*Kethuvim*), of the Hebrew canon.

The narrative prologue (chaps. 1–2) and epilogue (chap. 42) are necessary frames for the extended body of the book. The poetic dialogues and monologues (chaps. 3–41) were composed entirely in the form of Hebrew parallelism found in the other wisdom books and the Psalms (as well as elsewhere in the Old Testament). (See *Genre and Literary Style* for *Proverbs* for more information on Hebrew parallelism.)

The Hebrew vocabulary and style was so challenging to the Greek translators of Job (second century B.C.) that they skipped translating a number of lines, further suggesting an earlier date for the composition of Job.

Themes:

The character of God; the character of humanity; the problem of evil

The long central section of dialogues and monologues shows the futility of supposing that humans can understand the purposes of God apart from divine revelation. Job's "friends" were heartless and arrogant. Job sank into despair and complained bitterly to God. Only when God revealed himself to Job (chaps. 38–41) did Job return to a confident trust that the Creator—supreme in power and goodness—was his true Friend.

Book Features and Structure

Chapters 3–26 contain three cycles of dialogues between Job and his counselors, Eliphaz, Bildad, and Zophar. Chapter 28 is noted as Job's beautiful poem on wisdom. In chapters 32–37, a previously unmentioned fourth friend, Elihu, gives a masterful monologue. God's speeches (chaps. 38–41) provide the spiritual climax to the book.

The entire book may be organized into five sections, each with either a God-centered or a human-centered perspective: Job's suffering (chaps. 1–2, God-centered); Job's disputes with his counselors (chaps. 3–26, human-centered); Job's and Elihu's monologues (chaps. 27–37, human-centered); God's answer (chaps. 38–41, God-centered); Job's restoration (chap. 42; God-centered).

"Those who sow in tears will reap with shouts of joy. Though one goes along weeping, carrying the bag of seed, he will surely come back with shouts of joy, carrying his sheaves" (Ps. 126:5-6).

PSALMS

THE BOOK OF PSALMS OR THE PSALTER

The English title is based on the name given by the Greek translators of this book in the second century B.C. The name could be translated "Songs." The original Hebrew title is *Tehillim*, "Hymns" or "Praises."

○ KEY TEXT: 150:6

"Let everything that breathes praise the LORD. Hallelujah!"

○ KEY TERM: "HALLELUJAH"

The Psalter became Israel's hymnal. Not all psalms were hymns (songs honoring or about God), but praise to God was their dominant theme. The well-known *hallelujah* means "praise Yah(weh)."

○ ONE-SENTENCE SUMMARY

God, the true and glorious King, is worthy of all praise and prayer, thanksgiving and confidence—whatever the occasion in personal or community life.

A girl prays the psalms at Jerusalem's Western Wall.

GOD'S MESSAGE IN THE BOOK

Purpose

The purpose of the individual poems as well as the entire collection process for the Psalter was to preserve the inspired words of Israelite songwriters as they expressed the heights (and depths) of their relationship with God. Their poems were preserved to guide God's people in later times in how to approach him no matter what experiences they were undergoing. Thus there are songs of exultation and high worship, songs of respect for God's Word, songs of trust when evil prevails, songs of confession, and other expressions of true religion. Although the Psalms contain doctrine, prophecy, and instruction, above all they were meant to be sung to God as expressions of delight in him. God's people today should use the Psalms in light of their original purpose.

Christian Worldview Elements

Every worldview element is taught in the Psalms! The book focuses, however, on the worldview categories of *community* (God's people worshiping and serving him together with others) and *discipleship* (living a personal life of worship and devotion to God).

God
Creation
Sovereignty and Providence
Faith and Reason
Revelation and Authority
Humanity
Rebellion and Sin
Covenant and Redemption
○ **Community** and Church
○ **Discipleship**
Ethics and Morality
Time and Eternity

Teachings about God

Psalms celebrates God as Creator. He is also Redeemer and Covenant-maker. Many attributes of God are praised throughout the book of Psalms. The Spirit is God's active agent in accomplishing his purposes (Pss. 51:11-12; 104:30; 139:7; 143:10).

Teachings about Humanity

The essential teaching of Psalms about the human race is that God desires (and enables) people to praise and thank him. Humans reach their highest potential only when they seek joy and fulfillment in the Creator rather than in the creation. The Psalter notes the extremes of human existence. Psalm 8 shows the glory of humanity as made by God. On the other hand, the many psalms that mention enemies of God and of God's people show the shameful sinfulness to which humans may fall.

Teachings about Salvation

The quotation of Ps. 32:1-2 by Paul in Rom. 4:7-8 demonstrates that justification by faith was the same in Old Testament times as in New Testament times. Other passages, such as Ps. 51, confirm that the perspective of the psalmists was that salvation was initiated by the God of the covenant and was his gift to those who trusted in his *chesed* (usually translated "faithful love," "mercy," or "loving-kindness").

CHRIST IN PSALMS

Both Christ's first and second comings are prophesied. For example, Ps. 22 looks ahead to the crucifixion and Ps. 2 looks forward to the time when his kingdom is universally acknowledged.

 GOD'S STORY

When the Events of This Book Happened:
Timeless, although historical events are mentioned
A few psalms, such as Ps. 105, refer to events in Israel's history. Others, such as Ps. 3, refer to a historical event in the inscription. Because God's people throughout the ages have seen the psalms as the songs that they too are to sing, it is best to recognize the timeless quality of this part of Scripture.

How Psalms Fits into God's "Story"
Psalms does not fit into the narrative of the story of the kingdom. On one hand, it preserves songs of worship for those already committed to the King of the kingdom of God. On the other hand, it looks forward to the time when "All the nations you have made will come and bow down before you, Lord,

"The Lord is my shepherd" (Ps. 23:1).

"LORD, my heart is not proud; my eyes are not haughty. I do not get involved with things too great or too wondrous for me. Instead, I have calmed and quieted my soul like a weaned child with its mother; my soul is like a weaned child" (Ps. 131:1-2). *Under the Elderberry* by Hans Thoma.

and will honor your name" (86:9). The book was compiled for those who were already in God's kingdom and were seeking to express themselves to the Lord, their King. The book of Psalms shows kingdom citizens how to worship God in this life, both as the gathered community and the individual. Even the seven penitential psalms (6; 32; 38; 51; 102; 130; 143) express how those already numbered among God's people may repent and be restored to fellowship with him. The royal psalms (e.g., 2; 18; 20; 45; 72; 89; 110) in honor of Israel's earthly kings will find their greatest fulfillment when the unending King reigns unopposed forever and ever (Rev. 11:15). The New Testament commends the singing of psalms for Christians (Eph. 5:19; Col. 3:16), showing their ongoing value.

 ## ORIGINAL HISTORICAL SETTING

Author and Date of Writing:
Many authors, perhaps finally compiled ca. 400 B.C.
The titles of more than 70 psalms mention David, a noted musician and poet (1 Sam. 16:23; 2 Sam. 1:17). Both Asaph and "the sons of Korah" wrote several. Other named authors are Moses, Solomon, Heman, and Ethan. Of these, Moses was the earliest (1400s B.C.). Some psalms may have been composed after Israel returned from exile.

The collection grew gradually over time. For example, "Book I" (Pss. 1–41) could have been completed early in Solomon's time. The Asaph Collection (Pss. 73–83) and the Songs of Ascents (Pss. 120–134) were perhaps added as a group. The final compilation probably did not occur until after the second temple had been completed.

First Audience and Destination:
The Israelite people living in their land
Each of the 150 psalms was first intended for a particular audience. Sometimes the psalm title is suggestive, for example, the Songs of Ascents (Pss. 120–134) were evidently composed as songs for Israelite travelers to sing as they were going up (literally) to Jerusalem. The Psalter in its final form was designed as the "Hymnal of Second-Temple Judaism."

Occasion
Only 14 psalms provide a historical occasion in the title (3; 7; 18; 30; 34; 51; 52; 54; 56; 57; 59; 60; 63; 142). For others, the content is suggestive but not conclusive. The final editors of the collection were prompted by the need to preserve the psalms they had. Many scholars believe that the final editors composed Pss. 1, 2, and 150 as the formal introduction and conclusion to the Psalter.

LITERARY FEATURES

Genre and Literary Style:
An anthology of poetry in honor of Israel's God and Israel's faith, written in Hebrew

The poetic style of the book of Psalms has much in common with the poetry of every culture: the rich use of figurative language and hyperbole that comes from thoughtful use of the imagination. Who can forget the metaphor, "The Lord is my shepherd" (23:1), or the hyperbole, "Let the rivers clap their hands" (98:8)? (See *Genre and Literary Style* for *Proverbs* for more information on Hebrew parallelism.) Psalms was the first book in the Writings (*Kethuvim*), the third section of the Hebrew canon. Jesus referred to this threefold organization in Luke 24:44: "everything written about me in the Law of Moses, the Prophets, and the Psalms must be fulfilled."

Themes:
Praise and thanksgiving, lament and trust, wisdom, kingship

By careful observation, most psalms may be assigned to one of the themes or "psalm types" listed above. Many psalms exalt God for who he is (praise) and what he has done (thanksgiving). Some psalms are laments or calls to God for help, either because of personal or national distress. These are prayers of petition more than psalms of praise, but they express confident trust in God. A few psalms exhort the righteous to live in wisdom along the lines of the book of Proverbs. The royal psalms have already been noted.

Book Features and Structure

Of the 150 psalms, 116 have a title of some sort. (The other 34 are called "orphan psalms.") These 116 psalms provide information about authorship, historical context, musical notations, or original usage. For the most part, the meaning of the musical terms (e.g., *shiggaion*, *maskil*, *miktam*, and *selah*) is lost.

The present five-section organization of Psalms was possibly meant to echo the five books of Moses. Each section ends on a note of praise to the Lord.

Book I (mainly by David):	Pss. 1–41
Book II (mainly by David):	Pss. 42–72
Book III (mainly by Asaph):	Pss. 73–89
Book IV (mainly anonymous):	Pss. 90–106
Book V (Davidic and anonymous):	Pss. 107–150

PROVERBS
THE BOOK OF PROVERBS

The longer title translates the name found in Latin Bibles (*Liber Proverbiorum*). In Hebrew the title was "Proverbs of Solomon." Solomon was named as the main contributor. Proverb (*mashal* in Hebrew) may be rendered "maxim" or "wise saying."

○ KEY TEXT: 3:5-6

"Trust in the LORD with all your heart, and do not rely on your own understanding; in all your ways know him, and he will make your paths straight."

○ KEY TERM: "WISDOM"

This book shows God's people how to live life skillfully: "The fear of the LORD is the beginning of knowledge" (1:7). These principles for everyday life combine common sense as well as proper reverence for God, resulting in true wisdom. Wisdom (Hebrew *hokmah*) goes beyond theoretical knowledge into practical guidelines for facing life's challenging issues successfully.

○ ONE-SENTENCE SUMMARY

Those who follow God's wise design for living—particularly in areas of sexual purity and integrity of speech—avoid the perils that others fall into and enjoy life on earth as God meant it to be lived.

"Wisdom calls out in the street; she makes her voice heard in the public squares. She cries out above the commotion; she speaks at the entrance of the city gates: 'How long, inexperienced ones, will you love ignorance?'" (Prov. 1:20-22a).

GOD'S MESSAGE IN THE BOOK

Purpose

Proverbs gives positive and negative principles for successful living, no matter the situation. The book applies to everyday life the great commandments to love God supremely and to love one's neighbors as oneself (Deut. 6:5; Lev. 19:18). Because proverbial teachings, by their nature, tell what works in human relationships, they cannot be treated as absolutes or as prophecies. The book assumes but does not explicitly mention covenant and redemption or Israel's history. Living well means enjoying successful relationships now, whatever happened in history or whatever the future brings.

Christian Worldview Elements

Proverbs presents two worldview categories extremely well. First, *sovereignty and providence* are taught by the laws of cause and effect in the moral realm. Second, the book provides practical insight on *ethics and morality*. No Bible book more fully teaches that God's people are to have a different quality of life than the ungodly.

God
Creation
o **Sovereignty and Providence**
Faith and Reason
Revelation and Authority
Humanity
Rebellion and Sin
Covenant and Redemption
Community and Church
Discipleship
o **Ethics and Morality**
Time and Eternity

Teachings about God

In Proverbs, God is the one who has set up the world so that those who live by his principles will find blessing and success. The highest virtue is "the fear of the Lord."

Teachings about Humanity

Proverbs shows that humans may live by a right way or a wrong way, a wise way or a foolish way. The right way is not the easy way, but those who live by it find great reward. All of life's relationships may be governed by the wise teachings of this book.

Teachings about Salvation

Proverbs assumes God's covenant but does not teach about it directly. This surely serves to demonstrate that the wisdom coming from the people of God is superior to and results in greater blessing than the wisdom coming from others—even without explicitly referring to the mighty acts of God on behalf of his people.

CHRIST IN PROVERBS

Wisdom as an attribute of God is pictured as a person in Proverbs. In light of the New Testament, we know that Wisdom as Jesus Christ, the Word by whom the worlds were created and are sustained (John 1:1; Heb. 1:3).

GOD'S STORY

When the Events of This Book Happened:
Timeless
These principles are operative in human relationships without reference to time.

How Proverbs Fits into God's "Story"

Proverbs does not fit into the narrative of the story of the kingdom. Rather, it offers timeless principles for those already committed to the King of the kingdom of God. Although Jesus is "greater than Solomon" (Matt. 12:42), the wisdom teachings of this book apply directly to all kingdom citizens, whether ancient Israelites or contemporary believers. The book of Proverbs shows how to live with love for God foremost and love for others second. Proverbs does not tell how to get into the kingdom of God; rather, it tells those already in the kingdom how to live in right relationship to others. This is essentially the same approach that Jesus took in the Sermon on the Mount (Matt. 5–7) and the approach taught in the letter from James.

ORIGINAL HISTORICAL SETTING

Author and Date of Writing:
Primarily Solomon, but also others, ca. 950–700 B.C.
Solomon ruled Israel ca. 970–931 B.C. He "spoke 3,000 proverbs, and his songs numbered 1,005" (1 Kgs. 4:32). Many of these were preserved in this book. Solomon wrote the first section (1:8–9:18) and the second section (10:1–22:16). More than two centuries later, more of Solomon's proverbs were compiled by scholars working for King Hezekiah (25:1–29:27). Unnamed wise men wrote the proverbs collected in 22:17–24:22. Two others, unknown outside this book, contributed short sections: Agur (30:1-33) and King Lemuel (31:1-9). The final compiler of Proverbs evidently wrote the prologue, stating the book's purpose (1:1-7) and the epilogue about the wife of noble character (31:10-31).

Solomon may have collected his own proverbs and put them into written form. The later contributions could have been completed by 700 B.C. Some scholars believe that the book of Proverbs was not edited into its final form until after the Jews returned from their Babylonian exile, perhaps the fifth century B.C.

First Audience and Destination:
The Israelite people living in their own land
The first hearers were the Israelite people who came to admire the wisdom of their great king Solomon (1 Kgs. 3:28). According to 1 Kgs. 4:29-34, representatives of "all peoples" of the surrounding nations came to Jerusalem to hear Solomon's divinely inspired wisdom.

Occasion

When God asked Solomon at the beginning of his reign to name a gift, he asked for "wisdom and knowledge" to rule the Israelite people well (2 Chr. 1:10). God granted this, and over the course of years Solomon's wisdom became legendary so that it "was greater than the wisdom of all the East, greater than all the wisdom of Egypt" (1 Kgs. 4:30). Perhaps most of Solomon's proverbs were written during his early years as king, before he was led astray by "many foreign women" (1 Kgs. 11:1).

 LITERARY FEATURES

Genre and Literary Style:

Wisdom literature emphasizing short maxims, written entirely in Hebrew poetry

People of the ancient Near East greatly admired the wise men who collected and published guidelines for successful living. Wisdom literature was of two types: proverbial (such as the present book, stating principles for living well) and speculative (such as Job or Ecclesiastes, pondering deep issues of human existence). Both the Mesopotamians and the Egyptians developed wisdom traditions. Israelite wisdom, however, based on the fear of the Lord, surpassed that of other nations. Proverbs was placed in the third section, he Writings (*Kethuvim*), of the Hebrew canon.

Hebrew poetry characteristically had two (sometimes three) lines that are parallel in thought (rather than in rhyme). In *synonymous* parallelism, the second line repeated the essence of the first in different words (see 5:7). In *antithetic* parallelism, the second line stated the opposite of the first (see 10:3). When the later line built on the first without either repeating or contrasting, it is referred to as synthetic parallelism (see 31:15).

Themes:

Fear of the Lord; cause and effect in the moral realm; wisdom and folly (each personified as a woman)

Although common sense does not take God into account, true wisdom is based on reverence and trust in the God who has revealed himself. He has built into the moral world the relentless law of sowing and reaping, cause and effect. Good choices result in good ends; evil choices result in evil ends. One way to understand these is to contrast those who follow Wisdom and those who follow Folly.

Book Features and Structure

Beyond the parallelism of Hebrew poetry, this book has a number of noteworthy literary features. Vivid comparisons abound: "A word spoken at the right time is like gold apples in silver settings" (25:11). Another device is to use numbers; especially striking is the "x plus 1" pattern: "Three things are never

FORMS OF WISDOM TEACHING IN PROVERBS

1.	Proverb	A proverb is a short, carefully constructed ethical observation (13:7) or teaching (14:1).
2.	Admonition	An admonition is a command written either as a short proverb or as part of a long discourse.
3.	Numerical Saying	The numerical pattern lists items that have something in common after an introduction like, *"The LORD hates six things; in fact, seven are detestable to him"* (6:16).
4.	Better Saying	A better saying follows the pattern "A is better than B" (21:19).
5.	Rhetorical Question	A rhetorical question is a question with an obvious answer that still draws the reader into deeper reflection (30:4).
6.	Wisdom Poem	Wisdom poems or songs teach a series of moral lessons (31:10-31). These poems are often acrostic which means that the first letter of the first line begins with the first letter in the Hebrew alphabet. The first letter of the second line is the second letter of the Hebrew alphabet, and so on.
7.	Example Story	An example story is an anecdote meant to drive home a moral lesson (7:6-27).

satisfied; four never say, 'Enough!'" (30:15). Chapters 1–9 feature several long wisdom poems that use striking female imagery. Not only are wisdom and folly portrayed as attractive women, but there are also warnings against the immoral woman. These chapters were crafted as instructions to youth. Chapters 10–30 contain a string of two-line sayings unrelated to their immediate context. The epilogue (31:10-31) was written as an acrostic, with each verse beginning with successive letters of the Hebrew alphabet.

Lemuel and His Mother by Ephraim Moses Lilien (1874-1925). Proverbs 31 are words that King Lemuel's mother taught him. "What should I say, my son? What, son of my womb? What, son of my vows? Don't spend your energy on women or your efforts on those who destroy kings. . . .Speak up for those who have no voice, for the justice of all who are dispossessed. Speak up, judge righteously, and defend the cause of the oppressed and needy" (Prov. 31:2-3, 8-9).

ECCLESIASTES

The Greek translators used this name when they titled it in the second century B.C. It was their rendering of the Hebrew title, *Qoheleth*, "Teacher" or "Preacher." Ecclesiastes means "One Who Assembles People," akin to *ekklesia*, "assembly."

○ KEY TEXT: 1:2 (WHICH IS THE SAME AS 12:8)

"Absolute futility. Everything is futile."

○ KEY TERM: "FUTILITY" (USELESSNESS OR ABSURDITY)

The Hebrew term *hebel* literally meant "breath" or "vapor." It referred to something without meaning or something absurd or useless. The term occurs more than 30 times in the book but only once elsewhere in the Bible.

"All things are wearisome, more than anyone can say. The eye is not satisfied by seeing or the ear filled with hearing. What has been is what will be, and what has been done is what will be done; there is nothing new under the sun" (Eccl. 1:8-9). *La Tasse de Chocolat* by Pierre Auguste Renoir.

○ ONE-SENTENCE SUMMARY

Although human beings can accumulate many things, accomplish much, and achieve great wisdom, these are without profit and ultimately pointless unless one has lived in fear and obedience to God.

 GOD'S MESSAGE IN THE BOOK

Purpose

Ecclesiastes answers the question, what is the meaning of life? The way *Qoheleth* (the "Teacher") argued was to show at length the failure of the answers offered by those who live life "under the sun," that is, apart from revealed religion. Materialists find life's object in the abundance of possessions or achievements. Sensualists discover meaning in physical pleasure (food, sex, excitement, adventure). Scholars seek purpose through intellectual inquiry (wisdom). All these answers are "absolute futility" or "utterly meaningless." Life's meaning cannot be discovered; it is only revealed by God. Life is brief; judgment is coming; God is sovereign. *Qoheleth's* answer is that of divine revelation: "When all has been heard, the conclusion of the matter is this: fear God and keep his commands, because this is for all humanity. For God will bring every act to judgment, including every hidden thing, whether good or evil" (12:13-14).

Christian Worldview Elements

Ecclesiastes focuses attention on the worldview categories of *God* first and *humanity* second. When the order is reversed, the result is "absolute futility." No other Bible book does a better job of teaching that the meaning of life is found only outside oneself and only in right relationship to God.

○ **God**
  Creation
  Sovereignty and Providence
  Faith and Reason
  Revelation and Authority
○ **Humanity**
  Rebellion and Sin
  Covenant and Redemption
  Community and Church
  Discipleship
  Ethics and Morality
  Time and Eternity

Teachings about God

In Ecclesiastes God is referred to simply as "God" (*Elohim*) or "Creator." He is not called "the Lord/LORD." This emphasizes God in relationship to all humanity—their Creator and the One to whom they are ultimately accountable—as opposed to God in relationship to Israel as the covenant people.

Teachings about Humanity

Ecclesiastes has an optimistic view of human capacity apart from God. Materialists, sensualists, and scholars alike can reach worthwhile goals that bring temporary satisfaction and the appearance of meaning. Yet the book is pessimistic about the ability of persons to understand their true purpose unaided by divine revelation. Left to themselves, humans never reach right answers to the question, why am I here?

Teachings about Salvation

Salvation in Ecclesiastes is addressed in terms of proper fear (reverence, awe, respect) of God (see 3:14; 5:7; 8:12; 12:13). Ultimately only those who "fear God and keep his commands" (12:13) give evidence of experiencing salvation, which like existence itself comes from the Creator. The meaning of human life is displayed when redeemed people magnify the glory of God by joyfully fearing and obeying him.

 ## CHRIST IN ECCLESIASTES

Ecclesiastes gives a graphic picture of life's emptiness and futility apart from God. Jesus uses the image of a vine with branches to underscore this truth: "The one who remains in me and I in him produces much fruit, because you can do nothing without me" (John 15:5).

 ## GOD'S STORY

When the Events of This Book Happened:
Timeless
The questions and answers about life's purpose discussed in Ecclesiastes are valid in all times and places.

How Ecclesiastes Fits into God's "Story"

Ecclesiastes does not fit into the narrative of the story of the kingdom. Rather, people already in the kingdom need to know that he gladly gives them exuberant human experiences to savor when their priority is fearing and obeying him.

Ecclesiastes must be considered from two different perspectives. Much of the book focuses on the emptiness of everything done apart from God. "For what does it benefit someone to gain the whole world and yet lose his life?" (Mark 8:36).

But are human accomplishments inherently evil? Not at all. For those already in the kingdom—who fear God and obey his commands—human life is a wondrous and good gift from God to be enjoyed to the fullest (9:7-10). This is true despite the harsh realities of life; those in the kingdom may delight in the material possessions, life's pleasures, and wisdom that this present life offers: "Whatever your hands find to do, do with all your strength" (9:10). Ecclesiastes serves kingdom purposes by reminding God's people that they are to enjoy this present existence fully.

ORIGINAL HISTORICAL SETTING

Author and Date of Writing:
Probably Solomon, perhaps near the end of his reign (ca. 935 B.C.)
The author called himself *Qoheleth*, "Teacher" or "Preacher" in the sense of one who assembles people for instruction. He was also "son of David, king in Jerusalem" (1:1). Jewish and Christian traditions alike have identified him as Solomon, and the perspective of an experienced old man is certain (see 12:1-7).

On the other hand, several features of the book point to a writer other than and later than Solomon. The Hebrew style is unusual and considered late; the reference to "all who were before me in Jerusalem" (2:9) seems odd for Solomon, Jerusalem's second Israelite king; and the writer expressed negative views about rulers (see 4:13; 5:8-9; 7:19; 8:2-3) that are hard to imagine coming from Solomon.

It may be, as is clear in the case of Proverbs, that the material was mainly written by Solomon but that it was expanded and revised by an unknown editor at a later time, perhaps as late as the 400s B.C. There is nothing in the book that Solomon could not have written, and he certainly is the best Old Testament character to fit the description of one who "taught the people knowledge . . . and arranged many proverbs" (12:9; see 1 Kgs. 4:32).

First Audience and Destination:
The Israelite people living in their own land
The first hearers were the Israelite people who came to admire the wisdom of Solomon (1 Kgs. 3:28). According to 1 Kgs. 4:29-34, representatives of "all peoples" of the surrounding nations came to hear Solomon's divinely inspired wisdom.

Occasion
Solomon reigned ca. 970–931 B.C. The precise occasion for Ecclesiastes is unknown. The teachings of Ecclesiastes come from late in Solomon's reign— after he had experienced everything life had to offer and was contemplating once again, "what's it all about?" (The book of Proverbs was evidently his wisdom from early in his reign.)

LITERARY FEATURES

Genre and Literary Style:
Wisdom literature composed in a mixture of prose and poetry, written in unusual Hebrew
Ancient wisdom literature was of two types: proverbial (such as the book of Proverbs, stating principles for living well) and speculative (such as Job or the present book, pondering deep issues of human existence). In the Hebrew canon, Ecclesiastes was placed in the third section, the Writings or *Kethuvim*

"Remember your Creator in the days of your youth: Before the days of adversity come, and the years approach when you will say, 'I have no delight in them'" (Eccl. 12:1).

(the other two sections are the Law and the Prophets). Among the Writings it was one of the Five Scrolls. Each of these Five Scrolls became associated with one of the Israelite festivals and was read publicly during that festival. Ecclesiastes was identified with *Sukkoth*, "Shelters" or "Tabernacles," a happy time that celebrated the completion of all agricultural labors. The Hebrew style is markedly different from anything else in the Old Testament.

Themes:
Vanity (uselessness), under the sun, profit

The theme of the uselessness of humanity's work apart from God has already been considered. The phrase "under the sun" occurs 27 times in the text and seems to refer to life lived independently of God. The theme of "profit" sometimes occurs in rhetorical questions in the modern sense of "what's the use of that?" with the expected answer, "no use at all."

Book Features and Structure

Ecclesiastes is easy to read, but it is almost impossible to give a satisfactory outline of how the topics develop. The prose and poetry sections shift without warning. Many of the statements, taken by themselves, are enigmas. Memorable passages include "There is an occasion for everything . . ." (3:1-8) and "Wise Sayings" (7:1-14). Because *Qoheleth* referred to himself in the third person only at the beginning and end of the book, a three-part structure—which admittedly does not show the inner development of the book—may be suggested: introduction and theme (1:1-11); discourses on the meaning of life—with and without God (1:12–12:8); "the conclusion of the matter" (12:9-14).

SONG OF SONGS
SONG OF SOLOMON OR CANTICLES

The Hebrew title is *Shir Hashirim*, "Song of Songs," meaning "The Best Song." Because 1:1 mentions Solomon, English Bibles have often included his name in the title. *Canticles* is Latin for "Songs."

O KEY TEXT: 6:3

"I am my love's and my love is mine; he feeds among the lilies."

O KEY TERM: "BELOVED"

Song of Songs is a book of romantic love poetry. The lovers—bride and groom—refer to each other passionately. The bride calls him "the one I love," an expression that occurs six times; the groom calls her "my darling."

O ONE-SENTENCE SUMMARY

A bride and groom (or wife and husband) celebrate with exuberant passion God's wonderful gift of the love they share by describing the intimate dimensions of their love—physical, emotional, and spiritual.

The Caring Young Shepherdess by Otto Gebler. The setting for Song of Songs is pastoral. The main characters are a shepherdess and a shepherd.

GOD'S MESSAGE IN THE BOOK

Purpose

Many parts of Scripture address human sexuality, and a number of divine commands regulate marriage, adultery, divorce, and sexual immorality. Other than this book, however, little is noted in Scripture about whether a man and woman should enjoy or merely endure romance. In the tradition of ancient Near Eastern wisdom literature, Song of Songs explores one of the "big issues" of life. It definitively answers the question, should a husband and wife enjoy the amorous dimension of their relationship? The answer is, yes, indeed! Although people often abuse or distort erotic love, it is a wondrous and normal part of marriage to be savored as God's gift. Strikingly, the dominant speaker is the wife, whose delight in the intimacies she enjoys demonstrates that the biblical view of sex is neither negative nor repressed. It is not claiming too much to call this book "The Bible's Romance Manual for Marriage." God's people should enjoy the Song of Songs today in light of its original purpose.

Christian Worldview Elements

This book deals with the worldview categories of *humanity* and *ethics and morality*. No other Bible book more fully teaches that human beings may enjoy rich and sensual love. On the other hand, this love is suitably expressed only within the marriage of a man and a woman, according to the standards God revealed elsewhere in Scripture.

God
Creation
Sovereignty and Providence
Faith and Reason
Revelation and Authority
o **Humanity**
Rebellion and Sin
Covenant and Redemption
Community and Church
Discipleship
o **Ethics and Morality**
Time and Eternity

Teachings about God

God is not directly named in this book.
None of his usual names are found, such as God, Lord, the Lord, or the Almighty. God is affirmed indirectly as the Creator who conceived of romantic love between husband and wife, as in the account of the first man and woman coming together as one flesh (Gen. 2:18-25).

Teachings about Humanity

Song of Songs celebrates the glory of wedded bliss possible for human beings, despite the many obstacles to true love. The climax of the book shows how strong and wonderful romantic love is: "A huge torrent cannot extinguish love; rivers cannot sweep it away. If a man were to give all his wealth for love, it would be utterly scorned" (8:7).

Teachings about Salvation

The book does not teach directly about redemption. If the love of a husband for his wife can be as rich and satisfying as the book describes, however, how much greater is the love of God for his beloved people? (see Rev. 21:9).

CHRIST IN SONG OF SONGS

Love between a husband and wife is taken by Paul as a picture of the love Christ has for his bride, the church (Eph. 5:32).

GOD'S STORY

When the Events of This Book Happened:
Timeless
The romantic love celebrated by this book is authentic for all times and places.

How Song of Songs Fits into God's "Story"

Song of Solomon does not fit into the narrative of the story of the kingdom. However, for those already part of God's kingdom, when true love is aroused, it is to be enjoyed (see 2:7; 3:5; 8:4 in contemporary versions). It says nothing about how to get into God's kingdom, but it shows one important aspect of earthly life to those already in the kingdom. This wisdom book serves kingdom purposes by reminding God's people that they are to savor the bliss of married love while they look forward to the consummation of God's redemptive purposes in eternity.

The juicy fruit of the pomegranate (*Punica granatum*), about the size of a tennis ball, is full of seeds and sweet pulp. It develops from beautiful scarlet flowers that cover the twiggy bush in spring. Pomegranate bushes were often grown in gardens and beside houses (Deut. 8:8; Song 6:11). Pomegranates were symbols of lovemaking and fertility.

ORIGINAL HISTORICAL SETTING

Author and Date of Writing:
Probably Solomon, perhaps near the beginning of his reign (ca. 965 B.C.)

The author wrote the most exquisite romantic poetry in the Bible, and the perspective of a young couple captivated with each other is transparent. The inscription (1:1) as well as Jewish and Christian tradition identified the author as Solomon. According to 1 Kgs. 4:32, Solomon's "songs numbered 1,005." Many believe that the pure and passionate words of love expressed in this book were necessarily written early in his life—before he was married to so many women (1 Kgs. 11:1-8).

Some scholars have argued that the title is a dedication to Solomon (rather than a statement of authorship) and find it hard to imagine that a polygamous king wrote such beautiful celebration of monogamous love. Although their arguments for later anonymous authorship have merit, there is no reason that a young Solomon could not have written the song in its entirety.

First Audience and Destination:
Israelites living in their own land

The first hearers were the Israelite people who admired both the proverbs and the songs of their great king Solomon (1 Kgs. 4:32).

"Set me as a seal on your heart, as a seal on your arm. For love is as strong as death; jealousy is as unrelenting as Sheol. Love's flames are fiery flames—an almighty flame!" (Song 8:6).

Occasion

Scholars have a variety of opinions about what prompted the composition of this book. Two major suggestions follow. Some believe that the book describes an ideal romance composed for a royal occasion, such as a state wedding. In this view, the bride and groom were not individuals but Every-Bride and Every-Groom, depicting the possibilities of human romance with all its challenges and glories. Others have argued that this is Solomon's poem about an actual, historical romance and marriage between an unnamed young woman (called the "Shulammite," 6:13) and her beloved (either Solomon himself or an unnamed lover). The former view of the occasion appears preferable.

 LITERARY FEATURES

Genre and Literary Style:
Wisdom literature emphasizing the value of romantic love, written entirely in Hebrew poetry

Although some scholars have questioned whether this book is properly "wisdom literature," it answers one of the grand questions of life: should a husband and wife enjoy the erotic dimension of their relationship? (See earlier discussion under *Purpose*.) As such, it belongs to the literary category "speculative wisdom." The poetic imagery is exquisite, lavish, and delicate, even if modern lovers do not fully appreciate the vivid metaphors from the ancient Near East (see 4:1-7; 5:10-16; 6:4-10; 7:1-10). The lines of poetry are short, and the Hebrew style is appropriate to the subject matter.

In the Hebrew canon, this book was placed in the third section, the Writings or *Kethuvim* (the other two sections are the Law and the Prophets). Among the Writings, it was the first of the Five Scrolls, each of which became associated with one of the Israelite festivals and was read publicly during that festival. Song of Songs was associated with *Pesach*, "Passover." Although this connection seems strange, this can be understood in light of the Jewish allegorical interpretation of the book. Its deeper (and truer) meaning was said to be its declaration of God's love for Israel, of which the greatest historical evidence was the exodus at the first Passover. This view was also taken up by Christians in the medieval period, but revised and seen as an allegory of Christ's love for the church. Bible scholars today generally reject such allegorical readings as a misunderstanding of the book's purpose by theologians unwilling to admire as literally true the frankly erotic elements of the book.

Themes:
Desire, commitment, giving of self to one's lover despite obstacles

The passionate desire of the woman for her husband and of the husband for his wife is the major theme of the book. This passion, however, lies in the mutual commitment of one to the other. (See *Key Text*.) True love is so strong that it overcomes all obstacles (see 5:6-8), yet it should not be wakened until "the appropriate time" (2:7; 3:5; 8:4).

Book Features and Structure

Although it was originally a song, no clues about the original musical notation have survived. The Hebrew text distinguishes the characters by changing gender and number in certain verbs and pronouns. On this basis, many translations have added subheadings to clarify changes in speaker from "Woman" to "Man" (with "Young Women," "Brothers," and a "Narrator" talking in places).

ISAIAH

Isaiah, the eighth-century B.C. Israelite prophet from Judah, has given his name to this book as its composer. His name means "The Lord Saves" in Hebrew.

○ KEY TEXT: 1:19-20

"If you are willing and obedient, you will eat the good things of the land. But if you refuse and rebel, you will be devoured by the sword.' For the mouth of the LORD has spoken."

○ KEY TERM: "JUDGMENT"

Isaiah's vision of the heavenly throne compelled him to proclaim God's case against his people before their earthly throne in Jerusalem. Although divine judgment was inevitable, Isaiah offered hope, comfort, and a glorious future for God's kingdom.

○ ONE-SENTENCE SUMMARY

Isaiah prophesied that because of continued idolatry God would send Judah into Babylonian captivity, yet he would graciously restore them (through the work of his Servant, who would bear away their sins by his death), so that his kingdom would be unending in the new heavens and the new earth.

GOD'S MESSAGE IN THE BOOK

Purpose

This book preserves the divinely inspired prophecies Isaiah made during his ministry of more than 40 years. These prophecies were originally for the people of Judah facing Assyrian invasions. Because of rebellion and idolatry, their kingdom would be destroyed—even though individuals could still repent and seek the Lord.

The last part of Isaiah (chaps. 40–66) was really addressed to later generations. On the one hand, it would comfort exiles returning to the land after Babylonian captivity (late sixth century B.C.); on the other hand, it speaks to every later generation of God's people who long for God's kingdom to be revealed to all in its holiness and righteousness.

Christian Worldview Elements

Isaiah deals with the worldview categories of *rebellion and sin*; *covenant and redemption*; and *time and eternity*. Judah's sin—like all sin—had tragic consequences. Yet judgment was not the final word, only the means of bringing God's people to ultimate salvation. Isaiah gives the big picture of redemption from his own day until the consummation of all things.

Isaiah by Michelangelo

Teachings about God

God expects his people to fulfill his requirements. He is outraged by sin and will judge it. Yet he is also the God of help and hope. Isaiah's portrait of God is thus one of tension between judgment and comfort. The book is famous for its detailed prophecies about Messiah, especially his birth (7:14; 9:6-7) and his death (52:13–53:12). The Spirit will empower both the Servant and the servants of the Lord (11:2; 32:15; 42:1; 44:3; 61:1).

> God
> Creation
> Sovereignty and Providence
> Faith and Reason
> Revelation and Authority
> Humanity
> ○ **Rebellion and Sin**
> ○ **Covenant and Redemption**
> Community and Church
> Discipleship
> Ethics and Morality
> ○ **Time and Eternity**

Teachings about Humanity

Aside from its general teachings that humans are fallen sinners whom God must redeem, the book provides personal glimpses into the lives of two people God used. Isaiah shows that God may call and use someone who is well educated. The section on Hezekiah (chaps. 36–39) shows a ruler who valued trust in God more than military or economic success.

Teachings about Salvation

In Isaiah, salvation is based on God's forgiveness of sins (1:18; 6:5-6). The passage on the suffering Servant (52:13–53:12) is the most detailed biblical prophecy about Jesus's death as a substitute, and the New Testament writers quoted it often. Ultimately, however, salvation includes the restoration of Zion (chap. 62) as well as the nations (chap. 60). The goal is for the nations to "proclaim the praises of the Lord" (60:6). This will be brought to completion in the eternal state (Isa. 65:17; cp. Rev. 21:1).

CHRIST IN ISAIAH

Isaiah is the only Old Testament book to prophesy the virgin birth of Christ (7:14). Christ as Suffering Servant is foretold in Isaiah (52:13–53:12).

GOD'S STORY

When the Events of This Book Happened:

Isaiah prophesied during the reigns of four kings of Judah: Uzziah, Jotham, Ahaz, and Hezekiah (mainly ca. 740–700 B.C.)

Second Kings 15–20 and 2 Chr. 26–32 provide the historical narrative for the four kings mentioned in Isa. 1:1. The kingdom of Judah was isolated, with powerful enemies especially to the north. From Samaria, idolatrous kings

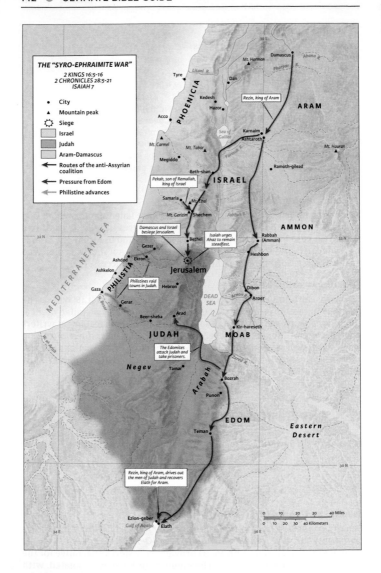

THE "SYRO-EPHRAIMITE WAR"
2 KINGS 16:5-16
2 CHRONICLES 28:5-21
ISAIAH 7

- • City
- ▲ Mountain peak
- ☼ Siege
- Israel
- Judah
- Aram-Damascus
- ← Routes of the anti-Assyrian coalition
- ← Pressure from Edom
- ← Philistine advances

Damascus

Mt. Hermon

Abana R.

Tyre

Dan

Rezin, king of Aram

ARAM

PHOENICIA

Kedesh

Hazor

Acco

Karnaim

Sea of Galilee

Ashtaroth

Mt. Carmel

Mt. Tabor

Yarmuk R.

Mt. Hauran

Megiddo

Ramoth-gilead

Beth-shan

Pekah, son of Remaliah, king of Israel

ISRAEL

Samaria

Mt. Ebal

Mt. Gerizim

Shechem

Jabbok R.

AMMON

Damascus and Israel besiege Jerusalem.

Isaiah urges Ahaz to remain steadfast.

Rabbah (Amman)

Bethel

Gezer

Ashdod

Ekron

Ashkelon

Heshbon

PHILISTIA

Jerusalem

Philistines raid towns in Judah.

Hebron

Gaza

W. el-Besor

DEAD SEA

Dibon

Gerar

Arnon R.

Aroer

Beer-sheba

Arad

JUDAH

Kir-hareseth

MOAB

The Edomites attack Judah and take prisoners.

Negev

Tamar

Bozrah

Arabah

Zered R.

Punon

EDOM

Eastern Desert

Teman

MEDITERRANEAN SEA

32 N

33 N

30 N

Rezin, king of Aram, drives out the men of Judah and recovers Elath for Aram.

Ezion-geber

Gulf of Aqaba

Elath

34 E

36 E

0   10   20   30   40 Miles
0   10   20   30   40 Kilometers

ruled over the kingdom of Israel. North of there, the power of Aram (Syria, KJV), with its capital in Damascus, was a constant threat. Beyond all these was the terrible world superpower, the Assyrians, with their capital in Nineveh.

How Isaiah Fits into God's "Story"

The events of Isaiah's time belong to "chapter 2" of the story: God educates his nation (disobedient Israel disciplined). Judah was weak and impotent because it had become like the surrounding nations: self-sufficient and selfish. There was little sense that it was part of God's kingdom of righteousness and holiness. Yet Isaiah prophesied the coming of a righteous King—a descendant of David—who would one day rule God's kingdom forever (9:7).

 ## ORIGINAL HISTORICAL SETTING

Author and Date of Writing:
Isaiah, perhaps finally compiled ca. 680 B.C.

Because of the message of good news in the last section of his book, the author has been called the "Evangelist of the Old Covenant." Isaiah the son of Amoz was evidently from Jerusalem. According to Jewish tradition, he was from a noble family. He had a wife and at least two sons with symbolic names, "A Remnant Will Return" and "Speeding to the Spoil; Hastening to the Plunder" (*Shear-jashub* and *Maher-shalal-hash-baz*, 7:3; 8:3). He was possibly martyred by being sawed in half (see Heb. 11:37). The kings Isaiah mentioned ruled almost a century, from 792 to 686 B.C. Isaiah's years of influence were ca. 740–700 B.C.

For the past two centuries, critical scholars have argued that chapters 40–66 were necessarily written later than Isaiah's lifetime. These chapters focus on return from Babylonian exile (which did not happen until centuries after Isaiah) and name Cyrus (44:28; 45:1), the Persian king who allowed the Jewish exiles to return (Ezra 1:1-2). Isaiah 40–55 is designated "Deutero-Isaiah" (an unknown prophet with an exilic perspective) and Isa. 56–66 viewed as "Trito-Isaiah" (an unknown postexilic prophet). The basic assumption of this critical view appears to be that Scripture does not contain true predictive prophecy. For Bible students who accept that God gave specific revelations of the distant future to his prophets, there is no reason to doubt that Isaiah wrote all the book that bears his name.

First Audience and Destination:
The people of Judah living during Isaiah's lifetime

The first hearers were people living in Judah near the end of the 700s B.C.

Occasion

The specific occasion of a few parts of Isaiah are clear, for example, chapter 7 was prompted by the Syrian-Israelite coalition against Judah (734–732 B.C.), and chapters 36–39 were prompted by Sennacherib's invasion of Judah (701 B.C.).

"As a mother comforts her son, so I will comfort you, and you will be comforted in Jerusalem" (Isa. 66:13).

The last event that may be dated in Isaiah's lifetime is the murder of Sennacherib (681 B.C.). By this time, Isaiah was an old man, for he had been commissioned ca. 740 B.C., the year of King Uzziah's death. Isaiah did not tell what prompted his compilation of the entire book.

LITERARY FEATURES

Genre and Literary Style:
Prophecies and a few historical narratives written in excellent Hebrew poetry and prose

The genius of Hebrew prophecy was that it both "forth tells" and "foretells." The essence of the prophetic message was its clear "This is what the Lord GOD says." Isaiah includes the three classic elements of prophecy: (1) call to people to turn from their sins in the face of divine judgment, (2) predictions of near events (such as the fall of Damascus), and (3) predictions of remote events (such as the coming of the Servant of the Lord).

The book is mainly Hebrew poetry. The main prose section, the narrative about King Hezekiah (chaps. 36–39), skillfully makes the transition from the challenges Judah faced from the Assyrians to those Judah would later face from the Babylonians. Isaiah was a master of Hebrew vocabulary and style. His book has a larger vocabulary than any other Old Testament book. He particularly used the literary technique of personification, such as the sun being ashamed or the mountains singing (24:23; 44:23). In the Hebrew Scriptures, the book of Isaiah was the first of the four Latter Prophets.

Themes:
The Holy One of Israel, judgment, comfort, the Servant of the Lord

Isaiah's special name for God was "the Holy One of Israel" (26 occurrences), found only six times elsewhere in Scripture. The first section of the book describes the coming of divine judgment. The last section emphasizes comfort and hope, looking forward to Zion's restoration. Isaiah is noted for four "Servant Songs" in which the Messiah representatively fulfills the responsibilities of Israel as the Lord's son.

Book Features and Structure

Isaiah predicted important details of the first coming of the Messiah. Especially noteworthy are his prophecies of the virgin birth (7:14); the child born to be Prince of Peace (9:6-7); God's Spirit on the Branch (11:1-2); the gentleness of the Servant (42:1-4); and the suffering of the Servant (52:13–53:12).

In addition to Isaiah's oracles against Judah, chapters 13–23 are noted as prophecies of coming judgment against the surrounding nations, especially the taunt against Babylon in chapter 14. Isaiah is readily divided into two major sections, the "Book of Judgment" (chaps. 1–39) and "Book of Comfort" (chaps. 40–66).

HEZEKIAH'S TUNNEL
CA. 700 B.C.

PATH OF TUNNEL

1. Gihon Spring (ENTRANCE TO CAVE PROTECTED BY "SPRING GATE TOWERS")
2. Gihon Pool and Pool Towers
3. Pool of Siloam
4. Runoff Pool (RUNOFF FROM POOL OF SILOAM)

In 711 B.C. Sargon II of Assyria captured Ashdod. Hezekiah foresaw a time when the Assyrian army might besiege Jerusalem. He fortified Jerusalem and organized an army. Knowing that a source of water was crucial within the city walls, Hezekiah constructed a 1,750-foot tunnel through solid rock from the Gihon Spring to the Siloam pool. On the east wall of the tunnel conduit, about 20 feet from the Pool of Siloam, an inscription was found that represents one of the oldest Hebrew inscriptions of significant length. Although the inscription was broken in an attempt to steal it, the fragments are now in the Istanbul Archaeology Museum.

JEREMIAH

Jeremiah, the sixth- and seventh-century B.C. Israelite prophet from Judah, has given his name to this book as its composer. His name probably means either "The Lord Exalts" or "The Lord Throws Down" in Hebrew.

⦿ KEY TEXTS: 30:15 AND 31:31

"Why do you cry out about your injury? Your pain has no cure! I have done these things to you because of your enormous guilt and your innumerable sins."

"'Look, the days are coming'—this is the LORD's declaration—'when I will make a new covenant with the house of Israel and with the house of Judah.'"

⦿ KEY TERM: "CURSE"

Jeremiah was the original "doomsday prophet." He called people to repent, but his main message was that Judah had fallen under the curse of God and was doomed to Babylonian exile because of its refusal to turn from sin.

⦿ ONE-SENTENCE SUMMARY

Anguished by the burden of his prophetic call and the rejection of his message, Jeremiah witnessed what he warned about, the Babylonian captivity, yet he prophesied God's gracious restoration through the new covenant.

"For my people have committed a double evil: They have abandoned me, the fountain of living water, and dug cisterns for themselves—cracked cisterns that cannot hold water" (Jer. 2:13). Nabatean cistern north of Makhtesh Ramon, southern Israel.

GOD'S MESSAGE IN THE BOOK

Purpose

This book preserves both the divinely inspired prophecies Jeremiah made during his long ministry and a great many of his personal experiences. These prophecies were originally for people of Judah facing invasions and then Babylonian captivity. They were facing the curse that Deut. 27 had predicted for rejecting the covenant. Although he prophesied doom, Jeremiah foretold that the exile would be limited, that Babylon would fall, and that salvation lay on the other side of divine wrath.

Christian Worldview Elements

Jeremiah deals especially with the worldview categories of *rebellion and sin*; *covenant and redemption*; and *humanity*. The consequences of rebelling against God cannot be postponed indefinitely. Although the covenant people would be judged, God would provide a new covenant. Because there is so much biographical material on the prophet, the book shows the importance of individuals coming to terms with their personal significance.

God
Creation
Sovereignty and Providence
Faith and Reason
Revelation and Authority
○ **Humanity**
○ **Rebellion and Sin**
○ **Covenant and Redemption**
Community and Church
Discipleship
Ethics and Morality
Time and Eternity

Teachings about God

Jeremiah's understanding of God explicitly included such attributes as his omnipresence (he is everywhere) and his omnipotence (he is all powerful). The classic text is 23:24: "'Can a person hide in secret places where I cannot see him?'—the LORD's declaration. 'Do I not fill the heavens and the earth?'—the LORD's declaration."

Neither Christ nor the Spirit is explicitly present in the book. Jesus, however, liked to quote Jeremiah and taught that his crucifixion established the "new covenant" that Jeremiah had predicted (31:31-34).

Teachings about Humanity

The book manifests both the wickedness and the greatness possible in human beings. King Jehoiakim's destruction of the scroll and King Zedekiah's mistreatment of Jeremiah (chaps. 36—38) show the great evil that political leaders can fall into. On the other hand, more is known about the godly Jeremiah than any other writing prophet.

Teachings about Salvation

Individuals in Jeremiah's own time, at least early in his ministry, could still turn from sin and avoid destruction (7:5-7; 18:7-8). Later on he announced that doom was inevitable. The overall perspective of the book is that redemption will happen only after judgment (29:10-14). The passage on the new covenant (31:31-34), the longest text quoted in the New Testament (Heb. 8:8-12), looked forward to what Christ would accomplish by his coming and death, as the argument of Hebrews makes clear.

✚ CHRIST IN JEREMIAH

Jeremiah's own sufferings anticipate the sufferings of Jesus, Israel's Messiah. There are numerous parallels between Jeremiah and Jesus. Both wept over Jerusalem (Jer. 9:1; Luke 19:41) and both foretold the imminent destruction of the temple (Jer. 7:11-15; Matt. 24:1-2).

🕊 GOD'S STORY

When the Events of This Book Happened:
Jeremiah prophesied during the reigns of the last five kings of Judah and during the early days of Judah's exile (ca. 626–585 B.C.)
Second Kings 22–25 and 2 Chr. 34–36 provide the historical narrative for the kings of the Davidic dynasty of Jeremiah's ministry (Josiah, Jehoahaz, Jehoiakim, Jehoiachin, and Zedekiah). At the time of Jeremiah's call, the great empires

A potter at work (Jer. 18:1-6)

of Egypt, Assyria, and Babylon were vying for dominion. Judah was an insignificant player, but the geography of the ancient Near East meant that Judah could not be ignored. Jeremiah lived to see Babylon defeat its rivals: Assyria (fall of Nineveh, 612 B.C.); Egypt (battle of Carchemesh, 605 B.C.); and Judah (fall of Jerusalem, 586 B.C.). By the end of Jeremiah's ministry, Babylon had become the single superpower in the ancient Near East.

How Jeremiah Fits into God's "Story"

Jeremiah tells about the end of "chapter 2" of the story: God educates his nation (disobedient Israel disciplined). He understood God's sovereignty in determining the rise and fall of all earthly nations. Mighty Babylon would fall (25:11-12; 29:10). God's plans to establish a new covenant form a magnificent vision for the future of God's people and kingdom. Through Jeremiah God pledged, "I will give them a heart to know me, that I am the LORD. They will be my people, and I will be their God because they will return to me with all their heart" (24:7). The last two chapters of the Bible describe the final fulfillment of this promise.

 ORIGINAL HISTORICAL SETTING

Author and Date of Writing:
Jeremiah, perhaps finally compiled around 585 B.C.
Because of his personal anguish over the coming captivity, Jeremiah has often been called the Weeping Prophet. Jeremiah, son of Hilkiah the priest, was from Anathoth, a town near Jerusalem in the territory of Benjamin. God required him to remain unmarried and childless (16:2). His prophetic call came ca. 626 B.C., when he was still young (1:6). His message of coming doom isolated him and exposed him to danger time and again. For 40 years he proclaimed God's word in Judah and stayed there even after Jerusalem fell. According to chapter 43, finally he was forcibly taken to Egypt and probably died there. Although many critical scholars believe that portions were written by other anonymous prophets, there is no good reason to doubt that Jeremiah authored the entire book.

First Audience and Destination:
The people of Judah living during Jeremiah's lifetime
The first hearers were the kings and people living in Judah during the 40 years before the Babylonian captivity. A few parts were originally for Jews living just after the fall of Jerusalem.

Occasion
This book records its origins as a piece of literature more than any other prophetic work. That Jeremiah caused his prophecies to be put in scroll form is explicitly told in several passages, for example, 25:13; 30:2; 36:2; 45:1; 51:60.

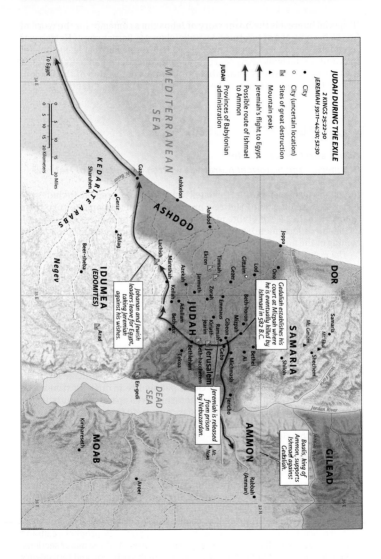

JUDAH DURING THE EXILE

2 KINGS 25:22-30
JEREMIAH 39:11-44:30; 52:30

• City
○ City (uncertain location)
▦ Sites of great destruction
▲ Mountain peak
→ Jeremiah's flight to Egypt
→ Possible route of Ishmael to Ammon
JUDAH Provinces of Babylonian administration

Gedaliah establishes his court at Mizpah where he is eventually killed by Ishmael in 582 B.C.

Johanan and Jewish leaders leave for Egypt, taking Jeremiah against his wishes.

Jeremiah is released from prison by Nebuzaradan.

Baalis, king of Ammon, supports Ishmael against Gedaliah.

Of special interest is the bitter story of Jehoakim's contempt for the word of God by burning one of Jeremiah's scrolls (chap. 36). Baruch son of Neriah was Jeremiah's personal assistant, who physically wrote down at least some of the words of the book (45:1). Since he accompanied Jeremiah to Egypt (43:6), the two may have worked together on the final compilation of the book of Jeremiah, the longest book in the Bible composed by a single author.

LITERARY FEATURES

Genre and Literary Style:
Prophecies and historical narratives written in a mixture of Hebrew poetry and prose

Jeremiah's prophecies both "forth tell" and "foretell." Jeremiah includes the three classic elements of Hebrew prophecy: (1) call to people to turn from their sins in the face of divine judgment, (2) predictions of near events (such as the fall of Jerusalem), and (3) predictions of remote events (such as the coming of the new covenant).

The majority of the book is poetic. The prose sections are mainly found in chapters 7; 11; 16; 19; 21; 24–29; 32–45; 52. The biographical sections were written in the third person, perhaps evidence of Baruch's input. Jeremiah's style included repetition, such as "sword . . . famine . . . plague" (16 times), and the use of cryptograms ("Sheshach" for Babylon in 25:26). Memorable phrases abound, for example, "Can the Cushite change his skin, or a leopard his spots?" (13:23). In the Hebrew canon, Jeremiah was the second of the four Latter Prophets.

Themes:
God's judgment and salvation; Jerusalem's fall; Jeremiah's personal life

The tension between judgment on sin and salvation yet to come make Jeremiah a book of hope, especially when God's people live in difficult times. The material on Jerusalem's last days is agonizing. Even apart from studying the content of his prophecies, believers today can benefit from tracing the course of Jeremiah's life as one filled with self-doubt and misgivings, yet faithful to his calling from God.

Book Features and Structure

One of the striking features of the book is its inclusion of symbols to which Jeremiah supplied an interpretation. Of note are the linen undergarment ("girdle," KJV) that was ruined (chap. 13), the potter and clay (chap. 18), and the hiding of stones (chap. 43).

The organization of the book is challenging to determine. It is not at all chronological, but seems to be topical. Between chapter 1 (the prophet's call) and chapter 52 (an appendix parallel to 2 Kgs. 24–25), there are three major sections: prophetic warnings to Judah (chaps. 2–35), Jeremiah's suffering and Jerusalem's fall (chaps. 36–45) and prophetic warnings to the nations (chaps. 46–51).

LAMENTATIONS

The English title renders the name given by the Greek translators of this book in the second century B.C. *Thrénoi*. The original Hebrew title is simply the first word of the book, *'Ekah*, "How!"

O KEY TEXT: 1:1

"How she sits alone, the city once crowded with people! She who was great among the nations has become like a widow. The princess among the provinces has been put to forced labor."

O KEY TERM: "LAMENT"

A "lament" or "lamentation" is a formal expression of grief in the face of loss or death. This book expresses the anguish the author felt over the fall of Jerusalem.

O ONE-SENTENCE SUMMARY

A skillful and emotional poet described the devastation of the city of Jerusalem—brought by the Babylonians but ultimately caused by the Lord's anger against his people—and poured out his own personal expressions of sorrow.

 ## GOD'S MESSAGE IN THE BOOK

Purpose

This book comes to grips with the destruction of Jerusalem on several levels, especially the emotional and the theological. On one hand, Lamentations shows that bitter grief is a fitting response to loss and death. On the other hand, it shows that the prophets who had warned "repent or be destroyed" had given a true message from God after all. God's people who study Lamentations today should view it with its original purpose in mind, but it can also help them to express their own grief in times of sorrow.

Christian Worldview Elements

Lamentation deals particularly with the worldview categories of *sovereignty and providence* and *rebellion and sin*. This Bible book, like the book of Job, explores the relationship of human sin to God's sovereignty.

Teachings about God

God's holiness resulted in his destroying Jerusalem for her many sins. Yet

God
Creation
O **Sovereignty and Providence**
Faith and Reason
Revelation and Authority
Humanity
O **Rebellion and Sin**
Covenant and Redemption
Community and Church
Discipleship
Ethics and Morality
Time and Eternity

Jeremiah Lamenting the Destruction of Jerusalem by Rembrandt Harmenzoon van Rijn

at the very center of the book the author emphasized God's mercy and faithfulness (3:22-26). The most often quoted text is 3:22-23: "Because of the LORD's faithful love we do not perish, for his mercies never end. They are new every morning; great is your faithfulness!" There is no specific reference to Christ or to the Holy Spirit.

Teachings about Humanity

Because human beings are moral agents responsible to God, their sins will be punished. The destruction of Jerusalem and the temple is the chief Old Testament event showing that rebellion against God cannot go on indefinitely. Yet because God made humankind in his image, they are capable of emotion, including sorrow and despair. Even when the loss is deserved, intense expressions of grief are a normal part of human experience.

Teachings about Salvation

Despite the grief he expressed, the author did not waver in his faith in God (see 3:26). The author's steadfast trust in God in the presence of national catastrophe and personal disaster makes him one of the greatest heroes of faith found in Scripture.

✝ CHRIST IN LAMENTATIONS

Lamentations shows God's wrath poured out on the city he loves just as his wrath was later poured out on his beloved Son. Lamentations 1:12 has often been used of Christ as he suffered on the cross: "Is this nothing to you, all you who pass by? Look and see! Is there any pain like mine, which was dealt out to me, which the LORD made me suffer on the day of his burning anger? "

GOD'S STORY

When the Events of This Book Happened:
Jerusalem was destroyed in 586 B.C.

The Chaldean (Babylonian) army under Nebuchadnezzar came against Jerusalem three times before the city was finally destroyed. The first siege (605 B.C.), at which King Jehoiakim surrendered, resulted in his becoming a vassal of Babylon. Nebuchadnezzar looted the temple and deported a number of the nobility, such as Daniel and his friends (Dan. 1:1-7). The second siege (597 B.C.), at which King Jehoiachin surrendered, resulted in his deportation to Babylon along with 10,000 others, including Ezekiel (2 Kgs. 24:8-17; Ezek. 1:1-3). The third siege (586 B.C.), at which Zedekiah, the last king, surrendered, resulted in Zedekiah's deportation to Babylon, along with many others (Jer. 52). The temple and city were plundered and burned on August 14, 586 B.C.

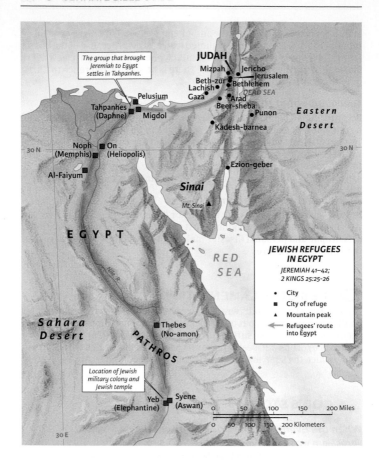

The group that brought Jeremiah to Egypt settles in Tahpanhes.

JUDAH

Mizpah • Jericho
Beth-zur • • Jerusalem
Lachish • • Bethlehem
Gaza • • Arad DEAD SEA
Beer-sheba •
Punon •
Kadesh-barnea •

Eastern Desert

Pelusium
Tahpanhes (Daphne) • Migdol

Noph (Memphis) ■ ■ On (Heliopolis)

Al-Faiyum ■

Ezion-geber •

Sinai

Mt. Sinai ▲

30 N   30 N

EGYPT

RED SEA

Sahara Desert

PATHROS

Thebes (No-amon) ■

JEWISH REFUGEES IN EGYPT
JEREMIAH 41–42;
2 KINGS 25:25-26
• City
■ City of refuge
▲ Mountain peak
← Refugees' route into Egypt

Location of Jewish military colony and Jewish temple

Yeb (Elephantine) ■ Syene (Aswan)

0   50   100   150   200 Miles
0   50 100 150   200 Kilometers

30 E

How Lamentations Fits into God's "Story"

Lamentations was written in response to the end of "chapter 2" of the story: God educates his nation (disobedient Israel disciplined). It shows how to live in submission to the discipline that God sends his people, even when disciplinary suffering and evil fall on them. The book does not tell how to get into the kingdom of God; rather, it expresses for those already in the kingdom important aspects of living in right relationship to God. If the author of Lamentations could hope in God, then God's people today can do the same no matter what happens to them.

ORIGINAL HISTORICAL SETTING

Author and Date of Writing:

Unknown, perhaps Jeremiah, written soon after 586 B.C.

The book is anonymous. Jewish and Christian tradition alike affirmed that Jeremiah the prophet wrote this book. According to 2 Chr. 35:25, Jeremiah was a writer of laments. (For more information, see *Author and Date of Writing* for *Jeremiah*.)

On the other hand, both the literary style and some of the content of Lamentations is unlike the book of Jeremiah. In particular, it is hard to imagine that the composer of the longest prophetic book would also write, "instruction is no more, and even her prophets receive no vision from the LORD," (2:9). If Jeremiah did not write the book, then one of his contemporaries, now unknown, wrote it. Ultimately there is no reason Jeremiah could not have written the book. If so, this confirms his reputation as the Weeping Prophet.

Because the book expresses such raw emotions, it was almost certainly composed shortly after Jerusalem's demise. It was necessarily written before the Jews returned from exile in 516 B.C.

Tisha B'Av, a day of mourning at Jerusalem's Western Wall. *Tisha B'Av*, the ninth day of Av (July–August), is the day on which the first and second temples were destroyed in 586 B.C. and A.D. 70, respectively.

First Audience and Destination:
Jewish witnesses to Jerusalem's fall
If an unknown author wrote the book, his audience could have been exiles newly arrived in Babylon. If Jeremiah wrote the book, he composed it for those who had remained in the ruined Jerusalem or else for those who fled Jerusalem for Egypt after Gedaliah's assassination (Jer. 40–42).

Occasion
The book does not tell what prompted it to be written other than the fall of Jerusalem. It is possible that Lamentations was originally composed in order to be read on the Ninth of Av, the annual summertime commemoration of the temple's destruction.

 ## LITERARY FEATURES

Genre and Literary Style:
A lament written in Hebrew poetry with acrostic features
People of the ancient Near East often composed laments in the face of tragedy. "Lamentation over the Destruction of Ur" (Sumerian) is an early example. The Old Testament has many examples: David's "Song of the Bow" (2 Sam. 1:19-27); psalms of lament (e.g., Pss. 44; 60; 88); and expressions by the prophets (Isa. 63–64; Ezek. 19; Amos 5; Mic. 1).

The entire book is Hebrew poetry, and, more than in any other book, the poetry seems to have a definite rhythm or meter. Many of the lines follow the *qinah* (lament) meter: lines of five beats, divided into three beats and then two. An example is 5:14:

> "The elders have left the city gate,   (3 beats)
> the young men, their music."   (2 beats)

In English Bibles, Lamentations follows the Greek translators by placing it after Jeremiah. In Hebrew Scripture, it was placed in the third section, the Writings or *Kethuvim*. Among the Writings, it was one of the Five Scrolls (*Megilloth*). Lamentations became the scroll read publicly on the Ninth of Av, the solemn annual Jewish remembrance of both the destruction of Solomon's temple (586 B.C.) and of the second temple (A.D. 70). The month of Av corresponds to July–August.

Themes:
Descriptions of devastation, the writer's emotions, God's justice and mercy
Nothing is more horrible than destruction that results in mothers cannibalizing their own children (2:20; 4:10). Other descriptions are equally vivid. The writer's weeping (1:16; 2:11) comes to full expression in chapter 3. Although

God's justice in punishing his people is in the foreground, the background note is one of his mercy, so that the book ends with an appeal for God to restore his people.

Book Features and Structure

Each of the five chapters is dominated by alphabetical considerations. The Hebrew alphabet has 22 letters—and chapters 1, 2, 3, and 5 all have 22 verses. Further, chapters 1–4 are acrostic (not chap. 5). In chapters 1–3, the first verse begins with the letter '*aleph*; the second verse begins with *beth* and so on alphabetically to the end. (See Ps. 119 and Prov. 31:10-31 for other 22-part Hebrew acrostic poems.) In Lamentations 3, with 66 verses, the acrostic is triple. Verses 1-3 begin with '*aleph*; verses 4-6 begin with *beth*, and so on. By this means, the author has said everything "from A to Z" (or '*aleph* to *taw*) on his subject.

Ruins of this temple at Nippur, the city where Ezekiel and some of the exiles from Judah settled when they were deported in 597 B.C. Sumerian tradition was that this was the site where Sumerian gods met and the place where man was created.

Ezekiel, the sixth-century Israelite prophet exiled to Babylon, has given his name to this book as its composer. His name means "God Strengthens" in Hebrew.

○ KEY TEXT: 38:23

"I will display my greatness and holiness, and will reveal myself in the sight of many nations. Then they will know that I am the LORD."

○ KEY TERM: "VISIONS"

This book is built around the three "visions of God" (1:1; 8:3; 40:2) that Ezekiel received. The first vision revealed God's glory (chaps. 1–3); the second, God's judgment (chaps. 8–11); the third, God's people and temple idealized (chaps. 40–48).

○ ONE-SENTENCE SUMMARY

From exile in Babylon, Ezekiel's stunning visions and startling symbolic acts were prophecies for the Israelites to teach God's sovereign plan over them in the history of his kingdom, so that "they will know that I am the LORD."

Ezekiel settled with a group of Jewish exiles near the city of Nippur by the Chebar River. *By the Waters of Babylon* by Gebhard Fugel (1863-1939). See Ps. 137:1.

GOD'S MESSAGE IN THE BOOK

Purpose

This book preserves the divinely inspired prophecies that Ezekiel made during his ministry of more than 20 years. These prophecies were originally for Israelites who had been exiled to Babylon shortly before the final fall of Judah. Ezekiel warned that God's destruction of Jerusalem was looming, but that God responded to individuals based on their relationship to him. Ezekiel also foresaw the distant time when God would act decisively so that Israel and all the nations would know that the Lord alone is God.

Christian Worldview Elements

Ezekiel deals with a number of world-view categories. Especially prominent are *God*; *covenant and redemption*; and *time and eternity*. The book begins with Ezekiel's remarkable vision of the glory of God, unequaled in the Old Testament. The entire book makes sense only in the context of God's covenant with his people and his great redeeming purpose. Ezekiel's final vision looks down through time to portray the ideal temple and people of God.

○ **God**
　Creation
　Sovereignty and Providence
　Faith and Reason
　Revelation and Authority
　Humanity
　Rebellion and Sin
○ **Covenant and Redemption**
○ Community and Church
○ Discipleship
○ Ethics and Morality
○ **Time and Eternity**

Teachings about God

All that God does on behalf of people is ultimately for the sake of his name or glory (39:7). He is absolutely sovereign in the affairs of all people and all nations. Prophecies of a coming Davidic king, fulfilled by Christ, are scattered throughout the book (17:22-24; 37:24-28). In the future, the Spirit will enable God's people to obey his laws from their heart (36:27; 39:29).

Teachings about Humanity

One of the clearest biblical passages about the responsibility of each individual before God is Ezek. 18. This is famously stated in 18:4: "The person who sins is the one who will die." Ezekiel illustrates one whom God used in a time of crisis and whose intimate family life became a symbol of God's dealing with his people (24:15-18).

Teachings about Salvation

Ezekiel teaches both the individual and the corporate dimensions of salvation. Chapter 18 teaches that the wicked child of a righteous parent will die (18:10-13). A person showing the fruit of righteousness—even if the parents are wicked—will live (18:14-17). Corporately salvation is the sovereign act of God's Spirit, who breathes on people ("dry bones," chap. 37), giving them spiritual life and enabling them to follow God's ways.

 CHRIST IN EZEKIEL

The expression "son of man" is used more than 90 times in Ezekiel. God uses the term to address Ezekiel. "Son of Man" is the expression Jesus uses most frequently to refer to himself. The phrase has two different meanings. First, it simply designates a human being. Second, it refers to a divine being. When used of Jesus, it carries both of these meanings.

 GOD'S STORY

When the Events of This Book Happened:

Ezekiel prophesied during the first part of the Jews' Babylonian captivity (ca. 593–571 B.C.)

At this time, the Chaldean Empire (Babylonians) dominated the world under Nebuchadnezzar (ruled 605–562). Twelve times Ezekiel listed the exact day that he received messages from God, and all of these can be transferred into dates using modern calendar equivalents. Called to minister at age 30, Ezekiel prophesied for seven years before the temple was destroyed (593–586) and for fifteen years after (586–571). (See *When the Events of This Book Happened* for *Lamentations* for more details.)

How Ezekiel Fits into God's "Story"

The events of Ezekiel's time belong to the first part of "chapter 3" of God's story: God keeps a faithful remnant (Messiah's space and time prepared). Ezekiel saw God's glory depart from Israel (chap. 10). After Jerusalem was destroyed, with no temple, no king, and no capital, the people had no hope. Had the covenant failed? Was God's promise of an everlasting dynasty for David a cruel joke? Through Ezekiel, God promised that he would be merciful to a remnant. In a wonderful new era of the kingdom of God, God's people would be indwelt by the Spirit and would have new hearts of obedience (36:24-27). God would live in their midst (48:35) and a Davidic king (37:24-28) would rule in righteousness (34:23-24).

 ORIGINAL HISTORICAL SETTING

Author and Date of Writing:

Ezekiel, perhaps finally compiled ca. 570 B.C.

Ezekiel, the son of Buzi, was born into a priestly family and grew up in Judah. As a young adult, he was taken captive by the Babylonians in 597 and deported, along with King Jehoiachin and 10,000 others (2 Kgs. 24:14-17). He settled in Tel-abib by the Chebar Canal (River Chebar, KJV). At age 30, Ezekiel was called as a prophet (1:1-3). He was married, but his wife died suddenly just before Jerusalem's final fall (24:15-18). God called Ezekiel "son of man" ("human being") more than 90 times.

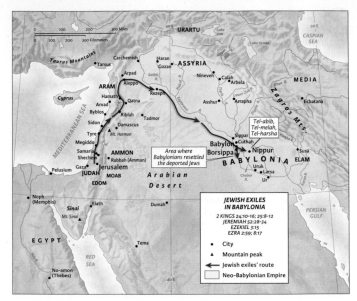

Ezekiel's unusual visions and symbolic actions marked him as strange both in his own day and by modern people. His message was not well received (3:25; 33:31-32). Some recent scholars have even suggested he suffered from mental illness. Other scholars accept that Ezekiel wrote parts of the book, but that many editorial insertions were made at a later date. The only prophetic work written entirely in the first person, the book claims to be Ezekiel's work. Scholars who accept the testimony of Scripture at face value continue to affirm that Ezekiel, under divine inspiration, composed the entire book. He perhaps compiled the work shortly after the last dated prophecy (571 B.C.; 29:17-21).

First Audience and Destination:
Israelite exiles living in Babylon

The first hearers were Israelites who had been taken into exile along with Ezekiel. By the time of Ezekiel's first vision, five years had elapsed, so the people had begun to establish themselves in a foreign land. After the final fall of Jerusalem, recently arriving exiles also heard Ezekiel's message.

Occasion

The messages God sent to Ezekiel were at God's initiative, not the prophet's. His references to specific dates on which he received messages are as follows: 1:1-2; 8:1; 20:1-2; 24:1; 26:1; 29:1,17; 30:20; 31:1; 32:1,17; 40:1. Ezekiel did not tell what prompted his compilation of the entire book.

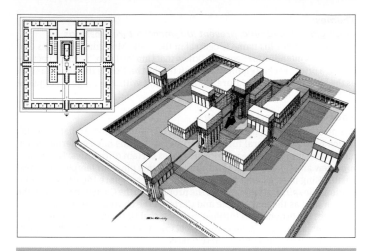

Ezekiel's Visionary Temple.

 LITERARY FEATURES

Genre and Literary Style:
Prophecies, including visions and symbolic actions, written mainly in Hebrew prose but with some poetry

Ezekiel's prophecies both "forth tell" and "foretell." Ezekiel includes the classic elements of Hebrew prophecy: (1) call to people to turn from their sins, (2) predictions of near events (such as the destruction of the temple, chap. 24), and (3) predictions of remote events (such as the coming of the new temple, chaps. 40–48).

Ezekiel's three visions (chaps. 1–3; 8–11; 40–48) are a special kind of prophecy. The first "forth tells" God's glory; the second "foretells" a near disaster; the third "foretells" a remote blessing. More than any other prophet, Ezekiel performed actions with symbolic meaning, which he then interpreted. The best known of these include his lying on one side (chap. 4), shaving his head with a sword (chap. 5), and the death of his wife (chap. 24). Ezekiel also told a number of parables. Chapters 7; 17; 19; 21; 24; 26–32 are the main poetic sections; the rest are in Hebrew prose.

Themes:
God's glory; the temple; present judgment; future blessings
God's concern for his name is central in the book. More than 60 times God declares his intention for people to "know that I am the LORD." Perhaps because he was a priest, Ezekiel emphasized both the destruction of the temple as well as the ideal temple of the future. His book begins with a message of judgment and ends with hope.

Book Features and Structure
The most challenging feature is the vision of a future temple (chaps. 40–48), which has had no literal fulfillment. Interpretations have generally fallen along one of three lines, each of which faces certain difficulties. The *millennial* view anticipates a literal fulfillment, with a physical temple and a real earthly King in Jerusalem for an intermediate era before the final consummation. The *spiritual* view applies the prophecy to the Christian age, with the church seen as the new temple and Christ as the church's Lord. The *eternal* view sees the prophecy as fulfilled in the eternal state, understood along the same lines as Rev. 21–22. No matter what interpretation is taken, the important truth is that "The LORD Is There" (48:35).

The book follows a topical order rather than a chronological sequence. There are three main sections: prophecies against Israel (chaps. 1–24); prophecies against the nations (chaps. 25–32); future blessings for God's people (chaps. 33–48).

Daniel, the sixth-century Judahite prophet exiled to Babylon, has given his name to this book as its composer. His name means "God Judges" or "God's Judge" in Hebrew.

O KEY TEXT: 4:3

"How great are his miracles, and how mighty his wonders! His kingdom is an eternal kingdom, and his dominion is from generation to generation."

O KEY TERM: "KINGDOMS"

This book contrasts all earthly kingdoms, both in Daniel's day and those of the future, with God's glorious everlasting kingdom. Of all the Old Testament books, this one has a more sharply defined kingdom perspective than any other.

O ONE-SENTENCE SUMMARY

Daniel demonstrated remarkable trust in God and revealed God's plans for the future, not only for his own day but also for the Maccabean period and on through the time that God's kingdom is fully established by the Son of Man.

GOD'S MESSAGE IN THE BOOK

Purpose

This book preserves the divinely inspired prophecies Daniel made during his long ministry of more than 60 years. These prophecies were originally for the assurance of Israelites who had been exiled to Babylon at the fall of Judah. The book looks at God's kingdom through three lenses: the lens of the present, the lens of the second century B.C. (the Maccabean period), and the remote lens of the completion of God's kingdom.

Christian Worldview Elements

Daniel deals with the worldview categories of *sovereignty and providence; ethics and morality;* and *time and eternity.* This book shows God's sovereignty in all things, perhaps like no other. Daniel's obedience to God shows godly behavior when it would have been easier to follow the crowd. The panorama of the future broadly reveals the direction of history.

God
Creation
O **Sovereignty and Providence**
Faith and Reason
Revelation and Authority
Humanity
Rebellion and Sin
Covenant and Redemption
Community and Church
Discipleship
O **Ethics and Morality**
O **Time and Eternity**

Daniel's Visionary Statue
DANIEL 2

1. Head of Gold

2. Chest & Arms of Silver

3. Stomach & Thighs of Bronze

4. Legs of Iron

5. Feet of Iron and Fired Clay

Abe Goolsby

Nebuchadnezzar's Dream (Dan. 2)

Teachings about God

God is both the revealer of secrets and the sovereign of the universe. His ultimate purpose is to give dominion to the son of man (7:13-14), fulfilled by Jesus, who deliberately called himself "Son of Man." Daniel was recognized as having "a spirit of the holy gods" (e.g., 4:8), but this appears to fall short of a clear reference to the Holy Spirit.

Teachings about Humanity

Daniel and his friends modeled living as God's people in a pagan world. The kings in the book—Nebuchadnezzar, Belshazzar, and Darius—are all seen to be agents of God. Truly evil characters are predicted, yet they too are unwittingly God's agents. The clearest Old Testament statement about a future bodily resurrection is Dan. 12:2-3.

Teachings about Salvation

Daniel 9:26 ("after those sixty-two weeks the Anointed One will be cut off and will have nothing") refers to Christ's crucifixion on behalf of his people. Some scholars believe that 9:27 predicts Christ's first coming, when he established the new covenant, resulting in the end of animal sacrifices. (Other scholars believe that the covenant referred to will be made not by Christ but by the antichrist shortly before Jesus's second coming.) In any event, 9:24 anticipates "everlasting righteousness."

DANIEL 2	DANIEL 7	MEANING
Head of gold	Lion	Babylon
Breast and arms of silver	Bear (ram in chap. 8)	Medo-Persia
Belly and thighs of bronze	Leopard (goat in chap. 8)	Greece (also Egypt and Syria)
Legs of iron; feet of clay	Dreadful beast	Rome
Great mountain	Son of man	God's eternal kingdom

☧ CHRIST IN DANIEL

Daniel has a vision of "one like a son of man was coming with the clouds of heaven" (7:13). This is a prophecy of Christ's second coming at which time he will be given glory and dominion over all people.

GOD'S STORY

When the Events of This Book Happened:
Daniel prophesied during the reigns of Babylonian kings and one Persian king (ca. 605–530 B.C.)

Daniel was taken to Babylon as part of the first deportation from Jerusalem (605 B.C.). In exile he influenced Nebuchadnezzar and later Belshazzar (son and vice-roy of the emperor Nabonidus). After Babylon fell to the Medo-Persians in 539 B.C., Daniel served "Darius the Mede," perhaps an alternate title for Cyrus the Great.

Daniel 8 details wars between a "ram" (the Persians) and a "male goat" (the Greeks, led by Alexander the Great, who would defeat the Persians in 330 B.C.). Daniel 11 gives particulars about the Hellenistic (Greek) kingdoms that succeeded Alexander. The "king of the South" (the Ptolemies in Egypt) would war against "the king of the North" (the Seleucids in Syria), with Palestine caught between them. The "despised person" (11:21) who would arise in the north was Antiochus IV (Epiphanes). His hatred of the Jews would lead to the infamous sacrilege at the second temple, December 15, 168 B.C., which led to the Maccabean Revolt of the Jews.

How Daniel Fits into God's "Story"

The events in Daniel belong to "chapter 3" of God's story: God keeps a faithful remnant (Messiah's space and time prepared). Daniel predicted the progress of the kingdoms of the world from his own time until the arrival of God's kingdom. This is seen chiefly in the visions of chapters 2 and 7.

 ORIGINAL HISTORICAL SETTING

Author and Date of Writing:
Daniel, perhaps finally compiled ca. 530 B.C.

The book is technically anonymous, although much of it is recorded as the first-person memoirs of Daniel. According to uniform Jewish and early Christian belief, Daniel wrote the book. In Matt. 24:15, Jesus affirmed this view. Critical scholarship for the past two centuries has uniformly rejected that a sixth-century author could have written detailed accounts of events centuries in the future. Therefore an unknown prophet living in the Maccabean era (second century B.C.) necessarily composed large parts of the book. The basic assumption of this critical view appears to be that Scripture does not contain true predictive prophecy. For Bible students who accept that God gave specific revelations of the distant future to his prophets, there is no reason to doubt that Daniel wrote all the book that bears his name.

First Audience and Destination:
Israelite exiles living in Babylon

The first hearers were Israelites who had been taken into exile along with Daniel. After the final fall of Jerusalem, recently arriving exiles would also have heard Daniel's message. By the time of Daniel's last prophecies, Babylon was no more, and the time had come for the exiles to be permitted to return to their homeland (9:2).

Occasion

Daniel's early ministry as a young man was initiated by Nebuchadnezzar (chaps. 1–4). During the last years of Babylon, God initiated visions of the future (chaps. 7–8), and then Daniel was called to interpret the handwriting on the wall (chap. 5). Daniel's encounter with the lions (chap. 6) and his final visions of the future (chaps. 9–12) came when he was a very old man, shortly after the time the Persians defeated Babylon.

Belshazzar's Feast by Rembrandt Harmenszoon van Rijn (1609-1669)

LITERARY FEATURES

Genre and Literary Style:

Prophecies, including visions and interpretations, written partly in Hebrew and partly in Aramaic

Daniel included little "forth telling," emphasizing instead "foretelling" prophecies. He predicted near events (such as the destruction of Babylon) and remote events (such as the coming of the Son of Man). The book was written in two languages. Chapters 1 and 8–12, written in Hebrew, deal with God's people and their future. Chapters 2–7, written in Aramaic, the international trade language of the day, deal with the kingdoms of the world as they carry on apart from acknowledging the true God.

In English Bibles, Daniel comes after Ezekiel as one of the Major Prophets, following the order of the Greek translators. In Hebrew Scripture, it was placed in the third section, the Writings or *Kethuvim*. The Greek translation added sections with no Hebrew original. These "Additions to Daniel" are considered scriptural by Roman Catholics, but Protestants believe them to be merely interesting parts of the Apocrypha.

Themes:

Sovereignty, kingdoms of the world, God's kingdom

God's sovereignty in individual lives is seen by the personal history of Daniel. In the case of Nebuchadnezzar, God took the most powerful man in the world and sent him through a period of insanity. The prophecies of four world kingdoms (chaps. 2; 7) is the most extensive "philosophy of history" in the Old Testament. The message of God's kingdom triumphing through the Son of Man became a dominant feature of Jesus's preaching.

Book Features and Structure

Daniel's famous prophecies of "the abomination of desolation" (11:31; 12:11) and of the "seventy weeks" (9:24) are two of the most difficult elements of the book. The original abomination occurred in 168 B.C., when swine were sacrificed at the Jerusalem temple. Jesus predicted a second abomination (Matt. 24:15) that occurred in A.D. 70, when the second temple was burned. Both Daniel and Jesus may also point to a third abomination to be perpetrated by the future antichrist. The "seventy weeks" (490 years) may have been completely fulfilled in the first century A.D., but some believe the "seventieth week" (seven years) will happen only in the days before Christ's return.

The content of Daniel neatly divides into halves. The first half (chaps. 1–6) collects stories about Daniel; the second half (chaps. 7–12) contains four visions of Daniel.

HOSEA

Hosea, the eighth-century prophet to the northern kingdom of Israel, has given his name to this book as its composer. His name means "Salvation" in Hebrew.

○ KEY TEXT: 1:10

"Yet the number of the Israelites will be like the sand of the sea, which cannot be measured or counted. And in the place where they were told: You are not my people, they will be called: Sons of the living God."

The Prophet Hosea by Moretto da Brescia

○ KEY TERM: "UNFAITHFULNESS"

The marital unfaithfulness of Gomer, Hosea's wife, became a symbol that Hosea used to proclaim his message. The people of the northern kingdom had become unfaithful to the Lord by aligning with Baal, yet God longed to take them back.

○ ONE-SENTENCE SUMMARY

Hosea's marriage to an adulterous wife and the children she bore graphically demonstrated God's "marriage" to his spiritually adulterous people Israel, who must respond to his covenant love and repent or face severe judgment.

 GOD'S MESSAGE IN THE BOOK

Purpose

This book preserves the divinely inspired prophecies that Hosea made during his ministry of more than 35 years. (He and Amos were the only writing prophets to target the northern kingdom of Israel.) Hosea warned Israel that because of rebellion and idolatry, their kingdom faced destruction, yet God still loved his covenant people.

Christian Worldview Elements

Hosea deals particularly with the worldview categories of *rebellion and sin* and *covenant and redemption*. God's case against Israel was put in terms of a woman's unfaithfulness to her husband (the Lord) and seeking liaison with another (Baal). Yet no Bible book more fully teaches God's love in reaching out to people who cannot save themselves.

God
Creation
Sovereignty and Providence
Faith and Reason
Revelation and Authority
Humanity
○ **Rebellion and Sin**
○ **Covenant and Redemption**
Community and Church
Discipleship
Ethics and Morality
Time and Eternity

Teachings about God

Hosea's doctrine of God is based mainly on the analogy of a husband-wife relationship. The Lord is jealous and will not forever tolerate his people "lusting" after other deities. He must judge unfaithfulness. At the same time, his love for his covenant people endures forever, and one day Ephraim (the northern kingdom of Israel) will be healed of rebelliousness (chap. 14). Matthew recognized Hosea's historical note about Israel's exodus from Egypt as a picture foreshadowing Jesus's coming from Egypt (Hos. 11:1; Matt. 2:15). The Spirit is not directly present in the book.

Teachings about Humanity

The adultery of Gomer and the idolatry of Israel both paint rather dark portraits of human shame and sinfulness. Hosea's exceptional love for Gomer provides a stark contrast and shows something of what it means to experience the love of God.

Teachings about Salvation

The clearest text in this book on the nature of salvation is 6:6: "For I desire faithful love and not sacrifice, the knowledge of God rather than burnt offerings." Offering sacrificial animals without an inner heart of love for God and one's neighbors was never a part of the biblical understanding of salvation. The word translated "faithful love" (Hebrew, *chesed*) included loyalty to God as well as compassionate actions toward others.

✝ CHRIST IN HOSEA

Matthew tells of Joseph and Mary taking the child Jesus to Egypt to escape the wrath of Herod. Following Herod's death, Jesus's family returned to Nazareth. Matthew quoted Hos. 11:1 to show the parallel between God's calling Israel and his calling Jesus: "Out of Egypt I called my son" (Matt. 2:15).

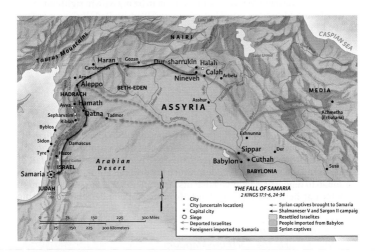

"Samaria's king will disappear like foam on the surface of the water. . . . Samaria will bear her guilt because she has rebelled against her God" (Hos. 10:7; 13:16).

GOD'S STORY

When the Events of This Book Happened:
Hosea prophesied during the last decades of the northern kingdom of Israel (at least 753–715 B.C.; mainly ca. 750–722 B.C.)

Second Kings 14–17 provides the historical background for the times of Hosea. In general, it was the time when Assyria was asserting itself as the world superpower. Hosea's earliest prophecies and marital woes came from the end of the rule of Jeroboam II of Israel (593–753 B.C.). He continued to minister in Israel during the reigns of the last kings there and on through the conquest of Israel by the Assyrians in 722. Afterward, he evidently ministered in the southern kingdom of Judah, judging from his reference to Hezekiah (1:1), who became king in Jerusalem in 715.

How Hosea Fits into God's "Story"

The events of Hosea's time belong to "chapter 2" of the story: God educates his nation (disobedient Israel disciplined). Israel had forgotten that the Lord had called them into existence and blessed them. They were offering bounty sent by God to Baal (2:8). In order to break them, for a time God would call them Lo-ammi ("not my people," 1:9). Yet his purposes were settled. One of the great statements of God's everlasting kingdom plan is Hos. 2:19: "And I will take you to be my wife forever. I will take you to be my wife in righteousness, justice, love, and compassion." Both Peter and Paul applied Hosea's message to God's inclusion of Gentiles among his people (1 Pet. 2:10; Rom. 9:25-26).

 ORIGINAL HISTORICAL SETTING

Author and Date of Writing:
Hosea, perhaps ca. 715 B.C.

Hosea was a contemporary of Isaiah and Micah. The son of Beeri, he was evidently from the northern kingdom of Israel. (See *Occasion,* below, for information about Hosea's marriage.) The book does not mention the fulfillment of Hosea's prophecies against Israel, but he witnessed the fall of Samaria and the northern kingdom. Since his prophecies also include calls for Judah to repent, it is believed that his last ministry was to people of Judah after the northern kingdom had fallen. He probably compiled his book during that time.

First Audience and Destination:
Israelites living in the northern kingdom

Hosea's first audience was people living in the northern kingdom—also called Ephraim or Samaria—in the mid-700s B.C.

Occasion

Hosea's tragic marriage to Gomer—who left the prophet and became a slave, only to be bought back by her own husband—is one of the great love stories (but hardly a romance) in Scripture. Gomer bore three children: Jezreel ("God Sows," a son); Lo-ruhamah ("No Mercy," a daughter); and finally Lo-ammi ("Not My People," a son). The last two children may have been fathered by one of Gomer's lovers; if so, it makes Hosea's personal story that much more poignant.

Hosea's marriage experiences and the names of his children were at the Lord's command. Other than this, no precise occasion can be offered for his prophecies, but clearly he spoke in the name of the Lord. No one knows exactly what prompted Hosea to compile his writings at the end of his long ministry.

 LITERARY FEATURES

Genre and Literary Style:
Prophecies and a few historical narratives, written mainly in Hebrew poetry

Hosea's prophecies both "forth tell" and "foretell." He includes the three classic elements of Hebrew prophecy: (1) call to people to turn from their sins in the face of divine judgment, (2) predictions of near events (such as the fall of Samaria), and (3) predictions of remote events (such as the coming of ideal peacetime conditions).

The majority of the book is Hebrew poetry. The prose sections are limited to chapters 1 and 3, the narrative about Hosea's marriage and children. The Hebrew style reveals an author with rhetorical skill. In English Bibles, Hosea is the first of the 12 Minor Prophets, "minor" in the sense that they are shorter than Isaiah, Jeremiah, or Ezekiel. In the Hebrew canon, the Minor Prophets were compiled as a composite book called "The Twelve." Thus "The Twelve" was the last book of the Latter Prophets (following Isaiah, Jeremiah, and Ezekiel). These four Latter Prophets balanced the four Former Prophets in the Hebrew Bible (Joshua, Judges, Samuel, and Kings).

Themes:
Faithfulness versus unfaithfulness, the Lord versus Baal; judgment versus restoration

Hosea is a book of contrasts. God was faithful to Israel; Israel was unfaithful. In terms of the marriage analogy, one of the Hebrew words for "husband" (*baal*) was the same as the name of the deity the Israelites found so attractive. God longed for Israel to call him *Ishi* ("My husband") instead of *Baali* ("My Baal"); see 2:16-17. Like many other prophetic books, Hosea contrasts present judgment with the promise of future restoration.

Book Features and Structure

The most challenging feature of the book is the nature of Hosea's relationship to Gomer. As a "woman of promiscuity" (1:2), was she already a prostitute when Hosea married her, or was he simply told by God in advance that his bride would betray him? The evidence is not clear, and Bible scholars have argued for both interpretations. Another question concerns chapter 3, in which Hosea was told to "show love to a woman . . . an adulteress" (3:1). Does this (1) retell the story of chapter 1 from a first-person perspective, or (2) tell a later episode in the story of Hosea and Gomer, or (3) describe Hosea's second marriage to an unnamed slave woman after Gomer's death? In this instance the most reasonable answer seems to be number 2.

Hosea is readily divided into two major sections. The first is narrative about an unfaithful wife (chaps. 1–3); the second contains prophecies against an unfaithful nation (chaps. 4–14).

Joel, an otherwise unknown Israelite prophet to Judah, has given his name to this book as its composer. His name means "The Lord Is God" in Hebrew.

○ KEY TEXT: 1:4

"What the devouring locust has left, the swarming locust has eaten; what the swarming locust has left, the young locust has eaten; and what the young locust has left, the destroying locust has eaten."

○ KEY TERM: "LOCUSTS"

Joel described a locust swarm that devoured the crops of Judah. He understood them to be an army sent by God to judge his people for their sins.

○ ONE-SENTENCE SUMMARY

Joel proclaimed that the people of Judah should interpret a severe locust plague as a forerunner of "the great and terrible day of the LORD," which would consume the pagan nations and also unfaithful Judah unless the people repented.

GOD'S MESSAGE IN THE BOOK

Purpose

This book preserves the divinely inspired prophecies that Joel made during his ministry to Judah. Although the era in which he ministered is not clear, the people were evidently assuming that the coming "day of the LORD" would involve God's judgment on the pagan nations and not on God's people. Joel proclaimed that this view was wrong. The people of Judah would be restored only after they had been judged and repented of their sins.

Christian Worldview Elements

Joel deals with the worldview categories of *rebellion and sin* and *covenant and redemption*. Judah's sin was not trivial. Yet judgment was to be the means of bringing God's people to ultimate salvation. Joel gives a long-term picture of redemption from his own time until the day that God poured out his Spirit on all people.

God
Creation
Sovereignty and Providence
Faith and Reason
Revelation and Authority
Humanity
○ **Rebellion and Sin**
○ **Covenant and Redemption**
Community and Church
Discipleship
Ethics and Morality
Time and Eternity

Teachings about God

God is a righteous judge, and in the coming "day of the *Lord*" he will bring

The Prophet Joel sculpted by Aleijadinho. The sculpture is in front of the Sanctuary of Jesus of Matosinhos in Congonhas, Minas Gerais, Brazil.

sure and swift devastation on all who have opposed him. Yet he also will become "jealous for his land" and spare "his people" (2:18).

Teachings about Humanity

Joel explicitly denied the (usual) tendencies of God's people to presume that the Lord is lenient with them concerning their lifestyles and that they are therefore immune from the times he comes in judgment. Although God's judgment will utterly destroy the pagan nations (3:1-13), it will also be a decisive turning point that his people must also go through—on the way to ultimate blessing.

Teachings about Salvation

This short book contains two profound passages on salvation. First, "everyone who calls on the name of the LORD will be saved" (2:32; compare Rom. 10:13). Second, Joel describes repentance as a tearing ("rending," KJV) of one's heart rather than external actions such as tearing clothes (2:12-14).

✕ CHRIST IN JOEL

Peter and Paul taught that prophecies about the "day of the Lord" applied to the second coming of Jesus (1 Thess. 5:2; 2 Pet. 3:10). Joel also prophesied the coming of God's Spirit on all flesh: "Your sons and your daughters will prophesy, your old men will have dreams, and your young men will see visions" (2:28). According to Peter, this prediction began to be fulfilled on the day of Pentecost when the Holy Spirit filled the followers of Jesus (Acts 2:16-21).

 GOD'S STORY

When the Events of This Book Happened:
Unknown, perhaps either the ninth century or the fifth century B.C.

This prophet is not mentioned in any other Old Testament book, and there is insufficient information in the book to date the locust plague or the ministry of Joel. Traditionally, he has been thought of as the earliest writing prophet. Evidence for an early date includes references to Tyre, Sidon, and Philistia (see 3:4 in contemporary translations), Judah's military enemies during the ninth century. There are no references to Assyria or Babylon, Judah's enemies later on. Evidence for a later date is found in Joel's call to the elders and priests, who led the nation to repent after the return from exile (1:9,13; 2:17). There is no mention of a king, which also fits the postexilic situation. Ultimately the message of the book does not depend on when the locust plague occurred, but there is no reason to reject the traditional early date for the book.

How Joel Fits into God's "Story"

Depending on the date of its composition, Joel belongs either to "chapter 2" of God's story: God educates his nation (disobedient Israel disciplined) or "chapter 3" of God's story: God keeps a faithful remnant (Messiah's space and time prepared).

The people of Joel's day supposed that religiously they were all right. Joel's book is a reminder that sin always threatens God's people. Although the iniquities were not specified, all the people, not just the leaders, were to acknowledge their sins, repent with fasting and broken hearts, and turn to God. Such a kingdom message is ongoing until "the day of the LORD." Joel's long-term prophetic lens looks forward to the time when all God's people will have his Spirit, a kingdom reality since the day of Pentecost (Rom. 8:9). Like other prophets, Joel anticipated a glorious future for the kingdom: "But Judah will be inhabited forever, and Jerusalem from generation to generation" (3:20).

 ## ORIGINAL HISTORICAL SETTING

Author and Date of Writing:
Joel, perhaps either ninth or fifth century B.C.

Although there are numerous Joels in the Old Testament, the prophet bearing this name is known only from this book. He identified himself only as "the son of Pethuel" and did not name his hometown or the kings of his ministry. Because of his frequent references to Jerusalem (six times in 73 verses), he may have lived there. No other personal details of his life are known. (See *When the Events of This Book Happened* for information on the era in which Joel prophesied.)

First Audience and Destination:
The people of Judah living in Jerusalem

The first hearers were people and priests living in Judah, perhaps ca. 800 B.C. or ca. 500 B.C.

Occasion

Swarms of locusts were a constant threat to farmers of the ancient Near East. Hordes consisting of millions of the creatures could strip everything green in a short period of time. The successive stages of locust life span (or else four varieties of locusts) that he mentioned in 1:4 and 2:25 show that this was a long-lasting scourge. Locusts easily symbolized an invading human army that could wreak utter destruction. As early as Exod. 10, locusts were a divinely sent plague, as was the swarm of Joel's day (see also Rev. 9). God used the locust plague of Joel's day as the occasion to warn of a coming day of even greater disaster.

"I will repay you for the years that the swarming locust ate, the young locust, the destroying locust, and the devouring locust—my great army that I sent against you. You will have plenty to eat and be satisfied. You will praise the name of the LORD your God, who has dealt wondrously with you" (Joel 2:25-26).

 LITERARY FEATURES

Genre and Literary Style:
Prophecy written entirely in Hebrew poetry

Even as one of the shortest prophetic works, the book includes two of the classic elements of Hebrew prophecy: (1) call to people to turn from their sins, and (2) predictions of remote events (the coming "day of the LORD").

Joel's poetry is vivid and visual. He also uses sarcasm, for example, when God summons the nations to assemble for their own destruction (3:9-11). In 3:10, his call to arms uses the opposite of Isaiah's and Micah's peaceful images: "Beat your plows into swords and your pruning knives into spears."

In English Bibles, Joel is the second of the 12 Minor Prophets. In the Hebrew canon, it belonged to the composite book called "The Twelve" (See *Genre and Literary Style* for *Hosea* for more information.)

Themes:
Locusts, "the day of the Lord"
The matter of the locusts has already been mentioned. Joel's prophecy is really more about "the day of the LORD" than about locusts. (See the section that follows.)

Book Features and Structure
If Joel is early, he was the first prophet to use the phrase "the day of the LORD." The exact phrase occurs more often (five times) than in any other book of the Bible. (In the Old Testament, only the major or minor prophets use the phrase; they may also use the equivalent phrase "that day.") In general, the term points to events that take place at history's decisive turning points, in which God intervenes to accomplish specific aspects of his kingdom plan. In Joel, as well as in the other prophets, "the day of the LORD" usually refers to the final times (just before and including Christ's return). It will involve the nations as well as God's people, but afterward there will be unending blessing.

The book, consisting of only 73 verses, has two sections. The first interprets the locust plague as a preview of "the day of the LORD" (1:1–2:17); the second focuses on "the day of the LORD" as a time of judgment for the nations but restoration for God's people (2:18–3:21).

AMOS

Amos, the eighth-century prophet from Judah to the northern kingdom of Israel, has given his name to this book as its composer. His name means "Burden Bearer" in Hebrew.

○ KEY TEXT: 5:24

"But let justice flow like water, and righteousness, like an unfailing stream."

○ KEY TERM: "INJUSTICE"

Amos proclaimed God's disgust with both the pagan nations and the people of Israel because of their many acts of injustice. God holds all people everywhere, even those who do not recognize him, responsible for practicing social justice.

○ ONE-SENTENCE SUMMARY

Although Amos prophesied against the nations surrounding Israel, including Judah, his main message was against Israel, who must repent of injustice and idolatry or else go into exile—but then be restored to divine favor.

 GOD'S MESSAGE IN THE BOOK

Purpose

This book preserves the divinely inspired prophecies that Amos made during his ministry of undetermined length. (He and Hosea were the only writing prophets to the northern kingdom of Israel.) During Amos's day, the people of the northern kingdom felt politically, economically, and religiously secure. Amos announced that these were false securities. Politically Assyria would soon assert itself as the major threat to Israel; economically the good times had led to social corruption, violence, and injustice; religiously the worship of the Lord had been compromised by idolatry. Amos warned that injustice, immorality, and idolatry would bring divine judgment in the form of exile.

Christian Worldview Elements

Amos deals especially with the worldview categories of *rebellion and sin* and *ethics and morality*. Disloyalty to God is sin, but so is the selfish lack of concern for the needs of others. In other words, failure to live by either of the Great Commandments (Matt. 22:37-39) offends God. Amos's emphasis on personal ethics and morality should be seen in this light.

Teachings about God

God is absolutely sovereign. He raises up and puts down nations. He is also a God who reveals himself and his plans to "his servants the prophets" (3:7).

The Prophet Amos by Gustave Doré

Therefore, he has revealed himself to be the judge of all, pagan and people of God alike. He is also—and not least—a God who has a wonderful future for his people when they are restored at last (9:11-15).

Teachings about Humanity

The people of Amos's day showed the universal human tendency to do the wrong thing rather than the right thing. In particular, this often evidences itself in religious compromise and compla-

cency (4:4-5). On the other hand, humanity will be salvaged! Both Israel and "all the nations that bear my name" (9:12) will one day experience unmeasured blessings. (James declared that this prophecy began to be fulfilled by Gentiles turning to Jesus, Acts 15:5-18.)

Teachings about Salvation

In Amos, redemption is based entirely on God's initiative. God reminded them that they were "the entire clan that I brought from the land of Egypt" and that "I have known only you out of all the clans of the earth" (3:1-2). What God desires from redeemed people is righteous living and obedience. Religious rituals and festivals, even those that God commanded, cannot substitute for a right relationship with him (5:21-24).

 CHRIST IN AMOS

Amos proclaimed the righteousness of God and called on God's people to turn from their unrighteousness and return to God. The high standards of God's righteousness were a passion with Jesus who told his followers he had not come to put aside the Law as an expression of God's righteousness; rather, he had come to fulfill God's righteous requirements.

 GOD'S STORY

When the Events of This Book Happened:

Amos prophesied during the reign of Jeroboam II of Israel (793–753 B.C.) while Uzziah king of Judah ruled (792–740 B.C.)

Second Kings 14:23–15:6 and 2 Chr. 26 provide the historical narrative for the two kings mentioned in Amos. Under Jeroboam II, the northern kingdom of Israel experienced its golden age of peace and prosperity. Jeroboam ruled a kingdom from the city of Samaria that extended to Damascus in the north

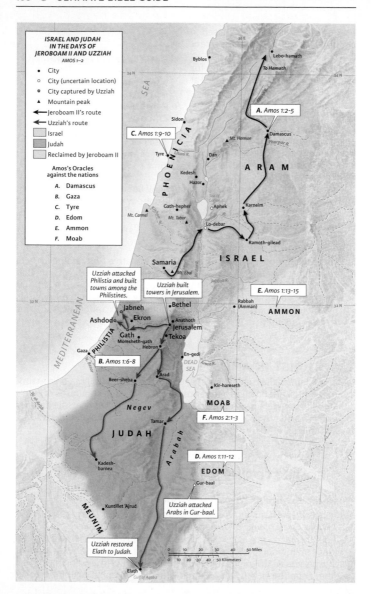

ISRAEL AND JUDAH
IN THE DAYS OF
JEROBOAM II AND UZZIAH
AMOS 1–2

- • City
- ○ City (uncertain location)
- • City captured by Uzziah
- ▲ Mountain peak
- ← Jeroboam II's route
- ← Uzziah's route
- Israel
- Judah
- Reclaimed by Jeroboam II

Amos's Oracles
against the nations

A. Damascus
B. Gaza
C. Tyre
D. Edom
E. Ammon
F. Moab

A. Amos 1:2–5

C. Amos 1:9–10

E. Amos 1:13–15

B. Amos 1:6–8

D. Amos 1:11–12

F. Amos 2:1–3

Uzziah attacked
Philistia and built
towns among the
Philistines.

Uzziah built
towers in Jerusalem.

Uzziah attacked
Arabs in Gur-baal.

Uzziah restored
Elath to Judah.

Lebo-hamath
To Hamath
Byblos
Sidon
Damascus
Pharpar R.
Tyre
Litani R.
Mt. Hermon
Dan
Kedesh
Hazor
Gath-hepher
Aphek
Karnaim
Mt. Carmel
Mt. Tabor
Kishon R.
Lo-debar
Ramoth-gilead
Samaria
Mt. Ebal
ISRAEL
Jabbok R.
Rabbah
(Amman)
AMMON
Jabneh
Bethel
Anathoth
Ashdod
Ekron
Jerusalem
Gath
Tekoa
Moresheth-gath
Hebron
Gaza
PHILISTIA
En-gedi
DEAD
SEA
Arnon R.
Kir-hareseth
MOAB
Beer-sheba
Arad
Negev
Tamar
JUDAH
Arabah
EDOM
Kadesh-barnea
Gur-baal
Kuntillet 'Ajrud
MEUNIM
Elath
Gulf of Aqaba

PHOENICIA
ARAM
MEDITERRANEAN
SEA

0 10 20 30 40 50 Miles
0 10 20 30 40 50 Kilometers

and to the Dead Sea in the south. (Both Aram [Syria, KJV] and Assyria, which would later threaten Israel, were politically weak during Amos's time.)

How Amos Fits into God's "Story"

The events of Amos's time belong to "chapter 2" of the story: God educates his nation (disobedient Israel disciplined). It reminds God's people that peace and prosperity can be threats to their behaving like God's people. Whenever plenty leads God's people to religious complacency or lack of concern for others, they should read the book of Amos. This book claims that "the day of the LORD" will take such people into judgment (5:18-20). On the other hand, the book looks forward to the ultimate time of the kingdom's fullness when the earth will be restored to an Eden-like bounty (9:13-15).

 ORIGINAL HISTORICAL SETTING

Author and Date of Writing:
Amos, perhaps ca. 750 B.C.

Amos was a contemporary of Jonah. He was from Tekoa, a small town about 10 miles south of Jerusalem. He was a rural person, by profession a shepherd and a gatherer of sycamore figs. He was not especially trained for religious work: "I was not a prophet or the son of a prophet" (7:14). Nothing is known of his family life. He evidently preached to the northern cities of Samaria (Israel's capital, 3:12; 4:1) and Bethel (a center for idolatry, 7:13). Amos's message was perhaps as startling and as well received as would be a farm boy from Nebraska preaching in Manhattan. His ministry was probably short, limited to the period "two years before the earthquake" (1:1), an event otherwise unknown. The year 750 is a best-guess estimate.

First Audience and Destination:
Israelites living in the northern kingdom

Amos's first audience was people living in the northern kingdom of Israel in the mid-700s B.C.

Occasion

Amos's only explanation of what prompted his prophetic ministry was "The LORD God showed me this" (7:1,4; 8:1) and "I saw the Lord" (9:1). Thirteen times he declared, "the LORD says." The only personal incident of his ministry that he recorded was his confrontation with Amaziah, the priest of Bethel (7:10-17). Amos did not explain what prompted him to commit his prophecies to writing.

LITERARY FEATURES

Genre and Literary Style:
Prophecies and one short narrative, written mainly in Hebrew poetry

Amos may be the earliest writing prophet to complete his ministry. (Joel might have preceded him.) He includes all the elements of prophecy: a clear "the LORD says," which includes "forth telling" and "foretelling." Amos's announcement that God despised the people's deeds implicitly included a call to repentance. Further, he predicted both near events (such as the fall of Samaria) and remote events (such as the coming restoration of "the fallen shelter of David," 9:11).

Except for 7:10-16, the book is written in vigorous Hebrew poetry. Amos created startling word pictures, from his opening salvo ("the LORD roars from Zion," 1:2) to his bold reference to the women of Samaria ("cows of Bashan," 4:1). His opening chapters are memorable for repeated use of the formula, "I will not relent . . . for three crimes, even four" (1:3,6,9,11,13; 2:1,4,6).

In English Bibles, Amos is the third of the 12 Minor Prophets. In the Hebrew canon, it belonged to the composite book called "The Twelve." (See *Genre and Literary Style* for *Hosea* for more information.)

Themes:
Social justice, true religion, "the day of the Lord"

With his attacks on the violent and those who oppressed the poor, Amos spoke not only for his own era, but for all eras to come. He understood the enduring truth that genuine religion is not based on ritual but a heart desiring to please God. If Amos preceded Joel, his references to "the day of the LORD" (5:18,20) are the earliest in Scripture. (See *Book Features and Structure* for *JOEL* for further information.)

Book Features and Structure

One of the striking features of Amos is the last section, which records five brief visions, along with the divine interpretation of each. Collectively they add to the striking nature of the book: the locusts (grasshoppers, KJV, 7:1-3), the fire (7:4-6), the plumb line (7:7-9), the basket of summer fruit (8:1-14), and the Lord by the altar (9:1).

The book has three major sections. First, there are eight brief announcements of judgment on individual nations (chaps. 1–2). Second, there are oracles of judgment against Israel (chaps. 3–6). Third, there are five visions of coming wrath (chaps. 7–9).

OBADIAH

Obadiah, the sixth-century Israelite prophet against Edom, has given his name to this book as its composer. His name means "Servant of the Lord" in Hebrew.

⊙ KEY TEXT: VERSE 15

"For the day of the LORD is near, against all the nations. As you have done, it will be done to you; what you deserve will return on your own head."

⊙ KEY TERM: "EDOM"

The people of Edom were descendants of Esau who lived southeast of Israel. God's wrath against Edom for its sins is the single concern of this book.

⊙ ONE-SENTENCE SUMMARY

Obadiah prophesied that God would destroy the nation of Edom because of its pride and violence, particularly in looking down on Judah's misfortune, and ultimately "the kingdom will be the LORD's."

GOD'S MESSAGE IN THE BOOK

Purpose

This book preserves the divinely inspired prophecies Obadiah made during his (perhaps) brief ministry. These prophecies served a twofold purpose. First,

"This is what the Lord GOD has said about Edom: . . . 'Your arrogant heart has deceived you, you who live in clefts of the rock in your home on the heights, who say to yourself, *Who can bring me down to the ground?*' Though you seem to soar like an eagle and make your nest among the stars, even from there I will bring you down.' This is the LORD's declaration" (Obad. 1,3-4). View of Petra in the southeast region of Edom.

they were meant to warn the people of Edom of their coming doom. Second, they were an encouragement to the people of Judah to believe that God would punish one of their enemies for their sins against God's people.

Christian Worldview Elements

Obadiah deals particularly with the worldview categories of *sovereignty and providence* and *community*. God's sovereignty in the rise and fall of nations is clearly addressed here. The matter of the covenant community's identity as God's people under his protection is also in view.

God
Creation
○ **Sovereignty and Providence**
Faith and Reason
Revelation and Authority
Humanity
Rebellion and Sin
Covenant and Redemption
○ **Community** and Church
Discipleship
Ethics and Morality
Time and Eternity

Teachings about God

God's justice in dealing with human sin is displayed in Obadiah. His promised destruction of Edom will be based on the criterion noted in the *Key Text above.*

Teachings about Humanity

On one hand, Obadiah continues the biblical emphasis that there are only two kinds of people: those who belong to "Mount Zion" (God's covenant people) and all the rest. On the other hand, the book shows that when God judges people and nations, he will have enough evidence to condemn based on their (mis)treatment of others.

Teachings about Salvation

In Obadiah, salvation is thought of in terms of God's ultimate deliverance of his people based on his sovereign care: "But there will be a deliverance on Mount Zion" (v. 17). Nothing is said about personal conversion.

✄ CHRIST IN OBADIAH

Obadiah prophesied that Edom would be judged and destroyed for its pride against God and its treachery against God's people. Herod the Great who ruled Judea during the time of Jesus's birth had Edomite ancestry. The old treachery of Edom against Israel is seen in Herod's attempt to kill Jesus when he was younger than two years old.

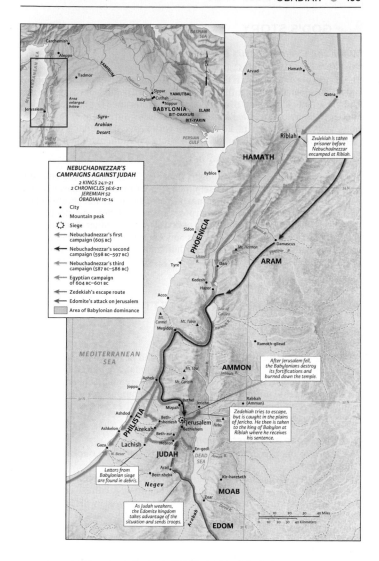

NEBUCHADNEZZAR'S
CAMPAIGNS AGAINST JUDAH

2 KINGS 24:1-21
2 CHRONICLES 36:6-21
JEREMIAH 52
OBADIAH 10-14

• City
▲ Mountain peak
✧ Siege

→ Nebuchadnezzar's first
campaign (605 BC)
→ Nebuchadnezzar's second
campaign (598 BC–597 BC)
→ Nebuchadnezzar's third
campaign (587 BC–586 BC)
→ Egyptian campaign
of 604 BC–601 BC
→ Zedekiah's escape route
→ Edomite's attack on Jerusalem
▢ Area of Babylonian dominance

Zedekiah is taken prisoner before Nebuchadnezzar encamped at Riblah.

After Jerusalem fell, the Babylonians destroy its fortifications and burned down the temple.

Zedekiah tries to escape, but is caught in the plains of Jericho. He then is taken to the king of Babylon at Riblah where he receives his sentence.

Letters from Babylonian siege are found in debris.

As Judah weakens, the Edomite kingdom takes advantage of the situation and sends troops.

GOD'S STORY

When the Events of This Book Happened:
Probably ca. 605–586 B.C.

The context is one in which the people of Edom, relatives of the people of Judah, had gloated about a military disaster that had befallen Jerusalem. They had even helped ransack the city (v. 13). The reference is probably to the successive Babylonian attacks on Jerusalem (in 605, 597, and 586). According to Ps. 137:7 and Ezek. 35:1-15, Edom joined with Babylon in Judah's downfall. (See *When the Events of This Book Happened* for *Lamentations* for more details.)

How Obadiah Fits into God's "Story"

The events of Obadiah's time belong to "chapter 2" of the story: God educates his nation (disobedient Israel disciplined). Sometimes God judges his own people because of their sins. Sometimes they are persecuted not because of sin but because it suits God's kingdom purposes. In such situations, evil people may gloat in satisfaction at the humiliation of God's people. In either case, however, such people have become God's enemies. Sooner or later God's sovereign justice will prevail. His kingdom purposes for human history will succeed, not the purposes of evil. Obadiah's last word is, "The kingdom will be the LORD's" (v. 21).

ORIGINAL HISTORICAL SETTING

Author and Date of Writing:
Obadiah, perhaps ca. 590 B.C.

Obadiah did not name his father or any king, and he left no personal traces in his prophecy. If the Babylonian invasions of Judah are indeed the context for Obadiah's ministry, he was a contemporary of Jeremiah. Scholars can only make a reasonable judgment about the date of composition. The year 590 would fit the evidence. This was the period after the first two Babylonian invasions, but before the final disaster of 586.

First Audience and Destination:
The Edomite people of "Mount Seir" and the Judahite people of "Mount Zion"

The first hearers of Obadiah were evidently the descendants of Esau. Ultimately, however, this was a message for the descendants of Jacob (i.e., the people living in and around Jerusalem). This book was preserved by the Israelites as part of their canon of Scripture at least partly because it contained a message relevant to them.

Occasion

There was an ancient and bitter hatred between the Israelites and the Edomites, going all the way back to the rivalry between their respective patriarchs,

Jacob and Esau (Gen. 27; 32–33). The descendants of Esau had settled southeast of the Dead Sea. From there, they had caused grief to the Israelites both in the last days of Moses and in the days of King Saul (Num. 20; 1 Sam. 22). Now they had once again demonstrated their hostility against a nation whose ethnic identity was not so different from their own. (See *When the Events of This Book Happened,* above.)

The book of Obadiah was prompted by divine revelation. It explicitly claimed to originate as a divinely sent "vision." The prophet had no doubt that his words were simply relaying, "This is what the Lord GOD has said" (v. 1).

 LITERARY FEATURES

Genre and Literary Style:
A brief prophecy written in Hebrew poetry
Obadiah is one of three prophetic books written for an initial audience outside of God's people. (The other two are Jonah and Nahum, both directed against the Assyrian capital of Nineveh.) His book "forth tells" the sins of Edom and God's displeasure. Then it "foretells" the coming ruin of Edom and the ultimate greatness of God's kingdom. Interpreters disagree about whether the prediction of Edom's destruction was fulfilled in the intertestamental period or whether it still waits for an end-time fulfillment.

The entire book is written in Hebrew poetry. In English Bibles, Obadiah is the fourth of the 12 Minor Prophets. In the Hebrew canon, it belonged to the composite book called "The Twelve." (See *Genre and Literary Style* for *Hosea* for more information.)

Themes:
Judgment on Edom; triumph of God's kingdom
Obadiah was the only prophet whose message focused extensively on Edom's coming judgment. Others, however, pronounced God's judgment against Edom as a secondary theme (see Jer. 49:7-22; Ezek. 35:1-15; Joel 3:19; Amos 1:11-12). Ultimately God will judge all his enemies and his kingdom will triumph. This book has an ongoing message for God's people when their enemies seem to be in control. In the end, "there will be a deliverance on Mount Zion, and it will be holy" (v. 17).

Book Features and Structure
There is great similarity between verses 1-9 and Jer. 49:7-22. Since the two men were probably contemporaries, it may be that they collaborated, although Obadiah wrote the shortest prophetic book while Jeremiah wrote the longest.

The book has two sections. The first (vv. 1-16) describes Edom's sins and coming destruction. The second (vv. 17-21) describes ultimate deliverance for "Mount Zion."

Illustration of Assyrian relief of Tiglath-Pileser III besieging a town.
Tiglath-Pileser III came to power after Jonah prophesied. The century
before Jonah lived, the Assyrians sent savage military expeditions west
into Syria-Palestine. Assyrian brutality and cruelty were legendary. This
knowledge would have shaped Jonah's view of the world. When he was
called to prophesy in Nineveh, he was reluctant to call the Assyrians to
repentance. What if they repented and were spared God's judgment?

JONAH

Jonah, the eighth-century B.C. Israelite prophet who initially spoke out against Nineveh, has given his name to this book as its central character and composer. His name means "Dove" in Hebrew.

○ KEY TEXT: 4:11

"But may I not care about the great city of Nineveh, which has more than a hundred and twenty thousand people who cannot distinguish between their right and their left, as well as many animals?"

○ KEY TERM: "FISH"

Although this book is not about the fish, clearly Jonah's being swallowed by the fish is the most exciting and memorable incident in the book. This is what keeps interest in the book alive and makes it the best known of all the Minor Prophets.

○ ONE-SENTENCE SUMMARY

After Jonah's disobedience to God's command for him to preach in Nineveh resulted in his being swallowed by a fish, he then obeyed God and preached in Nineveh, with the result that the entire city repented and turned to God.

Jonah the Prophet, sculpture by Sargis Babayan (b. 1986). "Jonah prayed to the LORD his God from the belly of the fish" (Jonah 2:1).

GOD'S MESSAGE IN THE BOOK

Purpose

Jonah was the Missionary Prophet. This book preserves the experiences of a reluctant preacher who, of all the prophets, had the most visibly positive results. The people of Israel had forgotten that God is concerned for all people. God meant for Israel to "declare his glory among the nations, his wondrous works among all peoples" (1 Chr. 16:24). Even though the people of Nineveh were the enemy (and would destroy the northern kingdom within a century), they were not beyond God's mercy. This book teaches that the most unlikely, most evil people in the world may respond favorably when they are given an opportunity to know the one true God. It also teaches that salvation is a matter of undeserved forgiveness, a truth that God's people have sometimes forgotten.

Christian Worldview Elements

Jonah deals principally with the worldview categories of God and *sovereignty and providence*. No Bible book more fully demonstrates God's mercy on the undeserving.

- **○ God**
- Creation
- **○ Sovereignty and Providence**
- Faith and Reason
- Revelation and Authority
- Humanity
- Rebellion and Sin
- Covenant and Redemption
- Community and Church
- Discipleship
- Ethics and Morality
- Time and Eternity

Teachings about God

Jonah reveals God as Creator. He is sovereign over the storms and fish of the sea, as well as the plants and worms of the land. The book also shows God as loving and compassionate. God's unanswered question that ends the book (see *Key Text*) is meant to provoke readers to think about how his mercy relates to "the nations."

Teachings about Humanity

God's enumeration of the vast city of Nineveh shows that each human life is valuable in the eyes of God. Jonah was personally a mass of contradictions—a prophet known mainly for disobeying God; a preacher angry at the success of his ministry; a believer more concerned about "creature comforts" than about people dying without knowing God. As such, he certainly demonstrates that God may use imperfect and reluctant persons to accomplish his plans.

Teachings about Salvation

Jonah demonstrates the principle that those whom God saves respond to hearing the word of God. No salvation occurs apart from the proclamation—whether willingly or reluctantly, partially or completely—of a word from God. The apostle Paul (who also knew about storms on the Mediterranean Sea) would later ask, "How, then, can they call on him they have not believed in? And how can they believe without hearing about him? And how can they hear without a preacher?" (Rom. 10:14).

CHRIST IN JONAH

Some crowds who heard Jesus clamored for a sign. Jesus told them that the only sign they would be given is the sign of Jonah. As Jonah was in the belly of the fish for three days, so Jesus was in the earth for three days and then was resurrected (Luke 11:29-32).

GOD'S STORY

When the Events of This Book Happened:

Sometime during the reign of Jeroboam II of Israel (ruled 793–753 B.C.)
According to 2 Kgs. 14:25, Jonah was a prophet during the days of Jeroboam II. (See 2 Kgs. 14:23-29 for the biblical narrative of his reign.) This was a time of unprecedented peace and prosperity in the northern kingdom of Israel. Aram (Syria in the KJV) to the north was so weak that Israel was able to expand, even taking control of Damascus. The Assyrians, with their capital in Nineveh, were in a period of retrenchment and inner turmoil. At the same time, they were well known throughout the ancient Near East as a potent military threat. (Shortly after Jeroboam's death and the ministry of Jonah, Assyria entered a period of aggression and expansion under Tiglath-Pileser III. Assyria would conquer Samaria and exile the people of the northern kingdom in 722.)

How Jonah Fits into God's "Story"

The events of Jonah's time belong to "chapter 2" of the story: God educates his nation (disobedient Israel disciplined). Jonah shows that God's kingdom purposes were never meant to be limited to only one ethnic entity. God's mercy in sending his prophet to the Assyrians foreshadowed his plan to send the good news of the gospel "to the end of the earth" (Acts 1:8).

ORIGINAL HISTORICAL SETTING

Author and Date of Writing:

Jonah, perhaps ca. 780 B.C.
The book is anonymous. On the other hand, according to uniform Jewish and early Christian belief, Jonah wrote this narrative of which he was the central human figure. If so, he likely wrote down the account of his ministry shortly after completing it.

Jonah was a contemporary of Amos. The only information known of his background is that his father was Amittai and he was from Gath-hepher, an Israelite town originally in the tribal allotment of Zebulun (2 Kgs. 14:25; Josh. 19:13). Because critical scholars dismiss the narrative as nonhistorical, they suppose the book was composed by some unknown writer, probably after the Jews returned from exile.

A relief from the palace of Ashurbanipal at Nineveh showing Assyrian soldiers subjecting captives to a series of tortures. In spite of the ruthlessness of the Assyrians, God sent his servant Jonah to offer them mercy. Jonah attempted to run in the opposite direction.

First Audience and Destination:

The people of the Northern Kingdom living in and around Samaria

Although the people of Nineveh heard and responded to Jonah's message, the book was written for the benefit of the people of Israel. According to 2 Kgs. 14:25, Jonah was involved in a prophetic ministry to Jeroboam II, presumably early in his reign.

Occasion

The book did not tell what prompted it to be written. Unlike all the other major and minor prophets, it is essentially a narrative. The only prophecy as such in the book is Jonah's warning, "In forty days Nineveh will be demolished!" (3:4).

LITERARY FEATURES

Genre and Literary Style:
A compact narrative written in Hebrew

Although this book contains almost none of the elements of Hebrew prophecy (see, e.g., *Genre and Literary Style* for *Isaiah*), this book is listed among the prophetic books for two reasons. First, its central character was a prophet (2 Kgs. 14:25); second, it issued a call to repentance. It contains no predictions at all. As a compact, well-written narrative, it has literary parallels with the book of Ruth or the stories about Elijah or Elisha (see 1 Kgs. 17–2 Kgs. 8).

Because taking the story as history requires believing the astonishing miracle of Jonah's survival in the fish and the otherwise unreported repentance of Nineveh, most critical scholars have suggested that the book belongs to a different genre. It has variously been called a parable or an allegory of God's love, that is, it is fictional in one way or another. Jesus himself, however, affirmed both Jonah's being swallowed by the fish and the repentance of Nineveh (Matt. 12:39-41), so there can be no doubt that the events reported in this book happened in history. If one believes in God's sovereignty over nature and history, then he can intervene supernaturally whenever it pleases him.

The entire book is written in Hebrew prose except for Jonah's prayer. In English Bibles, Jonah is the fifth of the 12 Minor Prophets. In the Hebrew canon, it belonged to the composite book called "The Twelve." (See *Genre and Literary Style* for *Hosea* for more information.)

Themes:
God's mercy; God's sovereignty over nature

The mercy of God to those who do not deserve it is one of the great themes of the Bible. In this book it is cast in a new light. God's sovereignty is seen explicitly in four things: God "appointed a great fish" (1:17); "appointed a plant" (4:6); "appointed a worm" (4:7); and "appointed a scorching east wind" (4:8).

Book Features and Structure

Jonah's prayer of thanksgiving from inside the fish (2:1-9) is a remarkable statement of trust in God. From that uncomfortable place, he affirmed, "Salvation belongs to the LORD" (2:9). It should also be noted that the text does not identify the kind of fish that swallowed Jonah, though it may have been a whale, as has been popularly imagined.

The book reflects a very wide geographical spread, from Tarshish (probably in southern Spain) in the far west to Nineveh on the Tigris River in Mesopotamia. In fact, the four chapters can be organized on the basis of Jonah's movements: (1) Jonah travels west (away from God); (2) Jonah sinks down (inside the fish); (3) Jonah travels east (to Nineveh to preach); (4) Jonah sits down (outside Nineveh to wait for its destruction).

"He will settle disputes among many peoples and provide arbitration for strong nations that are far away. They will beat their swords into plows and their spears into pruning knives. Nation will not take up the sword against nation, and they will never again train for war" (Micah 4:3). *Let Us Beat Swords into Plowshares*, sculpture by Yevgeny Vuchetich, 1959 gift of the Soviet Union to the United Nations. It's located in the garden of the United Nations Headquarters in New York City along the East River at 46th Street and 1st Avenue.

MICAH

Micah, the eighth-century B.C. Israelite prophet from Judah, has given his name to this book as its composer. His name is a short form of Micaiah, meaning "Who Is like the Lord" in Hebrew.

○ KEY TEXT: 3:8

"As for me, however, I am filled with power by the Spirit of the Lord, with justice and courage, to proclaim to Jacob his rebellion and to Israel his sin."

○ KEY TERM: "IDOLATRY"

The essential sin of Judah was idolatry, a rejection of the "First Table" of the Ten Commandments (the first four commandments). This brought about corruption, violence, and many other sins, a rejection of the "Second Table" (the last six commandments).

"Shepherd your people with your staff, the flock that is your possession. They live alone in a woodland surrounded by pastures. Let them graze in Bashan and Gilead as in ancient times" (7:14). Bashan is in the distance beyond the Sea of Galilee. *Lake Galilee, Looking Towards Bashan, Israel* by David Roberts.

⚪ **ONE-SENTENCE SUMMARY**

Although Micah also prophesied against Israel, his main message was against Judah, which must repent of idolatry and injustice or else go into exile—but then be restored to divine blessing under the Ruler from Bethlehem.

 GOD'S MESSAGE IN THE BOOK

Purpose

This book preserves the divinely inspired prophecies that Micah made during his ministry of at least 20 years. These prophecies were originally for the people of Judah facing Assyrian invasions. Micah warned that because of idolatry and injustice, God's case against Judah (and Israel) was severe. Their kingdoms would be destroyed—even though individuals could still repent and seek the Lord. Like Isaiah his colleague, Micah looked beyond the Assyrian captivity of Israel and the Babylonian captivity of Judah to the time when they would be forgiven and restored in righteousness, living under the Davidic Ruler that God would send.

Christian Worldview Elements

Micah deals with the worldview categories of *rebellion and sin*; *covenant and redemption*; and *time and eternity*. Judah's sin was about to have catastrophic consequences. Yet exile was not the final word. Micah offered a broad understanding of redemption from his own day until the time that "their King will pass through before them, the LORD as their leader" (2:13).

God
Creation
Sovereignty and Providence
Faith and Reason
Revelation and Authority
Humanity
o **Rebellion and Sin**
o **Covenant and Redemption**
Community and Church
Discipleship
Ethics and Morality
o **Time and Eternity**

Teachings about God

God's wrath against idolatry and all forms of human sin against others (violence, corruption, exploitation) is manifest in this book. The Assyrian and Babylonian captivities were the result of God's justice. Yet he is also a merciful God who does not retain anger forever. He will ultimately "cast all our sins into the depths of the sea" (7:19). Christ's birth in Bethlehem is specifically prophesied (5:2). The Spirit of God was present to empower the prophet (3:8).

Teachings about Humanity

Micah painted a dark picture of humanity as all too prone to wickedness. People from small to great were lying awake at night planning evil (2:1). The only hope was divine interference, which will happen when God personally takes responsibility for shepherding his flock (2:12).

Teachings about Salvation

In Micah, salvation is mainly corporate. It is based on God's forgiveness of sins (7:18-20) and restoring his people under the coming King. There is, however, an individual dimension. Those in a right relationship with God in this lifetime show it in the way they live now, reflected in perhaps the most beloved text from this book: "Mankind, he has told each of you what is good and what it is the LORD requires of you: to act justly, to love faithfulness, and to walk humbly with your God" (6:8).

 ## CHRIST IN MICAH

Micah repeats (4:1-5) Israel's messianic promise (4:2-4) centering in the exaltation of God's temple as a worship place for all nations and the end of war. Israel "will walk in the name of the LORD" (4:5). This is possible because God will once again visit David's birthplace in Bethlehem and bring forth a new, everlasting king (5:2-5a; compare Matt. 2:6).

 ## GOD'S STORY

When the Events of This Book Happened:

Micah prophesied during the reigns of three kings of Judah: Jotham, Ahaz, and Hezekiah (mainly ca. 740–700 B.C.)

Second Kings 15:32–20:21 and 2 Chr. 27–32 provide the historical narrative for the three kings mentioned in Mic. 1:1. In the city of Samaria, idolatrous kings ruled the northern kingdom of Israel. The power of Aram (Syria, KJV) with its capital in Damascus was a constant threat. Then there were the Assyrians, with their capital in Nineveh. Judah was isolated, with many powerful enemies.

During the rule of King Ahaz (735–715 B.C.), the Assyrians conquered Samaria, fulfilling Micah's word. Ahaz's son Hezekiah (715–686 B.C.) paid attention to the prophets Isaiah and Micah and instituted religious reform.

How Micah Fits into God's "Story"

The events of Micah's time belong to "chapter 2" of the story: God educates his nation (disobedient Israel disciplined). Judah was weak and impotent. It had become like the surrounding nations, idolatrous and corrupt to the core. There was little sense that it was part of God's kingdom of righteousness and holiness. They were a disobedient and sinful people who would be judged. Yet Micah prophesied the coming of a Ruler—a descendant of David to be born in Bethlehem—who would one day rule the kingdom in righteousness (5:2).

ORIGINAL HISTORICAL SETTING

Author and Date of Writing:
Micah, perhaps ca. 700 B.C.
Micah was a contemporary of Isaiah and Hosea. He was from the small town of Moresheth, probably Moresheth-gath in southern Judah (1:14). Almost nothing is known of his personal life. He saw the fulfillment of his predictions about the fall of Samaria to the Assyrians. Micah also witnessed the great religious revival initiated by Hezekiah, which delayed by a century the fulfillment of his prophecies about the coming fall of Jerusalem. He was one of the few prophets whose warnings of judgment were heeded. He probably wrote down his prophecies during the last years of Hezekiah.

First Audience and Destination:
The people of Judah living during Micah's lifetime
The first hearers were people living in Judah near the end of the 700s B.C.

Occasion
The specific occasion for Micah's prophecies is not known. They do, however, fit the period of religious and social corruption present during the rule of Ahaz (see 2 Kgs. 16). According to Jer. 26:18, Hezekiah repented in response to hearing Mic. 3:12, a prophecy of the coming fall of Jerusalem. The religious revival Hezekiah instituted marked a genuine return to worship of the Lord. (Later on, Isaiah worked with Hezekiah when the Assyrian army under Sennacherib laid siege against Jerusalem in 701 B.C., and God miraculously spared the city, Isa. 36–37.) Micah did not tell what prompted the collection of his writings.

 LITERARY FEATURES

Genre and Literary Style:
Prophecies written entirely in Hebrew poetry
Micah's prophecies both "forth tell" and "foretell." He includes the three classic elements of Hebrew prophecy: (1) call to people to turn from their sins in the face of divine judgment (which in fact happened), (2) predictions of near events (such as the fall of Samaria), and (3) predictions of remote events (such as the birth in Bethlehem of the coming ruler).

Micah's poetic style alternates between a hard-charging attack against sins and the promise of a coming restoration. Sometimes he uses "I" to voice God's own words (chap. 6); sometimes the "I" is his own voice (chap. 7). He is also known for quoting both false prophets (2:6-7) as well as the nations that will be converted (4:2).

Themes:

True religion, social justice, future restoration

Micah's message to Judah included basically the same themes as the message Amos had delivered to the northern kingdom half a century earlier. With his attacks on the violent and those who oppressed the poor, Micah spoke not only for his own era, but for all eras to come. He understood also the enduring truth that genuine religion is based on a heart desiring to please God, not ritual. Along with his contemporary, Isaiah, Micah foresaw an age of blessedness under a great Davidic ruler who would wisely lead God's people in righteousness.

Book Features and Structure

Micah 4:1-3 is almost exactly like Isa. 2:2-4, which demonstrates that these contemporaries indeed knew each other. Scholars disagree as to whether the time he referred to as the "last days" began with the first coming of Christ or yet awaits his return. These verses reverse the imagery of Joel 3:10.

One of the striking features of the book is the way it alternates between prophecies of judgment and prophecies of future blessing. This pattern occurs three times and provides a clue for organizing the book.

First cycle	Judgment (1:1–2:11)	Blessing (2:12-13)
Second cycle	Judgment (3:1-12)	Blessing (4:1–5:15)
Third cycle	Judgment (6:1–7:7)	Blessing (7:8-20)

Palace of Nineveh

NAHUM

Nahum, the seventh-century B.C. Israelite prophet against Nineveh, has given his name to this book as its composer. His name means "Comfort" in Hebrew.

○ KEY TEXT: 1:2

"The Lord is a jealous and avenging God; the Lord takes vengeance and is fierce in wrath. The Lord takes vengeance against his foes; he is furious with his enemies."

○ KEY TERM: "NINEVEH"

Nineveh was the capital of Assyria, the world superpower of the 600s B.C. God's wrath against Nineveh for its sins is the concern of this book. Nahum, the prophet of God's judgment, followed Jonah, the prophet of God's mercy, to Nineveh.

○ ONE-SENTENCE SUMMARY

Nahum prophesied that God would destroy Nineveh because of its wickedness and violence, never to rise again.

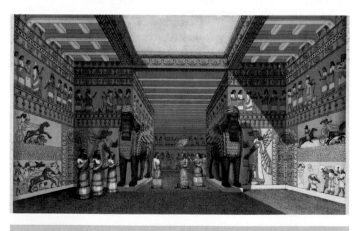

Reconstruction of a palace at Nineveh. Nahum prophesied the fall of this city of unparalleled wealth and power, built to withstand a 20-year siege. Nineveh fell when the Tigris and Khosr Rivers overflowed their banks. The resulting flood destroyed part of the city's wall. The Babylonians entered the breach in the wall, invaded the city, and destroyed it by fire. From 612 B.C. to the A.D. 1800s, Nineveh was lost in accumulating layers of dust.

GOD'S MESSAGE IN THE BOOK

Purpose

This book preserves the divinely inspired prophecies that Nahum made during his (perhaps) brief ministry. These prophecies served a twofold purpose. First, they were meant to warn the people of Nineveh of their coming doom. Second, they were an encouragement to people living in the kingdom of Judah to believe that God would punish their great enemy for their sins against God's people.

Christian Worldview Elements

Nahum focuses attention on the worldview categories of *sovereignty and providence* and *community*. God is supreme in the rise and fall of nations, as this book clearly addresses. The importance of God's people recognizing themselves as his people under his ultimate protection is also in view.

> God
> Creation
> ○ **Sovereignty and Providence**
> Faith and Reason
> Revelation and Authority
> Humanity
> Rebellion and Sin
> Covenant and Redemption
> ○ **Community** and Church
> Discipleship
> Ethics and Morality
> Time and Eternity

Teachings about God

God's wrath against every affront to his holiness is on full display in Nahum. He is patient, but this should not be misunderstood as weakness. His promised destruction of Nineveh was necessary because of the divine attributes noted in the *Key Text*, above.

Teachings about Humanity

On one hand, this book shows that human beings can achieve a great deal apart from God. The Assyrian civilization was highly advanced economically and militarily. On the other hand, the Assyrians were cruel and evil, an abomination to God. The book shows that God does not recognize as great (or good) any person or nation that measures success apart from obedience to him.

Teachings about Salvation

In Nahum, salvation is presented as God's final rescue of his people based on his sovereign care: "The LORD is good, a stronghold in a day of distress; he cares for those who take refuge in him" (1:7).

⊲⊳ CHRIST IN NAHUM

Nahum told Judah to look for a messenger who would bring the good news of Assyria's downfall, thus proclaiming peace for the world (1:15). The New Testament sees Jesus Christ as God's ultimate messenger, preaching God's peace for the world (Acts 10:36). As God is the one who rebukes seas and dries up rivers (1:4), so Jesus rebukes the sea and calms the storm (Matt. 8:26).

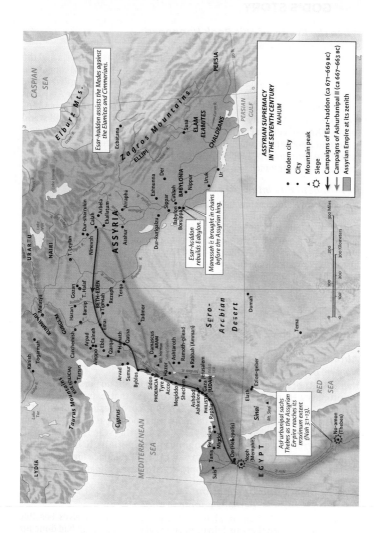

ASSYRIAN SUPREMACY
IN THE SEVENTH CENTURY
NAHUM

- ● Modern city
- ● City
- ▲ Mountain peak
- ⌂ Siege
- ↓ Campaigns of Esar-haddon (ca 671–669 BC)
- ↓ Campaigns of Ashurbanipal II (ca 667–663 BC)
- Assyrian Empire at its zenith

Esar-haddon assists the Medes against the Elamites and Cimmerians.

Esar-haddon rebuilds Babylon.

Manasseh is brought in chains before the Assyrian king.

Ashurbanipal sacks Thebes as the Assyrian Empire reaches its maximum extent (Nah 3:1-13).

 **GOD'S STORY**

When the Events of This Book Happened:
Sometime between 663 and 612 B.C.

During this time, Assyria dominated the ancient Near East. Samaria and the northern kingdom of Israel fell to Assyria in 722. In 663, Assyria had conquered the magnificent Egyptian stronghold of Thebes, located on the Nile River some 400 miles south of the Nile Delta. In Nah. 3:8, the prophet reminded the Assyrians of their great triumph. ("No" in the KJV is an alternate name for Thebes.) His argument was, if mighty Thebes fell, who are you to think you will stand forever? Nineveh did fall in 612 to the Babylonians, just as Nahum predicted.

Second Kings 21–23 and 2 Chr. 33–35 describe the three kings who ruled Judah between the fall of Thebes and the fall of Nineveh: Manasseh, Amon, and Josiah. It is unclear which one was reigning when Nahum prophesied.

How Nahum Fits into God's "Story"

The events of Nahum's time belong to "chapter 2" of the story: God educates his nation (disobedient Israel disciplined). When God judges his own people because of their sins, he may use evil people or powers. In this situation, however, such evil people are still subject to the vengeance of God. Sooner or later, God's sovereign justice prevails. His kingdom purposes for human history will succeed, not the purposes of evil. Although Assyria has long been destroyed, God's last enemy will not meet its final doom until Jesus's return to earth.

 ORIGINAL HISTORICAL SETTING

Author and Date of Writing:
Nahum, perhaps ca. 650 B.C.

Nahum did not name his father or any king, and he left no personal traces in his prophecy. He named himself as an "Elkoshite," that is, from the town of Elkosh, which is otherwise unknown. If Nahum prophesied soon after the fall of Thebes, the king of Judah was the idolatrous and long-reigning Manasseh, the "Ahab of Judah," who became a vassal of Assyria (2 Chr. 33:11-13). At this point Assyria was at its most arrogant and imperialistic height under Ashurbanipal (669–627). The year 650 would fit the evidence for the completion of Nahum's book, but this is simply a best-guess estimate.

First Audience and Destination:
People in Nineveh or perhaps people in Judah

The first hearers of Nahum may have been the Ninevites themselves. Possibly the prophet traveled there to deliver his message, just as Jonah had done for an earlier generation. Ultimately, however, this was a message for God's people. Nahum was preserved by the people of Judah in their canon of Scripture at least partly because it contained a message important to them.

Occasion

Assyria had long terrorized the ancient world. It had conquered Samaria and Thebes and appeared invincible. Nahum did not describe the specific occasion for his prophecy other than that it came as "the vision of Nahum." Like the other prophets, he was specifically aware of the divine origin of his ministry.

 LITERARY FEATURES

Genre and Literary Style:
A brief prophecy written in Hebrew poetry

Nahum is one of three prophetic books whose initial audience was outside of God's people. (The other two are Obadiah and Jonah, directed against Edom and Nineveh respectively.) His book "forth tells" the sins of Nineveh and God's wrath against it. Then it "foretells" the coming destruction of Nineveh, and indeed the entire Assyrian Empire. A secondary theme is the restoration of Judah (1:15; 2:2).

The entire book is written in Hebrew poetry. Nahum's style is vivid, with excellent use of metaphors and word pictures. In English Bibles, Nahum is the seventh of the 12 Minor Prophets. In the Hebrew canon, it belonged to the composite book called "The Twelve." (See *Genre and Literary Style* for *Hosea* for more information.)

Themes: Judgment on Nineveh, God's wrath against sin

Nahum was the only prophet whose message focused extensively on Nineveh's coming condemnation. In this way it complements the book of Jonah, in which God's judgment against Nineveh was averted. Ultimately God will judge all his enemies and his kingdom will triumph. Thus this book has an ongoing message for God's people. They should never doubt the seriousness of his wrath against sin, despite apparent delays in carrying out his justice.

Book Features and Structure

Nahum 1:2-8 is a psalm about God's awesome power. These verses are based on successive letters of the Hebrew alphabet, but the acrostic is incomplete. (See *Book Features and Structure* for *Lamentations* for information about acrostic poetry.) Of further interest is that this book concludes with a question, as does Jonah, the other prophetic book that focuses on Nineveh.

The three chapters of the book are suitable indications of its structure. Chapter 1 focuses on God's wrath; chapter 2 deals with Nineveh's condemnation; and chapter 3 presents Nineveh's coming destruction.

The prophet Habakkuk at The Cathedral of Santiago de Compostela, Galicia, Spain

HABAKKUK

Habakkuk, the seventh-century Israelite B.C. prophet to Judah, has given his name to this book as its composer. His name is possibly related either to the verb "embrace" in Hebrew or to an Assyrian plant called the *hambakuku*.

○ KEY TEXT: 2:4

"Look, his ego is inflated; he is without integrity. But the righteous one will live by his faith."

○ KEY TERM: "DIALOGUE"

The book reports a dialogue between the prophet and God. The prophet asked God questions about his ways, and God answered. The book shows one righteous way to bring concerns to God when his ways appear incomprehensible.

○ ONE-SENTENCE SUMMARY

When Habakkuk asked God questions about the nature of evil and its punishment, God answered by revealing his righteousness and sovereignty, and the prophet then responded with worship and faith.

Glazed brick relief of a striding lion from the Ishtar Gate of the palace of Nebuchadnezzar II who fulfilled Habakkuk's prophecy (Hab. 1:6-8a)

GOD'S MESSAGE IN THE BOOK

Purpose

This book preserves the divinely inspired dialogues and prayers of Habakkuk. These originated as a one-on-one conversation between the prophet and God, but they no doubt reflect the kinds of questions that many righteous people of Judah living in Habakkuk's time were also asking. The righteous of all eras may ask similar questions. God's people today will benefit from hearing God's replies to Habakkuk's questions: (1) why does evil seem to go unpunished for so long? and (2) why does God sometimes reprove the less evil by sending an even greater evil?

Christian Worldview Elements

Habakkuk focuses attention on the worldview categories of *God; sovereignty and providence*; and *ethics and morality*. The book causes readers to consider the attributes of God when their experience appears to deny that he is just. Further, the book addresses the issue of God's care for his people in the presence of great evil. The question of what is moral in international relations, particularly when one nation wars against another, is also in view.

> ○ **God**
> Creation
> ○ **Sovereignty and Providence**
> Faith and Reason
> Revelation and Authority
> Humanity
> Rebellion and Sin
> Covenant and Redemption
> Community and Church
> Discipleship
> ○ **Ethics and Morality**
> Time and Eternity

Teachings about God

The answers God gave the prophet show him as the Revealer of truth. The revelations God made focus on his absolute sovereignty over human history. Habakkuk's own passion was a concern for the glory of God's name to be known among all people: "His splendor covers the heavens, and the earth is full of his praise" (3:3).

Teachings about Humanity

Apart from divine revelation, human reasoning will never understand the ways of God. They will always be a mystery. It is fitting for people to ask God for revelation, but they must wait for the divine answers to their questions. When God reveals himself, people are to acknowledge his perfections by worship and praise.

Teachings about Salvation

The apostle Paul quoted Hab. 2:4 ("the righteous one will live by his faith") twice as evidence of the doctrine of justification by faith in the Old Testament (Rom. 1:17; Gal. 3:11). Steadfast, persevering trust in God for deliverance has always been the hallmark of God's people. The final verses of the book, a hymn of faith in the God who saves, includes the remarkable confession, "Yet I will rejoice in the Lord; I will rejoice in the God of my salvation!" (3:18).

Babylon's King Nebuchadnezzar II took thousands of Judean residents as captives to Mesopotamia in three deportations: 605, 597, and 586 B.C. The third deportation took place when Jerusalem, its walls, and the temple were destroyed.

CHRIST IN HABAKKUK

Habakkuk stood in awe at God's holiness and power. His reaction to the presence of God (3:16) is similar to that of the apostle John when the risen Christ appeared to him on the Isle of Patmos (Rev. 1:17).

GOD'S STORY

When the Events of This Book Happened:
At the time Babylon was becoming the world superpower (ca. 612–605 B.C.)

The book appears to belong to a time after Babylon (Chaldea) had risen to power (1:6) but before Babylon had directly attacked Judah. Babylon conquered Assyria in 612, and in 605 they defeated the Egyptians at the battle of Carchemish on the Euphrates River. Later that same year, Nebuchadnezzar made his first attack against Jerusalem.

The kings of Judah during this period were Josiah (640–609, killed in battle by the Egyptians), Jehoahaz (ruled three months in 609), and Jehoiakim (609–598), who changed loyalties from Egypt to Babylon. Second Kings 22:1–24:7 and 2 Chr. 34:1–36:8 describe the rule of these three kings. It is unknown which of these was king when Habakkuk prophesied.

How Habakkuk Fits into God's "Story"

The events of Habakkuk's time belong to "chapter 2" of the story: God educates his nation (disobedient Israel disciplined). God has a plan for his people that cannot be defeated. The essence of that plan is for them to acknowledge his greatness, his goodness, and his glory. These attributes are revealed by his sovereign acts in history. Such events are on his schedule, "for the appointed time," and "it will certainly come and not be late" (2:3). Although this book does not highlight the future completion of God's kingdom (as many prophetic books do), it does emphasize God's majesty as the King (see 3:1-6).

 ## ORIGINAL HISTORICAL SETTING

Author and Date of Writing:

Habakkuk, perhaps ca. 610 B.C.

Habakkuk is unknown apart from this book. He did not name his father or town of origin. Because of what he includes about the international military scene (see *When the Events of This Book Happened,* above), he almost certainly prophesied near the end of the seventh century. As such, he was a contemporary of Jeremiah and Zephaniah and probably lived to see his prophecy of the Chaldean conquest of Judah fulfilled (with Jerusalem and the temple burned in 586). The year 610 fits the evidence for the completion of Habakkuk's book—after the fall of Assyria to Babylon but before King Josiah's death or the battle of Carchemish—but this is simply a best-guess estimate.

First Audience and Destination:

People in Judah living during Habakkuk's lifetime

The first hearers were the kings and people living in the land of Judah during the years before the Babylonian captivity.

Occasion

Habakkuk did not tell what prompted him to write down his book. He recorded the private dialogue of himself with God and his personal response as a written account for the benefit of the people. Because the last chapter contains liturgical notations (3:1,19), those verses were probably included in worship services at the temple.

LITERARY FEATURES

Genre and Literary Style:
Prophetic dialogue, woes, and prayer written in Hebrew poetry

As a prophetic writer, Habakkuk included materials in an unusual format, although he included classic elements of "forth telling" and "foretelling." His "forth telling" included great declarations of God's attributes as well as woes on the wicked (see especially 2:9-17). His "foretelling" predicted both near events (Judah's devastation by Chaldea (fulfilled in 586), as well as the more remote event of the destruction of Chaldea (fulfilled in 539 by the Persians).

The entire book is written in Hebrew poetry. Habakkuk's style reveals him as one whose greatest concern was for the honor of God's name (1:12; 3:3). In English Bibles, Habakkuk is the eighth of the 12 Minor Prophets. In the Hebrew canon, it belonged to the composite book called "The Twelve." (See *Genre and Literary Style* for *Hosea* for more information.)

Themes:
God's honor, God's sovereignty in the face of evil

The majestic glory of God is evident throughout the book, in particular in Habakkuk's confession that has become a standard in Christian worship: "But the Lord is in his holy temple; let the whole earth be silent in his presence" (2:20). The supremacy of God in international events is especially evident in the dialogue section of the book.

Book Features and Structure

The dialogue of Habakkuk with God makes this book noteworthy among the prophetic works of Scripture. This is seen in the following organizational scheme:

Habakkuk's first question: Why is evil in Judah not being punished? (1:1-4).

God's first answer: God will use Chaldea to punish evil in Judah (1:5-11).

Habakkuk's second question: How can God righteously use the more wicked (Chaldea) to punish the less wicked (Judah)? (1:12–2:1).

God's second answer: Chaldea will also be punished for its evil (2:2-20).

The book has two major sections. First is the dialogue between the prophet and God (chaps. 1–2). Second is the prophet's prayer of faith (chap. 3).

"The court secretary Shaphan told the king (Josiah), 'The priest Hilkiah has given me a book, and Shaphan read it in the presence of the king. When the king heard the words of the book of the law, he tore his clothes" (2 Kings 22:10-11). Josiah initiated reforms in Judah in light of hearing the book of the law. Zephaniah may well have supported this reform. He called on the people of Judah to "Seek the Lord, all you humble of the earth, who carry out what he commands. Seek righteousness, seek humility; perhaps you will be concealed on the day of the Lord's anger" (Zephaniah 2:3).

ZEPHANIAH

Zephaniah, the seventh-century prophet from Judah, has given his name to this book as its composer. His name means "The Lord Hides" in Hebrew.

○ KEY TEXT: 3:17

"The LORD your God is among you, a warrior who saves. He will rejoice over you with gladness. He will be quiet in his love. He will delight in you with singing."

○ KEY TERM: "DAY OF THE LORD"

Zephaniah predicted the future "day of the LORD" as a time of ruin for Jerusalem. The initial coming of the "day of the LORD" was manifested by Judah's fall to Babylon; its final fulfillment lies in the future in the context of Christ's return.

○ ONE-SENTENCE SUMMARY

Although Zephaniah prophesied coming judgment against the nations, his main message was against Judah, whose sins were so serious that they would go into exile on the "day of the LORD," but later they would be restored to righteousness.

"And at that time I will search Jerusalem with lamps and punish those who settle down comfortably, who say to themselves: The LORD will not do good or evil" (Zeph. 1:12).

GOD'S MESSAGE IN THE BOOK

Purpose

This book preserves the divinely inspired prophecies that Zephaniah made during his ministry to Judah about four decades before Jerusalem's fall to Babylon. He argued that the coming "day of the LORD" would involve God's judgment on God's people as well as on the pagan nations. God would later restore a remnant of his people, who would then worship him forever as the King of Israel.

Christian Worldview Elements

Zephaniah focuses on the worldview categories of *rebellion and sin* and *covenant and redemption*. The people of Judah had sinned greatly, particularly the religious and political leaders. God's judgment would ultimately result in the surviving remnant coming to salvation. Zephaniah demonstrates a long-term view of redemption from his own day until the time of restoration.

> God
> Creation
> Sovereignty and Providence
> Faith and Reason
> Revelation and Authority
> Humanity
> ○ **Rebellion and Sin**
> ○ **Covenant and Redemption**
> Community and Church
> Discipleship
> Ethics and Morality
> Time and Eternity

Teachings about God

God is righteous and jealous for his people. In the coming "day of the LORD," he will bring about justice on all who have opposed him by living in violence and treachery, including those who claimed to belong to him. Although there is no direct prediction of Christ or the coming of the Holy Spirit, Christians have understood Zephaniah's prediction of the day when "the King of Israel, the LORD, is among you" (3:15) to refer to Jesus.

Teachings about Humanity

Zephaniah shows the universal tendency toward evil present among humans. All kinds of people—Jerusalemites, Philistines, Moabites, Assyrians, and Ethiopians—will alike be condemned because of their sins against God. Arrogance, oppression, and violence deserve God's judgment, no matter what persons or nations have committed them. The "day of the LORD" will come against them all (see 2:11).

Teachings about Salvation

Because of Zephaniah's emphasis on the "day of the LORD," his understanding of salvation focuses on God's subsequent blessing on the righteous remnant of Israel. God's restoration of the covenant people, however, also means that all the nations of the earth will know him: "so that all of them may call on the name of the LORD and serve him with a single purpose" (3:9).

CHRIST IN ZEPHANIAH

Zephaniah announced that the King of Israel was in their midst (3:15). Jesus was crucified as King of the Jews (Mark 15:26). As Judah did not recognize the presence of the divine king in their circumstances, so many Jewish leaders failed to recognize the presence of God in Jesus Christ.

GOD'S STORY

When the Events of This Book Happened:
During the reign of King Josiah (ruled 640–609 B.C.)

Second Kings 22–23 and 2 Chr. 34–35 provide the historical narrative for Josiah's reign. In international affairs, Josiah saw the shift of world power move from Assyria and Egypt to Babylon. The most significant religious event in Judah was the revival and restoration of temple worship led by Josiah (ca. 622 B.C.). Tragically, Josiah's reforms were unable to undo the damage done by his idolatrous grandfather Manasseh. After Josiah's untimely demise, three

Sunset on the beach at Ashdod, one of the major cities of the Philistines. Zephaniah prophesied judgment for Israel and surrounding nations including the Philistines (Zeph. 2:4-7).

of his sons and one grandson reigned as the last of the Davidic dynasty in Jerusalem. Within 25 years of Josiah's death, the Babylonians completely destroyed the temple and carried the people into exile (586 B.C.). It is not clear whether Zephaniah prophesied before or after Josiah's reforms.

How Zephaniah Fits into God's "Story"

The events of Zephaniah's time belong to "chapter 2" of the story: God educates his nation (disobedient Israel disciplined). Zephaniah's use of "day-of-the-Lord" language shows that he meant it as a decisive turning point in God's dealings with people. One such turning point for his people was the "day of the Lord" that sent them into Babylonian captivity. But, as New Testament writers came to know, in some ways the day of the Lord will not reach its fullest expression until the days before Christ's return. God's plans to be the King in the midst of his people is a magnificent prophecy that will ultimately be fulfilled in the final expression of God's kingdom. The last two chapters of the Bible describe the complete realization of this promise.

ORIGINAL HISTORICAL SETTING

Author and Date of Writing:
Zephaniah, perhaps ca. 625 B.C.

Zephaniah was a contemporary of Jeremiah and Habakkuk. He identified himself by a more complete genealogy than any other prophet (1:1) and ministered during the reign of Josiah. He was the great-great-grandson of a certain Hezekiah, probably the famous king. If so, Zephaniah belonged to the royal family. (King Josiah was Hezekiah's great-grandson.) Zephaniah's attacks on the sins of the elite—princes, priests, judges, and false prophets—suggest that he was acquainted with the powerful and that he had true boldness (see 3:3-5). The evils of Judah that he described match the religious corruption rooted out by Josiah's reform. If, as appears likely, Zephaniah preached shortly before 622, he contributed greatly to the reforms of Josiah's rule.

First Audience and Destination:
People in Judah living during Zephaniah's lifetime

The first hearers were the kings and people living in Judah some 40 years before the Babylonian captivity.

Occasion

The specific occasion for Zephaniah's prophecies is not known. He stated only that "the word of the Lord" came to him (1:1). As noted above, however, his message fits the period of religious and social corruption present during the early rule of Josiah (see 2 Kgs. 22—23). The revival Josiah instituted marked a genuine return to worship of the Lord. Zephaniah did not tell what prompted the collection of his writings.

LITERARY FEATURES

Genre and Literary Style:
Prophecies written entirely in Hebrew poetry

Zephaniah's prophecies both "forth tell" and "foretell." He includes the three classic elements of Hebrew prophecy: (1) call to people to turn from their sins in the face of divine judgment (which in fact happened), (2) predictions of near events (such as the fall of Judah and Jerusalem), and (3) predictions of remote events (such as the restoration of a remnant in righteousness).

The entire book is written in Hebrew poetry. Zephaniah's poetic style is largely dark: the coming "day of the LORD" will be bitter; the penalties will be sure and severe. On the other hand, there are rays of light when he speaks of the coming time of renewal. In English Bibles, Zephaniah is the ninth of the 12 Minor Prophets. In the Hebrew canon, it belonged to the composite book called "The Twelve." (See *Genre and Literary Style* for *Hosea* for more information.)

Themes:
Day of the Lord, repentance, judgment, restoration

The "day of the LORD" looms large in Zephaniah (see also Joel). Because of the certainty of this day, people should take heed and repent of their sins. Yet judgment (both on Judah and the nations) appears inevitable. While the theme of restoration is not developed as fully as it is in other prophetic books (such as Isaiah), it is unmistakably and clearly the note on which the book concludes.

Book Features and Structure

One often overlooked biblical theme is that of the happiness of God. Zephaniah noted God's coming pleasure in the full ingathering of his people. Just as these people are urged to "sing" and "shout" to God when they are restored (3:14), so God himself will "rejoice over you with gladness" and "delight in you with singing" (3:17). Just as God's people find bliss in God, so one source of bliss for God is his people.

The book consists of only 53 verses. They may be organized into three sections: the day of the Lord (1:1–2:3); the judgment of the nations (2:4–3:8); the restoration of the remnant (3:9-20).

Haggai prophesied during the reign of Darius I, king of Persia. Darius sought documentation that Cyrus had authorized the rebuilding of the temple in Jerusalem. A scroll was found in the archives at Ecbatana that contained Cyrus's authorization (Ezra 6). On that basis, Darius issued a decree permitting the rebuilding of the Jerusalem temple on its original site.

HAGGAI

Haggai, the sixth-century prophet who returned to Judah from Babylonian exile, has given his name to this book as its composer. His name means "Festive" in Hebrew.

○ KEY TEXT: 1:8

"'Go up into the hills, bring down lumber, and build the house; and I will be pleased with it and be glorified,' says the Lord."

○ KEY TERM: "REBUILDING"

The primary focus of this book is rebuilding the Jewish temple in Jerusalem after the return from Babylonian captivity.

○ ONE-SENTENCE SUMMARY

When Haggai proclaimed God's command to rebuild the temple, giving God's promises that the glory of the second temple would exceed that of the first temple, the people obeyed with a willing heart.

Ruins of Persepolis, the Persian royal retreat built by Darius, during whose reign the second temple in Jerusalem was completed (515 B.C.).

GOD'S MESSAGE IN THE BOOK

Purpose

This book preserves the divinely inspired sermons that Haggai gave during his ministry in the last months of 520 B.C. These prophecies were originally for the people of Judah who had recently returned from the Babylonian captivity and were lethargic about their primary duty: to reestablish the true worship of God at his temple. Unlike most biblical prophets, Haggai's message was obeyed, and his sermons were kept as a permanent reminder of his ministry. From a broader perspective, the second temple, the Jewish community, and a stable Jerusalem were important contexts for the coming of Jesus more than five centuries later.

Christian Worldview Elements

Haggai deals particularly with the worldview categories of *covenant and redemption* and *community*. Despite the Babylonian captivity, the returned exiles were still the covenant people. Their return was evidence that God had not forsaken them. As the covenant community, they were called on to worship as a community in the way that God commanded.

God
Creation
Sovereignty and Providence
Faith and Reason
Revelation and Authority
Humanity
Rebellion and Sin
○ **Covenant and Redemption**
○ **Community** and Church
Discipleship
Ethics and Morality
Time and Eternity

Teachings about God

God desires to be honored by his people (see *Key Text)*. Because of this, he has the right to prescribe what pleases him. His concern in the time of Haggai was to be worshiped properly in his temple. Ultimately, the greatness of the rebuilt temple was that it would one day receive "the treasures of all the nations" (2:7). Further, God's promise to Zerubbabel that he was "like my signet ring" (2:23) was a promise of the coming Messiah (a direct descendant of Zerubbabel, Matt. 1:12).

Teachings about Humanity

On one hand, the people whom Haggai addressed needed to be rebuked. They were under a divine curse because of their inactivity concerning the things of God. It was not so much that they were actively evil but that they were passive when they should have been passionate. On the other hand, the book shows that people can be moved to do right things, but even this must be at God's initiative: "And the Lord roused . . . the spirit of all the remnant of the people" (1:14).

Teachings about Salvation

The people who returned from exile were cured of the idolatry that took their ancestors into captivity. Haggai revived an emphasis from the era of the

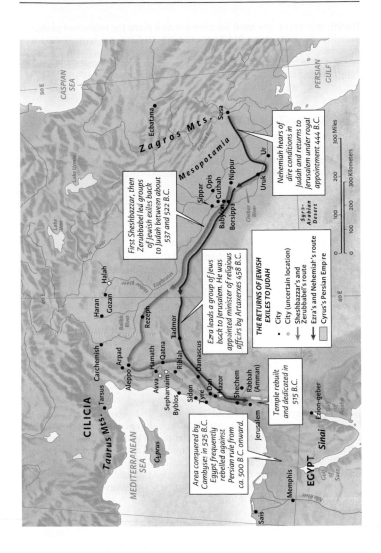

First Sheshbazzar, then Zerubbabel led groups of Jewish exiles back to Judah between about 537 and 522 B.C.

Nehemiah hears of dire conditions in Judah and returns to Jerusalem under royal appointment 444 B.C.

Ezra leads a group of Jews back to Jerusalem. He was appointed minister of religious affairs by Artaxerxes 458 B.C.

THE RETURNS OF JEWISH EXILES TO JUDAH

• City
○ City (uncertain location)
→ Sheshbazzar's and Zerubbabel's route
→ Ezra's and Nehemiah's route
   Cyrus's Persian Empire

Temple rebuilt and dedicated in 515 B.C.

Area conquered by Cambyses in 525 B.C. Egypt frequently rebelled against Persian rule from ca. 500 B.C. onward.

Davidic monarchy: the need for a temple as a place for redeemed people to worship. As throughout Old Testament times, personal trust in God was expressed through participation in right sacrifices and through obeying God's law. Thus the blessings of salvation are promised in this book to those who fully obey the divine commands.

 CHRIST IN HAGGAI

Through Haggai the Lord says he will shake the elements of creation and the nations. Then the nations will come to worship at the new temple that God will fill with his glory (2:6-7). Simeon saw in the baby Jesus a light for the Gentile nations and glory for Israel (Luke 2:32).

 GOD'S STORY

When the Events of This Book Happened:
Between August and December, 520 B.C.
The Persians defeated the Chaldean Empire and the city of Babylon in 539, then initiated the policy of allowing exiles of all ethnic groups to go back to their homeland. The first Israelites returned during Cyrus's rule. They rebuilt the altar and laid the foundations for the temple about 536 (Ezra 6:3-5). The work then halted until after Darius the Great came to the throne of Persia (522–486 B.C.). The prophetic ministry of Haggai is carefully dated in the second year of Darius. Haggai's ministry was successful in spurring the work, but the second temple was not dedicated until 516, exactly 70 years after Solomon's temple was destroyed (2 Chr. 36:21; Ezra 6:15). The walls of Jerusalem were rebuilt much later, in the time of Nehemiah (445 B.C.).

How Haggai Fits into God's "Story"
Haggai tells part of "chapter 3" of God's story: God keeps a faithful remnant (Messiah's space and time prepared). Although there was no Davidic king, that did not keep the returning exiles from worshiping properly or doing what they were able to do. The second temple was a pale replica of Solomon's temple, but it would be more important. Jesus, the Son of God and Son of David, was presented in this temple and ended his public ministry by teaching there. The book of Haggai shows how one of God's prophets played a key role in bringing this temple into being.

ORIGINAL HISTORICAL SETTING

Author and Date of Writing:
Haggai, ca. 520 B.C.

Haggai was a contemporary of Zechariah. Hardly anything is known about him. He did not note his lineage or his hometown. Presumably he was one of the exiles from Babylon who returned to Judah in the 530s. He did, however, date precisely the four occasions on which "the word of the LORD came" to him (1:1; 2:1,10,20). In modern equivalents, these dates are (1) August 29, 520; (2) October 17, 520; (3) and (4) December 18, 520. According to Ezra 6:14, Haggai saw the successful conclusion of his ministry in the completion of the temple. Presumably he wrote down his messages as they were given to him, and he compiled them shortly thereafter.

First Audience and Destination:
Israelites in Jerusalem after they returned from exile

The original hearers and destination are clearly stated. The first audience was the people of Jerusalem who had returned to exile. In particular, Zerubbabel the governor and Joshua the high priest were recipients of some of Haggai's exhortations.

Occasion

Ezra 4–5 describes the opposition that the returning exiles faced when they attempted to rebuild the temple. Opposition, however, became an excuse for inactivity. For more than 15 years, inertia set in. God raised up Haggai to rouse the Jews from their doldrums.

LITERARY FEATURES

Genre and Literary Style:
Prophetic sermons written in Hebrew prose

Although Haggai was clearly a postexilic prophet, his prophecies both "forth tell" and "foretell" in the classic manner of the Hebrew prophets: (1) call to people to turn from their sins (in this case, the sin of unconcern for the temple) and (2) predictions of future events (such as the glory that would come to the second temple).

The book is written in Hebrew prose, rather than poetry. In English Bibles, Haggai is the tenth of the 12 Minor Prophets. In the Hebrew canon, it belonged to the composite book called "The Twelve." (See *Genre and Literary Style* for *Hosea* for more information.)

Themes:

Lord of hosts, rebuilding the temple, future blessings

Haggai, Zechariah, and Malachi all emphasize God's name as "LORD of hosts." (See *Book Features and Structure,* below.) The conviction that he was in charge of all armies logically led to confidence that he would enable the rebuilding of the temple and bring about the blessings that were promised.

Book Features and Structure

The last three books of the Old Testament use the name "LORD of Armies" more than 90 times, although Isaiah and Jeremiah—as well as some of the historical books—also make use of it. "Armies" can refer to earthly armies, heavenly bodies (such as stars and planets), and angelic armies. The name emphasizes God's supremacy over all things on earth and in heaven. Such a God deserves to be worshiped in a temple of his choosing, and he can enable his worshipers to construct such an edifice, despite any opposition.

The book has only 38 verses. In the Old Testament, only Obadiah is shorter. It is organized around the four divinely given messages that the prophet dated. (See *Author and Date of Writing,* above.)

ZECHARIAH

Zechariah, the sixth-century prophet who returned to Judah from Babylonian exile, has given his name to this book as its composer. His name means "The Lord Remembers" in Hebrew.

⭕ KEY TEXT: 8:3

"The LORD says this: 'I will return to Zion and live in Jerusalem. Then Jerusalem will be called the Faithful City; the mountain of the LORD of Armies will be called the Holy Mountain.'"

⭕ KEY TERM: "JERUSALEM"

This book focuses on the city of Jerusalem, which still lay in ruins in Zechariah's day. Both the near-term rebuilding of the city and the ultimate, everlasting destiny of Jerusalem as the city in which God delights are in view.

⭕ ONE-SENTENCE SUMMARY

Through night visions and prophetic oracles, Zechariah predicted the welfare of Jerusalem as God's beloved holy city into which the King would enter riding a donkey, the one also called God's servant, "the Branch" (3:8).

 GOD'S MESSAGE IN THE BOOK

Purpose

This book preserves the divinely inspired prophecies that Zechariah received during his ministry in 520–518 B.C. (or possibly extending later). These prophecies were originally for the people of Judah who had recently returned from the Babylonian captivity and were uncertain about the future prospects for the city of Jerusalem, once great but still in ruins from the Babylonian invasion. His message was essentially one of encouragement: the greatest days of Jerusalem lay in the glorious future. Because of Zechariah's messianic prophecies that Jesus fulfilled, the greatest glory of Jerusalem was that Jesus blessed the city with his presence.

Christian Worldview Elements

Zechariah draws attention to the worldview categories of *covenant and redemption* and *community*. Despite the Babylonian captivity, the returned exiles were still the covenant people. Their return was evidence that God had not forsaken them. The "glory days" for the covenant community were still in the future, not in the past, which had implications for how they should function together as a community in the present.

The Prophet Zechariah by Michelangelo

Teachings about God

Zechariah emphasizes God's mercy—for his name's sake—on his beloved people. For this reason, they will one day dwell in security and blessing in Jerusalem forever. God's Spirit is present to enable his servants (4:6). Jesus is predicted in a number of places: his royal entrance into Jerusalem (9:9); his betrayal for 30 silver pieces (11:12); and his role as shepherd (13:7) and Branch (3:8; 6:12).

> God
> Creation
> Sovereignty and Providence
> Faith and Reason
> Revelation and Authority
> Humanity
> Rebellion and Sin
> ○ **Covenant and Redemption**
> ○ **Community** and Church
> Discipleship
> Ethics and Morality
> Time and Eternity

Teachings about Humanity

In general, Zechariah looks forward to the time when God's people—having been punished for their sins—will be restored in righteousness. In particular, the book shows what God can accomplish through individuals committed to obedience. These exemplary people are Zechariah the prophet, Joshua the priest (3:1-10), and Zerubbabel the governor (4:6-10). These men foreshadow the coming of the Messiah, the greatest Prophet, Priest, and King.

Teachings about Salvation

Zechariah draws attention to the future redemption of God's people corporately, as they live safely in the land and he lives among them (chap. 8). This salvation will follow the horrible "day of the LORD" when God will defeat the nations that have come against Jerusalem (chap. 14). All those who share in this salvation will enjoy a city where the holiness that once resided in the temple will be pervasive throughout the city.

⋉ CHRIST IN ZECHARIAH

The Gospels incorporate more passages from Zechariah than from any other prophet. In Zechariah we see foreshadowed the piercing of Jesus's body (12:10; compare John 19:34,37; Rev. 1:7).

GOD'S STORY

When the Events of This Book Happened:
The dated prophecies are 520–518 B.C.

Zechariah dated several of his prophecies. He began about the same time as Haggai, but continued for at least two years longer. The last six chapters possibly come from the time after the temple was completed in 516. (See *When the Events of This Book Happened* for *Haggai*.)

"Ask the LORD for rain in the season of spring rain. The LORD makes the rain clouds, and he will give them showers of rain and crops in the field for everyone" (Zech. 10:1).

How Zechariah Fits into God's "Story"

Zechariah tells part of "chapter 3" of God's story: God keeps a faithful remnant (Messiah's space and time prepared). This book looks at the kingdom of God from three time frames. The first is the time present to the prophet (God's people living in a ruined Jerusalem, wondering whether they had any future at all). The second is the time of the King's coming to Jerusalem on a donkey (fulfilled by Jesus in his first coming). The third is the ultimate glory of the city (yet to be fulfilled by Jesus at his second coming; see the last two chapters of Revelation). Thus Zechariah has an extremely broad kingdom focus.

 ## ORIGINAL HISTORICAL SETTING

Author and Date of Writing:
Zechariah, perhaps ca. 518 B.C.
Zechariah was a contemporary of Haggai. The only thing really known about him is that he was the son of Berechiah and grandson of Iddo (1:1). Presumably

he was one of the exiles who returned to Judah in the 530s. He dated two of his visions, which enables scholars to integrate his ministry with that of Haggai. His initial call came in October or November of 520 (1:1); the eight night visions came on February 15, 519 (1:7); a third message came on December 7, 518. Zechariah almost certainly did not live long enough to see the walls of Jerusalem rebuilt (in 445 B.C., some 75 years after his initial call).

Most critical scholars have argued that Zech. 9–14 were written by a later, unknown prophet, a "Deutero-Zechariah," with a different style and perspective. (This is parallel to the argument for a "Deutero-Isaiah." See *Author and Date of Writing* for *Isaiah*.) There are, however, no really strong arguments for denying that the sixth-century prophet wrote the entire book. Presumably he wrote down his messages as they were given to him, and they were compiled shortly thereafter.

First Audience and Destination:
Israelites in Jerusalem after they returned from exile
The first audience was the people of Jerusalem who had returned to exile. In particular Zerubbabel the governor and Joshua the high priest received some of Zechariah's messages of encouragement.

Occasion
Zechariah described his prophetic call as simply "the word of the LORD." For more than 15 years, the Jews had been back in Jerusalem, but the city was still in physical disarray. The walls were still ruined, and the people were questioning the future of the city. God raised up Zechariah to encourage these Jews with a vision of Jerusalem's glorious future. He did not tell what prompted the collection of his writings.

 LITERARY FEATURES

Genre and Literary Style:
Prophecies, including visions and words from God, written mainly in Hebrew prose but with some poetry
Zechariah's prophecies both "forth tell" and "foretell." The book includes the three classic elements of Hebrew prophecy: (1) call to people to turn from their sins, (2) predictions of near events (such as God's blessing on Zerubbabel), and (3) predictions of remote events (such as the coming of the King to Jerusalem riding a donkey).

Like Ezekiel and Daniel, Zechariah received symbolic visions as a part of his ministry. These included both near and distant prophetic elements. The book is written mainly in good Hebrew prose, rather than poetry. Chapters 9–10 are the main poetic section. In English Bibles, Zechariah is the eleventh of the 12 Minor Prophets. In the Hebrew canon, it belonged to the composite book called "The Twelve." (See *Genre and Literary Style* for *Hosea* for more information.)

Themes:

Lord of hosts, Jerusalem, the Servant

Haggai, Zechariah, and Malachi all emphasize God's name as "LORD of Armies." (See *Book Features and Structure* for *Haggai*.) The Jerusalem theme should be compared with the similar theme of Nehemiah. Zechariah's messianic prophecies, particularly on Jesus as the coming "servant" are similar to those in the book of Isaiah.

Book Features and Structure

One feature of predictive prophecy in several biblical books but especially prominent in Zechariah is "telescoping." Sometimes near and remote prophecies are so compressed together that it is difficult to tell whether a specific prediction is near or distant. (This is like looking at two mountaintops through a telescope: they appear to be close together, but they are many miles apart.) Thus Zechariah's prophecies about the future of Jerusalem are often telescoped. They include events all the way from his lifetime to the final glorious days of the city.

The book has two distinct parts. Part 1 (chaps. 1–8) focuses on Zechariah's night visions and concludes with God's blessings on Jerusalem. Part 2 (chaps. 9–14) focuses on Zechariah's oracles (sermons) and concludes with God's victory in the final war against Jerusalem.

MALACHI

Malachi, the fifth-century prophet to Judah, has given his name to this book as its composer. His name means "My Messenger" in Hebrew.

○ KEY TEXT: 1:11

"'My name will be great among the nations, from the rising of the sun to its setting. Incense and pure offerings will be presented in my name in every place because my name will be great among the nations,' says the LORD of Armies."

○ KEY TERM: "MESSENGER"

Malachi, God's messenger, noted that while true priests of God served as God's messengers (2:7), God would one day send "my messenger" (3:1, John the Baptist) to prepare the way for "the Messenger of the covenant" (3:1, Jesus).

○ ONE-SENTENCE SUMMARY

Malachi rebuked God's people for specific violations of the covenant, such as laws concerning sacrifices, divorce, and tithes, but he also prophesied the coming of the Messenger who will set all things right.

"'My name will be great among the nations, from the rising of the sun to its setting. Incense and pure offerings will be presented in my name in every place because my name will be great among the nations,' says the Lord of Armies" (Mal. 1:11).

GOD'S MESSAGE IN THE BOOK

Purpose

The book of Malachi preserves the divinely inspired words received by the prophet during his (possibly brief) ministry ca. 450 or 420 B.C. These prophecies were originally for the second or third generation of people in Judah after the return from the Babylonian captivity. The temple was functioning; the city was rebuilt; and people had become perfunctory in their worship and lifestyles. His message was essentially one of accusation: as God's messenger, he charged them with violations of the covenant and gave specific examples. But he also looked ahead to a time of wonderful blessing.

Christian Worldview Elements

Malachi deals particularly with the worldview categories *covenant and redemption* and *ethics and morality*. Those who have been included in God's covenant have a serious obligation to live in obedience to the covenant terms. Those claiming to be God's people cannot tolerate negligent living.

God
Creation
Sovereignty and Providence
Faith and Reason
Revelation and Authority
Humanity
Rebellion and Sin
○ **Covenant and Redemption**
Community and Church
Discipleship
○ **Ethics and Morality**
Time and Eternity

Teachings about God

Malachi presents God's immutability. (He does not change.) For this reason, his promises are enduring. Further, he is one who judges rightly, beginning with his own people. The eternal God, moreover, is personal, as frequent use of the pronoun "I" in this book emphasizes. Christ is prophesied as the Messenger who will purify priests and people alike (3:1-5). The Holy Spirit is not mentioned.

Teachings about Humanity

God's people were addressed in this book, yet they were disheartened and disillusioned. The promises that earlier prophets had made of a coming golden age seemed empty. These people illustrate that in times when God does not appear to be acting on behalf of his people, it is easy for them to become complacent. It is even easy for them to be apathetic about obeying God's specific moral commands. This book offers God's cure for such doubtful people.

Teachings about Salvation

Redemption in Malachi has two aspects. First is the notion of the covenant (mentioned six times). Salvation comes because God has initiated it in his covenant. Second is the work of the coming Messenger. Malachi predicted that his coming would bring cleansing: "He will be like a refiner's fire, and like launderer's bleach" (3:2). The implications of this prophecy would not be entirely clear until Jesus fulfilled it by his atoning death.

"But for you who fear my name, the sun of righteousness will rise with healing in its wings, and you will go out and playfully jump like calves from the stall" (Mal. 4:2).

✄ CHRIST IN MALACHI

Malachi describes Christ as the sun of righteousness who brings healing to his people. He also comes as a refiner's fire to purify the sons of Levi so they can make an offering in righteousness.

 GOD'S STORY

When the Events of This Book Happened:
Shortly before (or after) Nehemiah's governorship, ca. 450 or 420 B.C.
The context of this book is the generation after the prophets Haggai and Zechariah. Persia was the superpower of the ancient Near East. The Jerusalem temple was functioning; there was a Persian governor (1:8); Judah was an unimportant backwater. The people had become complacent. Sins that Malachi condemned match some of those that Nehemiah attacked. The priests were corrupt (Mal. 1:6–2:9; Neh. 13:7-8); the tithe was neglected (Mal. 3:8-10; Neh. 10:37-39); Jewish men had married pagan wives (Mal. 2:11-15; Neh. 10:30; 13:23-27).

(See *When the Events of This Book Happened* for *Nehemiah*.) Malachi's ministry may have preceded Nehemiah's arrival in Judah, or perhaps he challenged people who had reverted to their old ways after Nehemiah's time.

How Malachi Fits into God's "Story"

Malachi tells part of "chapter 3" of God's story: God keeps a faithful remnant (Messiah's space and time prepared). As the last book of the Old Testament to be written, Malachi gives a discouraging picture of God's people. When the action opens on the New Testament four centuries later, the picture is still bleak for the people as a whole. Malachi, however, prophesied events that would shake up the Jewish world and begin a new way of thinking about God's kingdom. John the Baptist, the messenger who prepared the way for the Lord (Mal. 3:1; Mark 1:2), came announcing the coming of God's kingdom (Matt. 3:2). Then, also in fulfillment of Malachi, Jesus came as the Messenger of the covenant preaching the kingdom (Mark 1:15). Malachi also looks ahead to the final day, when the Lord will burn up wickedness, but God's people will be set free (Mal. 4:1-3; see also the *Key Text*).

ORIGINAL HISTORICAL SETTING

Author and Date of Writing:
Malachi, perhaps ca. 450 or 420 B.C.
The prophet did not name his parents or the rulers of his day, which makes precise dating of his life impossible. Almost nothing is known about him. He was probably born in the land of Judah after the exiles began returning from Babylon in the 530s. Presumably he wrote down his messages as they were given to him, and they were compiled shortly thereafter.

First Audience and Destination:
Israelites in Judah after the Babylonian exile
The first audience was the people of Judah of the second or third generation after the return from captivity who had become lethargic in their relationship to God.

Occasion

Malachi described his prophecy as "A pronouncement: The word of the Lord to Israel" (1:1). He did not tell about receiving visions or describe the mechanism by which God spoke to him. Malachi had as strong a sense of being God's mouthpiece as any of the prophets who had preceded him, and he often spoke as the voice of God using the pronoun "I." He did not tell what prompted the collection of his writings.

LITERARY FEATURES

Genre and Literary Style:
Disputations and prophecies written in Hebrew prose

As a prophetic writer, Malachi included materials in an unusual format (see *Book Features and Structure,* below), although he included classic elements of "forth telling" and "foretelling." His "forth telling" emphasized the sins of the people caused by their indifference to God. His "foretelling" focused on distant events (such as the coming of John the Baptist and Jesus).

The entire book is written in Hebrew prose. The prophet used a number of vivid metaphors, however. In English Bibles, Malachi is the last of the 12 Minor Prophets. In the Hebrew canon, it belonged to the composite book called "The Twelve." (See *Genre and Literary Style* for *Hosea* for more information.)

Themes:
Lord of hosts, messenger, proper sacrifices, proper marriage, proper giving

Haggai, Zechariah, and Malachi all emphasized God's name as "LORD of Armies." The messenger theme has been noted as the *Key Term.* The specific covenant violations (2:10) had to do with offering unblemished animals in sacrifice, marrying only within the covenant family, and keeping the tithing regulations.

Book Features and Structure

Malachi's most unusual feature was his style of disputation as God's spokesman. He accused the people of doubting God by quoting their own words, sometimes prefaced by "you ask." Examples include the following:

- "Yet you ask 'How have you loved us?'" (1:2)
- "Yet you ask: 'How have we despised your name?'" (1:6).
- "Yet you ask, 'How have we wearied him?'" (2:17).
- "'How do we rob you?' you ask" (3:8).

To these questions (and more) the prophet gave God's answer, but sometimes he answered a question with a question (1:2), adding to the adversarial feel of this book.

The book may be organized into two sections. Chapters 1–2 are God's rebuke on the people's present neglect of God. Chapters 3–4 are God's announcement of the expected Messenger and the coming day of judgment (and blessing).

MATTHEW
THE GOSPEL ACCORDING TO MATTHEW

This title has been associated with the First Gospel as long as it has been known. It was named this because its author was believed to be Matthew, the apostle of Jesus.

⦿ KEY TEXT: 16:16,18

"Simon Peter answered, 'You are the Messiah, the Son of the living God.' Jesus responded, '...And I also say to you that you are Peter, and on this rock I will build my church, and the gates of Hades will not overpower it.'"

⦿ KEY TERM: "MESSIAH"

This book shows Jesus's fulfillment of the Scriptures as the promised Messiah more emphatically than any other Gospel.

⦿ ONE-SENTENCE SUMMARY

In his life, death, and resurrection, Jesus fulfilled the prophecies about the Jewish Messiah and created the church.

Sea of Galilee from the traditional location for the Sermon on the Mount on the northwestern shore of the Sea of Galilee, between Capernaum and Gennesaret

GOD'S MESSAGE IN THE BOOK

Purpose

The original purpose of this Gospel was to provide a written proclamation of the redemption God brought about through Jesus with an emphasis suitable for Jewish Christians: Jesus is the promised Messiah. God's people who read and study Matthew today should view it with this original purpose in mind.

Christian Worldview Elements

Matthew touches on almost every element involved in developing a Christian worldview. In particular, this Gospel develops the categories of *covenant and redemption*; *discipleship*; *ethics and morality*; and *time and eternity*.

> God
> Creation
> Sovereignty and Providence
> Faith and Reason
> Revelation and Authority
> Humanity
> Rebellion and Sin
> ○ **Covenant and Redemption**
> Community and Church
> ○ **Discipleship**
> ○ **Ethics and Morality**
> ○ **Time and Eternity**

Teachings about God

The First Gospel shows God in action, taking the initiative in fulfilling the Scriptures about the coming Messiah.

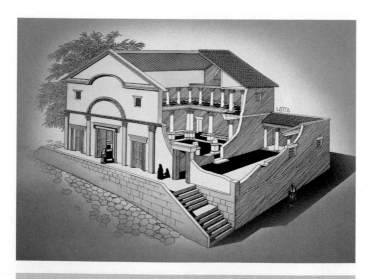

Reconstruction of a typical first-century synagogue

It teaches about the Trinity, and it contributes greatly to the Christian understanding of the deity of Christ. Jesus's constant reference to himself as the Son of Man plays a key role in understanding Jesus's earthly mission.

Teachings about Humanity

The author documented the sinfulness of humans in stark terms: Both Jews and Romans were responsible for Jesus's crucifixion. Yet he also showed that humans committed to following Jesus can accomplish great good. Matthew noted the importance of people putting faith in Jesus; he also showed Jesus's criticism of those with little faith.

Teachings about Salvation

Salvation is presented mainly in terms of belonging to the kingdom of God, which arrived in a fresh way in the person of Jesus (12:28). The death and resurrection of Jesus were the divine means by which God provided salvation. Although Jesus took the message of the kingdom only to Jews during his lifetime, his last act in this Gospel was to commission his followers to go to Gentiles ("all nations") as well (28:18-20).

 ## CHRIST IN MATTHEW

When the wise men came to Jerusalem, they asked, "Where is he who has been born king of the Jews? (2:2). "THIS IS JESUS, THE KING OF THE JEWS" (27:37) was placed in writing above Jesus as he was crucified. Matthew presents Jesus as King and Israel's Messiah. More than any other Gospel writer, he quotes from the Old Testament to make his case.

 ## GOD'S STORY

When the Events of This Book Happened:
During Jesus's earthly life, 6 B.C.–A.D. 30

Matthew's Gospel begins with the announcement of Jesus's coming birth, ca. 6 B.C., and ends with his postresurrection ministry in the spring of A.D. 30. (See *When the Events of This Book Happened* for *Luke* for further details about dates.)

How Matthew Fits into God's "Story"

Matthew tells "chapter 4"—the most important chapter—of God's story: God purchases redemption and begins the kingdom of God through Jesus Christ. Jesus's original hearers had no concept of a Messiah with two comings. One of his great concerns was to explain for his followers that the kingdom was not arriving in a single, one-step manner. Most first-century Jews supposed that the Messiah would usher in the kingdom of God (or "age to come") in an

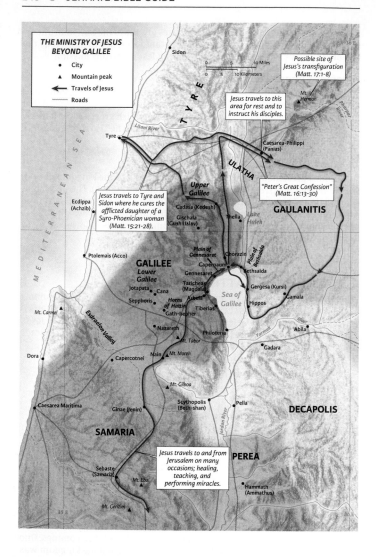

THE MINISTRY OF JESUS
BEYOND GALILEE
● City
▲ Mountain peak
← Travels of Jesus
— Roads

Possible site of
Jesus's transfiguration
(Matt. 17:1-8)

Jesus travels to this
area for rest and to
instruct his disciples.

Jesus travels to Tyre and
Sidon where he cures the
afflicted daughter of a
Syro-Phoenician woman
(Matt. 15:21-28).

"Peter's Great Confession"
(Matt. 16:13-30)

Jesus travels to and from
Jerusalem on many
occasions; healing,
teaching, and
performing miracles.

irresistible, visible, dramatic way on the day of the Lord (Dan. 2). Especially in his parables, Jesus taught that God's kingdom had truly come, but in a resistible, invisible, gradual way. In Matthew, at Jesus's first coming, only a few wise men acknowledged him as king (2:1-12); at his second coming, he will be the King who judges all people (25:31-46).

 ORIGINAL HISTORICAL SETTING

Author and Date of Writing:
Matthew the apostle, perhaps ca. A.D. 55–65
The book is anonymous, but early Christian tradition uniformly affirmed that Matthew composed this Gospel. He was also known as Levi, a tax collector ("publican") whom Jesus called to be an apostle (Matt. 9:9; Mark 2:14). The organization and fondness for numbers in the book point to an author interested in mathematical precision. Many scholars of the past two centuries have denied that Matthew wrote this book, partly because of their belief that the author fabricated many of the details, such as the miracles of Jesus. Such invention is harder to explain if the account was written by an eyewitness to Christ's life. The Christian tradition of authorship by Matthew is surely correct.

Because most scholars believe Matthew used Mark's Gospel as a source, Matthew should be dated in the A.D. 50s or later. Matthew quoted Jesus's prophecy of the coming destruction of the temple (24:2; fulfilled in A.D. 70) without mentioning that it had come to pass as Jesus said. This leads many conservative scholars to conclude that Matthew published his Gospel before 70. Others, however, accept the decade of the 70s. Critical scholars uniformly date Matthew after 70, perhaps near the end of the first century. A typical conservative estimate for its composition is the decade from 55 to 65.

First Audience and Destination:
Jewish Christians, perhaps living in Antioch of Syria
Matthew did not directly mention his audience, but his interest in showing that Jesus fulfilled the Scriptures points to a Jewish-Christian audience. He began his Gospel with a genealogy that recalls the entire history of the Jewish people, also pointing in this direction. This understanding has generally been held throughout Christian history.

Antioch of Syria is a "best-guess" deduction. This major Roman city had a significant number of Greek-speaking Jewish Christians involved in carrying out Jesus's missionary commission (Matt. 28:18-20; Acts 11:19; 13:1-3). Further, the first known quotation from this Gospel was made by Ignatius of Antioch around A.D. 110.

Occasion
Matthew did not explain what prompted him to write. The assessment of many students is that he composed his Gospel largely to help Jewish Christians

interpret Jesus as the fulfillment of the Scriptures. Most scholars believe that the author was prompted by reading Mark's Gospel plus a (now lost) record of Jesus's teachings (sometimes called "Q"). There is much to commend the view that Matthew interwove Mark, "Q," his own research, and eyewitness memories into his own careful account.

LITERARY FEATURES

Genre and Literary Style:
A Gospel composed in ordinary Greek

The question, what, exactly, are the Gospels in comparison to other literary genres? has been discussed at length by scholars. The Gospels are more like biographies than any other ancient literary type. Yet they lack many features common to biography (such as regular attention to place and date), and they omit many years of the central character's life. The best suggestion is that the

Heel bone and nail from the ossuary of "Yehonahan, son of Hagdol," a victim of crucifixion, Jerusalem, first century A.D.

Gospels are a unique literary genre brought into being by the coming of the unique Son of God to the world. As such, the Gospels may be defined as "kerygmatic history." The Greek term *kerygma* meant "proclamation," a reminder that the Gospels proclaim the good news about Jesus in written form—just as the apostles orally proclaimed the good news and called people to commitment to Jesus. The term "history" indicates that the author—like every historian—selected and arranged his material to suit his own purposes.

Matthew wrote in the ordinary (*Koinē*) Greek spoken throughout the Roman world of the first century. His style is both more concise and more polished than Mark. It is less sophisticated in vocabulary and precision than Luke. Christian tradition records that Matthew composed material in Hebrew or Aramaic, but the present Gospel bears no marks of being a translated document.

Themes:
Jesus as Messiah, the kingdom of God, the church, prophecy
Matthew focuses on Jesus as the Messiah (Christ), the Anointed One. He penned the term "kingdom" more than 50 times, usually in the phrase "kingdom of heaven" or "kingdom of God." Of the four Gospels, only Matthew mentions the "church" (16:18; 18:17). The Olivet Discourse (chaps. 24–25) is the most extensive prophetic portion found in any New Testament book except Revelation.

Book Features and Structure
Matthew loved to quote Scripture, particularly with reference to how the birth and death of Jesus fulfilled prophecy. He is also well known for presenting the teachings of Jesus in five major discourses. Matthew signaled the end of every discourse with words such as "when Jesus had finished saying these things" (see 7:28; 11:1; 13:53; 19:1; 26:1).

Matthew noted a transition to a new aspect of Jesus's ministry by using the words, "from then on Jesus began to" (4:17; 16:21). This observation may be used to organize this Gospel into three sections: (1) introduction to the Messiah (1:1–4:16); (2) development of the Messiah's ministry (4:17–16:20); and (3) completion of the Messiah's ministry (16:21–28:20).

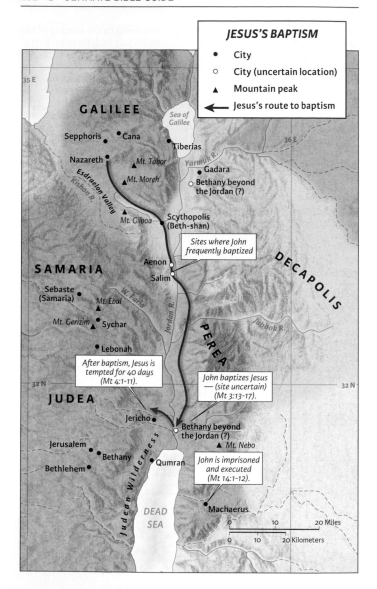

JESUS'S BAPTISM

- ● City
- ○ City (uncertain location)
- ▲ Mountain peak
- ← Jesus's route to baptism

GALILEE

Sea of Galilee

Sepphoris ● ●Cana

●Tiberias

Nazareth ● ▲*Mt. Tabor*

Esdraelon Valley

▲*Mt. Moreh*

Kishon R.

●Gadara

○Bethany beyond the Jordan (?)

Yarmuk R.

▲*Mt. Gilboa* Scythopolis (Beth-shan)

Sites where John frequently baptized

DECAPOLIS

SAMARIA

Aenon ○

Salim ○

Sebaste (Samaria) ●

▲*Mt. Ebal*

W. Faria

Mt. Gerizim ▲ ●Sychar

Jordan R.

PEREA

Jabbok R.

●Lebonah

After baptism, Jesus is tempted for 40 days (Mt 4:1-11).

John baptizes Jesus — (site uncertain) (Mt 3:13-17).

JUDEA

Jericho ●

Jerusalem ● ●Bethany

Bethany beyond the Jordan (?) ○

▲*Mt. Nebo*

Bethlehem ●

Qumran ●

John is imprisoned and executed (Mt 14:1-12).

Judean Wilderness

DEAD SEA

●Machaerus

| 0 | 10 | 20 Miles |

| 0 | 10 | 20 Kilometers |

MARK
THE GOSPEL ACCORDING TO MARK

This title has been associated with the Second Gospel as long as it has been known. It was named this because its author was believed to be (John) Mark, the first-century Christian associated especially with Peter and Paul.

⊙ KEY TEXT: 10:45

"For even the Son of Man did not come to be served, but to serve, and to give his life as a ransom for many."

⊙ KEY TERM: "SERVANT"

Omitting Jesus's birth and reporting relatively few of his teachings, this Gospel emphasizes Jesus's deeds as One who actively served the needs of people.

⊙ ONE-SENTENCE SUMMARY

In his life, death, and resurrection, Jesus did the deeds of the (suffering) Servant of the Lord, notably through his death as a "ransom for many."

"Very early in the morning, while it was still dark, he got up, went out, and made his way to a deserted place; and there he was praying" (1:35).

GOD'S MESSAGE IN THE BOOK

Purpose

The main purpose of this Gospel was to provide a written proclamation of the redemption brought about through Jesus with an emphasis suitable for Gentile Christians: Jesus is the perfect Servant of the Lord. God's people who read and study Mark today should view it with its original purpose in mind.

Christian Worldview Elements

Mark deals particularly with the worldview categories of *covenant and redemption* and *discipleship*. The death of Jesus to save sinners is the event to which the entire Gospel drives. Further, the original disciples of Jesus—often slow to learn, yet transformed by Jesus—can be seen as modeling for all generations what following Jesus really means.

God
Creation
Sovereignty and Providence
Faith and Reason
Revelation and Authority
Humanity
Rebellion and Sin
o **Covenant and Redemption**
Community and Church
o **Discipleship**
Ethics and Morality
Time and Eternity

Teachings about God

Jesus emphasized God as "your Father" in this Gospel. He is also the Father of Jesus, and from his opening words Mark declared Jesus to be "the Son of God." The Holy Spirit is present, empowering Jesus's ministry and mission. This is seen especially in his triumph over every unholy spirit.

Teachings about Humanity

Jesus encountered both the sick and the sinful in this Gospel. He healed the sick and forgave the sinful. Multitudes (at the feeding of the 5,000 and the triumphal entry) and small groups (the apostles) were transformed by Jesus. Yet other large crowds (at Jesus's trial and crucifixion) and small groups (Jewish religious leaders) utterly rejected him. Mark emphasized that humans could not remain neutral about Jesus. They had to decide either for him or against him.

Teachings about Salvation

A higher percentage of this book is given over to the events of Jesus's suffering and death than any other Bible book. By quoting the three times that Jesus predicted his death, Mark emphasized the necessity of the cross, that he must die (8:31; 9:31; 10:33). At the Last Supper, Jesus explained his death was as a substitute: "for many" (14:24).

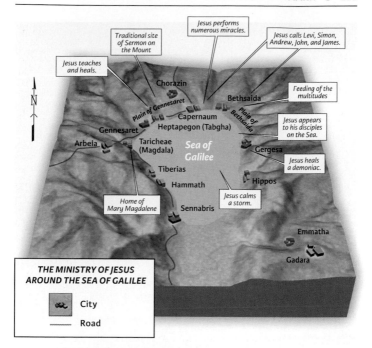

THE MINISTRY OF JESUS AROUND THE SEA OF GALILEE

City

Road

✝ CHRIST IN MARK

Mark's presentation of Jesus is action packed and fast paced. He emphasizes Jesus's mighty acts and his role as Suffering Servant who calls followers to take up their own cross and follow him.

🕊 GOD'S STORY

When the Events of This Book Happened:
Jesus's earthly ministry, A.D. 26–30

Mark began his account with the preaching of John the Baptist, who came on the scene probably in the year 26. The crucifixion and resurrection occurred in the spring of A.D. 30. (See *When the Events of This Book Happened* for *Luke*.)

How Mark Fits into God's "Story"

Mark tells "chapter 4"—the most important chapter—of God's story: God purchases redemption and begins the kingdom of God through Jesus Christ.

Healing of the Blind Man by A.N. Mironov (Mark 8:22-26)

As with all the Gospels, Mark prominently featured the kingdom of God in the teachings of Jesus. (See *How Matthew Fits into God's Story*.)

ORIGINAL HISTORICAL SETTING

Author and Date of Writing:
John Mark, perhaps ca. A.D. 50–60

The book is anonymous, but early Christian tradition uniformly asserted that Mark composed this Gospel in conjunction with Peter's memories. Mark was a secondary figure in Acts. Mark became infamous for deserting Paul and Barnabas on their first missionary journey (Acts 12:25; 13:5; 15:37-39). He later did mission work with Barnabas and eventually won his way back into Paul's good graces (Col. 4:10; 2 Tim. 4:11). At the time Peter wrote his first letter, perhaps a few years after Mark wrote his Gospel, the aged apostle called Mark "my son" (1 Pet. 5:13). Most critical scholars deny that Mark was the author or that he wrote on the basis of Peter's recollections, but there are a number of incidental details in the book that support this conclusion. In particular, Bible students have noted that Mark's outline is identical to the outline that Peter used in his preaching (Acts 3:13-15; 10:36-41).

During the past two centuries, a general, but not universal, consensus has emerged (among all kinds of scholars, both critical and conservative, Protestant and Roman Catholic) that Mark was the first canonical Gospel written. The reasons focus on Mark's more elementary chronology and style of writing as compared to the other Gospels. In any event, most conservative scholars conclude that Mark published his Gospel before A.D. 70, prior to the temple's

Roman denarius (Mark 12:15) bore the image of Tiberius Caesar who reigned A.D. 14–37.

destruction (Mark 13:2). A good estimate for its composition is the decade from 50 to 60, when both Peter and Mark were still alive and certainly had opportunities for collaboration on this project.

First Audience and Destination:
Probably Gentile Christians living around Rome

The original hearers and destination are not stated but are believed from tradition. Irenaeus and Clement of Alexandria (both late second century) each identified Rome as the place of origin. A number of details in the Gospel support this conclusion, such as the quick, business-like pace with which Jesus is presented, heightened by Mark's frequent use of "immediately." Several terms with Latin origins also point in this direction.

Occasion

Scholars have long debated the human factors that prompted the composition of this Gospel. Frankly this is all a matter of conjecture. Some have suggested that the impetus was the growing realization that Jesus's return might be in the distant future. Until then, his followers had a need for a written account of the life of their Master. Since Peter was an eyewitness to almost everything recorded in this Gospel, his memories provided Mark with an outstanding historical basis for writing. Another suggestion is that this Gospel was written for Christians facing persecution, perhaps the Roman persecution

"Then they came to a place named Gethsemane, and he told his disciples, 'Sit here while I pray'"(Mark 14:32).

instigated by Emperor Nero in A.D. 64. The Christians would thus be encouraged. Since their Master had faced the injustice of religious and political authorities victoriously, they too could triumph no matter what they had to suffer.

 LITERARY FEATURES

Genre and Literary Style:
A Gospel composed in ordinary Greek
See *Genre and Literary Style* for *Matthew* for information about what a "Gospel" is. Assuming Mark was the first to compose a Gospel, he may be credited as the one who innovated this genre. Mark wrote in ordinary (*Koinē*) Greek, in a style characterized by frequent use of the present tense to describe the action. His vigorous, vivid vocabulary is generally wordier than Matthew or Luke (when these Gospels are parallel). The style is consistent with someone who is writing down the memories of another as they are recounted to him.

Themes:
Jesus as Servant, the kingdom of God, Jesus's suffering and death, Galilee
The first three of these are so evident as not to require comment. Interestingly, Mark centered his account of the ministry of Jesus entirely in Galilee, with the exception of his suffering and death (see 1:14; 16:7).

Book Features and Structure
One of the most striking features of this Gospel is the "Messianic Secret." This refers to the times that Jesus asked his disciples or someone for whom he had worked a miracle to keep the secret about his identity or what he had done (1:34,44; 3:12; 5:43; 7:36-37; 8:26,30; 9:9). These reflect Jesus's desire to accomplish his primary mission of dying for sin, which could have been hindered by people who wanted him to behave as a political deliverer (the Messiah-King) or as a miracle worker. (Critical scholars view this feature as a fictional device by Mark to "explain" why Jesus was not acknowledged as the Messiah during his earthly ministry.)

Another feature that should be mentioned briefly is the manuscript history of the last 12 verses of this Gospel (16:9-20). Because the earliest and best handwritten copies of Mark omit these verses, some contemporary interpreters (and translations) have concluded that they are a later addition to the Gospel.

The *Key Text* (10:45) provides a useful organizational basis for this Gospel. The first section, "Jesus the Servant," shows Jesus in action through the occasion of Peter's confession (8:30). The second section, "Jesus the Ransom," begins in 8:31 with Jesus's prediction of his crucifixion and goes to the end of the book.

The Annunciation by Carl Heinrich Bloch

THE GOSPEL ACCORDING TO LUKE

This title has been associated with the Third Gospel as long as it has been known. Its author was believed to be Luke, the first-century Christian physician who was a traveling companion of Paul.

○ KEY TEXT: 19:10
"For the Son of Man has come to seek and to save the lost."

○ KEY TERM: "SAVIOR"
The saving activity of Jesus, both in his ministry and in his death, is the focus of this book. Because his mission was to save others, he did not save himself (23:35).

○ ONE-SENTENCE SUMMARY
Jesus not only lived and ministered as the perfect human, but he also died and rose to new life as the Savior for sinners.

 GOD'S MESSAGE IN THE BOOK

Purpose
The author explicitly stated his purpose in the preface (1:1-4). He wrote his Gospel to provide an orderly account of the beginnings of Christianity so that the reader will have reliable information about Jesus Christ. Every fair understanding of this Gospel accepts this as a beginning point for understanding.

Christian Worldview Elements
Luke focuses attention on a number of worldview elements. In particular, he focuses on *humanity*; *covenant and redemption*; and *ethics and morality*. Luke's special ability to portray individuals vividly with a few words and his unique presentation of Jesus's teachings contribute to these emphases.

God
Creation
Sovereignty and Providence
Faith and Reason
Revelation and Authority
○ **Humanity**
Rebellion and Sin
○ **Covenant and Redemption**
Community and Church
Discipleship
○ **Ethics and Morality**
Time and Eternity

✝ CHRIST IN LUKE
Luke writes primarily for Gentiles and focuses on Jesus as offering salvation to Jew and Gentile alike. Luke shows Jesus's compassion for the poor and the oppressed.

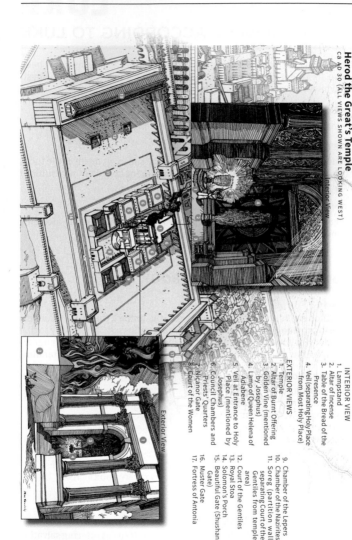

Herod the Great's Temple
CA AD 30 (ALL VIEWS SHOWN ARE LOOKING WEST)

Interior View

Exterior View

INTERIOR VIEW
1. Lampstand
2. Altar of Incense
3. Table of the Bread of the Presence
4. Veil (separating Holy Place from Most Holy Place)

EXTERIOR VIEWS
1. Temple
2. Altar of Burnt Offering
3. Golden Vine (mentioned by Josephus)
4. Lamp of Queen Helena of Adiabene
5. Veil at Entrance to Holy Place (mentioned by Josephus)
6. Council Chambers and Priests' Quarters
7. Nicanor Gate
8. Court of the Women

9. Chamber of the Lepers
10. Chamber of the Nazirites
11. Soreg (partition wall separating Court of the Gentiles from temple area)
12. Court of the Gentiles
13. Royal Stoa
14. Solomon's Porch
15. Beautiful Gate (Shushan Gate)
16. Muster Gate
17. Fortress of Antonia

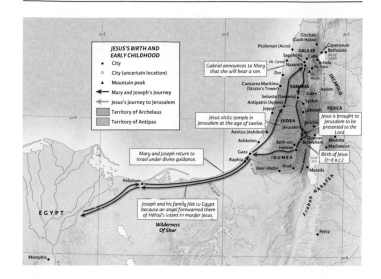

*JESUS'S BIRTH AND
EARLY CHILDHOOD*

• City
○ City (uncertain location)
▲ Mountain peak
◀— Mary and Joseph's journey
◀— Jesus's journey to Jerusalem
▓ Territory of Archelaus
▓ Territory of Antipas

Gabriel announces to Mary
that she will bear a son.

Jesus visits temple in
Jerusalem at the age of twelve.

Mary and Joseph return to
Israel under divine guidance.

Jesus is brought to
Jerusalem to be
presented to the
Lord.

Birth of Jesus
(7–6 B.C.)

Joseph and his family flee to Egypt
because an angel forewarned them
of Herod's intent to murder Jesus.

GOD'S STORY

When the Events of This Book Happened:
During Jesus's earthly life, 7 B.C.–A.D. 30

Luke's Gospel begins earlier than either Matthew or Mark, with the announcement of John's birth, around 7 B.C. It ends with his ascent to heaven in the spring of A.D. 30. Jesus was born before Herod the Great died in 4 B.C., possibly two or three years earlier. The probable year of Jesus's birth is 6 B.C.

The years 30 and 33 are the only years when Pontius Pilate governed Judea that Passover fell on a Friday. So discussion of the year of Jesus's crucifixion centers on these two years. John's ministry began in "the fifteenth year of the reign of Tiberius Caesar" (3:1). This probably refers to the fifteenth year after beginning his authority over the provinces (A.D. 11), giving a date of A.D. 25–26 for the beginning of John's ministry. Jesus's ministry from baptism to crucifixion probably lasted about three-and-a-half years. (See *When the Events of This Book Happened* for *John*.) If so, he was baptized late in A.D. 26 (when he was age 32; see Luke 3:23), and he was crucified on Passover of A.D. 30 (Friday, April 7, in modern calendar notation).

How Luke Fits into God's "Story"

Luke tells "chapter 4"—the most important chapter—of God's story: God purchases redemption and begins the kingdom of God through Jesus Christ. (See *How Matthew Fits into God's Story.*)

Simeon in the Temple by Rembrandt Harmenszoon van Rijn (Luke 2:25-35)

Jesus to Simon the Pharisee: "'Therefore I tell you, her many sins have been forgiven; that's why she loved much. But the one who is forgiven little, loves little.' Then he said to her, 'Your sins are forgiven'" (Luke 7:47-48). *Christ and the Sinner* by Andrei Mironov.

Teachings about God

In this Gospel, God initiates everything concerning salvation. The glory of God is especially emphasized, from the song of the angels (2:14) to the triumphal entry (19:38). Equally important is the glory of Jesus himself, from the transfiguration (9:32) to his resurrection splendor (24:26). Jesus is, of course, the virgin-born Son of God in this book. The Spirit is active from Jesus's conception to the great power of his ministry (1:35; 4:14). The Spirit is also the gift Jesus promised to his followers (11:13).

Teachings about Humanity

This Gospel focuses on humanity in two ways. First, Jesus is the ideal or perfect Human. Luke shows what a Spirit-filled person, wholly obedient to God, is like. (Note the centurion's confession at Jesus's death: "This man really was righteous!"; 23:47.) Second, Luke painted a vivid portrait of a number of individuals Jesus impacted, showing the value of each human life.

Teachings about Salvation

The turning point in this Gospel is 9:51, when "he determined to journey to Jerusalem"—the proper place for Jesus to offer himself as a sacrifice. In his own words, "Wasn't it necessary for the Messiah to suffer these things and enter into his glory?" (24:26). On the night he was betrayed, he taught his disciples that his death was a substitute and that it brought about the new covenant (see Jer. 31:31-34).

ORIGINAL HISTORICAL SETTING

Author and Date of Writing:
Luke, perhaps ca. A.D. 60–61

The book is anonymous, but early Christian tradition uniformly affirmed that Luke composed this Gospel as well as Acts. (See *Author and Date of Writing* for *Acts* for reasons supporting Luke's authorship of Acts.) The dedications to Theophilus, the similar Greek style and vocabulary, and special shared emphases of the books (such as prayer and joy) all point to common authorship.

Luke was a secondary figure in the book of Acts, known not by name but by his use of the pronouns "we" and "us" when he was present to the actions he was describing. Paul named him three times in his letters (Col. 4:14; 2 Tim. 4:11; Phlm. 24). He was a Gentile, a medical doctor, and a loyal supporter of Paul. His home city and the nature of his conversion are unknown. Most critical scholars believe that the author of the Third Gospel and Acts was someone other than the Luke of Paul's letters or the "we" of Acts.

The date of Luke must be after Mark (which Luke almost certainly used as a source) but before Acts, which was perhaps published ca. 61–62. If Luke researched his Gospel while Paul was imprisoned in Caesarea, then perhaps he wrote and published from Caesarea (ca. A.D. 59) or possibly after he arrived in Rome with Paul after the famous shipwreck (ca. A.D. 61). Other scholars have argued that Luke, like all the Gospels, must be dated later, from the A.D. 70s or 80s.

First Audience and Destination:
Theophilus, a Gentile whose residence is unknown

Luke explicitly dedicated this Gospel to Theophilus ("God's friend"), whom he called "most honorable." Mentioned only in the prefaces to Luke and Acts, he appears to have been a Gentile of high social status who had been "instructed" in Christianity but wanted more detailed information about Jesus. Theophilus may have provided financial patronage for Luke, underwriting his research expenses.

Occasion

The needs of Theophilus provided the immediate prompting for Luke's writing. Already "many" had written of Jesus's life, and in his preface Luke said that he used sources, including eyewitnesses. Luke possibly used the two years Paul was imprisoned in Caesarea (Acts 24:26-27; 27:1) to research the Gospel. He had access to any number of witnesses to Jesus's life, possibly including Jesus's mother (2:19,51). Most scholars believe that he was also aided by reading Mark's Gospel plus a (now lost) record of Jesus's teachings (sometimes called "Q"). There is much to commend the view that Luke interwove Mark, "Q," and his own research findings into his own careful account.

LITERARY FEATURES

Genre and Literary Style:

A Gospel composed in outstanding Koinē *Greek*

See *Genre and Literary Style* for *Matthew* for information about what a "Gospel" is. Luke was the most versatile of all the Gospel writers. The preface is classical Greek, and the rest of chapters 1–2 resembles a Hebrew style. The body of the Gospel is in excellent *Koinē* Greek. Luke's large vocabulary and careful style mark him as an educated "man of letters." Luke was more self-conscious that he was writing "a history" than the other Gospel writers, as shown by his attention to dating certain events.

Themes:

Jesus as Savior, universal good news, the poor and outcast, prayer, joy

Luke's portrait of Jesus concentrates on him as the Savior. As such, his birth brought good news to all people, and at his ascension he commissioned his followers to go to all the nations. Luke drew a particularly sympathetic portrait of those on the fringes of society whom Jesus changed: a leper, a sinful woman, Zacchaeus, a widow with only two mites. This Gospel shows Jesus at prayer more than the other Gospels, and it clearly demonstrates the joy that Jesus brought to people.

Calvary by John Martin. "Then [one of the criminals] said, 'Jesus, remember me when you come into your kingdom.' And he said to him, 'Truly I tell you, today you will be with me in paradise'" (Luke 23:42-43).

Book Features and Structure

This is the longest and most inclusive of the Gospels. Luke is known for a number of striking literary features. In the first two chapters, he reported four wonderful poems (often set to music). In the middle section, he included a number of Jesus's parables found nowhere else (in particular, the prodigal son and the good Samaritan). At the end of his narrative, he reported resurrection appearances found in no other Gospel.

Luke's emphasis on Jerusalem may serve as a structural guideline. First, Jesus's childhood and early ministry (1:1–9:50); second, Jesus's journey toward Jerusalem (9:51–19:27); third, Jesus's ministry and passion in Jerusalem (19:28–24:53).

Landscape with Christ and His Disciples on the Road to Emmaus by Jan Wildens. "He said to them, 'How foolish and slow you are to believe all that the prophets have spoken! Wasn't it necessary for the Messiah to suffer these things and enter into his glory?' Then beginning with Moses and all the Prophets, he interpreted for them the things concerning himself in all the Scriptures" (Luke 24:25-27).

JOHN
THE GOSPEL ACCORDING TO JOHN

This title has been associated with the Fourth Gospel as long as it has been known. It was named this because its author was believed to be John, the apostle of Jesus.

○ KEY TEXT: 3:16

"For God loved the world in this way: He gave his one and only Son, so that everyone who believes in him will not perish but have eternal life."

○ KEY TERM: "LORD"

From the opening prologue to the end of the Gospel, Jesus is portrayed as Lord and God, with a proportionately greater emphasis on his deity than in the other Gospels.

○ ONE-SENTENCE SUMMARY

Jesus is the sign-working Son of God who gives eternal life on the basis of his death and resurrection to all who believe in him.

Marriage at Cana by Johann Georg Platzer, (John 2:1-12)

GOD'S MESSAGE IN THE BOOK

Purpose

The author explicitly states his purpose near the end of his book (20:30-31). He wrote his Gospel to provide an account of Jesus's life and the signs he performed so that people will believe in him and experience eternal life. Because the verb "believe" may be translated "continue to believe," his purpose no doubt included building up Jesus's followers as well as converting unbelievers.

Christian Worldview Elements

John deals particularly with the worldview categories of *covenant and redemption*, *discipleship*, and *time and eternity*. Jesus's death as an "appointment with destiny" is especially emphasized. The importance of believing in Jesus in order to be his disciple and to receive eternal life is pronounced.

God
Creation
Sovereignty and Providence
Faith and Reason
Revelation and Authority
Humanity
Rebellion and Sin
○ **Covenant and Redemption**
Community and Church
○ **Discipleship**
Ethics and Morality
○ **Time and Eternity**

Teachings about God

John emphasized the sovereignty and the love of God in sending Jesus. Jesus perfectly reveals God (1:18). In particular, Jesus's astounding proclamations that begin with "I am" are remarkable claims about both his person and work. Jesus's teaching on the Spirit (the "Counselor") is more extensive than in any other Gospel (chaps. 14–16). This Gospel especially reveals the glory and the name of the Father and the Son.

Teachings about Humanity

Humans are sinners in need of a Savior. They are unable to do anything toward their salvation but are wholly dependent on God's initiative through Jesus. Many individuals demonstrate this: Nicodemus, the Samaritan woman, the man born blind.

Teachings about Salvation

This Gospel, more than the others, emphasizes strongly a personal relationship with Jesus that's built on faith in him and his sacrificial death. Faith in Jesus is salvation and eternal life. One such text is 10:27-28: "My sheep hear my voice, I know them, and they follow me. I give them eternal life, and they will never perish. No one will snatch them out of my hand." John balances between God's sovereign election of some for eternal life (6:44) and the invitation to "everyone who believes" (3:16).

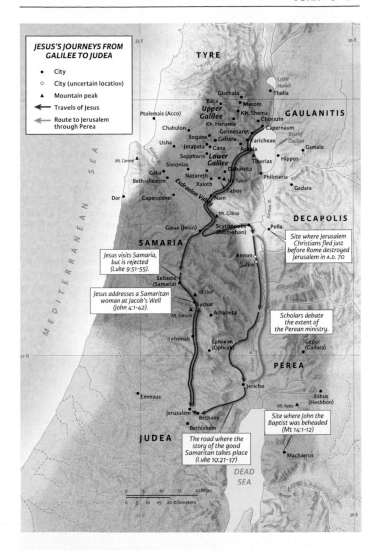

JESUS'S JOURNEYS FROM GALILEE TO JUDEA

- • City
- ○ City (uncertain location)
- ▲ Mountain peak
- ← Travels of Jesus
- ← Route to Jerusalem through Perea

TYRE

Lake Huleh

Thella

Gischala

Baca   Merom

Upper Galilee   Kh. Shema

Ptolemais (Acco)   Chorazin   GAULANITIS

Chabulon   Kh. Hanania   Capernaum

Gennesaret

Usha   Sogane   Gabara   Sea of Galilee

Jotapata   Cana   Taricheae   Gamala

Sepphoris   Arbela

Simonias   **Lower Galilee**   Tiberias   Hippos

Mt. Carmel   Geba   Nazareth   Dabaritta   Philoteria

Beth-shearim   Xaloth   Mt. Tabor   Gadara

Dor   Capercotnei   Nain   DECAPOLIS

Esdraelon Valley

Mt. Gilboa   Pella

Ginae (Jenin)   Scythopolis (Beth-shan)

Site where Jerusalem Christians fled just before Rome destroyed Jerusalem in A.D. 70

SAMARIA

Aenon

Jesus visits Samaria, but is rejected (Luke 9:51-55).   Salim

Sebaste (Samaria)

Jesus addresses a Samaritan woman at Jacob's Well (John 4:1-42).   Mt. Ebal

Sychar

Mt. Gerizim   Acrabeta

Scholars debate the extent of the Perean ministry.

Lebonah

Ephraim (Ophrah)   Gedor (Gadara)

PEREA

Jericho

Emmaus   Esbus (Heshbon)

Mt. Nebo

Jerusalem   Bethany   *Site where John the Baptist was beheaded (Mt 14:1-12).*

Bethlehem

JUDEA   *The road where the story of the good Samaritan takes place (Luke 10:21-37).*

Machaerus

DEAD SEA

0   5   10   15   20 Miles

0   5   10   15   20 Kilometers

MEDITERRANEAN SEA

☉ CHRIST IN JOHN

In John, Jesus is the Logos, the Word of God who was with God and was God. Jesus is God in flesh. Jesus's deity is further amplified in his seven "I am" sayings (I am the bread of life; the light of the world; the gate for the sheep; the good shepherd; the resurrection and the life; the way, the truth, and the life; the true vine).

GOD'S STORY

When the Events of This Book Happened:
During Jesus's earthly ministry, A.D. 26–30

Although the prologue goes back to "in the beginning," the narrative of Jesus's life begins with John the Baptist's recognition of Jesus as the Lamb of God and concludes with Jesus's post-resurrection reinstatement of Peter by the Sea of Tiberias (Galilee). (See *When the Events of This Book Happened* for *Luke* for more information on the dates for Jesus's birth and crucifixion.)

John's Gospel helps determine the development of Jesus's ministry (from his baptism to his death) by describing Jesus's trips to Jerusalem to participate in various Jewish festivals. The probable date for these is as follows:

2:13—Passover of the first temple cleansing	Spring A.D. 27
5:1—Passover of the healing by the pool	Spring A.D. 28
6:4—Passover just before the feeding of 5,000	Spring A.D. 29
12:1,12—Passover of the triumphal entry	Spring A.D. 30

The Resurrection of Lazarus by Andrei Mironov (John 11).

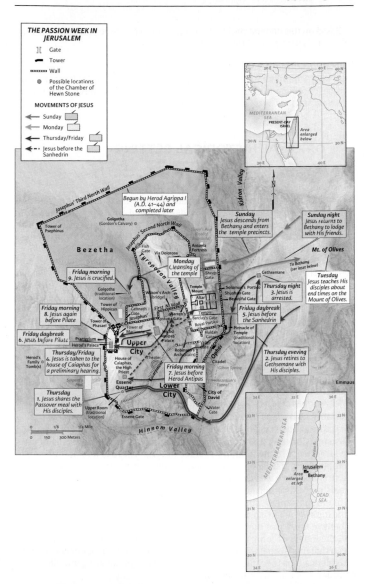

THE PASSION WEEK IN JERUSALEM

Gate
Tower
Wall
Possible locations of the Chamber of Hewn Stone

MOVEMENTS OF JESUS

Sunday
Monday
Thursday/Friday
Jesus before the Sanhedrin

Begun by Herod Agrippa I (A.D. 41–44) and completed later

Josephus' Third North Wall

Tower of Psephinus

Bezetha

Golgotha (Gordon's Calvary)

Josephus' Second North Wall

Sunday
Jesus descends from Bethany and enters the temple precincts.

Sunday night
Jesus returns to Bethany to lodge with His friends.

Tyropoeon Valley

Fish Gate

Via Dolorosa

Antonia Fortress

Kidron Valley

Mt. of Olives
(see inset below)

To Bethany

Monday
Cleansing of the temple

Gethsemane

Tuesday
Jesus teaches His disciples about end times on the Mount of Olives.

Golgotha (traditional location)

Wilson's Arch (bridge)

Tower of Hippicus

Gennath Gate

Tower of Phasael

Tower of Mariamne

Josephus' First N. Wall

Kystus Gate

Herod Antipas' Palace

Warren's Gate

Barclay's Gate

Temple Mount

Altar

Temple

Royal Portico

Solomon's Portico

Shushan Gate

Beautiful Gate

Sheep Gate

Thursday night
3. Jesus is arrested.

Friday daybreak
5. Jesus before the Sanhedrin

Friday morning
9. Jesus is crucified.

Friday morning
8. Jesus again before Pilate

Friday daybreak
6. Jesus before Pilate

Praetorium

Herod's Palace

Herod's Family Tomb(s)

Thursday/Friday
4. Jesus is taken to the house of Caiaphas for a preliminary hearing.

Upper City

House of Caiaphas, the High Priest

Theater

Robinson's Arch (stairs)

Huldah Gates

Pinnacle of Temple (traditional location)

Thursday evening
2. Jesus retires to Gethsemane with His disciples.

Ophel

Citadel

Gihon Spring

Essene Quarter

Lower City

Friday morning
7. Jesus before Herod Antipas

City of David

Hezekiah's Tunnel

Emmaus

Serpent's Pool

Thursday
1. Jesus shares the Passover meal with His disciples.

Upper Room (traditional location)

Essene Gate

Water Gate

Siloam

Hinnom Valley

0   1/8   1/4 Mile
0   150   300 Meters

MEDITERRANEAN SEA

PRESENT-DAY ISRAEL

Area enlarged below

MEDITERRANEAN SEA

Jerusalem
Bethany

Area enlarged at left

DEAD SEA

Jordan R.

Based on this understanding, Jesus ministered for three years plus the time between his baptism and the first temple cleansing.

How John Fits into God's "Story"

John tells "chapter 4"—the most important chapter—of God's story: God purchases redemption and begins the kingdom of God through Jesus Christ. (See *How Matthew Fits into God's Story*.)

 ## ORIGINAL HISTORICAL SETTING

Author and Date of Writing:
John the apostle, possibly ca. A.D. 80–90

As with all the Gospels, the book is anonymous. Early Christian tradition uniformly affirmed that John composed this Gospel. He was a fisherman from Galilee, son of Zebedee and brother of James, whom Jesus called to be an apostle (Mark 1:19; 3:17). According to Acts, John and Peter were the prominent leaders of early Christianity.

Many scholars of the past two centuries have denied that John wrote this book, partly because of their belief that the author fabricated many details, such as the miracles and the discourses of Jesus. Such invention is harder to explain if the account was written by an eyewitness of Jesus's life. The author, however, claimed to be an eyewitness (21:24) and referred to himself in the third person as "the disciple Jesus loved" (13:23; 19:26; 20:2; 21:7,20). The tradition of authorship by John is undoubtedly correct.

This Gospel was the last to be written, for it assumes knowledge of many events in Jesus's ministry (which are omitted). On the other hand, it offers much new material. The decade of the A.D. 80s is a good estimate for the composition of this Gospel.

First Audience and Destination:
Probably Christians living in Roman Asia

This issue has been vigorously debated by scholars. According to strong and consistent Christian tradition John lived a long life and ministered in Ephesus, the largest city in the Roman province of Asia. There is no good reason to doubt this original destination. Scholars, however, are divided as to whether the first audience was Greek, Jewish, or simply Christian. Those who see a Greek (non-Christian) audience note, among other things, that John began with emphasizing Jesus as the Logos, the "Word," a concept from Greek philosophy. The Jewish audience view emphasizes that John wanted people to believe Jesus was the Messiah (20:31). The similarities between this book and the letters of John, which were clearly written for believers, probably mean that this Gospel was first intended for the benefit of believers. In God's providence, it has become remarkably effective in persuading unbelievers to embrace Jesus as Lord and Savior.

What Is Truth? Christ Before Pilate by Nikolai Ge (John 18:38)

Occasion

John did not relate the human factors that led him to write. It appears evident, however, that he wanted to give a fuller account of some aspects of Jesus's ministry than the other Gospels related. This may have been prompted by John's advancing age and awareness that he had a unique perspective on Jesus's life to preserve.

 ## LITERARY FEATURES

Genre and Literary Style:

A Gospel composed in simple but elegant Koinē *Greek*

See *Genre and Literary Style* for *Matthew* for information about what a "Gospel" is. John wrote with a limited vocabulary, joining his sentences with "and." His style lent itself to developing a number of contrasting concepts: love versus hate; light versus dark; life versus death; truth versus falsehood; above versus below.

Themes:

Jesus as Lord and God, Jesus's signs, Jesus's "I am" teachings, Jesus's "hour"

John's emphases on Jesus's lordship and deity have already been noted. Yet this Gospel related far fewer of Jesus's miracles than did the others. John selected a limited number because of their sign value in pointing to Jesus's true identity. The "I am" teachings also point to Jesus's identity, in particular because of their connection with the earlier revelation of God as "I AM" (Exod. 3:14). In this Gospel, Jesus calls his appointment with death his "hour" (contrast 2:4; 7:30 with 13:1; 17:1).

Book Features and Structure

John wrote about many incidents missing from the other Gospels. These include a number of miracles (water to wine; the man born blind; Lazarus raised), a number of teachings (the "I am" sayings; the new birth discourse with Nicodemus; the upper room discourse); and other incidents (meeting the Samaritan woman; washing the disciples' feet). John tells nothing of Jesus's birth, baptism, temptation, casting out demons, teaching in parables, or instituting the Lord's Supper.

Another feature that should be mentioned briefly is the manuscript history of John 7:53–8:11 (the adulterous woman story). Because the earliest and best handwritten copies of John omit these verses, some contemporary interpreters (and translations) have concluded that they are a later addition to the Gospel.

The organization of the book is straightforward. The main body is sandwiched between a formal prologue (chap. 1) and epilogue (chap. 21). The first main section focuses on Jesus's signs and his conflicts with "the Jews" (chaps. 2–12). The second section describes Jesus's "glorification" as he is crucified and accomplishes the purpose for which God sent him into the world (chaps. 13–20).

ACTS
THE ACTS OF THE APOSTLES

This title has always been associated with this book. It refers to the deeds Jesus's apostles did in the 30 or so years following his return to heaven.

○ KEY TEXT: 1:8

"But you will receive power when the Holy Spirit has come on you, and you will be my witnesses in Jerusalem, in all Judea and Samaria, and to the end of the earth."

○ KEY TERM: "SPIRIT"

This book records what the apostles and early Christians accomplished as they were empowered by the Holy Spirit. The author understood that none of this would have been possible apart from the Holy Spirit.

○ ONE-SENTENCE SUMMARY

Christianity spread from Jerusalem to Rome and from Jews to Gentiles by the power of the Holy Spirit, working especially through Peter and Paul.

 GOD'S MESSAGE IN THE BOOK

Purpose

The author's purpose was twofold. First, he wrote as a historian, penning "Volume 2" of his two-part work. The first part told what Jesus "began to do and teach" (Acts 1:1); the second part is a selective record of what Jesus continued to do through his Spirit and his apostles. The second part of his purpose was theological. He showed that Christianity and the church had become the legitimate heir of Israel (and of the Scriptures of Israel). This is seen especially in the biblical quotations in the book, for example, in Peter's citation of Joel (Acts 2:16-21); James's quotation of Amos (Acts 15:16-17); and Paul's reference to Isaiah (Acts 28:25-28).

Christian Worldview Elements

Acts offers insight into a number of worldview categories. In particular, the categories of *sovereignty and providence*; *community and church*; and *discipleship* are pushed to the forefront. Without the contribution of Acts there would be little biblical basis for understanding the historical origins of the church as the new people of God.

God
Creation
○ **Sovereignty and Providence**
Faith and Reason
Revelation and Authority
Humanity
Rebellion and Sin
Covenant and Redemption
○ **Community and Church**
○ **Discipleship**
Ethics and Morality
Time and Eternity

Pentecost by Juan Bautista Mayno (Acts 2)

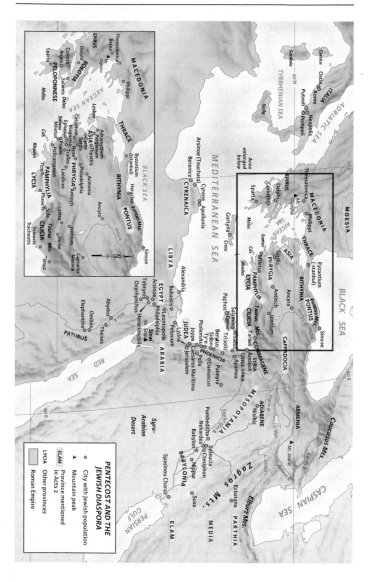

PENTECOST AND THE JEWISH DIASPORA

● City with Jewish population

▲ Mountain peak

ELAM Province mentioned in Acts 2

LYCIA Other provinces
Roman Empire

Teachings about God

The Father is in particular the Sender of the Holy Spirit. The book shows that from the beginning of Christianity Jesus has been the center of proclamation. His life, death, and resurrection were the essence of the good news. Above all, however, this book reveals the Holy Spirit more extensively than any other book. The age of Christianity is the era in which all that believe receive the gift of the Spirit.

Teachings about Humanity

By tracing the spread of Christianity from Jews to Samaritans and then to Gentiles, this book shows that all kinds of people are included in salvation. A Pharisee who persecuted Jesus's followers, an African official, a Roman centurion, and a slave girl in Philippi were all touched by the power of Jesus. On the other hand, some leading authorities (both Jewish and Gentile) rejected the proclamation about Jesus.

Teachings about Salvation

Over and over in this book, the basic Christian message is presented: Jesus fulfilled the prophecies of Scripture by his deeds and life; he was crucified; God raised him; the necessary human response is to repent of sins and believe in him; those who do so receive God's good gift of the Spirit. Salvation in Acts focuses on the Spirit's filling believers so that they live holy lives and do God's will.

 CHRIST IN ACTS

Jesus, triumphant over death, spends 40 days in conversation with his disciples. He then ascends to the Father and sends, 10 days later, the Holy Spirit to indwell and empower believers. Acts is an account of what Jesus continued to do through his church in the wisdom and power of the Holy Spirit.

 GOD'S STORY

When the Events of This Book Happened:
During the church's first decades, A.D. 30–61

The crucifixion and resurrection of Jesus occurred in A.D. 30. (See *When the Events of This Book Happened* for *Luke*.) The last event recorded is Paul's two-year imprisonment in Rome while he was waiting for his case to come before the emperor. This imprisonment occurred ca. 60–61. The approximate year of key events in Acts are as follows: A.D. 33, death of Stephen (chap. 7) and conversion of Saul (chap. 9; A.D. 49, council in Jerusalem concerning circumcision (chap. 15); A.D. 57, Paul's arrest in Jerusalem on a false charge (chaps. 21–22).

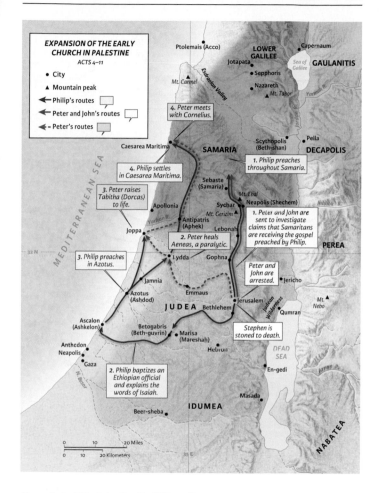

EXPANSION OF THE EARLY CHURCH IN PALESTINE
ACTS 4–11

- City
- ▲ Mountain peak
- ← Philip's routes
- ← Peter and John's routes
- ← - Peter's routes

4. Peter meets with Cornelius.

4. Philip settles in Caesarea Maritima.

3. Peter raises Tabitha (Dorcas) to life.

1. Philip preaches throughout Samaria.

1. Peter and John are sent to investigate claims that Samaritans are receiving the gospel preached by Philip.

2. Peter heals Aeneas, a paralytic.

3. Philip preaches in Azotus.

Peter and John are arrested.

Stephen is stoned to death.

2. Philip baptizes an Ethiopian official and explains the words of Isaiah.

MEDITERRANEAN SEA

LOWER GALILEE — Ptolemais (Acco), Jotapata, Sepphoris, Nazareth, Mt. Tabor, Capernaum, Sea of Galilee, GAULANITIS

Mt. Carmel, Esdraelon Valley

Scythopolis (Beth-shan), Pella, DECAPOLIS

SAMARIA — Caesarea Maritima, Sebaste (Samaria), Mt. Ebal, Mt. Gerizim, Sychar, Neapolis (Shechem), Lebonah, Apollonia, Antipatris (Aphek), Joppa, Lydda, Gophna, Jamnia, Emmaus, Azotus (Ashdod), Bethlehem, Jerusalem, Jericho, PEREA

JUDEA — Ascalon (Ashkelon), Betogabris (Beth-guvrin), Marisa (Mareshah), Hebron, Qumran, Mt. Nebo

Anthedon, Neapolis, Gaza, N. Besor, En-gedi, DEAD SEA

IDUMEA — Beer-sheba, Masada

NABATEA

32 N, 35 E

0   10   20 Miles
0   10   20 Kilometers

How Acts Fits into God's "Story"

Acts begins "chapter 5" of God's story: God spreads the kingdom through the church. It is the exciting record of the spread of God's kingdom during the transition from Israel to the church. The book opens with Jesus's explanation of the kingdom of God (1:3) and closes with Paul's "proclaiming the kingdom of God" (28:31). Peter discharged the responsibility Jesus entrusted to him in giving him the "keys of the kingdom" (Matt. 16:19). He was the human instru-

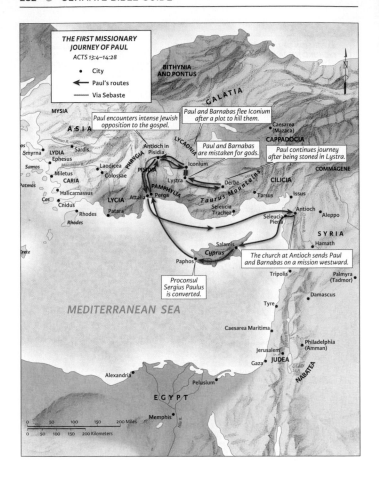

THE FIRST MISSIONARY JOURNEY OF PAUL
ACTS 13:4–14:28

- City
- Paul's routes
- Via Sebaste

Paul encounters intense Jewish opposition to the gospel.

Paul and Barnabas flee Iconium after a plot to kill them.

Paul and Barnabas are mistaken for gods.

Paul continues journey after being stoned in Lystra.

The church at Antioch sends Paul and Barnabas on a mission westward.

Proconsul Sergius Paulus is converted.

ment through whom the Holy Spirit was poured out on three successive ethnic groups: Jews (chap. 2); Samaritans (chap. 8); and Gentiles (chap. 10). The time had come when forgiveness of sins was proclaimed through faith in Jesus, Israel's Messiah, rather than through animal sacrifices and justification through the law of Moses (13:16-40).

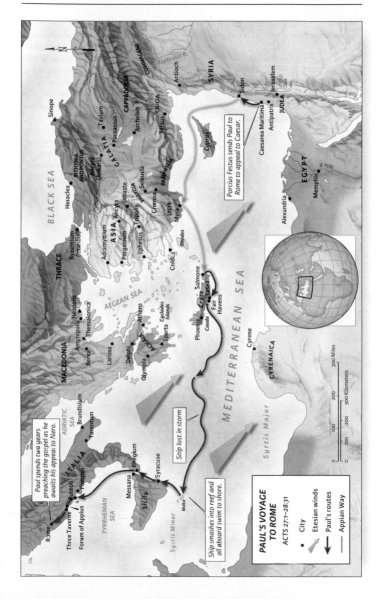

Porcius Festus sends Paul to Rome to appeal to Caesar.

Ship lost in storm.

Ship smashes into reef and all aboard swim to shore.

Paul spends two years preaching the gospel as he awaits his appeal to Nero.

PAUL'S VOYAGE TO ROME
ACTS 27:1–28:31

· City
Etesian winds
Paul's routes
Appian Way

Roman Grain Ship
ACTS 27

[5]After sailing through the open sea off Cilicia and Pamphylia, we reached Myra in Lycia. [6]There the centurion found an Alexandrian ship sailing for Italy and put us on board . . .[37]In all there were 276 of us on the ship. [38]When they had eaten enough, they began to lighten the ship by throwing the grain overboard into the sea . . . [40]After cutting loose the anchors, they left them in the sea, at the same time loosening the ropes that held the rudders. Then they hoisted the foresail to the wind and headed for the beach. [41]But they struck a sandbar and ran the ship aground. The bow jammed fast and remained immovable, while the stern began to break up by the pounding of the waves.

Roman Grain Ship by Abe Goolsby (Acts 27)

ORIGINAL HISTORICAL SETTING

Author and Date of Writing:
Luke, perhaps ca. A.D. 61–62

Like the Gospel according to Luke, this book is anonymous. On the other hand, uniform Christian tradition affirms that Luke wrote both. The evidence for Lukan authorship within the book is found in three "we" sections in which "we" and "us" occurs (16:10-17; 20:5–21:18; 27:1–28:16). At these times, the writer was an eyewitness of Paul's ministry (from Troas to Philippi on Paul's second journey; from Philippi to Jerusalem on the third journey; and from Caesarea to Rome). By a process of deduction, all the associates of Paul except for Luke can be eliminated. If Luke was the author of the "we" sections, then by extension he wrote the rest of Acts (since the Greek style and vocabulary is noticeably the same). By further extension, Luke must also be the author of the Third Gospel. (See *Author and Date of Writing* for *Luke* for more information.)

Determining the date for Acts depends on what to make of the end of the book. From Acts 25:11, the primary historical question raised by the book is, what happened to Paul when he appeared before Caesar? Yet Acts does not tell. Many Bible students are persuaded that, in his desire to publish, Luke was unwilling to wait on the outcome of Paul's case. He went ahead with publication at the end of Paul's two-year detention described in 28:30. If this is true, Acts is to be dated at 61 or 62. Other scholars, particularly those who reject the traditional understanding of authorship, date the book in the 80s. (The influential nineteenth-century radical critic F. C. Baur believed Acts was written in the second century as an imaginative fiction.)

First Audience and Destination:
Theophilus, a Gentile whose residence is unknown

Both Luke and Acts were written for Theophilus. (See *First Audience and Destination* for *Luke*.)

Occasion

The needs of Theophilus and perhaps his ongoing financial patronage provided the immediate occasion for Acts. If Luke began researching Acts while Paul was detained in Caesarea (see *Occasion* for *Luke*), then he had direct access to Philip, who was an eyewitness of most of the events for chapters 1–12 (21:8; 23:33; 24:27). Luke also had direct access to Paul, the central character for chapters 13–28, and was himself an eyewitness of some of the events he recorded.

LITERARY FEATURES

Genre and Literary Style:
A historical narrative written in excellent Koinē *Greek*

The overall genre of Acts is "historical narrative." In this sense, Acts parallels other works from antiquity, especially those also known as "Acts." Luke's work (like his Gospel) was not simply a recounting of facts, but a careful theological interpretation. He included summaries of important early Christian speeches, giving samples of a variety of speakers (Peter, Stephen, Paul), audiences (Jewish, Greek, Christian), and circumstances (friendly, hostile). Luke used a large vocabulary and carefully polished Greek style.

Themes:
Lordship of Jesus in building the church, activity of the Spirit, Peter and Paul

Jesus, who sent out the apostles, closed doors and opened new ones, always as "Lord of the harvest" sending out people to spread the gospel. The Spirit's work in filling Jesus's followers is a prominent theme. The two central characters are Peter (1–12) and Paul (13–28), entrusted with different responsibilities, but equally empowered and equally obedient to their specific commissions from Jesus.

Book Features and Structure

In the Christian canon, Acts fills a pivotal role. As "Part 2" of a two-part work, it looks back to the life of Jesus. By virtue of its description of Paul's conversion and ministry, it provides a historical context for understanding Paul's letters. Without Acts, there would be no firm basis for understanding the origins of Christianity.

The *Key Text*, Acts 1:8, provides a useful way of organizing the book. The apostles proclaim Jesus in Jerusalem (chaps. 1–7); the apostles proclaim Jesus in Judea and Samaria (chaps. 8–10); the apostles go "to the end of the earth" (chaps. 11–28).

ROMANS
THE EPISTLE TO THE ROMANS

As with all the New Testament letters written by Paul the apostle, this epistle is titled according to its first recipients, in this case the Christians in Rome.

O KEY TEXT: 1:16-17

"For I am not ashamed of the gospel, because it is the power of God for salvation to everyone who believes, first to the Jew, and also to the Greek. For in it the righteousness of God is revealed from faith to faith, just as it is written: The righteous will live by faith."

O KEY TERM: "RIGHTEOUSNESS"

The Greek noun translated "righteousness" is *dikaiosunē*. It is closely related to the verb *dikaioō*, usually translated "justify." This book is a long theological argument about how unrighteous sinners may receive right standing with God (are justified).

O ONE-SENTENCE SUMMARY

Righteousness with God is given freely (imputed) to all those who have faith in Jesus Christ for salvation according to God's eternal plan.

GOD'S MESSAGE IN THE BOOK

Purpose

Paul wrote to the Roman Christians in order to give them a substantial résumé of his theology. This epistle stands as Paul's "theological self-confession." Behind this was his concern to prepare the Roman believers for his intended ministry there and to create interest in his planned preaching mission to Spain.

Christian Worldview Elements

As the greatest doctrinal presentation of salvation in the Bible, Romans touches on almost every element of a Christian worldview. Among the most prominent are God; *rebellion and sin*; *covenant and redemption*; *community and church*; and *ethics and morality*.

o **God**
Creation
Sovereignty and Providence
Faith and Reason
Revelation and Authority
Humanity
o **Rebellion and Sin**
o **Covenant and Redemption**
o **Community and Church**
Discipleship
o **Ethics and Morality**
Time and Eternity

Teachings about God

In Romans, God is supreme in all matters of salvation, which serves his glory

Saint Paul by Rembrandt Harmenszoon van Rijn

and the good of his people. He is both "righteous," and One who declares "righteous the one who has faith in Jesus" (3:26). There is no fuller presentation of the person and work of Christ. The Holy Spirit is the One by whose indwelling believers are enabled to live holy lives (chap. 8).

A view of the Roman Forum at night

Teachings about Humanity

There are only two kinds of human beings: sinners who are condemned "in Adam" and believing sinners "in Christ" who are therefore declared righteous. Those who have been justified by faith are expected to live holy personal lives and to live in Christian community with each other by the power of the Spirit.

Teachings about Salvation

Salvation is a complex concept that includes past, present, and future. For individual believers, Christ has saved from the penalty of sin (justification, chaps. 4–5); he is saving from the power of sin (sanctification, chaps. 6–7); and he will save from the presence of sin (glorification, chap. 8). For the community of believers, salvation came first to Israel (chaps. 9–10), and in the present era it is coming to both Jews and Gentiles who make up the church (chap. 11).

✄ CHRIST IN ROMANS

In this letter to the Romans, Paul presents Christ as "a descendant of David according to the flesh and was appointed to be the powerful Son of God according to the Spirit of holiness by the resurrection from the dead" (1:3-4). Through Jesus's death, we are reconciled to God and by his life we are saved (5:10).

GOD'S STORY

When the Events of This Book Happened:
ca. A.D. 57
The historical events recorded in this book concern Paul's personal situation and travel plans. Romans fits the period near the end of Paul's third missionary journey, when he was anticipating traveling to Rome once he had finished accompanying the "love offering" from the Gentile churches to the Jerusalem church.

How Romans Fits into God's "Story":
Romans is part of "chapter 5" of God's story: God spreads the kingdom through the church. It explains how Jesus, the greatest descendant of Abraham and David (who are illustrations in this book), is also the One by whose death sinners may be justified—and so become part of God's kingdom. The parable of the olive tree (chap. 11) shows that God's kingdom plan includes both Jews and Gentiles, but especially Gentiles in the present age. The only specific mention of the kingdom of God in Romans notes its spiritual rather than its material nature (14:17).

ORIGINAL HISTORICAL SETTING

Author and Date of Writing:
Paul the apostle, ca. A.D. 57
This book claims to be written by "Paul, a servant of Christ Jesus." All New Testament scholars accept this claim. He was a devout Pharisee converted to faith in Jesus and called to become apostle to the Gentiles on the famous Road to Damascus (Acts 9). Paul's ministry may be divided into three parts:

- The period of personal growth in discipleship, ca. A.D. 33–47 (Acts 9–12)
- The period of three missionary journeys, ca. A.D. 48–57 (Acts 13–21)
- The period of consolidating the churches, ca. A.D. 58–65 (Acts 22–28)

Romans was written near the end of Paul's third missionary journey, which culminated in his arrest in Jerusalem.

First Audience and Destination:
Christians worshiping in house churches in Rome
Little is known about how Christianity first arrived in Rome. No biblical evidence supports the tradition that Peter was the first to preach the gospel in Rome. The gospel may have been taken there by Jews from Rome who believed in Jesus on Pentecost (Acts 2:10). It was already present in A.D. 49, when Emperor Claudius expelled Jews from the city, among whom were the Christian couple Priscilla and Aquila (Acts 18:2).

By the time Paul wrote Romans, the majority of believers there were probably Gentile. Paul knew a number of Roman Christians by name (chap. 16), and his greeting pattern indicates that they met in house churches scattered throughout the city (16:5; vv. 14 and 15 probably each reflect a house church group).

The city of Rome was a splendid if corrupt monument to centuries of Roman military success. It may have had a million people, over one-third of whom were slaves. Rome was the economic and political center of the world. Truly all roads led to Rome.

Occasion

Paul had never preached in Rome, and he had long desired this privilege. He had finished his great endeavor of the third missionary journey, the collection for the saints in Jerusalem. (See *Occasion* for *2 Corinthians*.) He was at this time spending the winter in Corinth (A.D. 56–57), for the Mediterranean Sea

Nero at Baiae by Jan Styka. Baiae was a popular resort. It lies on Gulf of Puteoli in the northwestern Gulf of Naples. Nero had been emporer three years when Paul wrote the Romans: "Let everyone submit to the governing authorities, since there is no authority except from God, and the authorities that exist are instituted by God" (Rom. 13:1). The evidence is strong that both Paul and Peter died during the persecution advanced by Nero.

was unsafe for travel for three months (Acts 20:3). Paul's mind was now turning to Rome (where he wanted to preach and to encourage the Roman Christians) and to Spain. With "time on his hands" in Corinth, he penned this letter to the Roman Christians in order to introduce himself and his theology. He was aided by Tertius the scribe (16:22).

 LITERARY FEATURES

Genre and Literary Style:
A long, formal epistle written in Koinē *Greek*

See *Genre and Literary Style* for *1 Thessalonians* for information about the genre "epistle." All four standard parts of a first-century epistle appear in Romans: salutation (1:1-7); thanksgiving (1:8-17); main body (1:18–16:18); farewell (16:19-24). Some scholars designate Romans as a tractate (a formal treatise rather than a pastoral letter). Paul's Greek is careful, and Romans reflects Paul at his most typical writing style.

Themes:
Righteousness, law, sin, justification, sanctification

Romans is rightly called the "Mount Everest of Christian Theology." The themes listed, of course, are all doctrinal. Because the Reformation of the sixteenth century was driven by a recovery of the doctrines of Romans, a few words are in order. Martin Luther's initial understanding of "the righteousness of God" referred to God's own righteousness—that perfection by which he judges sinners. Later he came to see "the righteousness of God" as God's righteousness offered to sinners as a gift and received by faith as opposed to a righteousness achieved by humans. Through God's free gift, humans are reconciled to God.

Book Features and Structure

Romans is the longest of Paul's letters, and it has always had "pride of place" in the Pauline collection. It stands as the most comprehensive statement of the gospel in all the Bible. His passion for his subject led him to emotional outbursts, especially the famous, "Absolutely not!" In developing his argument, he often (1) appealed to Scripture and (2) argued with an imagined opponent employing a rhetorical convention called a "diatribe," using phrases such as "every one of you" and "you, a mere man" (2:1; 9:20).

Like so many of Paul's epistles, the body of the letter has two parts. The first section may be called "God's provision of righteousness" (chaps. 1–11); the second may be called "the saint's fruit of righteousness" (chaps. 12–16).

1 CORINTHIANS

THE FIRST EPISTLE TO THE CORINTHIANS

This book is so named because it is the first canonical letter that Paul the apostle wrote to the Christians in Corinth.

○ KEY TEXT: 15:58

"Therefore, my dear brothers and sisters, be steadfast, immovable, always excelling in the Lord's work, because you know that your labor in the Lord is not in vain."

○ KEY TERM: "CHARITY" [LOVE]

Although this letter reflects a church facing many difficult issues, the solution always involves love ("charity" in the KJV; *agapē* in Greek). The "Love Chapter" (13) is the best known and most beloved part of the letter.

○ ONE-SENTENCE SUMMARY

The many problems a congregation may have, whether doctrinal or practical, will be resolved as that church submits properly to the lordship of Christ and learns to love one another genuinely.

A view of the Gulf of Corinth from the Acrocorinth that rises nearly 1,900 feet above Corinth

GOD'S MESSAGE IN THE BOOK

Purpose

Paul wrote to the Corinthian Christians to address the difficulties they were facing. (See *Occasion*, below.) His desire, of course, was for the church to change where it needed to change and to be encouraged where it was doing the right things.

Christian Worldview Elements

First Corinthians deals particularly with the three worldview categories of *community and church*; *discipleship*; and *ethics and morality*. No Bible book more fully develops the interrelationship among these three categories.

God
Creation
Sovereignty and Providence
Faith and Reason
Revelation and Authority
Humanity
Rebellion and Sin
Covenant and Redemption
○ Community and Church
○ Discipleship
○ Ethics and Morality
Time and Eternity

Teachings about God

God the Father is the supreme Lord, for whose glory all things are to be done (10:31). The theological centrality of Jesus's bodily resurrection is developed in the sustained argument of the "Resurrection Chapter" (15). His lordship over the church means that he has the right to order its life and worship. The Spirit's life-giving presence has brought the church into existence, has given each of its members "spiritual gifts," and enables its members to live holy lives because he is the Holy Spirit.

Teachings about Humanity

Humanity in this book is seen mainly within the context of Christian community. Redeemed people have been transformed by Christ, are called and enabled to love each other, and are destined for resurrection. Such persons, however, still struggle with sins such as divisiveness, sexual immorality, and disorder in worship.

Teachings about Salvation

This letter contains what may be the first-composed written summary of the New Testament understanding of redemption: "For I passed on to you as most important what I also received: that Christ died for our sins according to the Scriptures" (15:3). Further, this book emphasizes that God saves only those individuals who believe in Christ's death (1:21-25).

CHRIST IN 1 CORINTHIANS

To a church fascinated by wisdom and power, Paul declares Christ to be both the power (1:18,24) and the wisdom (1:21,24,30) of God.

Entrance to the stadium at Olympia, Greece. In 1 Corinthians (9:24-27), Paul uses imagery from the Panhellenic Games, of which there were four: Olympic, Pythian, Nemean, and Isthmian.

 GOD'S STORY

When the Events of This Book Happened:
From A.D. 50 to 55

Paul reached Corinth in A.D. 50 as part of his second missionary journey. After preaching in Macedonian cities (Philippi, Thessalonica, and Berea), he traveled south to Athens and then arrived in Corinth (Acts 17–18). He stayed for more than a year in Corinth, capital of Achaia. The date of Paul's ministry in Corinth is fixed by the reference in Acts 18:12 to Gallio as the proconsul (KJV "deputy") of Achaia, known from an inscription to have governed in Corinth in 51–52. Paul wrote 1 Corinthians some five years after he had first preached there. (See *Author and Date of Writing*, below.)

How 1 Corinthians Fits into God's "Story"

First Corinthians is part of "chapter 5" of God's story: God spreads the kingdom through the church. This epistle shows that proclaiming the kingdom of God did not end with Jesus but continued as a major theme of the apostles. In 1 Corinthians, Paul mentioned the kingdom of God five times (4:20; 6:9-10; 15:24,50). The kingdom is a powerful present reality, yet its glorious future lies after "flesh and blood" have been laid aside at the resurrection. Paul explicitly thought of the kingdom in moral terms. There is no place in the kingdom for those who practice immorality in this life.

ORIGINAL HISTORICAL SETTING

Author and Date of Writing:
Paul the apostle, ca. A.D. 55

This letter claims to be written by "Paul, called as an apostle of Christ Jesus by God's will." All New Testament scholars accept this claim. (See *Author and Date of Writing* for *Romans* for more information about Paul.) The apostle wrote this letter ca. A.D. 55, probably near the end of his long ministry in Ephesus on his third missionary journey (Acts 19).

First Audience and Destination:
Christians in Corinth

Acts 18 describes how Christianity first came to Corinth through Paul's preaching. Silas, Timothy, Priscilla, Aquila, and Apollos also helped establish the church in Corinth. The members had come from both Jewish and pagan backgrounds.

Corinth was a large and splendid commercial city, with Greek roots and a Roman overlay in the first century. Its population was perhaps 500,000. Because of its location at the Corinthian isthmus, it benefited from both land and sea routes. Corinth, rather than Athens, was chosen as the Roman capital of Achaia. Like all large cities of the Roman Empire, Corinth was both very religious (with a number of pagan temples) and very immoral (with the worship of Aphrodite sanctioning religious prostitution).

Occasion

Paul's ministry in Corinth had resulted in a well-established, thriving congregation. He had moved on from there and now was living in Ephesus. Several factors converged to make this letter necessary.

1. Paul had written a (now lost) letter advising the believers not to associate with people claiming to be Christians but living immorally. The church misunderstood Paul's meaning (5:9-11).
2. Paul had received an oral report from "Chloe's people" that the church had divided into several competing factions (1:11-12).
3. Paul had learned that the church was tolerating open sexual immorality (5:1).
4. Paul had received a "committee" (composed of Stephanas, Fortunatus, and Achaicus) sent by the Corinthians. They brought him more information about the church and had a list of written questions for Paul to respond to (7:1; 16:17).

Paul therefore wrote this letter to respond to this great variety of issues. He apparently used the professional secretarial help of Sosthenes and sent the letter by Timothy (1:1; 4:17).

LITERARY FEATURES

Genre and Literary Style:
A long epistle written in Koiné *Greek*

See *Genre and Literary Style* for *1 Thessalonians* for information about the genre "epistle." The four standard parts of a first-century epistle all appear in 1 Corinthians: salutation (1:1-3); thanksgiving (1:4-9); main body (1:10–16:18); farewell (16:19-24). Like most of Paul's writings, this is a pastoral letter, driven by the occasion and needs of the recipients, rather than a tractate (a formal treatise). Paul's Greek is careful, and 1 Corinthians reflects the typical Pauline writing style.

Themes:
Christian unity, morality, women's roles, spiritual gifts, the resurrection

The variety of themes (and more could be mentioned) is imposed by the occasion of the epistle. Recently the issues of women's roles and spiritual gifts have been of great interest in evangelical Christianity, showing the abiding value of this book. Concerning women, Paul affirmed the value of women who prayed or prophesied in worship (11:2-16), yet limited women's leadership (14:33-38). Concerning spiritual gifts, Paul distinguished between spiritual gifts (sovereignly given by the Spirit to believers at the new birth) and natural talents. (The gift of "tongues" in Corinth was to be strictly regulated, but Paul's basic command was "do not forbid," 14:39.)

Book Features and Structure

The most noteworthy literary feature of this book is Paul's use of the expression variously translated in CSB as "now about" or "now concerning." Most scholars believe that he used this device to move through the list of questions brought to him by the committee (16:17). These items were as follows, with the verse containing "now concerning" indicated: male and female in marriage (7:1); virgins (7:25); food offered to idols (8:1); spiritual gifts (12:1); the collection for the saints in Jerusalem (16:1); Apollos (16:12).

The body of the letter is best seen containing three answers. First, Paul answered the matter of divisions in the church (received orally from Chloe's people), (chaps. 1–4). Second, Paul dealt with immorality (received in an oral report), (chaps. 5 6). Third, he answered the church's list of questions (brought in writing by the committee), (chaps. 7–16).

Remains of the Temple of Apollo in Corinth. This temple had been standing for over 500 years when Paul came to Corinth. Paul would likely have
seen the bronze statue of Apollo within the temple.

2 CORINTHIANS

This book is so named because it is the second canonical letter that Paul the apostle wrote to the Christians in Corinth.

○ KEY TEXT: 12:9

"But he said to me, 'My grace is sufficient for you, for my power is perfected in weakness.' Therefore, I will most gladly boast all the more about my weaknesses, so that Christ's power may reside in me."

○ KEY TERM: "DEFENSE"

Of all Paul's letters, this is the most personal—and the most defensive. In it Paul mounted a defense ("apology" in the good sense) of his apostolic authority and ministry.

Corinth is located on the southwest end of the Isthmus of Corinth, a narrow land bridge connecting the mainland of Greece with the Peloponnesian Peninsula. Corinth was a maritime city located between two seaports: the port of Lechaion on the Gulf of Corinth about two miles to the north and the port of Cenchreae on the Saronic Gulf about six miles east of Corinth. In Paul's day an overland ship road across the isthmus connected the ports of Lechaion and Cenchreae. Cargo from large ships was unloaded, transported across the isthmus, and reloaded on other ships. Small ships were moved across the isthmus on rollers. This enabled ships to avoid 200 miles of stormy travel around the southern part of the Peloponnesian Peninsula.

O ONE-SENTENCE SUMMARY

True Christian ministry, although it may have to be defended against false attacks, is commissioned by Christ and empowered by his Spirit.

GOD'S MESSAGE IN THE BOOK

Purpose

Paul wrote to the Corinthian Christians in order to express his relief at the success of his severe letter and the mission of Titus, to ask for money for the poor saints in Jerusalem, and to defend his ministry as an apostle to the minority of unrepentant Corinthians. (See *Occasion*, below.) His desire, of course, was to encourage the majority and to lead the minority to change their mind.

Christian Worldview Elements

Second Corinthians focuses attention on the worldview categories of *revelation and authority*; *community and church*; and *ethics and morality*. Of all Paul's letters, this one deals the most extensively with the matter of authority as it relates to a local church, an ongoing important issue.

> God
> Creation
> Sovereignty and Providence
> Faith and Reason
> O **Revelation and Authority**
> Humanity
> Rebellion and Sin
> Covenant and Redemption
> O **Community and Church**
> Discipleship
> O **Ethics and Morality**
> Time and Eternity

Teachings about God

God is the Father of Jesus Christ (1:3; 11:31) who sovereignly sent him as the great "indescribable gift" (9:15). Jesus is the source of all comfort for his people. By his death and resurrection, Jesus is Lord of the new creation (5:14-17). The life-giving Spirit has come as the "down payment" or deposit, guaranteeing the believer's future (5:5). "Where the Spirit of the Lord is, there is freedom" (3:17).

Teachings about Humanity

There were two kinds of people in the Corinthian church: those who submitted to genuine apostolic authority and those who did not. Paul sent blistering criticism on the latter (chaps. 10–11). This book contains the most extensive teaching in Scripture about the status of redeemed humans between the death of the body and the resurrection. This is referred to as the "intermediate state," when persons are "with the Lord" in conscious bliss while waiting for the consummation (5:1-8).

The Corinth Canal that was completed in 1893. Nero used 6,000 Judean slaves to attempt to build the canal but lacked the tools needed to complete the project. Today the canal is used for tourist vessels.

Teachings about Salvation

This letter contains Paul's most extensive discussion on the contrast between the "old covenant" and the "new covenant" (chap. 3). Although salvation was real in the Mosaic era, it came with fading glory, for the old covenant was meant to be temporary. The new covenant arrived with Jesus Christ, and its glory can never be surpassed. The benefit to the believer in the new covenant era is incomparable (3:18).

⚓ CHRIST IN 2 CORINTHIANS

Jesus Christ, God's Son, is not an ambiguous, fickle word from God, not "Yes and No" but "Yes." Conformity to Christ's image is the goal of the Christian life. Christ, working through the Spirit, brings this about.

GOD'S STORY

When the Events of This Book Happened:
From A.D. 50 to 56
See *When the Events of This Book Happened* for *1 Corinthians*. Paul wrote 2 Corinthians some six years after he had first preached there. (See *Author and Date of Writing, below.*)

How 2 Corinthians Fits into God's "Story"
Second Corinthians is part of "chapter 5" of God's story: God spreads the kingdom through the church. This book emphasizes the spiritual nature of what God is doing in spreading the kingdom of God. Paul rejected material or merely human resources (such as clever arguments). The Spirit of the Lord was accomplishing everything important. Thus Paul could boast about his own human weakness and argue that "the weapons of our warfare are not of the flesh, but are powerful through God for the demolition of strongholds" (10:4). Ultimately, in God's kingdom the invisible and eternal will triumph over what is visible and temporary (4:16-18).

ORIGINAL HISTORICAL SETTING

Author and Date of Writing:
Paul the apostle, ca. A.D. 56
This book claims to be written by "Paul, an apostle of Christ Jesus by God's will." All biblical scholars accept this claim. (See *Author and Date of Writing* for *Romans* for more information about Paul.) The apostle wrote this letter ca. A.D. 56, after he had concluded his ministry in Ephesus on his third missionary journey and had arrived in Macedonia (Acts 20:1-2; 2 Cor. 7:5-7).

First Audience and Destination:
The Christians in Corinth
See *First Audience and Destination* for *1 Corinthians*.

Occasion
See *Occasion* for *1 Corinthians*. Careful study of 2 Corinthians has resulted in the following understanding of the events that led to its composition.

1. First Corinthians had not been well received by the congregation. Timothy evidently returned to Paul in Ephesus with a report that the church was still greatly troubled. This was partly caused by the arrival in Corinth of "false apostles" (11:13-15). (These were evidently Jewish Christians who emphasized sophisticated rhetoric, perhaps also they were Judaizers, asking the Corinthians to live according to Mosaic regulations.)

2. Paul had visited Corinth, which he described as "painful"(2:1). Evidently the "false apostles" led the Corinthians to disown Paul.

3. Paul then wrote a (now lost) "Severe Letter" (7:8, NLT) of stinging rebuke to Corinth from Ephesus. He sent this letter by Titus (2:3-4). Sometime shortly after this, Paul left Ephesus and traveled on, first to Troas and then to Macedonia (2:12-13).

4. Titus finally tracked Paul down in Macedonia with good news. Most of the church had repented and returned to the gospel and accepted Paul's authority (7:5-7).

Paul decided to write the Corinthians one more time, his fourth known letter to them, expressing his relief but still pleading with the unrepentant minority. He apparently used the professional secretarial help of Timothy and sent the letter by Titus (1:1; 8:17).

 ## LITERARY FEATURES

Genre and Literary Style:
A long epistle written in Koinē *Greek*

See *Genre and Literary Style* for *1 Thessalonians* for information about the genre "epistle." The standard parts of a first-century epistle appear in 2 Corinthians, except that the thanksgiving is missing: salutation (1:1-2); main body (1:3–13:10); farewell (13:11-13). Like most of Paul's writings, this is a pastoral letter, driven by the occasion and needs of the recipients, rather than a tractate (a formal treatise).

Second Corinthians 2:14–7:4 is often referred to as the "Great Digression," because it could be removed without upsetting the narrative of Paul's travels. (This "digression" presents important doctrinal material found here only in Paul's writings.) Paul's Greek is typical, but in this letter given to passionate outbursts and irony.

Themes:
Apostolic authority, new covenant, intermediate state, sacrificial giving

The variety of themes is driven by the occasion of the epistle. The first three of these have already been mentioned. The matter of sacrificial giving is the focus of chapters 8–9, the most extensive teaching in the New Testament on Christian stewardship. Paul asked the churches he had founded to send a large, generous offering to the poor believers of Jerusalem. This occupied much of his energy during the last part of his third missionary journey. He mentioned it in his three longest epistles (Rom. 15:28,31; 1 Cor. 16:1-4; 2 Cor. 8–9).

Book Features and Structure
The most noteworthy literary feature of this book is the distinct change in tone and subject matter between chapters 1–9 and 10–13. The first section is

generally warm and friendly, while the last section is noticeably harsh. Many critical scholars have concluded that chapters 10–13 were originally the "Severe Letter" Paul wrote after 1 Corinthians but before 2 Cor. 1–9 (see *Occasion*, above). Because no Greek manuscript supports this separation, it is best to affirm the original unity of 2 Corinthians. The differences in tone may be accounted for by judging that Paul wrote the last section to an unrepentant minority of Corinthians.

The body of the letter has three major sections. First, Paul discussed his itinerary as an apostle, including the "Great Digression" on doctrine (chaps. 1–7). Second, Paul appealed for generous giving (chaps. 8–9). Third, he defended his ministry against the false apostles (chaps. 10–13).

GALATIANS
THE EPISTLE TO THE GALATIANS

As with all the New Testament letters written by Paul, this epistle is titled according to its first recipients, in this case Christians in the Roman province of Galatia.

KEY TEXT: 2:16

"Because we know that a person is not justified by the works of the law but by faith in Jesus Christ, even we ourselves have believed in Christ Jesus. This was so that we might be justified by faith in Christ and not by the works of the law, because by the works of the law no human being will be justified."

KEY TERM: "FAITH"

"Faith alone" is the heartbeat of this book. Paul's insistence that no human work can contribute to a person's right standing with God makes this book critical for all those who cherish the doctrine of salvation as a gift of God's grace.

The sunset reflected in Lake Eğirdir, the second-largest freshwater lake in Turkey. Lake Eğirdir is situated southwest of Pisidian Antioch where Paul preached in the Jewish synagogue on his first missionary journey. It is likely that Paul's letter to the Galatians was sent to the churches in this region that he and Barnabas planted and later revisited.

O ONE-SENTENCE SUMMARY

Sinners are justified (and live out a godly life) by trusting in Jesus Christ alone, not by keeping the law or by counting on good works.

 GOD'S MESSAGE IN THE BOOK

Purpose

Galatians was written to accomplish three purposes. First, Paul defended his authority as an apostle of Jesus. Second, he argued the doctrinal case for salvation by faith alone. Third, he showed that everyday Christian living is based on freedom from the law in the power of the Holy Spirit.

Christian Worldview Elements

Galatians directs attention to the world-view categories of *revelation and authority*; *covenant and redemption*; and *ethics and morality*. Chapters 1–2 focus on the first category (particularly Paul as an agent of divine revelation). Chapters 3–4 develop the second category. Chapters 5–6 show that Christian ethics are truly founded in the liberty of love.

> God
> Creation
> Sovereignty and Providence
> Faith and Reason
> o **Revelation and Authority**
> Humanity
> Rebellion and Sin
> o **Covenant and Redemption**
> Community and Church
> Discipleship
> o **Ethics and Morality**
> Time and Eternity

Teachings about God

God is the Father of Jesus who brings about all things related to salvation, including setting apostles apart for service (1:15). Jesus is the Son of God by whose death righteousness is provided (2:21). The Holy Spirit is given to all believers, enabling them to subdue "the flesh" and to grow in Christian character ("the fruit of the Spirit") (5:16-26).

Teachings about Humanity

Galatians contrasts two kinds of people in the world. First, there are those under God's curse (3:10). This includes people who suppose that they can attain salvation by doing good works. They are doomed to live according to the evil works of the flesh and will not be part of God's kingdom. Second, there are those who, by God's grace, have been set free from the curse by faith in Christ who bore the curse by his death (3:13). Such people live according to the Spirit's power and will "reap eternal life" (6:8).

Teachings about Salvation

Galatians stands as Paul's passionate testimony that salvation is a gift of God's grace. It is unearned and undeserved, and must be received by faith alone. Paul is careful not to turn faith into a work, for he argues that "faith came"

(3:23-25) to those who were helpless slaves (see also Eph. 2:8; Phil. 1:29). This view of salvation so strongly gripped the apostle that if someone offered a different doctrine, let "a curse be on him" (1:8).

 ## CHRIST IN GALATIANS

Christ became a curse for us so that he could redeem us from the curse of the law (3:13). Believers are crucified with Christ and yet they live. Christ himself becomes their very life (2:19-20).

GOD'S STORY

When the Events of This Book Happened:
From A.D. 47 to 49 (or from A.D. 50 to 55)
Two ways of understanding the events in Galatians have been presented. Scholars of all kinds (conservative, critical, Protestant, Catholic) have supported each view.

"Carry one another's burdens; in this way you will fulfill the law of Christ" (Gal. 6:2).

The South Galatian View. Paul established churches in cities of southern Galatia (Iconium, Lystra, and Derbe), ca. A.D. 47 on his first missionary journey (Acts 14). In his epistle to them, he described two visits to Jerusalem:

- Gal. 1:18-19 = Acts 9:26-30 (3 years after conversion)
- Gal. 2:1-10 = Acts 11:29-30 (14 years after conversion = famine relief)

After these two trips to Jerusalem, Paul began his missionary journeys and established the churches in Galatia.

The North Galatian View. Paul established churches in cities of northern Galatia (not mentioned in Acts, but see Acts 18:23), about A.D. 50 on his second missionary journey. The Jerusalem visits he noted in his letter are understood differently than above:

- Gal. 1:18-19 = Acts 9:26-30 (3 years after conversion)
- Gal. 2:1-10 = Acts 15:6-29 (14 years after first visit = Jerusalem Council)

Only after the Jerusalem Council (and after his first missionary journey to southern Galatia) did Paul establish the churches to which he was now writing.

How Galatians Fits into God's "Story"

Galatians is part of "chapter 5" of God's story: God spreads the kingdom through the church. Faith, not ethnic background or keeping the laws of Moses, determines citizenship in the kingdom. Believers in Jesus Christ now constitute "the Israel of God" (6:16). The only reference to the kingdom emphasizes its spiritual and moral character: "those who practice such things (the works of the flesh) will not inherit the kingdom of God" (5:21).

 ## ORIGINAL HISTORICAL SETTING

Author and Date of Writing:
Paul the apostle, ca. A.D. 49 (or ca. 52–55)

The book claims to be written by Paul, and no one doubts that he wrote this letter. (See *Author and Date of Writing* for *Romans* for more information about Paul's life.)

The date of writing depends on whether the North or the South Galatian View is true. The South Galatian View seems preferable because (1) Acts specifically mentions Paul's preaching only in southern Galatia; (2) the alternate view asserts that Paul deliberately (misleadingly?) omitted referring to his Jerusalem visit of Acts 11:29-30; and (3) the vehemence of the epistle makes better sense if it preceded the Jerusalem Council.

First Audience and Destination:
Christians living in the Roman province of Galatia

These Christians came mainly from a Gentile background. They had been believers in Christ for a few years at most. Galatia was a large Roman province snaking from north to south (in the center of modern Turkey). "Galatians" was originally an ethnic term for the original settlers of the northern part of the region who had migrated from Gaul. The Romans had extended the original Galatian region southward to become a large province whose capital was Ancyra in the north.

Occasion

After Paul had left the Galatian churches, troublemakers had come there proclaiming a different version of the gospel (1:6-9; 5:7-12). They criticized Paul as a self-appointed apostle who did not truly reflect the message of Jesus. These agitators evidently wanted Christianity to be a sect within current Judaism. Gentiles, they said, had to become Jews (accepting circumcision and living according to Mosaic laws, including dietary rules) before they could be saved and be a part of God's people. These false teachers are called "Judaizers," based on the verb translated "to live like Jews" in 2:14.

Paul understood Christianity as "the hope of Israel" (Acts 28:20), a culmination of what God began with Abraham, Moses, David, and the prophets. He reacted violently against the Judaizers by penning this letter (5:12). If Paul wrote at the earlier date, he probably composed from Antioch of Syria, his "home base," and Galatians is his earliest letter (written between his first and second missionary journeys). If he wrote to churches in northern Galatia, he probably composed from Corinth or Ephesus (during the second or third missionary journeys).

 ## LITERARY FEATURES

Genre and Literary Style:
An epistle written in Koinē Greek

See *Genre and Literary Style* for *1 Thessalonians* for information about the genre "epistle." The standard parts of a first-century epistle appear, except that the thanksgiving is missing: salutation (1:1-5); main body (1:6–6:15); farewell (6:16-18). This is a pastoral letter, driven by the occasion and needs of the recipients, rather than a tractate (a formal treatise). Paul's Greek is at its most passionate in this letter.

Themes:
Grace, faith, justification, freedom, fruit of the Spirit

Justification by grace alone through faith alone became the rallying cry of the Reformation. Galatians has been called "Luther's Book" because of these themes. Because of its emphasis on freedom from law, the Christian life,

Galatians has also been called the "Charter of Christian Liberty." By the power of the Spirit, Christians produce a harvest of righteous character, without which there is no evidence of eternal life.

Book Features and Structure

Contrasting concepts are more prominent here than in any other Pauline letter. The most evident of these are divine revelation versus human insight; grace versus law; justification versus condemnation; Jerusalem versus Mount Sinai; sons versus slaves; the fruit of the Spirit versus the works of the flesh; and liberty versus bondage.

The structure of the book is threefold, corresponding to the three parts of Paul's purpose for writing. (See *Purpose,* above.) The first two chapters are personal; the middle two chapters are doctrinal; and the last two chapters are practical.

EPHESIANS
THE EPISTLE TO THE EPHESIANS

As with all New Testament letters written by Paul the apostle, this epistle is titled according to its first recipients, in this case Christians in the city of Ephesus.

○ KEY TEXT: 3:10-11

"This is so that God's multi-faceted wisdom may now be made known through the church to the rulers and authorities in the heavens. This is according to his eternal purpose accomplished in Christ Jesus our Lord."

○ KEY TERM: "UNITY"

Ephesians focuses on the unity between Christ the head of the church and the church as the body of Christ, as well as the unity between Jew and Gentile in God's greatest masterpiece, the church.

○ ONE-SENTENCE SUMMARY

In God's eternal plan, God's great masterpiece, the church, has now been manifested, in which Christ is united with all the redeemed whether Jew or Gentile, transforming relationships in this life and leading to a glorious future.

The ancient amphitheater in Ephesus

GOD'S MESSAGE IN THE BOOK

Purpose

Paul wrote to the Christians in and around Ephesus to develop fully in writing his magnificent understanding of the doctrine of the church and to instruct believers about the importance of holy conduct, particularly in Christian family relationships. Ephesians presents the church as the focal point of displaying God's glory forever (3:21).

Christian Worldview Elements

Ephesians directs attention to the worldview elements of *sovereignty and providence*; *revelation and authority*; *community and church*; and *time and eternity*. God's sovereign eternal plan for the church, once a "mystery" but now revealed, is the heart of this book. This plan, conceived in the eternal past, is being developed in the present age and will endure into the eternal future.

> God
> Creation
> ○ **Sovereignty and Providence**
> Faith and Reason
> ○ **Revelation and Authority**
> Humanity
> Rebellion and Sin
> Covenant and Redemption
> ○ **Community and Church**
> Discipleship
> Ethics and Morality
> ○ **Time and Eternity**

Teachings about God

Ephesians is filled with texts that contribute to a fully orbed doctrine of the Trinity. God the Father is the One whose eternal plan for the church has now been revealed. Jesus the Son is the exalted Head of the body, the church, and for whose glory the church exists. The church is a house or temple in which God's Spirit lives, yet the Spirit fills each believer individually.

Teachings about Humanity

Ephesians shows the dreadful condition of all who are still in their natural condition: "dead in your trespasses and sins" (2:1). Paul summarizes this as "without hope and without God" (2:12). The alternate group is those whom God has changed and who are in a supernatural state: made alive together with Christ (2:5). Old distinctions between Jew and Gentile used to count for something, but now in the church they no longer apply.

Teachings about Salvation

The best known and most loved New Testament summary of the gospel is Eph. 2:8-9, with its emphasis on grace and faith. Ephesians also notes God's delight in electing persons to salvation. The language of predestination to eternal life is pronounced (1:5,11), as is Paul's notion that "Christ loved the church and gave himself for her" (5:25). (The long-standing theological dispute about divine election—predestination—is a matter of discerning the basis of God's choice. All students who take the Bible seriously affirm divine predestination; the debate is simply over its basis.)

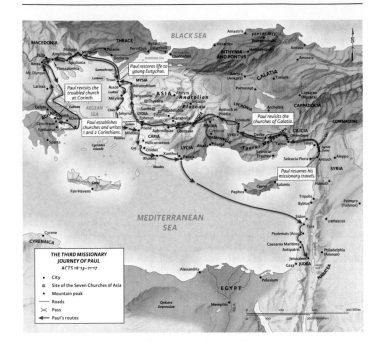

THE THIRD MISSIONARY
JOURNEY OF PAUL
ACTS 18:22–21:17

- City
- ⊡ Site of the Seven Churches of Asia
- ▲ Mountain peak
- — Roads
- ≍ Pass
- ← Paul's routes

 CHRIST IN EPHESIANS

Christ, through his death, brought peace between God and humankind and between Jew and Gentile. He is the cornerstone and head of the church, which is his body.

 GOD'S STORY

When the Events of This Book Happened:
From A.D. 53 to 61

Paul first proclaimed Christ in Ephesus on his third missionary journey, arriving there ca. A.D. 53 (Acts 19). He wrote this letter to the church at a time that he was imprisoned (6:20). Christian tradition is surely correct in affirming that Paul wrote from Rome while he was waiting for his appeal to come before the emperor, as Acts 28 describes. Paul's two-year detention in Rome was ca. A.D. 60–61.

How Ephesians Fits into God's "Story"

Ephesians is part of "chapter 5" of God's story: God spreads the kingdom through the church. Ephesians shows that there are really only two opposing kingdoms in the universe. The devil is "the ruler of the power of the air" (2:2), the ruler of a kingdom of sin and death. God's kingdom is diametrically opposed: "For know and recognize this: Every sexually immoral or impure or greedy person, who is an idolater, does not have an inheritance in the kingdom of Christ and of God" (5:5). The church (the body of Christ) is the expression of the kingdom in which God receives everlasting glory (3:21).

 ORIGINAL HISTORICAL SETTING

Author and Date of Writing:
Paul, ca. A.D. 61

The letter claims to be written by "Paul, an apostle of Christ Jesus by God's will." For the past two centuries, critical scholars have argued that Paul was not the author. The arguments against Pauline authorship of Ephesians include the following. (1) The Greek style and vocabulary are different from the undisputed Pauline letters. (2) The doctrine of the church is too advanced for Paul's time. (3) The parallels between Ephesians and Colossians open the possibility that a sincere admirer of Paul used Colossians as a source for writing a letter in his own (later) day, claiming Paul's name to lend his work greater authority. Each of these points may be refuted. The letter's self-claim and the unbroken Christian tradition of Pauline authorship should be accepted.

Assuming that Paul is the author, he wrote from Roman imprisonment as described at the end of Acts, ca. A.D. 60–61. Those who reject Pauline authorship date the letter toward the end of the first century.

First Audience and Destination:
Christians living in (and around) the city of Ephesus

The gospel came to Ephesus on Paul's third missionary journey. He stayed longer in Ephesus than he did in any other city (Acts 19:10). Paul's Ephesian work was the most visibly successful of all the places of his ministry. The church included both Jews and Gentiles. Because the words "in Ephesus" are missing from 1:1 in some of the earliest and best manuscripts, many believe that this was originally a circular letter, intended for several cities (as was Galatians). This would account for the fact that Paul made no reference to individuals and his note that he had only heard of the readers' faith (1:15).

Ephesus was the most important city in the Roman province of Asia and may have had a population of 600,000. Like Corinth, Ephesus was a great commercial center and port city. Although a number of governmental activities were in Ephesus, the official capital was Pergamum. Ephesus was the site of the famous temple to Diana (or Artemis), one of the Seven Wonders of the Ancient World.

Occasion

Paul had ample opportunity to think over the full implications of Christianity and the church during his Roman imprisonment. He had evidently just written the Colossians (to deal with the Colossian heresy; see *Occasion* for *Colossians*). He concluded that the doctrinal message of that letter was worth expanding and distributing to a wider audience. Thus he composed this letter and had it sent with the help of Tychicus (6:21) to Ephesus (and perhaps to other nearby churches; compare Rev. 1:11).

 LITERARY FEATURES

Genre and Literary Style:

An epistle written in Koinē *Greek*

See *Genre and Literary Style* for *1 Thessalonians* for information about the genre "epistle." All four standard parts of a first-century epistle appear in Ephesians: salutation (1:1-2); thanksgiving (1:3-23); main body (2:1–6:20); farewell (6:21-24). Some scholars designate Ephesians as a tractate (a formal treatise rather than a pastoral letter). Paul's Greek is at its most composed and dispassionate in this letter.

Themes:

Grace, heavenly places, mystery

Romans has been called the king of Paul's epistles, but Ephesians is the queen. "Grace" (Greek, *charis*) permeates the letter from first to last (1:2; 6:24). In fact, each of the 13 letters bearing Paul's name has the word "grace" at the beginning and end, like bookends. The term "in the heavens" is found here only in the New Testament (1:3,20; 2:6; 3:10; 6:12). It may have been a Pauline coinage for this book. "Mystery" does not mean something obscure or hard to understand but a divine truth previously hidden, now made known by God's agent of revelation.

Book Features and Structure

Paul's style is deliberative and reflective, in tone the "coolest" of his letters (in contrast to Galatians and 2 Corinthians, the "hottest"). His vocabulary and style are noticeably different. He also wrote sentences that are notorious in their length and complexity. In the original, 1:3-14 is a single sentence of 202 Greek words, followed immediately by 1:15-23, a single sentence of 169 Greek words.

The structure of the book is twofold, displaying Paul's typical outline. The first three chapters are doctrinal, describing the heavenly position of the church; the last three chapters are practical, describing the earthly condition of the church.

Philippi's acropolis seen from the hill where Cassius's forces camped in 42 B.C. The Battle at Philippi was one of the strategic engagements between Julius Caesar's assassins, Brutus and Cassius, and his avengers, Mark Antony and Octavius. The victory of the latter forces was a critical step toward Octavius becoming Caesar Augustus (Luke 2:1).

PHILIPPIANS
THE EPISTLE TO THE PHILIPPIANS

As with all New Testament letters written by Paul the apostle, this epistle is titled according to its first recipients, in this case Christians in the city of Philippi.

○ KEY TEXT: 3:10

"My goal is to know him and the power of his resurrection and the fellowship of his sufferings, being conformed to his death."

○ KEY TERM: "JOY"

Forms of the noun "joy" and the verb "rejoice" occur 16 times in this short letter. Philippians is the biblical book that most extensively defines and describes joy.

○ ONE-SENTENCE SUMMARY

Knowing Jesus Christ is much more joyful and important than anything else because God has exalted Jesus, the crucified servant, with the name above every name.

Western entrance to the ancient theater at Philippi. The mountain in the background is Pangaion from which gold and silver was extracted and then minted in Philippi.

GOD'S MESSAGE IN THE BOOK

Purpose

Paul wrote to the Philippians to thank them for the financial gift they had sent through Epaphroditus. He further wanted to report on Epaphroditus and to tell about Timothy's probable visit to them. As an added bonus, Paul wanted to give them some important doctrinal teaching about Christ (and knowing him) as well as to offer practical advice on living the Christian life vigorously and joyfully.

Christian Worldview Elements

Philippians directs attention to the worldview elements of *covenant and redemption*; *community and church*; and *discipleship*. Redemption as a personal relationship with God through knowing Jesus Christ is prominent in this book. So also is the concept of a local church as a worshiping and witnessing community.

God
Creation
Sovereignty and Providence
Faith and Reason
Revelation and Authority
Humanity
Rebellion and Sin
○ **Covenant and Redemption**
○ **Community and Church**
○ **Discipleship**
Ethics and Morality
Time and Eternity

Teachings about God

For his glory, God the Father has both exalted Jesus Christ and called a people to know him, whom he tenderly cares for. Jesus, by very nature God, humbled himself by death on a cross but thereby has been exalted with the greatest name. The Spirit of God enables all true worship and provides help for God's people.

Teachings about Humanity

In Philippians, there are two essential categories of human beings: enemies of the cross of Christ and those who know him (3:18-20). The former are destined for destruction, the latter for resurrection. Among those who know him, however, some proclaim him purely, but others do so from false motives (1:15-18).

Teachings about Salvation

Salvation is presented from the viewpoint of knowing Christ. Knowing Christ, more than just the remedy for sins, is a valuable treasure, for which everything else in life is to be happily cast aside. This applies not only to whatever good things one was and did before, but it also means that his followers will joyfully suffer as he did. They will ultimately share in his resurrection.

The map shows The Second Missionary Journey of Paul (Acts 15:36—18:22) with the following annotations:

- Paul establishes churches in Philippi, Thessalonica, and Berea.
- Paul is imprisoned. Luke joins Paul.
- Paul receives vision that encourages him to travel to Macedonia.
- Paul is brought on charges before Gallio.
- Paul speaks to the Areopagus.
- Paul asks Timothy to join him in his work.
- Paul returns from Jerusalem to plan his next venture.
- Jerusalem Conference, A.D. 49 (Ac 15:1-30; Gl 2:1-21)

THE SECOND MISSIONARY
JOURNEY OF PAUL

ACTS 15:36—18:22

- City
▲ Mountain peak
— Via Egnatia
✕ Pass
← Route of Paul and Silas

✝ CHRIST IN PHILIPPIANS

Christ, who existed in the form of God, emptied himself of his privileges as God and became a human being and a slave. After this, God exalted him and gave him the name that is above every name. At the name of Jesus all creatures will bow and confess him as Lord.

GOD'S STORY

When the Events of This Book Happened:
From A.D. 49 to 61

Paul first preached in Philippi on his second missionary journey, arriving there ca. A.D. 49 (Acts 16). He wrote this letter to the church while he was imprisoned (1:13-17). According to Christian tradition, he wrote from his two-year imprisonment in Rome while he was waiting to appear before the Emperor (Acts 28, ca. A.D. 60–61).

How Philippians Fits into God's "Story"

Philippians is part of "chapter 5" of God's story: God spreads the kingdom through the church. Although the terms "king" and "kingdom" are missing, the letter is filled with (future-oriented) kingdom concepts. First is the "day of Christ Jesus," clearly equivalent to the Old Testament "day of the LORD," that time when Paul and the Philippians will stand before him, complete at last (1:6,10; 2:16). Second is the glorious time when Christ's lordship is universally acknowledged (2:11).

ORIGINAL HISTORICAL SETTING

Author and Date of Writing:
Paul, ca. A.D. 61
The letter claims to be written by Paul, and all biblical students accept this testimony. (See *Author and Date of Writing* for *Romans* for more information about Paul's life.) Some scholars have argued that all or part of Phil. 3 was written at a different time than the main letter, but no Greek manuscript evidence supports this.

According to tradition, Philippians is one of the four Prison Epistles written from Rome. In the twentieth century, some scholars argued that the many travels implied in the letter make better sense if Paul wrote from Ephesus a few years earlier. They have conjectured an otherwise unknown imprisonment (not mentioned in Acts or anywhere in Paul's letters) during his third missionary journey, ca. 55–56. While this theory remains possible, it is an argument based on silence, and the traditional view that Philippians was written from Rome ca. 60–61 appears much more likely.

First Audience and Destination:
Christians living in the city of Philippi
The gospel came to Philippi on Paul's second missionary journey. This was the first church Paul planted after his Macedonian vision (Acts 16:9). Because Luke was an eyewitness of the founding of this church (as the "we's" of Acts 16 indicate), a great deal is known about the individuals who made up the original core of the congregation, such as Lydia and the city jailer. Paul did not stay in Philippi very long, but Luke himself probably stayed behind as the church's spiritual leader. (The "we's" stop after Acts 16:17.) By reading Acts and Philippians carefully, one discovers that Paul had visited the church at least twice since its beginning and that it was a true source of joy for him.

Philippi was an important commercial city in the province of Macedonia. (The capital was Thessalonica.) The city had a privileged status as a colony of Rome, so its citizens were considered citizens of Rome (note Paul's emphasis on heavenly citizenship in 3:20-21). According to Acts, there were evidently not enough Jews in the city to support a synagogue, so the city and the church were primarily Gentile.

Occasion
While Paul was imprisoned in Rome, the Philippian church had sent him a financial gift, perhaps to assist with his living expenses or his legal fees,

through Epaphroditus, one of their leaders (4:10-20). While Epaphroditus was with Paul, he experienced a near-fatal illness. The Philippians had received word of this, and Paul had learned that they were gravely concerned about Epaphroditus. At last, however, Epaphroditus had recovered, and Paul was ready to send him home (2:25-29). He took this occasion, therefore, to write the Philippians a thank-you letter in which he complimented Epaphroditus and brought them up to date on his own ministry. The doctrinal and practical emphases in the letter are probably a response to information brought by Epaphroditus. Paul composed this letter (probably with Timothy's help, whom he also wanted to send to Philippi at a later time, 1:1; 2:19-24) and sent it to Philippi with Epaphroditus.

 LITERARY FEATURES

Genre and Literary Style:
An epistle written in Koinē *Greek*

See *Genre and Literary Style* for *1 Thessalonians* for information about the genre "epistle." All four standard parts of a first-century epistle appear in Philippians: salutation (1:1-2); thanksgiving (1:3-11); main body (1:12–4:20); farewell (4:21-23). This is a pastoral letter, driven by the occasion and needs of the recipients, rather than a tractate (a formal treatise). Paul's Greek is at its most typical in this letter.

Themes:
Righteousness, humility, gratitude, Christ's exaltation and lordship

In Philippians (as in Romans), righteousness is a gift of grace to believers, and it is to bear fruit in the believer's life (1:11; 3:9). The humility of Christ is the pattern for believers to follow in this life. Since this included suffering in Jesus's life, it may very well include suffering in the believer. Paul's gratitude for the Philippians' gift is another theme where a pattern to follow is evident. There is no finer biblical presentation of the lordship of Jesus Christ (2:9-11).

Book Features and Structure

Most biblical students agree that 2:6-11 is a "Hymn about Christ" which Paul was quoting, probably something that he himself had composed earlier. A number of poetic features appear here. This is a six-stanza hymn in which stanzas 1–3 (vv. 6-8) focus on the humiliation of Jesus and stanzas 4–6 (vv. 9-11) focus on his exaltation. This hymn is the most concentrated New Testament passage to combine the doctrines of the person (identity—who he is) and the work (actions—what he did) of Christ.

The structure of the letter is less formal than is usual for Paul. Chapter 1 is personal; chapter 2 teaches humility; chapter 3 deals with true righteousness; chapter 4 contains Paul's thank-you note.

St. Paul by Jan Lievens (1607-1674). "Devote yourselves to prayer; stay alert in it with thanksgiving. At the same time, pray also for us that God may open a door to us for the word, to speak the mystery of Christ, for which I am in chains, so that I may make it known as I should" (Col. 4:2-4).

COLOSSIANS
THE EPISTLE TO THE COLOSSIANS

As with all New Testament letters written by Paul the apostle, this epistle is titled according to its first recipients, in this case Christians in the town of Colossae.

◯ KEY TEXT: 1:18
"He is also the head of the body, the church; he is the beginning, the firstborn from the dead, so that he might come to have first place in everything."

◯ KEY TERM: "PREEMINENCE"
Colossians declares the supremacy of Christ in all things, whether of creation or redemption. This teaching was the cure to a deadly heresy facing early believers.

◯ ONE-SENTENCE SUMMARY
Jesus Christ is supreme Lord of the universe and head of the church and therefore he is the only One through whom forgiveness is possible, making legal obligations or philosophical studies irrelevant in matters of salvation.

 GOD'S MESSAGE IN THE BOOK

Purpose
Paul wrote the Colossian Christians to combat a dangerous teaching, known only through his criticism of it in this letter. (See *Occasion,* below.) Although he condemned this heresy, his main approach was to exalt the person of Jesus Christ and to urge the Colossians to give up anything that denied Jesus his preeminent position as Lord.

Christian Worldview Elements
Colossians focuses on the worldview categories of *God; revelation and authority;* and *covenant and redemption.* No Bible book more explicitly teaches that Jesus is fully God. Paul was self-consciously an agent of divine revelation in this book. Jesus's uniqueness and the exclusiveness of Christianity as the only way to salvation are also prominent elements.

- **o God**
  - Creation
  - Sovereignty and Providence
  - Faith and Reason
- **o Revelation and Authority**
  - Humanity
  - Rebellion and Sin
- **o Covenant and Redemption**
  - Community and Church
  - Discipleship
  - Ethics and Morality
  - Time and Eternity

"For everything was created by him, in heaven and on earth, the visible and the invisible, whether thrones or dominions or rulers or authorities— all things have been created through him and for him. He is before all things, and by him all things hold together" (1:16-17). This image beautifully captures a triangular glow seen best in night skies free of overpowering moonlight and light pollution. The photograph was taken at European Southern Observatory's La Silla Observatory in Chile in September 2009, facing west some minutes after the sun had set.

Teachings about God

God is the Father of Jesus, and his fullness is in his Son (1:19; 2:9). Jesus is especially the "firstborn" (1:15,18). Colossians 1:15-18 is the most elevated passage in Paul's letters presenting the identity of Christ. When Jesus returns, his people "will appear with him in glory" (3:4). The Spirit is mentioned only once (1:8), as the source of love.

Teachings about Humanity

Because Colossians was first written to stop false teachings, it shows just how easy it is for people to be led astray from truth, particularly in matters of eternal destiny. In every age, powerful enemies of truth oppose genuine understanding of God and the human condition. Apart from Christ, all are "dead in trespasses" (2:13). Christ brings new life and transformation of relationships, particularly within the home (3:18–4:1).

Teachings about Salvation

Any understanding of salvation which is "Jesus plus" is defective. Good works, keeping Jewish law, accepting certain philosophical principles, and other positive human accomplishments cannot add anything to what Jesus has already achieved. Therefore salvation is a matter of being rightly related to him by faith and refusing to trust anything else, no matter how valuable. Christ allows nothing to rival him in redeeming sinners.

CHRIST IN COLOSSIANS

Christ is creator of all things, whether visible or invisible. He is the One who holds all creation together. The fullness of God lived in him, and through Christ's death God reconciled everything to himself.

GOD'S STORY

When the Events of This Book Happened:

From ca. A.D. 53 to 61

Paul had never been in Colossae. The gospel had evidently gone there from Ephesus, where Paul lived during his third missionary journey, arriving ca. A.D. 53 (Acts 19). He wrote while he was imprisoned (4:3,18). Christian tradition is surely correct in affirming that Paul wrote from Rome during the two years that he was waiting for his appeal to come before Nero (ca. A.D. 60–61), as Acts 28 describes.

How Colossians Fits into God's "Story"

Colossians is part of "chapter 5" of God's story: God spreads the kingdom through the church. Colossians shows that two kingdoms are in conflict.

On one hand is the domain of darkness, into which all humans are born. On the other hand, there is "the kingdom of the Son he loves" into which God's people have been transferred (1:13). This kingdom is a present reality, for which Paul and all other Christian ministers are working (4:11). Paul's use of the "firstborn" language is grounded in messianic prophecy: "I will also make him my firstborn, greatest of the kings of the earth" (Ps. 89:27).

ORIGINAL HISTORICAL SETTING

Author and Date of Writing:
Paul the apostle, ca. A.D. 61
The letter claims to be written by Paul the apostle. For the past two centuries, some (but not all) critical scholars have denied that Paul wrote this letter. They have argued that Colossians reflects the issues of a later time than Paul and was written by an unknown later Christian who used Paul's name to bolster his own authority. The basic arguments are (1) that the false teaching attacked is Gnosticism, which did not become a destructive influence until the end of the first century and (2) that the Christology is too highly developed for Paul. However, in response, (1) there is no proof that the Colossian heresy was directly related to Gnosticism, and (2) the Christology is no more exalted than Phil. 2:9-11, which is clearly Pauline. The letter's self-claim and the unbroken Christian tradition of Pauline authorship should be accepted.

Paul wrote from Roman imprisonment as described at the end of Acts, ca. A.D. 60–61. Those who reject Pauline authorship date it toward the end of the first century.

First Audience and Destination:
Christians living in the town of Colossae
Christianity came to Colossae through the ministry of Epaphras (1:7). He evidently brought the gospel while Paul was in Ephesus on his third missionary journey. Paul had only "heard" of the Colossian believers (1:4,9). The false teaching mixed Jewish and Greek elements (see *Book Features and Structure*, below), suggest that the believers were probably from both Jewish and Gentile backgrounds.

Colossae was an unimportant town in the province of Asia in the Lycus River Valley, about a hundred miles inland (east) from Ephesus. Its better-known sister cities were Hierapolis and Laodicea (2:1; 4:13-16).

Occasion
While Paul was imprisoned in Rome, Epaphras had visited him and brought news about the churches in the Lycus River Valley (4:12). Paul had learned from him about the presence of false teachers in the Colossian congregation who were threatening the survival of the church. He therefore wrote this letter, evidently with the secretarial assistance of Timothy, using Tychicus as the letter carrier.

This is one of four letters, called the Prison Epistles, written while Paul was waiting to appear before the emperor. Careful reading shows the following relationships:

- Colossians and Philemon were both sent to Colossae
  (Col. 1:1; 4:17; Phlm. 2).
- Colossians and Ephesians were carried by Tychicus (Col. 4:7; Eph. 6:21).
- Ephesians reflects a theological development of Colossians.

All three of these were probably written not long after Paul arrived in Rome; all three were perhaps carried together by Tychicus, who was also accompanying Onesimus. (See *Occasion* for *Philemon*.)

Philippians was likely the last of the four to be written because Paul was expecting to be released soon (Phil. 1:19).

 LITERARY FEATURES

Genre and Literary Style:
An epistle written in Koinē *Greek*

See *Genre and Literary Style* for *1 Thessalonians* for information about the genre "epistle." The standard parts of a first-century epistle appear: salutation (1:1-2); thanksgiving (1:3-8); main body (1:9–4:6); farewell (4:7-18). This is a pastoral letter, driven by the occasion and needs of the recipients, rather than a tractate (a formal treatise). This letter was written in Paul's typical style.

Themes:
Firstborn, fullness, freedom

Jesus Christ is the "firstborn" over all creation (1:15) as well as "firstborn" from the dead (1:18), showing that he is supreme over creation and supreme over the church. He is, furthermore, the "fullness" of the godhead (1:19; 2:9). Because of Christ's death, Christians are free from human regulations (2:13-23).

Book Features and Structure

The nature of the Colossian heresy must be inferred by Paul's attacks. The essential falsehood was that Jesus was a created being, someone less than God and more than human. There was a certain emphasis on Jewish elements: (1) legal restrictions concerning circumcision, diet, and holy days, 2:11-17; 3:11; (2) veneration of angels, 2:18. There were also Greek elements: (1) self-denial, 2:21-23; (2) adherence to philosophy and human wisdom, 2:4,8; (3) emphasis on secret knowledge, 2:18. The Colossians were what might be called "under the spell" of a syncretistic blend of Jewish and Hellenistic elements which Paul recognized as a serious threat to the survival of true Christianity.

The book follows Paul's classic pattern. The first two chapters are doctrinal (Christ as the head of the church). The last two are practical (holy Christian living).

The Ancient Agora, at the north end of Dikastirion Square, Thessaloniki

1 THESSALONIANS

THE FIRST EPISTLE TO THE THESSALONIANS

This book is so named because it is the first canonical letter that Paul the apostle wrote to the Christians in Thessalonica.

○ KEY TEXT: 4:16-17

"For the Lord himself will descend from heaven with a shout, with the archangel's voice, and with the trumpet of God, and the dead in Christ will rise first. Then we who are still alive, who are left, will be caught up together with them in the clouds to meet the Lord in the air, and so we will always be with the Lord."

○ KEY TERM: "COMING"

This book mentions the return of Christ in every chapter. The Greek noun *parousia*, here rendered "coming," can also be translated "arrival" or "presence."

○ ONE-SENTENCE SUMMARY

Whatever difficulties and sufferings believers experience in this life, the coming of Christ is the true hope of the Christian.

The view of Mount Olympus, Greece's highest mountain, from Thessaloniki, looking across the Thermaic Gulf. According to Greek mythology, Olympus was where the Greek gods lived. Paul reminded the Thessalonians how their turning from idols to the living God had become widely known in the region (1 Thess. 1:8-10).

GOD'S MESSAGE IN THE BOOK

Purpose

Paul wrote this letter mainly to correct a deficiency in the Thessalonians' understanding of the coming of Christ and related events. He also wanted to encourage these new converts in basic doctrine and to inspire them to make progress in holy living.

Christian Worldview Elements

First Thessalonians focuses attention especially on the worldview categories of *community and church*; *ethics*; and *time and eternity*. This is the only Bible book explicitly teaching that believers alive at the coming of Christ will be "caught up" to meet him.

God
Creation
Sovereignty and Providence
Faith and Reason
Revelation and Authority
Humanity
Rebellion and Sin
Covenant and Redemption
○ **Community and Church**
Discipleship
○ **Ethics** and Morality
○ **Time and Eternity**

Teachings about God

God is the Father who actively works to bring about salvation. He is presently working holiness into his children. Jesus died and rose again at his first coming, and he will return in glory at his second coming. The Spirit, the active agent by whom God makes the gospel alive, is God's gift enabling his people to have great joy (1:5-6; 4:8).

Teachings about Humanity

There are only two kinds of people: those who have received the word of God and those who have rejected it (2:13-16). The destiny of the one group is the experience of the wrath of God, leading to their destruction. The destiny of the other group is to be with the Lord forever. This latter group is called on to live a holy life that pleases God.

Teachings about Salvation

Jesus's death and resurrection is the basis of salvation (4:14; 5:10). The letter summarizes salvation as past, present, and future in this way: "You turned to God from idols to serve the living and true God and to wait for his Son from heaven, whom he raised from the dead—Jesus, who rescues us from the coming wrath" (1:9-10).

CHRIST IN 1 THESSALONIANS

Christ is a source of comfort because he is coming again. At his coming, those who have died in him will rise first. Then believers who are living will be caught up to join those who have died and be together with him.

GOD'S STORY

When the Events of This Book Happened:
ca. A.D. 50

After preaching in Philippi, Paul went next to Thessalonica (Acts 17). He reached the Thessalonians ca. A.D. 50 as part of his second missionary journey during a time when he was moving quickly, establishing churches in rapid succession. A short time later, he arrived in Corinth and stayed there more than a year (Acts 18). He wrote this letter from Corinth, probably within a few months of preaching to the Thessalonians.

How 1 Thessalonians Fits into God's "Story"

First Thessalonians is part of "chapter 5" of God's story: God spreads the kingdom through the church. When Paul first preached in Thessalonica, his opponents caused trouble because he proclaimed "that there is another king— Jesus" (Acts 17:7). Jesus's kingdom was understood as a rival to the kingdom of Caesar, yet Jesus's kingdom was not a political-military enterprise. In his letter, Paul emphasized the moral and spiritual nature of those who belong to King Jesus (2:12). The vocabulary Paul used to describe Jesus's return was the same as that describing a great king's arrival (*parousia*) at one of his cities.

ORIGINAL HISTORICAL SETTING

Author and Date of Writing:
Paul the apostle, ca. A.D. 50

All New Testament scholars accept the claim of the letter to be written by Paul. (See *Author and Date of Writing* for *Romans* for more information about Paul.) The apostle wrote this letter ca. A.D. 50 from Corinth. (See *Occasion*, below.)

First Audience and Destination:
Christians in Thessalonica

Acts 17:1-8 describes how Christianity first came to Thessalonica through Paul's preaching. Silas and Timothy had helped him. The believers had come from both Jewish and pagan backgrounds. Paul was forced by persecution to leave Thessalonica early, possibly staying there only three weeks. These new believers had enthusiastically embraced the gospel but were not taught in the way of the Lord.

Thessalonica was the capital of Macedonia and numbered perhaps 200,000 residents in the first century. It was a seaport and commercial center lying at the intersection of the Egnatian Way and the road leading north toward the Danube River.

Occasion

After Paul fled Macedonia, Timothy and Silas finally caught up with him in Athens. Paul was so concerned to learn about the spiritual state of the Thessalonians that he dispatched Timothy to them (3:1-5). Timothy stayed there for a time, strengthening and encouraging these new believers. At last Timothy caught up with Paul a second time, this time in Corinth (Acts 18:5; 1 Thess. 3:6).

Timothy's report was essentially positive. The congregation was thriving and growing in virtue, although they were enduring persecution of some kind. Paul's ministry there, however, had emphasized that Christ's coming could be very soon. Thus the Thessalonians were unprepared when some of their members had died (4:13). Had those who died missed the kingdom? Would they see the King? Paul found it important to expand his teaching on eschatology (end times) and to clarify their confusion. He penned this letter perhaps within months of first preaching in Thessalonica.

 LITERARY FEATURES

Genre and Literary Style:

An epistle written in Koinē Greek

Unlike the Gospels, which were a new literary genre inspired by Christianity, epistles were a well-known first-century literary form. First Thessalonians is one of the earliest of Paul's letters to survive, although Galatians may be earlier. This is the earliest Pauline epistle that contains all four standard elements of an epistle, of which many secular examples have been discovered.

- Salutation (1:1). The form is "From Sender to Recipient: Greetings." Paul always identified himself as the author and named the recipient. In place of the conventional word "greetings," Paul always used "grace to you and peace."
- Thanksgiving (1:2-3). This was a prayer directed to God on behalf of the readers. The secular examples invoked a variety of deities, depending on which god was served.
- Body (1:4–5:22). This obviously was the main point of the letter. Paul typically wrote a doctrinal argument followed by a shorter practical application.
- Farewell (5:23-28). The writer gave greetings and otherwise concluded the document. Paul always used the word "grace" (Greek, *charis*) in his farewell.

Like most of Paul's writings, this is a pastoral letter, driven by the occasion and needs of the recipients, rather than a tractate (a formal treatise). First Thessalonians represents Paul's typical careful use of the Greek language.

Themes:

Return of Christ, "the rapture," importance of holiness

Because Paul was writing in response to the needs of the congregation, their own concerns became the themes of the epistle. The doctrinal concern with right eschatology (beliefs about the end times) is balanced with Paul's practical concern with right living (holiness in light of Christ's return).

Book Features and Structure

This is the only Bible book that explicitly mentions that Christians who are alive at Christ's coming will be changed to resurrection life and rise to meet him in the air without dying (4:16-17). This doctrine is often called the rapture, based on the Latin term for "caught up." For the past two centuries, evangelical believers have had a lively debate concerning the relationship of the rapture to the second coming. Equally devout and Bible-believing scholars have disagreed. What is clear is (1) that Jesus will visibly, bodily return, (2) those who are already dead in Christ will one day be raised, and (3) Christians alive at Christ's parousia will be "raptured" (caught up) without dying.

This epistle is not organized by doctrinal material followed by practical advice. Instead, Paul moves back and forth. On the other hand, only practical material follows the transitional "so then" at 5:6.

Byzantine walls of Thessaloniki

2 THESSALONIANS
THE SECOND EPISTLE TO THE THESSALONIANS

This book is so named because it is the second canonical letter that Paul the apostle wrote to the Christians in Thessalonica.

○ KEY TEXT: 2:15

"So then, brothers and sisters, stand firm and hold to the traditions you were taught, whether by what we said or what we wrote."

○ KEY TERM: "STAND"

This book was written to believers who had been shaken by false teaching concerning the end times. The apostle's advice to "stand firm" applies no matter what doctrinal or practical challenge believers face.

○ ONE-SENTENCE SUMMARY

Whatever difficulties believers face, they should stand firm and continue living useful lives, since Christ's return may be in the distant future.

GOD'S MESSAGE IN THE BOOK

Purpose

Paul wrote this letter mainly to correct a new deficiency in the Thessalonians' understanding of the coming of Christ and related events. (See *Purpose* for *1 Thessalonians*.) He also wanted to correct the problem brought about because some had stopped working (in light of their belief that the day of the Lord had come).

Christian Worldview Elements

Second Thessalonians, like its sister letter, focuses attention especially on the worldview categories of *community and church*; *ethics*; and *time and eternity*.

God
Creation
Sovereignty and Providence
Faith and Reason
Revelation and Authority
Humanity
Rebellion and Sin
Covenant and Redemption
○ **Community and Church**
Discipleship
○ **Ethics** and Morality
○ **Time and Eternitt**

Teachings about God

God's supremacy in all things, particularly concerning salvation and the consummation of the world, is taught in this letter. His justice is especially taught in the way he will ultimately punish all evil doers. Jesus's coming is taught in this book, and he will easily overcome "the man of lawlessness," that is, "the man doomed to destruction" (2:3) as a display of his glory on "the

The Catacombs of St. John the Baptist in Thessaloniki are part of a network of subterranean passageways within the city. The severe persecution of Christians ordered by Emperor Diocletian in early A.D. 303 affected Thessaloniki in 304. Christians hid, gathered for worship, and buried their dead in catacombs like this. (2 Thess. 2:15)

day of the Lord." The Holy Spirit, mentioned only at 2:13, sanctifies (makes holy) those God has chosen to save.

Teachings about Humanity

This letter shows two sharply opposed groups of humanity. On one hand are those who know God and have come to obey the gospel. On the other hand are all others, "They will pay the penalty of eternal destruction from the Lord's presence and from his glorious strength" (1:9).

Teachings about Salvation

In 2 Thessalonians, salvation is seen from the future perspective of deliverance from judgment and destruction on the day of the Lord. In the end, those who perish do so "because they did not accept the love of the truth and so be saved" (2:10).

CHRIST IN 2 THESSALONIANS

Christ came the first time as a baby. His second coming will be different. He will come with his powerful angels who will punish God's enemies, those who refuse peace with God made possible by the death of Christ.

GOD'S STORY

When the Events of This Book Happened:
ca. A.D. 50 to 51

See *When the Events of This Book Happened* for *1 Thessalonians.* Second Thessalonians was probably written only a few months after the first epistle.

How 2 Thessalonians Fits into God's "Story"

Second Thessalonians is part of "chapter 5" of God's story: God spreads the kingdom through the church. Paul emphasized the spiritual nature of the kingdom of God in this letter. He urged the Thessalonians to "be counted worthy of God's kingdom, for which you also are suffering" (1:5). The portrait of Christ's return in a blaze of glory and wrath against his enemies is one of the most kingly portraits of Jesus in all the epistles (2:8-12).

ORIGINAL HISTORICAL SETTING

Author and Date of Writing:
Paul the apostle, ca. A.D. 50

The letter claims to be written by Paul the apostle. For the past two centuries, some (but not all) critical scholars have rejected that Paul wrote this letter. They have argued that the eschatology (end-times doctrine) of this letter contradicts the eschatology of 1 Thessalonians. This letter was therefore written by an unknown later Christian who used Paul's name to bolster his own authority. The basic argument is that in 2 Thessalonians Christ's coming appears to be distant, and a number of signs must precede it. Yet in the first epistle, his return appears to be imminent and without warning. Clearly the letters have differing emphases, but they are not incompatible. Down through the centuries, Christians have held that the day of the Lord may come at any time (imminence), but that it is not necessarily immediate. The letter's self-claim and the unbroken Christian tradition of Pauline authorship should be accepted.

Paul wrote from Corinth just a few months after he wrote 1 Thessalonians. Those who reject Pauline authorship date the letter toward the end of the first century.

First Audience and Destination:
Christians in Thessalonica

See *First Audience and Destination* for *1 Thessalonians*.

Occasion

After Paul sent 1 Thessalonians, the church had received a further report that the "day of the Lord"—the end times—had come. The return of Christ was immediate. This had come as if from Paul himself (2:2). The church was thrown into turmoil, and many of the members had quit their jobs and were waiting for the second coming. Paul therefore had to write them again to correct the doctrinal error and to urge them to settle down and get back to work.

 ## LITERARY FEATURES

Genre and Literary Style:
An epistle written in Koinē Greek

See *Genre and Literary Style* for *1 Thessalonians* for information about the genre "epistle." The standard parts of a first-century epistle appear: salutation (1:1-2); thanksgiving (1:3-11); main body (2:1–3:15); farewell (3:16-18). This is a pastoral letter, driven by the occasion and needs of the recipients, rather than a tractate (a formal treatise). It was written in Paul's typical style.

Themes:
Return of Christ, "day of the Lord," rejection of idleness

In this letter, Paul developed the "day of the Lord" theme that was already well established in the Old Testament prophets. (See *Joel* and *Zephaniah*.) The "day of the Lord" is now seen to be the time associated with Christ's return, when he will destroy God's enemies and bring God's people to glory. Paul's rejection of idleness is summarized in this instruction, ""If anyone isn't willing to work, he should not eat" (3:10).

Book Features and Structure

The literary "tone" of 2 Thessalonians is noticeably cooler than for the first epistle. In the first letter, he was warm with enthusiasm about their progress in the gospel and offered calm advice about congregational order in a series of staccato-like instructions (1 Thess. 5:12-22). In the second letter, he was gravely concerned about the spiritual state of the Thessalonians and offered them a sharp rebuke about maintaining congregational order (2 Thess. 3:6-15).

This epistle follows Paul's usual pattern of doctrinal material followed by practical. The doctrinal focus (on the day of the Lord) ends at 3:14; the practical advice begins at 2:15 (the *Key Text)* and goes to the end of the letter.

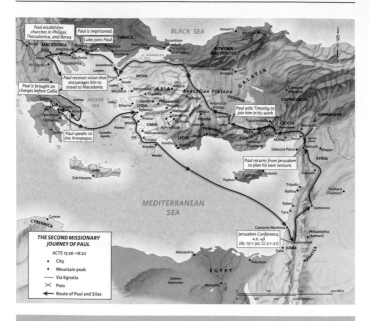

THE SECOND MISSIONARY
JOURNEY OF PAUL

ACTS 15:36–18:22

• City
▲ Mountain peak
— Via Egnatia
⤬ Pass
◄— Route of Paul and Silas

Paul probably first met Timothy on his first missionary journey. On his second missionary journey, Paul and Silas invited Timothy to join them as they traveled west.

1 TIMOTHY
THE FIRST EPISTLE TO TIMOTHY

This book is so named because it is the first canonical letter that Paul the apostle wrote to Timothy.

O KEY TEXT: 6:11

"But you, man of God, flee from these things, and pursue righteousness, godliness, faith, love, endurance, and gentleness."

O KEY TERM: "GODLINESS"

Godliness (Greek, *eusebeia*) is the virtue that sums up all others. Timothy's many ministry challenges would succeed only if he proceeded from godly character.

O ONE-SENTENCE SUMMARY

Whatever challenges Christian leaders face in life and ministry, they are to make progress in godliness and help maintain order in congregational life.

 GOD'S MESSAGE IN THE BOOK

Purpose

Paul wrote his dear friend Timothy to accomplish a number of objectives. First, he wished to encourage Timothy in his Christian growth. Second, he offered advice about being a better Christian leader. Third, he offered instructions about church organization, particularly congregational officers.

Christian Worldview Elements

First Timothy deals with the worldview categories of *community and church*; *discipleship*; and *ethics and morality*. This book, more fully than any other, instructs about organizing church life.

Teachings about God

This epistle contains the classic biblical summary of God's attributes: "the King eternal, immortal, invisible, the only God" (1:17). He is also "the blessed and only Sovereign, the King of kings, and Lord of lords" (6:15). Jesus is the

God
Creation
Sovereignty and Providence
Faith and Reason
Revelation and Authority
Humanity
Rebellion and Sin
Covenant and Redemption
o **Community and Church**
o **Discipleship**
o **Ethics and Morality**
Time and Eternity

only "mediator between God and humanity" (2:5). The Holy Spirit's person is clearly affirmed (3:16; 4:1).

Paul and Barnabas at Lystra by Nicolaes Pieterszoon Berchem. Paul and Barnabas's first missionary journey took them to Lystra (Acts 14:8-20), the home of Timothy who joined Paul and Silas on Paul's second mission- ary journey (Acts 16:1-5).

Teachings about Humanity

As one of the six New Testament letters first written to a single individual (1 and 2 Timothy, Titus, Philemon, 2 and 3 John), this book shows the importance of what one person can be and do. The individuals addressed in these books (Timothy, Titus, Philemon, "the elect lady," and Gaius) were all redeemed sinners working for the kingdom of God in one way or another. They all benefited from the advice and encouragement offered by the letter they received. These persons stand as examples of living out one's life for the glory of God and in the hope of eternal life.

Teachings about Salvation

Salvation in this letter, as everywhere in Paul's writings, focuses on Jesus Christ. Paul summarized his understanding by reminding Timothy of "the mystery of godliness," evidently an early Christian hymn or poem: "He was manifested in the flesh, vindicated in the Spirit, seen by angels, preached among the nations, believed on in the world, taken up in glory" (3:16).

 ## CHRIST IN 1 TIMOTHY

Christ's purpose for coming into the world is to save sinners. Paul says Christ took him as a worst-case scenario. He argues that if Christ can save Paul, he can save anyone.

 ## GOD'S STORY

When the Events of This Book Happened:
ca. A.D. 62–63

After Paul was released from the Roman imprisonment described in Acts 28, he engaged in further travel. One stop was Ephesus, where he ministered for a time before traveling on to Macedonia (1:3). From Macedonia Paul wrote to Timothy, whom he had asked to stay in Ephesus. The dates for these events are only approximate.

How 1 Timothy Fits into God's "Story"

First Timothy is part of "chapter 5" of God's story: God spreads the kingdom through the church. Although the term "kingdom" does not appear in this letter, God is called "King" twice (1:17; 6:15). While this language is more common in the Old Testament than the New, it is still appropriate in the era of the new covenant. God is not only the King as Sovereign of the universe; he is also the King of the people of God, whom he has called to know and worship him.

ORIGINAL HISTORICAL SETTING

Author and Date of Writing:
Paul the apostle, ca. A.D. 63

The book claims explicitly to be written by "Paul, an apostle of Christ Jesus" (1:1). Until about two centuries ago, all Bible students affirmed this belief. With the rise of critical approaches to Scripture, some scholars have adopted the position that an unknown admirer of Paul wrote 1 Timothy (as well as 2 Timothy and Titus). Opinions vary whether these letters contain any genuine Pauline fragments. The chief objection is historical. The travels mentioned in these three epistles do not fit into the framework provided by Acts. If Paul had died following his appeal to Caesar, he could not be the author of these books. It is also held that the congregational form encouraged in these letters (with bishops and deacons officially recognized) is too advanced for Paul's day. The Greek style is also noticeably different from that of the undisputed Pauline letters.

These objections may be satisfactorily answered. (1) It is by no means certain that Paul died at the end of the Acts 28 imprisonment. In fact, the evidence from Phil. 1:25 is that Paul expected to be released. (2) Little is actually known about the congregational form of the Pauline churches. Bishops and deacons certainly functioned in Philippi years before 1 Timothy was written (Phil. 1:1). (3) The difference in Greek style does not prove anything, for the Greek of 1 and 2 Timothy and Titus are more like the Greek of the undisputed Pauline letters than any other part of the Bible. The letter's self-claim and the unbroken Christian tradition of Pauline authorship should be accepted.

Paul wrote after he was released from the Roman imprisonment described at the end of Acts, ca. A.D. 63. Those who reject Pauline authorship date the letter toward the end of the first century.

First Audience and Destination:
Timothy, Paul's dearest friend, who was in Ephesus

Timothy had the task of being an apostolic representative. He was from Lystra (in modern Turkey). His father was Gentile, but his mother Eunice was a Jewish Christian (Acts 16:1; 2 Tim. 1:5). Timothy had probably come to the gospel through Paul during his first visit to Lystra (1 Tim. 1:2). Timothy joined Paul on his second missionary journey, helping Paul in Macedonia and Achaia (Acts 17–18). He traveled with Paul later on and was with him during his Roman imprisonment (Phil. 1:1; Col. 1:1).

After Paul's release, he assigned Timothy the responsibility of helping the church of Ephesus with its difficulties. Paul's comments about Timothy in Phil. 2:19-24 and his statements in 1 and 2 Timothy show Paul's affection for his loyal associate. Paul later asked Timothy to rejoin him (2 Tim. 4:9,21), and Heb. 13:23 indicates that Timothy was later imprisoned. (For information about Ephesus, see *First Audience and Destination* for *Ephesians.*)

Occasion

Paul had left Timothy in Ephesus when he found that false teaching had upset the stability of the church there. The exact nature of this teaching is impossible to determine, but it included both Jewish speculative elements ("myths and endless genealogies," 1:4) as well as Greek philosophical elements ("irreverent and empty speech and contradictions from what is falsely called knowledge," 6:20). Timothy had to deal with false teachers as well as organize the church along sound lines. Thus, from somewhere in Macedonia, Paul wrote to encourage Timothy and to remind him of his responsibilities.

 ## LITERARY FEATURES

Genre and Literary Style:
An epistle written in Koinē Greek

See *Genre and Literary Style* for *1 Thessalonians* for information about the genre "epistle." The standard parts of a first-century epistle appear in 1 Timothy, except that the thanksgiving is missing: salutation (1:1-2); main body (1:3–6:19); farewell (6:20-21). This letter, 2 Timothy, and Titus share certain vocabulary and style elements that make these three books distinctive. So clearly do they belong together that they are often considered as a unit, the Pastoral Epistles.

Themes:
Sound doctrine, bishops and deacons, widows

Sound doctrine is crucial as the cure for false teaching. This is the only New Testament book that gives qualifications for both the primary spiritual officers of a congregation (bishops = elders) and the secondary officers (deacons = helpers). Paul also instructed Timothy about widows, including women officially qualified to serve (5:9-13, compare with 3:8-13).

Book Features and Structure

See *Book Features and Structure* for *2 Timothy* for information about the "Faithful Sayings" in the Pastoral Epistles.

The letter moves through a variety of topics. In general, chapters 1–5 focus on Timothy's public responsibilities in the life of the congregation. Chapter 6 focuses on Timothy's private spiritual character as a "man of God" (6:11).

Interior of Rome's Mamertine Prison where Paul is believed to have been held in his last days—and from where he wrote his second letter to Timothy. The stairs descend into the Tullianum, an ancient dungeon where Rome incarcerated what it considered its most dangerous enemies.

2 TIMOTHY
THE SECOND EPISTLE TO TIMOTHY

This book is so named because it is the second canonical letter that Paul the apostle wrote to Timothy.

○ KEY TEXT: 2:2

"What you have heard from me in the presence of many witnesses, commit to faithful men who will be able to teach others also."

○ KEY TERM: "COMMITTED"

Timothy was to commit (entrust) the treasure of the gospel that had been committed to him to those who would faithfully transmit it to the next generation, just as he had committed his eternal destiny to the One who would keep it for "that day" (1:12).

○ ONE-SENTENCE SUMMARY

Christian leaders are to be unashamed of the gospel and to carry on faithfully with the message about Christ entrusted to them.

Rome in winter. In closing his second letter to Timothy, Paul urged Timothy to come from Ephesus: "When you come, bring the cloak I left in Troas with Carpus, as well as the scrolls, especially the parchments. ... Make every effort to come before winter" (4:13,21). As winter approached, the Mamertine Prison, the traditional site where Paul was incarcerated, would not have afforded protection as the temperature dropped.

GOD'S MESSAGE IN THE BOOK

Purpose

Paul wrote this letter as his "Last Will and Testament." He wished to remind Timothy of what mattered most to him in case he did not survive his imprisonment until Timothy arrived. He also urged Timothy (and Mark) to come to him in haste in order to be with him in his last days.

Christian Worldview Elements

Second Timothy deals particularly with the worldview categories of *revelation and authority* and *time and eternity*. This book especially sees God's revelation as a deposit—something that had been entrusted to Paul—which should not be tampered with but passed on faithfully. As Paul's last writing, it shows how an aged saint can live in the light of death's approach.

> God
> Creation
> Sovereignty and Providence
> Faith and Reason
> ○ **Revelation and Authority**
> Humanity
> Rebellion and Sin
> Covenant and Redemption
> Community and Church
> Discipleship
> Ethics and Morality
> ○ **Time and Eternity**

Teachings about God

God is the powerful Father who has graciously gifted his servants for ministry. Scripture is itself "inspired by God" (lit. "God-breathed," 3:16). Jesus is both God and man: "Remember Jesus Christ, risen from the dead and descended from David." (2:8). The Holy Spirit is the powerful presence of God indwelling believers and enabling them to continue their ministry (1:14).

Teachings about Humanity

See *Teachings about Humanity* for *1 Timothy*.

Teachings about Salvation

Salvation is both sovereignly determined by God and the divine gift to all who believe. Paul summarized the evangelistic aspect of his ministry with a statement combining both emphases: "This is why I endure all things for the elect; so that they also may obtain salvation, which is in Christ Jesus, with eternal glory" (2:10).

 CHRIST IN 2 TIMOTHY

God's saving grace through Christ was not an afterthought, a response to unforeseen developments in the world. It was planned before time. Christ has abolished death and brought life and immortality through his death and resurrection.

GOD'S STORY

When the Events of This Book Happened:
ca. A.D. 63–66

Paul had traveled to a number of places after he was released from the Roman imprisonment of Acts 28. He had written 1 Timothy and Titus during this time of liberty. Now, however, he had been rearrested and was facing his last imprisonment. From his Roman cell, Paul wrote to Timothy, whom he had asked to come to him, possibly from Ephesus. The dates for these events are only approximate.

How 2 Timothy Fits into God's "Story"

Second Timothy is part of "chapter 5" of God's story: God spreads the kingdom through the church. Because Paul was at the end of his life, he thought of the kingdom of God as a present heavenly reality, a destination at which he was about to arrive (4:18). Even so, he looked forward to the future glorious form of the kingdom that would be revealed in connection with Jesus's "appearing" on earth again (4:1). Thus at the end of his life, kingdom thinking was still prominent in Paul's theological framework.

ORIGINAL HISTORICAL SETTING

Author and Date of Writing:
Paul the apostle, ca. A.D. 66

See *Author and Date of Writing* for *1 Timothy* for information about objections to Pauline authorship. Assuming that Paul is the author, he wrote from his final Roman imprisonment, ca. A.D. 66. Those who reject Pauline authorship date the letter toward the end of the first century.

First Audience and Destination:
Timothy, Paul's dearest friend, possibly in Ephesus

See *First Audience and Destination* for *1 Timothy*. There is no definite indication in this letter concerning Timothy's location. Many students think it likely that he was still serving the Lord in Ephesus (1 Tim. 1:3).

Occasion

Paul had been rearrested in an unknown place and was back in Rome. The Roman government's official hostility to Christianity (which arose after the great fire of Rome in A.D. 64 when Nero decided to make Christians his scapegoats) was probably the context for Paul's final imprisonment. Paul was evidently in an imperial prison. He was not even given the benefit of adequate clothing against the cold and damp (4:13).

Paul was virtually alone. Only Luke had access to him; others had abandoned him or been sent out in ministry (4:10-12). Paul had been through a preliminary hearing that persuaded him that he would soon be executed (4:16). He therefore wanted company before he died and begged Timothy twice to come (4:9,21). He also wanted his books, his coat, and the fellowship of Mark (4:12-13). It is not known whether Timothy arrived in Rome in time to say good-bye to his beloved mentor face to face.

 ## LITERARY FEATURES

Genre and Literary Style:
An epistle written in Koinē Greek
See *Genre and Literary Style* for *1 Thessalonians* for information about the genre "epistle." The standard parts of a first-century epistle appear in 2 Timothy: salutation (1:1-2); thanksgiving (1:3-7); main body (1:8–4:18); farewell (4:19-22). This letter, like 1 Timothy and Titus, has certain vocabulary and style elements that make these three books distinctive. So clearly do they belong together that they are often considered as a unit, the Pastoral Epistles.

Themes:
Divine election, inspiration of Scripture, being unashamed, sound doctrine
The first two of these has already been noted. The need for courage in the gospel is noted repeatedly: Paul and Onesiphorus were not ashamed (1:12,16; 2:15). Timothy and all God-approved workmen must also be unashamed of Christ (1:8; 2:15). Sound doctrine is crucial as the cure for false teaching. Sound doctrine is prominent in this letter as it is in all the Pastoral Epistles.

Book Features and Structure
Scattered throughout 1 and 2 Timothy and Titus are five "Faithful Sayings," none of which is cited elsewhere. These were almost certainly confessions used publicly in worship. (The first and third of these add the words, "and deserves full acceptance," which was perhaps a congregational oral unison response to the words, "This saying is trustworthy," the leader's call to recitation.)

- "Christ Jesus came into the world to save sinners" (1 Tim. 1:15).
- "If anyone aspires to be an overseer, he desires a noble work" (1 Tim. 3:1).
- "Godliness is beneficial in every way, since it holds promise for the present life and also for the life to come" (1 Tim. 4:8) (possibly 4:10 is the "Faithful Saying").
- "For if we died with him, we will also live with him; if we endure, we will also reign with him; if we deny him, he will also deny us; if we are faithless, he remains faithful, for he cannot deny himself" (2 Tim. 2:11-13).
- "Not by works of righteousness that we had done, but according to his mercy—through the washing of regeneration and renewal by the Holy Spirit. He poured out his Spirit on us abundantly through Jesus Christ our

Savior so that, having been justified by his grace, we may become heirs with the hope of eternal life" (Titus 3:5-7).

The letter is organized into two main sections. Through 4:5, the general subject is commitment to ministry; from 4:6 to the end of the letter is Paul's personal farewell, the most poignant and personal words to come from the apostle.

The Basilica of Saint Titus, Gortyn, Crete

TITUS
THE EPISTLE TO TITUS

This book is so named as the letter that Paul the apostle wrote to Titus.

○ KEY TEXT: 2:1

"But you are to proclaim things consistent with sound teaching."

○ KEY TERM: "DOCTRINE"

This book emphasizes that sound doctrine is the necessary foundation for everything worthwhile in the life of a congregation or an individual.

○ ONE-SENTENCE SUMMARY

Whatever challenges they face in life and ministry, Christian leaders are to maintain order in the congregation, but only according to sound doctrine.

Crete is an island of great beauty and striking contrasts. Paul left his protégé Titus on Crete to "set right what was left undone" and "to appoint elders in every town" (1:5). According to Christian tradition, Titus lived into his 90s. Shown here is an archaeological site on the bay of Komos located in south-central Crete. This bay served as the harbor of Phaistos, Crete, one of the centers of Minoan civilization. Phaistos was inhabited as early as 10,000 B.C.

GOD'S MESSAGE IN THE BOOK

Purpose

Paul wrote to Titus, his friend in ministry, to accomplish a number of objectives. First, he wished to encourage Titus in his Christian growth. Second, he offered instructions about church organization, particularly congregational officers and various age groups. Finally, he wanted Titus to come to Nicopolis to spend the winter with him.

Christian Worldview Elements

Titus focuses on the worldview categories of *community and church*; *discipleship*; and *ethics and morality*. This book especially shows the necessary relationship between sound doctrine and sound behavior.

God
Creation
Sovereignty and Providence
Faith and Reason
Revelation and Authority
Humanity
Rebellion and Sin
Covenant and Redemption
○ Community and Church
○ Discipleship
○ Ethics and Morality
Time and Eternity

Teachings about God

Three times in this short letter the phrase "God our Savior" is used (1:3; 2:10; 3:4). The phrase "Christ Jesus our Savior" appears twice (1:4; 3:6). These two are combined remarkably in the expression, "our great God and Savior, Jesus Christ" (2:13), one of the strongest statements of the deity of Christ in Scripture. The only direct reference to the Spirit concerns his role in the regeneration of sinners (3:5).

Teachings about Humanity

See *Teachings about Humanity* for *1 Timothy*.

Teachings about Salvation

In his first coming, Jesus died to "redeem us from all lawlessness and to cleanse for himself a people for his own possession" (2:14). These people long for the day of full salvation at his return, the "blessed hope" (2:13) of his appearing. The vocabulary of salvation in this letter includes justification by grace (3:7), regeneration (3:5), and eternal life (3:7).

CHRIST IN TITUS

Christ came to redeem human beings from lawlessness, to create a special people, eager to do good works now and to look forward to Christ's appearing a second time.

GOD'S STORY

When the Events of This Book Happened:
ca. A.D. 62-63

After Paul was released from the Roman imprisonment described in Acts 28, he engaged in further travel. One place he stopped was Crete, where he ministered for a time (1:5). From an unknown location, Paul wrote to Titus, whom he had asked to continue on in Crete. The dates for these events are only approximate.

How Titus Fits into God's "Story"

Titus is part of "chapter 5" of God's story: God spreads the kingdom through the church. Although the term "kingdom" does not appear in this letter, the concept is evident. Local congregations of believers in Jesus Christ are like little kingdom outposts, waiting for the time that their King will appear gloriously (2:13). For this reason, it is important for local churches to be organized properly and to maintain sound doctrine.

ORIGINAL HISTORICAL SETTING

Author and Date of Writing:
Paul the apostle, ca. A.D. 63

See *Author and Date of Writing* for *1 Timothy* for information about critical objections to Pauline authorship. Assuming that Paul is the author, he wrote after he was released from the Roman imprisonment described at the end of Acts, ca. A.D. 63. Those who reject Pauline authorship date the letter toward the end of the first century.

First Audience and Destination:
Titus, Paul's trusted friend, who was on Crete

Titus had the task of being an apostolic representative. One of Paul's early converts (1:4), he was a Gentile, evidently from Antioch of Syria. Paul took Titus with him to Jerusalem to discuss the nature of the gospel (Gal. 2:1-3). Titus was so vibrant a disciple that the Jerusalem leaders were persuaded that Paul's law-free gospel was acceptable (Gal. 2:3-5). Titus was with Paul in Ephesus on his third missionary journey and was Paul's ambassador to the troubled church in Corinth, carrying both the "Severe Letter" and 2 Corinthians. (See *Occasion* for *2 Corinthians*.)

After Paul was released from his Roman imprisonment, he assigned Titus the responsibility of helping the churches on the island of Crete with their doctrinal and organizational difficulties. After this letter was written, Paul sent him to Dalmatia (2 Tim. 4:10). Titus proved to be a courageous and strong leader.

Crete is one of the largest islands in the Mediterranean Sea, lying directly south of the Aegean Sea. It is about 160 miles across, with a long history of civilization. In the Old Testament, it was called Caphtor, and the Philistine people probably migrated from there to southern Palestine. Paul's shipwreck adventure occurred after the captain of the ship he was on declined to spend the winter in Crete (Acts 27). Life in Crete was distressing because of the lying and laziness of the people (1:12).

Occasion

It is not known when the gospel first came to Crete. Paul had left Titus there when he discovered that false teaching had upset the stability of the churches there. The exact nature of this teaching is impossible to determine, but it was probably similar to the error facing the Ephesian church about the same time. (See *Occasion* for *1 Timothy*.) Both the false teaching and the Cretan character made Titus's task a big one. From an undisclosed location, possibly Macedonia or Ephesus, Paul wrote this letter to encourage Titus and to remind him of the responsibilities he faced on Crete.

 LITERARY FEATURES

Genre and Literary Style:
An epistle written in Koinē *Greek*

See *Genre and Literary Style* for *1 Thessalonians* for information about the genre "epistle." The standard parts of a first-century epistle appear in Titus, except that the thanksgiving is missing: salutation (1:1-4); main body (1:5–3:14); farewell (3:15). This letter, and 1 and 2 Timothy share certain vocabulary and style elements that make these three books distinctive. So clearly do they belong together that they are often considered as a unit, the Pastoral Epistles.

Themes:
Sound doctrine, elders, proper conduct for each age and gender

Sound doctrine is crucial as the cure for false teaching. This letter gives the qualifications for overseers (also called bishops), but not for other church officers (see 1 Tim. 3). The term "elder" (Greek, *presbyteros*) refers to the maturity and respect—the character qualities—that church leaders must have and was probably derived from the model of the Jewish synagogues. The term "bishop" (Greek, *episkopos*) is better translated "overseer" and refers to the ministry responsibilities entrusted to church leaders. This term was probably taken from Hellenistic (Greek) cultural patterns. Titus 2:1-9 catalogs appropriate relationships within the congregation.

Book Features and Structure

See *Book Features and Structure* for *2 Timothy* for information about the "Faithful Sayings" in the Pastoral Epistles.

The letter has three brief chapters and only 46 verses. Chapter 1 deals with church organization; chapter 2 gives advice to various groups in the church; chapter 3 is essentially a reminder of what sound doctrine includes.

PHILEMON
THE EPISTLE TO PHILEMON

This book is so named as the letter that Paul the apostle wrote to Philemon.

O KEY TEXT: VERSE 16

"No longer as a slave, but more than a slave—as a dearly loved brother. He is especially so to me, but how much more to you, both in the flesh and in the Lord."

O KEY TERM: "BROTHER"

When master and slave are both Christian, they are brothers, and therefore essentially equal. If Christian brotherhood extends this far, then it covers all relationships among the people of God.

O ONE-SENTENCE SUMMARY

Everyone who has repented of sin and come to Christ should be welcomed as a brother (or sister), treated gently, and forgiven by other believers.

Roman mosaic from Dougga, Tunisia (second century A.D.). The two slaves carrying wine jars wear typical slave clothing and an amulet against the evil eye.

GOD'S MESSAGE IN THE BOOK

Purpose

Paul wrote his friend Philemon to urge gentle treatment and forgiveness of a runaway slave, Onesimus. Some scholars believe that Paul's words in verse 21, "knowing that you will do even more than I say," are a strong hint for Philemon to set Onesimus free. Paul also asked Philemon for hospitality when he visited.

Christian Worldview Elements

Philemon deals particularly with the worldview categories of *covenant and redemption* and *ethics and morality*. This book focuses on the ethical responsibilities among redeemed individuals in the covenant community.

God
Creation
Sovereignty and Providence
Faith and Reason
Revelation and Authority
Humanity
Rebellion and Sin
○ **Covenant and Redemption**
Community and Church
Discipleship
○ **Ethics and Morality**
Time and Eternity

Teachings about God

In this epistle, God the Father is the source of grace and peace and the one to whom Christians pray (vv. 3-4). Jesus is the center of faith, on whose account Paul was in prison (vv. 5,9). The Holy Spirit is not specifically mentioned.

Teachings about Humanity

Philemon addresses slavery, an ethical problem that has vexed human life—and Christianity—for centuries. The book does not attack the institution of slavery as a sin, which could not have gained a hearing in the first century. Instead, it teaches that in Christ both master and slave are to consider each other as brothers. When the concept of the basic equality of all who are in Christ prevails, slavery will not endure as an institution. This truth has demonstrated its power in many cultures.

Teachings about Salvation

Salvation is seen through the perspective of two individuals, the master (Philemon) and the slave (Onesimus). Philemon was indebted to the apostle because Paul had brought the message of salvation to him (v. 19). Onesimus is a classic example of transformation because of the message of salvation: "Once he was useless to you, but now he is useful both to you and to me" (v. 11).

☧ CHRIST IN PHILEMON

Christ's grace is offered to master and slave alike. In Christ, master and slave become brothers.

GOD'S STORY

When the Events of This Book Happened:
From ca. A.D. 53 to 61

Philemon had come to Christ through Paul, evidently while Paul was in Ephesus on his third missionary journey. He had arrived there ca. A.D. 53 (Acts 19). Paul wrote at a time when he was imprisoned (vv. 10,13). This was the time he was in Rome for two years waiting to appear before Nero (ca. A.D. 60–61), as Acts 28 describes.

How Philemon Fits into God's "Story"

Philemon is part of "chapter 5" of God's story: God spreads the kingdom through the church. Although the term "kingdom" does not appear in this letter, its message is kingdom centered. All citizens of God's kingdom are brothers and sisters, and therefore they are under obligation to relate to one another with love and gentleness (see Matt. 5:1-10 for the character qualities of kingdom citizens).

ORIGINAL HISTORICAL SETTING

Author and Date of Writing:
Paul the apostle, ca. A.D. 61

This book claims to be written by Paul (v. 1). All scholars accept this claim. (See *Author and Date of Writing* for *Romans* for more information about Paul.) The apostle wrote from Roman imprisonment as described at the end of Acts, ca. A.D. 60–61.

First Audience and Destination:
Philemon, Paul's dear friend, who was in Colossae

Philemon was a wealthy Christian from Colossae with a wife, Apphia, and son, Archippus (Col. 4:17; Phlm. 2). Paul had led Philemon to faith in Christ, and they had worked together for the cause of Christ in ways not known (Phlm. 1,19). At the time Paul wrote Philemon, he was the host for one of the house churches of Colossae (Phlm. 2). (For information about Colossae, see *First Audience and Destination* for *Colossians.*)

Occasion

Onesimus, one of Philemon's slaves, had evidently stolen money from his master and then run away to Rome (v. 18). Somehow Onesimus had made his way to the house where Paul was under arrest, and he had been converted to Christ. His life had been transformed, and he had become a useful helper to Paul.

Paul, however, concluded that it was right for Onesimus to return to his master, even though Philemon had every legal right to deal with Onesimus harshly. Severe floggings were common punishments when runaway slaves were caught. Paul therefore wrote this letter to urge Philemon to forgive Onesimus and to treat him gently (vv. 17-18). Paul also alerted Philemon of his plans to visit him whenever he was released (v. 22). Philemon is one of the four Prison Epistles. (See *Occasion* for *Colossians*.)

According to Col. 4:7-9, Onesimus traveled to Colossae under the protection of Tychicus at the same time that Tychicus was carrying the letter to the Colossians. Thus when Tychicus traveled from Rome to Colossae, he was responsible for delivering two epistles to congregations (Ephesians and Colossians) as well as returning one slave (Onesimus), who probably hand-delivered the letter to Philemon.

 LITERARY FEATURES

Genre and Literary Style:
A brief epistle written in Koinē *Greek*
See *Genre and Literary Style* for *1 Thessalonians* for information about the genre "epistle." This letter has all four standard parts of a first-century epistle: salutation (vv. 1-3); thanksgiving (vv. 4-7); main body (vv. 8-22); farewell (vv. 23-25). The Greek of this letter is typical for Paul.

Themes:
Love, forgiveness
Paul's emphasis on love (Greek, *agapē*) as the motive for all relationships among Christians is striking (vv. 5,7,9). Interestingly, Paul's appeal for Philemon to forgive Onesimus's wrongs did not necessarily mean that he was to forget about his financial loss. Paul pledged that he would personally pay back what Onesimus had taken (v. 18).

Book Features and Structure
This is the shortest of all Paul's letters by far, at only 25 verses. It is the classic example of a personal communication, which, under the guidance of God's Spirit, has a place in the canon of Scripture as an inspired and abiding word from God to his people.

The body of the letter has two sections. First is Paul's request for Onesimus (through v. 21). Second is Paul's request for hospitality when he next visits Colossae.

HEBREWS
THE EPISTLE TO THE HEBREWS

This title is based on the belief that the first recipients were Hebrew (or Jewish) believers in Jesus as the Messiah.

○ KEY TEXT: 1:1-3

"Long ago God spoke to the fathers by the prophets at different times and in different ways. In these last days, he has spoken to us by his Son. God has appointed him heir of all things and made the universe through him. The Son is the radiance of God's glory and the exact expression of his nature, sustaining all things by his powerful word. After making purification for sins, he sat down at the right hand of the Majesty on high."

○ KEY TERM: "BETTER"

This book repeatedly makes the case that Christ and Christianity is better or superior to the old way of the old covenant. The word "better" (Greek, *kreitton* or *kreisson*) appears 12 times.

○ ONE-SENTENCE SUMMARY

Jesus Christ, who is better than the angels, Moses, Joshua, and the Hebrew high priests, made a better sacrifice and established a better covenant, ensuring that the old way is obsolete and that faith is the better way to live.

"During his earthly life, [Jesus] offered prayers and appeals with loud cries and tears to the one who was able to save him from death, and he was heard because of his reverence. Although he was the Son, he learned obedience from what he suffered" (Heb. 5:7-8).

GOD'S MESSAGE IN THE BOOK

Purpose

Hebrews was written to wean Jewish believers in Jesus from depending on the law of Moses or the old covenant, represented by the Old Testament, as the final rule for life. In order to do this, the author emphasized the superiority of Jesus Christ both in his person and in his work. The author also showed that the essential weakness of the old covenant was its "planned obsolescence" in God's purposes.

Christian Worldview Elements

Hebrews deals particularly with the worldview categories of *revelation and authority*; *covenant and redemption*; and *community and church*. No Bible book more fully teaches the superiority of Christ's person and work over all of God's previous dealings with humanity.

God
Creation
Sovereignty and Providence
Faith and Reason
○ **Revelation and Authority**
Humanity
Rebellion and Sin
○ **Covenant and Redemption**
○ **Community and Church**
Discipleship
Ethics and Morality
Time and Eternity

Teachings about God

God is the Father of Jesus Christ. He is wholly other and is to be approached with reverence and fear, "For our God is a consuming fire" (12:29). The superiority of Jesus to all possible rivals is the theme of the entire book. The full deity and complete humanity of Jesus is explicitly taught. The Holy Spirit in Hebrews is both the one who speaks in Scripture (3:7; 10:15) and the one alive among believers in the present age (6:4; 10:29).

Teachings about Humanity

A number of prominent Old Testament people are mentioned in Hebrews, and the "roll call of faith" in chapter 11 is an impressive reminder of what believing humans can do. The emphasis in Hebrews, however, is that Jesus has the glory and honor of being humanity at its best. In Psalm 8 God declared "man" as the crown of creation; Heb. 2 declares that this "man" is none other than Jesus Christ.

Teachings about Salvation

Jesus is a better high priest than the high priests of the old covenant. Further, Jesus's death was a superior sacrifice to any that had been made before, "For it is impossible for the blood of bulls and of goats to take away sins" (10:4). At the same time, however, Hebrews affirms that the human response to God's redemptive actions, faith, has always and forever been the single way that pleases God. This Bible book, more clearly than any other, shows the permanence of the new covenant state of affairs and the impermanence of the old covenant.

CHRIST IN HEBREWS

Christ is both God's agent of creation and the one for whom the universe is created. He is superior to angels, Moses, the priesthood, the old covenant, and the Levitical sacrificial system. Christ is both the source of our faith and the one who brings it to perfection. He is the same yesterday, today, and forever.

 GOD'S STORY

When the Events of This Book Happened:
Probably in the late A.D. 60s

The historical background is probably the persecution of Christians in Rome after the great fire of A.D. 64. The only contemporary events mentioned in the book are the persecutions the recipients have experienced and a few notices at the end of the book. These cannot be dated precisely, but late A.D. 60s seems to fit.

How Hebrews Fits into God's "Story"

Hebrews is part of "chapter 5" of God's story: God spreads the kingdom through the church. Language about the kingdom of God does not dominate this book, but it is striking when it exists. Jesus the Son of God is the King of God's everlasting kingdom (1:8; 7:1-2). The recipients are told about their future eternal state in explicit kingdom language: "Therefore, since we are receiving a kingdom that cannot be shaken, let us be thankful. By it, we may serve God acceptably, with reverence and awe" (12:28).

 ORIGINAL HISTORICAL SETTING

Author and Date of Writing:
Unknown, perhaps ca. A.D. 66

The secret of this book's authorship is one of the longest ongoing challenges for Bible students. In fact, scholarship has hardly advanced further today than Origen of the third century, who said that God alone knew who wrote the epistle. In the earliest centuries, Barnabas and Luke were mentioned as possible authors; in the Reformation era, Luther made the brilliant suggestion that Apollos may have been the author. From the fifth to the sixteenth centuries, Paul was believed to be the author, and many handwritten Greek manuscripts added Paul's name to the title, as did many translations.

The consensus of contemporary scholarship is that Paul could not have been the author. The strongest argument is historical: the author put himself in second-generation Christianity, distancing himself from eyewitnesses. In the eyes of many Bible students, it is impossible that the one who wrote Heb. 2:3-4 could also have written Gal. 1:11-12, Paul's vehement claim that he was an eyewitness.

The author was an expert in Scripture, quoting extensively from the Greek translation (the Septuagint). He was almost certainly Jewish, with an outstanding ability in Greek composition. Although knowing his name would be interesting, it would add little to the interpretation of the book's message. The date of composition may be ca. A.D. 66, almost certainly before the destruction of Jerusalem (A.D. 70).

First Audience and Destination:
Jewish believers, perhaps in Rome

As the title suggests, the letter was first "to the Hebrews." A number of features point in this direction, particularly the detailed arguments about the sacrificial system and the priesthood of the Old Testament. They were, however, now Christians. The greeting of 13:24 was sent from persons with the author to their fellow Italians "back home." This and the first citation of the epistle, by Clement of Rome ca. A.D. 96, suggests that the original recipients were Christians in Italy, perhaps Rome itself.

Occasion

The precise occasion has been debated because interpreters are limited to the data provided by the epistle, which is not entirely clear. These Jewish believers had been persecuted (10:32-39). They were now, however, considering giving up Christianity and returning to Judaism, which was legally recognized, unlike Christianity. Hebrews 10:25 may refer to some who had already withdrawn from meeting with the multiethnic congregation. The author, who knew their situation well, composed this letter about the superiority of Christ and Christianity and the danger of turning away to something that was clearly inferior.

 ## LITERARY FEATURES

Genre and Literary Style:
A long, formal epistle written in excellent Koinē Greek

Some scholars designate Hebrews as a tractate (a formal treatise rather than a pastoral letter). Two of the usual features of an epistle (salutation and thanksgiving) are missing, although there is a body (1:1–13:17) and farewell (13:18-25). In addition, it has a number of sermon-like features. It begins with a rhetorical statement of its thesis (1:1-3) and develops step-by-step arguments. The farewell shows that in its present form it was sent as a letter. The style of argument has parallels to the figurative interpretations made by Philo, the Jewish scholar of Alexandria. The Greek of Hebrews is outstanding, with a large vocabulary and excellent style, suggesting that the author was highly educated. The style is more like that of Luke and Acts than any other New Testament book.

Themes:

Superiority of Christ, the new covenant, Christ's priesthood, warnings
The author shows the superiority of Christ in a number of ways: he is better than angels (invisible and powerful spirit beings); than Moses (the great law-giver); than Joshua (the great land-giver); and than Aaron (the high priest). The new covenant Christ made is better because God designed it, unlike the Mosaic covenant, to last forever.

Book Features and Structure

Hebrews is memorable for its serious warning passages (2:1-4; 3:7-19; 4:11-13; 6:4-12; 10:19-31; 12:25-29). These should be understood as applying to all who profess Christ (but may not "possess" him). The plea is to prove the genuineness of faith by refusing the pressure to defect.

The structure of Hebrews revolves around three main points. First, Christ is superior in his person (chaps. 1–7). Second, Christ is superior in his sacrificial work (chaps. 8–10). Third, faith is the better way (chaps. 10–13).

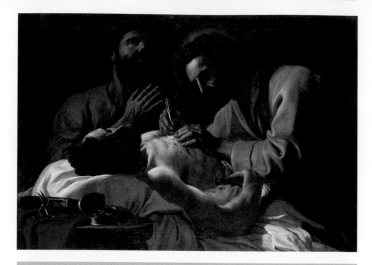

"Is anyone among you suffering? He should pray. Is anyone cheerful? He should sing praises. Is anyone among you sick? He should call for the elders of the church, and they are to pray over him, anointing him with oil in the name of the Lord. The prayer of faith will save the sick person, and the Lord will raise him up; if he has committed sins, he will be forgiven. Therefore, confess your sins to one another and pray for one another, so that you may be healed. The prayer of a righteous person is very powerful in its effect" (Jas. 5:13-16).

JAMES
THE EPISTLE OF JAMES

This letter is titled according to its author, James, who was probably the half brother of Jesus.

🔘 KEY TEXT: 2:26

"For just as the body without the spirit is dead, so also faith without works is dead."

🔘 KEY TERM: "WORKS"

This book focuses on the importance of good works as the evidence of genuine faith. As such, it perfectly complements Galatians.

🔘 ONE-SENTENCE SUMMARY

True faith must be lived out in everyday life by good deeds, especially in the face of trials or persecution, and such good works demonstrate the presence of faith and justification before God.

"You do not know what tomorrow will bring—what your life will be! For you are like vapor that appears for a little while, then vanishes" (James 4:14).

GOD'S MESSAGE IN THE BOOK

Purpose

James was originally composed to let (Jewish) believers in Jesus know the importance of having a practical, living, everyday faith. For James, practical faith equaled good works, and those who professed faith yet had no good works could not presume that they were truly God's people. James also wrote to give good advice about what to do in the presence of temptations, trials, and persecution.

Christian Worldview Elements

James focuses on the worldview categories of *community and church* and *ethics and morality*. This book teaches the importance of good works as the inevitable and essential fruit of salvation.

God
Creation
Sovereignty and Providence
Faith and Reason
Revelation and Authority
Humanity
Rebellion and Sin
Covenant and Redemption
o **Community and Church**
Discipleship
o **Ethics and Morality**
Time and Eternity

Teachings about God

God is good and the Father of his redeemed children. James often calls him "the Lord," evidently parallel to the Old Testament usage of "the Lord" (Yahweh), in particular calling him "the Lord of sabaoth" (meaning "hosts" or "armies," 5:4). Jesus is mentioned only twice (1:1; 2:1), which contributes to the distinctive Old Testament feel to this book. The Spirit is not referred to except in NASB, NKJV, and as an alternative translation in CSB (4:5).

Teachings about Humanity

James had a realistic, some would say pessimistic, view of the effects of sin in human life. The rich oppress the poor; temptation is a constant danger; all persons are possessed of an evil tongue. Even believers can be called "you adulterous people" (4:4) for being too friendly with the evil world, like the people of Israel who "prostituted themselves with other gods" (Judg. 2:17; 8:33). The advice James offered was to submit to God's sovereign goodness, to seek to live a life of true religion, and to do good deeds.

Teachings about Salvation

God saves through the action of "the implanted word" (1:21), bringing the response of faith. While Paul emphasized that faith alone saves, James emphasized that saving faith is never alone. For Paul, justification is a legal declaration of righteousness before God. (See *Romans.*) James, however, used justification in the sense of being righteous before people. Thus he can say, "You see that a person is justified by works and not by faith alone" (2:24). Good works are open to observation by others; faith is not; therefore, good works make faith visible. Good works are never the root (cause) of salvation, but they are always the fruit (result) of salvation.

CHRIST IN JAMES

Salvation made James a slave of his half-brother Jesus, the resurrected Lord (1:1). Jesus the Lord shares God's unique glory (2:1). Looking forward to his return will be a source of patience with the trials and tests of life.

GOD'S STORY

When the Events of This Book Happened:
Probably in the A.D. 40s
The only events mentioned in the book are the persecutions the recipients have experienced. These cannot be dated precisely, but the decade of the A.D. 40s seems to fit.

How James Fits into God's "Story"
James is part of "chapter 5" of God's story: God spreads the kingdom through the church. The kingdom of God is mentioned only once in this book. This instance is consistent with the letter's overall teaching that God's values and the wicked world's values oppose each other. Those who are rich in this world are likely to miss the kingdom; those who are poor in this world will be "heirs of the kingdom" (2:5). This is strikingly like the teaching of Jesus in the Gospels (Luke 6:20).

ORIGINAL HISTORICAL SETTING

Author and Date of Writing:
James, perhaps ca. A.D. 45
The author identified himself as "James, a servant of God and of the Lord Jesus Christ" (1:1). James is the English translation of the Hebrew name "Jacob" when it appears in the New Testament, *Iakōbos* in Greek. There were several Jameses in the New Testament, including two apostles (Matt. 10:2-3). This letter was almost certainly written by the James who rose to prominence in the church of Jerusalem (Acts 12:17; 15:13; 21:18). This was "James, the Lord's brother" (Gal. 1:19; 2:9). The son of Mary and Joseph, James had not believed that Jesus his older half brother was the Messiah until after the resurrection, when Jesus appeared to him (Matt. 13:55; John 7:5; 1 Cor. 15:7).

James was an effective leader as Acts and this letter shows. He apparently rose to leadership in the Jerusalem church sometime around the time that Peter left Jerusalem, ca. A.D. 44 (see Acts 12, especially v. 17). The tenor of his letter is such that it must predate the Jerusalem Council of A.D. 49 that opened Christianity officially and fully to Gentiles (Acts 15). So the epistle is likely to be dated between 44 and 49, with the year 45 being a reasonable estimate, perhaps composed in Jerusalem. James was probably one of the first New Testament book written.

According to the Jewish historian Josephus, James was martyred in A.D. 62. Christian tradition indicates that he was thrown from the pinnacle of the temple.

First Audience and Destination:
Jewish believers living somewhere outside Palestine

This letter was written to Jewish followers of Jesus. Their meeting was called a *synagōgen* in the original (2:2), and they were led by "elders" (5:14). They were part of "the twelve tribes dispersed abroad" (1:1), meaning Jews living outside Palestine. They lived in an unknown city of the Roman Empire where they spoke Greek. No reference is made to Gentiles.

Occasion

No one knows how James came to know about these believers. They had been victims of harassment of some kind and were being taken advantage of by their rich neighbors (1:2; 2:6). He wrote these discouraged disciples to encourage them not to lose heart. They also needed to know that the elements of true religion taught both in the Old Testament and by Jesus—giving, praying, fasting, living a holy life, and caring for widows, orphans, and the poor—were still part of the royal law of love that they were to live by (Matt. 6:1-18; Jas. 1:27; 2:8).

 ## LITERARY FEATURES

Genre and Literary Style:
An epistle written in Koinē Greek

James is the first of seven General Epistles in the New Testament, all of which are titled according to their author. Two of the usual features of an epistle (thanksgiving and farewell) are missing, although there is a salutation (1:1) and body (1:2–5:20). James is a pastoral letter, driven by the occasion and needs of the recipients, rather than a tractate (a formal treatise). Many scholars have noted the parallels in style between Proverbs and James. Many practical truths are presented, but they are only very loosely connected by the general theme of everyday Christian living. The Greek style is considered above average for the books of the New Testament.

Themes:
Faith and works, trials and temptations, rich and poor, the tongue, patience

These themes are all developed to encourage believers disheartened by their circumstances. All these themes deal with living successfully in this life, being aware that everything happens according to God's providence (4:15). Thus doctrinal truths are presented only when they help the reader understand how they relate to living effectively in everyday life.

Book Features and Structure

James is noted not only for its similarity to Proverbs, but also for its similarity to the Sermon on the Mount. (It is at least possible that James heard his brother Jesus give this sermon, even though he was not yet a follower.) The following points of connection are noteworthy:

- The poor to be rich in faith and inherit the kingdom (Jas. 2:5; Matt. 5:3)
- Contrasting plant pairs, such as grapes versus thorns (Jas. 3:10-12; Matt. 7:15-20)
- Blessing promised to peacemakers (Jas. 3:18; Matt. 5:9)
- The ease with which earthly riches are corrupted (Jas. 5:2-3; Matt. 6:19-20)
- Swearing prohibited ("let your 'yes' mean 'yes'") (Jas. 5:12; Matt. 5:33-37)

The structure of James is very loose. Each chapter may be characterized by a key term, however: (1) trials, (2) works, (3) tongue, (4) wisdom, (5) patience.

Asia Minor in the first century A.D.

1 PETER
THE FIRST EPISTLE OF PETER

Titled according to its author, this is the first canonical letter by Simon Peter, the apostle of Jesus.

⭕ KEY TEXT: 4:13

"Instead, rejoice as you share in the sufferings of Christ, so that you may also rejoice with great joy when his glory is revealed."

⭕ KEY TERM: "HOPE"

This epistle emphasizes hope for suffering believers. Hope (Greek, *elpis*) means "future certainty" rather than a vague expectation of some future occurrence.

⭕ ONE-SENTENCE SUMMARY

As Christians grow in understanding their privileges in salvation, their blessings of election, and the theology of suffering, they will live in holiness and humility, waiting for their great future hope of sharing Christ's glory.

Cappadocia (in Turkey) is one of the provinces to which Peter's letter circulated. During persecutions in larger cities, Christians fled to Cappadocia where the many caves provided places of safety. By the time of Constantine's reign (A.D. 313–337), Christianity had become the primary religion in this region.

GOD'S MESSAGE IN THE BOOK

Purpose

First Peter was written to encourage suffering Christians to live in light of the future. The apostle wanted to give a number of doctrinal insights and also provided many practical instructions, such as how to submit to those in authority. This book contains the most extensive New Testament development of a "theology of suffering," and it echoes the teaching of Job that God's glory is served when suffering is permitted.

Christian Worldview Elements

This book directs attention to the world-view categories of *sovereignty and providence*; *covenant and redemption*; and *ethics and morality*. No Bible book more clearly teaches the relationship between suffering and salvation.

God
Creation
○ **Sovereignty and Providence**
Faith and Reason
Revelation and Authority
Humanity
Rebellion and Sin
○ **Covenant and Redemption**
Community and Church
Discipleship
○ **Ethics and Morality**
Time and Eternity

Teachings about God

This book notes many attributes of God, from his foreknowledge (1:2) to his grace (5:12). The glory of God is the goal of all things (4:11). Jesus's suffering and death for sinners is highly empha-sized, as is his resurrection and return in glory. The Holy Spirit, who inspired the prophets of old, has now been sent to God's people (1:11; 4:14). First Peter 1:2 is an important text for understanding the Trinity.

Teachings about Humanity

First Peter dignifies all classes of human life by showing that living by the gospel makes a great difference in relationships. Christians submit both to government and to masters to the glory of God. In the Christian family, hus-bands and wives have a mutual responsibility to respect each other. In the congregation, spiritual leaders ("elders," 5:1) lead their flocks by being humble servants, creating a context of mutual submission.

Teachings about Salvation

Salvation in this book is past, present, and future. The past aspect involves God's sovereign election as well as Jesus's suffering and death to purchase salvation (2:9; 3:18). The present aspect involves the regeneration and the ongoing faith of God's people (1:3,21; 5:9). At Christ's return, those who "are being guarded by God's power through faith" will receive the "salvation that is ready to be revealed in the last time" (1:5).

CHRIST IN 1 PETER

The Spirit of Christ was present in the Hebrew prophets pointing them to the sufferings of Christ and the glory that followed his sufferings. Christ is like a lamb without defect or blemish. His precious blood redeems believers from their futile ways. Believers can expect to suffer as he suffered and anticipate the joy of his coming in glory.

GOD'S STORY

When the Events of This Book Happened:
Probably in the A.D. 60s

The only contemporary events the book mentions are the persecutions the recipients have experienced. These cannot be dated precisely, but the decade of the A.D. 60s seems to fit.

How 1 Peter Fits into God's "Story"

First Peter is part of "chapter 5" of God's story: God spreads the kingdom through the church. The kingdom of God is not directly mentioned. Yet what had been said in Scripture about Israel as God's people is now fulfilled by God's new people: "But you are a chosen race, a royal priesthood, a holy nation, a people for his possession, so that you may proclaim the praises of the one who called you" (2:9). Israel was the chosen people (Isa. 44:1), so now are Christians; Israel was the royal priesthood (Isa. 61:6), so now are Christians; Israel was a holy nation (Deut. 28:9), so now are Christians; Israel was a peculiar (special) treasure to God (Deut. 14:2), so now are Christians. God's kingdom plan for Israel to praise him (Isa. 43:21) is now fulfilled by his new people, the church.

ORIGINAL HISTORICAL SETTING

Author and Date of Writing:
Simon Peter the apostle, perhaps ca. A.D. 64

The author called himself "Peter, an apostle of Jesus Christ" (1:1). He was the son of Jonah (or John), the brother of Andrew, and a Galilean fisherman by trade when Jesus called him to become an apostle. His birth name, Simeon (often shortened to Simon), was transformed by Jesus to "Rock" ("Peter" in Greek; "Cephas" in Aramaic).

Peter's role as one of the three most prominent apostles (along with James and John) is well known from the Gospels. Peter rose to become the most visible leader of Christianity in Jerusalem. According to Paul, Peter was the apostle to Jews (Gal. 2:8). Peter's contribution to the New Testament was two epistles and probably collaboration with John Mark in producing the Second Gospel. In this letter, Peter mentioned that he was in Rome (called "Babylon," as in

Revelation) and that Mark was with him (5:13). According to tradition, he was later crucified in Rome during the last years of Nero.

For the past two centuries, many critical scholars have argued that Peter could not be the author of this epistle, primarily for two reasons. First, the excellent Greek of this letter is thought to be beyond what a Galilean fisherman could produce (Acts 4:13). Second, the persecutions are thought to belong to a later era than Nero's. These objections may be satisfactorily answered. First, the Greek style is probably due to the help of Silvanus (Silas), which Peter acknowledged (5:12). Second, the suffering of the believers could just as easily have occurred in Nero's time as in a later era. There is no persuasive reason to deny that Simon Peter wrote this epistle.

First Audience and Destination:
Believers living in Roman provinces of Asia Minor
This letter was addressed "To those chosen, living as exiles dispersed abroad in Pontus, Galatia, Cappadocia, Asia, and Bithynia" (1:1). These five Roman provinces make up roughly the northern half of modern Turkey. The order is probably the route the letter carrier followed. Evidence within the letter suggests that these believers were primarily Gentile (and therefore pagan, 1:18) in background, although there was probably also a Jewish minority (accounting for the frequent Old Testament references).

Occasion
Peter knew a great deal about what these believers had gone through, but he did not tell his source of information. They had been victims of serious persecution and unjust suffering, something Peter called a "fiery ordeal" (4:12). This in all likelihood was the first official Roman persecution of Christians, instigated by Nero after the great fire in Rome of A.D. 64. These disciples needed to be encouraged not to lose heart. He wanted to remind them of a number of important doctrinal truths (about God and salvation) as well as to help them see that suffering within the plan of God serves his glory. Thus Peter wrote this letter with the help of Silvanus (Silas).

 ## LITERARY FEATURES

Genre and Literary Style:
An epistle written in Koinē Greek
First Peter is the second of seven General Epistles in the New Testament, all of which are titled according to their author. All four of the usual features of an epistle are present: salutation (1:1-2); thanksgiving (1:3-5); body (1:6–5:11); farewell (5:12-14). Some scholars designate 1 Peter as a tractate (a formal treatise rather than a pastoral letter), particularly since it originated as a circular letter intended for several churches. The Greek style is excellent, on a par with Luke, Acts, and Hebrews.

Themes:

Hope, suffering, holiness, humility, submission

The first of these themes is oriented to the future, and it drives the rest. When believers are absolutely certain that there is a glorious future ahead, they can endure whatever negative experiences they must face in the present. Suffering becomes a privilege; holiness means becoming like God; humility and submission in relationships model living according to Jesus's example, "that you should follow his steps" (2:21).

Book Features and Structure

This epistle is noted for careful composition and many Old Testament quotations. Rather than give one extensive doctrinal presentation followed by application (such as Paul often did), Peter goes back and forth between doctrinal and practical teachings.

The following structure is based on this doctrinal-practical alteration. *Doctrinal teaching*: 1:1-12, privileges of salvation; 2:4-10, blessings of election; 3:13–4:19, theology of suffering. *Practical teaching*: 1:13–2:3, holiness; 2:11–3:12, submission; 5:1-14, humility.

"Scoffers will come in the last days scoffing and following their own evil desires, saying, 'Where is his coming that he promised? Ever since our ancestors fell asleep, all things continue as they have been since the beginning of creation.' They deliberately overlook this: By the word of God the heavens came into being long ago and the earth was brought about from water and through water. Through these the world of that time perished when it was flooded. By the same word, the present heavens and earth are stored up for fire, being kept for the day of judgment and destruction of the ungodly" (2 Pet. 3:3-7). *Noah: The Eve of the Deluge* by John Linnell (1848).

2 PETER
THE SECOND EPISTLE OF PETER

Titled according to its author, this is the second canonical letter by Simon Peter, the apostle of Jesus.

○ **KEY TEXT: 1:12**

"Therefore I will always remind you about these things, even though you know them and are established in the truth you now have."

"For we did not follow cleverly contrived myths when we made known to you the power and coming of our Lord Jesus Christ; instead, we were eyewitnesses of his majesty. For he received honor and glory from God the Father when the voice came to him from the Majestic Glory, saying 'This is my beloved Son, with whom I am well-pleased!' We ourselves heard this voice when it came from heaven while we were with him on the holy mountain" (2 Pet. 1:16-18). *Transfiguration* by Duccio di Buoninsegna.

○ KEY TERM: "RETURN"

This epistle shows the importance of holding firmly to the truth in the face of false teachings, particularly the truth that Jesus will visibly, bodily, and gloriously return and bring about the consummation of all things.

○ ONE-SENTENCE SUMMARY

As Christians grow in understanding, they will be safeguarded from false teachers, especially those who deny the return of Christ and the end of the world as it now exists.

GOD'S MESSAGE IN THE BOOK

Purpose

Second Peter was written to warn Christians who were facing the coming of false teachers. The apostle wanted to arm them with true knowledge as opposed to the heresy that was threatening them (2:1). The false teaching that Peter particularly attacked concerned whether Christ's return and the end of the world would really happen.

Christian Worldview Elements

Second Peter focuses attention on the worldview categories of *revelation and authority* and *ethics and morality*. This book especially shows the nature of truth as revealed by God (rather than merely discovered by people) and that this view of truth has a bearing on behavior.

> God
> Creation
> Sovereignty and Providence
> Faith and Reason
> ○ **Revelation and Authority**
> Humanity
> Rebellion and Sin
> Covenant and Redemption
> Community and Church
> Discipleship
> ○ **Ethics and Morality**
> Time and Eternity

Teachings about God

God is the Father of Jesus, and he glorified his Son (1:17). He is the judge of all beings, human and superhuman (2:4). This is the only Bible book that uses the full title "our Lord and Savior Jesus Christ" (1:11; 2:20; 3:18), a magnificent confession by one who knew him face to face during his earthly life. The single reference to the Holy Spirit mentions his role in the inspiration of Scripture (1:21).

Teachings about Humanity

Second Peter shows the great evil of those who are enslaved by error and sin: "like irrational animals—creatures of instinct born to be caught and destroyed—slander what they do not understand, and in their destruction they too will be destroyed" (2:12). On the other hand, redeemed humanity can grow in every virtue (1:5-8).

Teachings about Salvation

This book provides an important definition of heresy as "denying the Master who bought them" (2:1). In other words, a heresy is a serious error about the person or work of Christ, in particular a denial that his death involved the purchase of salvation. There is little that the letter develops about Christ's work, but God's people are described as those "who have received a faith equal to ours" (1:1). The future dimension of salvation will be revealed on "the day of the Lord" and the coming of "new heavens and a new earth, where righteousness dwells" (3:10,13).

 CHRIST IN 2 PETER

Christ came to live, die, and rise again in space and time. This is not some myth cleverly made up by men. Peter says that he was an eyewitness of Christ's glory on the mount of transfiguration when he, James, and John heard the voice of the Father say, "This is my beloved Son, with whom I am well-pleased!" (1:17).

 GOD'S STORY

When the Events of This Book Happened:
Probably in the A.D. 60s

The only contemporary events the book mentions are the coming of false teachers. These cannot be dated precisely, but the decade of the A.D. 60s seems to fit.

How 2 Peter Fits into God's "Story"

Second Peter is part of "chapter 5" of God's story: God spreads the kingdom through the church. The kingdom of God is directly mentioned in this epistle as the glorious goal of God's chosen people: "Therefore, brothers and sisters, make every effort to confirm your calling and election, because if you do these things you will never stumble. For in this way, entry into the eternal kingdom of our Lord and Savior Jesus Christ will be richly provided for you" (1:10-11).

 ORIGINAL HISTORICAL SETTING

Author and Date of Writing:
Simon Peter the apostle, perhaps ca. A.D. 67

The author named himself "Simeon Peter," and after hesitation on the part of a few, this book was accepted as apostolic in the fourth century. (See *Author and Date of Writing* for *1 Peter.*) For the past two centuries, however, almost all critical scholars have denied that Peter could be the author of this epistle. Both the style and content of this letter are noticeably different from 1 Peter. The difference in style, however, may be accounted for by the loss of Silas's secretarial assistance (1 Pet. 5:12) and the difference in content may surely be attributed to the differing occasions of the two letters. Another argument has been based on the reference to Paul's epistles (3:15-16), which supposedly refer to a time after Paul's letters had been collected, which in turn must be after Peter's lifetime. Yet this reference only means that Peter knew some of Paul's letters.

There is no persuasive reason to deny that Simon Peter wrote this epistle. The date of 67 is a best guess, determined by noting the strong tradition that Peter died during the last part of Nero's reign (ruled A.D. 54–68).

First Audience and Destination:
Believers living in an unknown location
The recipients were not specified geographically. Peter knew these people well enough to call them "dear friends" and to have written them a previous letter (3:1). There is no way to know whether these were the same believers addressed in his first epistle.

Occasion

Peter was aware of his own approaching death (1:14). He may already have been imprisoned in Rome, but he did not allude to this. He had become aware that these Christian friends were facing the threat of false teachers who were denying the saving work of Christ. Along with this went a skepticism about the historical facts surrounding the first coming of Jesus. Others were denying the second coming of Christ. As an eyewitness to Christ's life (1:16), perhaps one of the few left alive, Peter determined to write this letter before he died to affirm the reality of the first and second coming of Jesus and to "stir up your sincere understanding by way of reminder" (3:1).

 LITERARY FEATURES

Genre and Literary Style:
An epistle written in Koinē Greek
Second Peter is the third of seven General Epistles in the New Testament, all of which are titled according to their author. One of the usual features of an epistle (thanksgiving) is missing, although there is a salutation (1:1-2), body (1:3–3:18a), and a farewell (in this letter, a brief doxology, 3:18b). Second Peter is a pastoral letter, driven by the occasion and needs of the recipients, rather than a tractate (a formal treatise). The Greek style is awkward but more like 1 Peter than any other part of the Scriptures.

Themes:
Election, false teachers, "day of the Lord"

The letter strongly emphasizes divine predestination in salvation. The material on false teachers should be compared with Jude. The teaching on the "day of the Lord" is in the last chapter. This theme was also developed by Paul (1 Cor. 5:5; 2 Cor. 1:14; 1 Thess. 5:2; 2 Thess. 2:2). It appears to be the same as the "day of God" (2 Pet. 3:12; Rev. 16:14) and the "day of Christ" (Phil. 1:6,10; 2:16). (See *Joel* and *Zephaniah* for this theme in the Old Testament.)

Book Features and Structure

This epistle, especially chapter 2, is noted for its similarity to Jude, and most Bible students agree that there is a literary relationship between the two epistles. (See *Book Features and Structure* for *Jude.*) Peter developed his letter around three main topics: truth (chap. 1); false teachers (chap. 2), and the return of Christ (chap. 3).

John the Theologian and Prokhor by Andrei Mironov (b. 1975)

1 JOHN
THE FIRST EPISTLE OF JOHN

Titled according to its author, this is the first canonical letter by John, the apostle of Jesus.

⭘ KEY TEXT: 1:3

"What we have seen and heard we also declare to you, so that you may also have fellowship with us; and indeed our fellowship is with the Father and with his Son Jesus Christ."

⭘ KEY TERM: "FELLOWSHIP"

Fellowship (Greek, *koinōnia*) is partnership with Jesus and partnership with other believers in Jesus. The best preventive against false doctrine is true fellowship.

⭘ ONE-SENTENCE SUMMARY

Christians have fellowship with Christ, who is God incarnate, through walking in the light and through living in love, and as a result they are secure in the eternal life that Christ has given them.

Baptistry in the Basilica of St. John, Ephesus, Turkey

GOD'S MESSAGE IN THE BOOK

Purpose

First John was written mainly to combat the false doctrines of denying either the incarnation of Jesus Christ (that he came with real humanity and a truly physical body) or the messiahship of Jesus (that he is the Christ). These heresies led to certain false behaviors, in particular a denial of the seriousness of sin. John wrote not only to correct these dangers but to give positive encouragement about true beliefs and true Christian behavior, centered on fellowship with Jesus Christ.

Christian Worldview Elements

This book directs attention to the worldview categories of *faith and reason*; *covenant and redemption*; and *ethics and morality*. Reality is not just what the senses or reasons indicate but what can be known through faith. First John especially focuses on believing in Jesus's true identity and the reality of eternal life.

> God
> Creation
> Sovereignty and Providence
> ○ **Faith and Reason**
> Revelation and Authority
> Humanity
> Rebellion and Sin
> ○ **Covenant and Redemption**
> Community and Church
> Discipleship
> ○ **Ethics and Morality**
> Time and Eternity

Teachings about God

God is seen especially in his relationship to Jesus Christ. He is "the Father." Jesus is, in perfect complement, "the Son" (1:3). He is as well "the Christ" (2:22) who came "in the flesh" (4:2-3). The Holy Spirit has been given to believers (3:24; 4:13), and he enables believers to recognize and reject every false spirit (4:1-6).

Teachings about Humanity

First John recognizes only two categories of human beings: those who believe in Jesus Christ and all others (who belong to the spirit of the antichrist). Believers confess when they sin, but their lives are not characterized by sin (1:7-9; 5:16-18). They live in fellowship with God and with each other. Those who continue to live in sin are giving evidence that they have never known God (3:6).

Teachings about Salvation

One of the great texts about salvation is 1 John 2:2: "He himself is the atoning sacrifice for our sins, and not only for ours, but also for those of the whole world." The term "atoning sacrifice" refers to removal of divine wrath because of sin, as also in Rom. 3:25. Christ's death propitiated God's wrath not only for "our sins," referring to the people to whom John was writing, but includes people from all ethnic, economic, and social groups (Gal. 3:28; Rev. 7:9-10). The benefits of Christ's death come only to those who believe (5:13).

CHRIST IN 1 JOHN

Jesus is the Word of life who has come to earth and has been seen, heard, and touched. He reveals to us who God is and what God has done for our salvation. He came to make it possible for us to have fellowship with the Father (1:3) and to have fellowship with other believers (1:7). That fellowship is possible because Christ's blood cleanses us and takes away the sin that separates us from God (1:7).

GOD'S STORY

When the Events of This Book Happened:
Probably in the A.D. 80s
The only contemporary events the book mentions are the teachings of the heretics. These cannot be dated precisely, but the decade of the A.D. 80s seems to fit.

How 1 John Fits into God's "Story"
First John is part of "chapter 5" of God's story: God spreads the kingdom through the church. The kingdom of God is not directly mentioned. However, Jesus is referred to as "Christ" 10 times. Two of these references explicitly use "Christ" as a title rather than a name, calling on the readers to acknowledge him as "the Christ" that is, the Messiah promised by the prophets of Scripture (2:22; 5:1). As "the Christ," Jesus is the Anointed One, King over the kingdom of God. Only those who believe Jesus is the Christ receive eternal life, mentioned six times in the letter (1:2; 2:25; 3:15; 5:11,13,20).

ORIGINAL HISTORICAL SETTING

Author and Date of Writing:
John the apostle, possibly ca. A.D. 80-90
This letter is actually anonymous, but the style and approach are so much like the Fourth Gospel that the epistle and the Fourth Gospel are generally acknowledged to be written by the same person. Thus, the rejection of John's authorship of the Fourth Gospel by critical scholars also applies to this epistle. Christian tradition, however, has uniformly asserted that this author was John the apostle, which certainly fits the claim that the writer personally saw Jesus (1:1-4). (See *Author and Date of Writing* for *John* for more information.) Most scholars believe that this epistle was written somewhat after the Fourth Gospel, but it is impossible to be certain. The decade of the A.D. 80s is a good estimate.

First Audience and Destination:
Probably Christians living in Roman Asia
This letter was written to Christians (2:12-14,19; 3:1; 5:13). It makes the best sense if it is seen as addressed to the same believers, living in and around

Ephesus, who had earlier received the Fourth Gospel. (See *First Audience and Destination* for *John* for a discussion.)

Occasion

John was intimately acquainted with these believers, whom he repeatedly called "little children." He had become aware of dangerous false teachings that threatened these believers. The foundational error appears to be the belief that "matter is sinful." If this is true then (1) Jesus could not have had a material body or else he was necessarily sinful, and (2) human beings are sinful because they have material bodies (rather than because of their sinful deeds or sinful nature), which in turn leads to errors about the relationship of believers to sin. Such dualism (spirit = good; matter = evil) later developed into Gnosticism, a heresy that challenged Christianity in the second and third centuries. John did not say how he became aware of this teaching. He penned his letter, however, as the response of an aged, beloved apostle to Christians in desperate need of his advice.

 LITERARY FEATURES

Genre and Literary Style:

An epistle written in Koinē Greek

First John is the fourth of seven General Epistles in the New Testament, all of which are titled according to their author. This epistle does not have the customary features of an epistle, such as salutation, thanksgiving, or farewell. For this reason, some scholars designate 1 John as a tractate (a formal treatise rather than a pastoral letter). As with the Fourth Gospel, John wrote with a limited vocabulary and a simple style. Also, as with the Gospel, his style lent itself to developing contrasting concepts: love versus hate; light versus dark; life versus death.

Themes:

The incarnation of Christ, the messiahship of Jesus, living in light and love

The first two of these themes are doctrinal: what Christians must believe. The last theme is behavioral: how Christians are to live. John taught that true believers cannot continue to live a sinful lifestyle but must live in God's moral light and his holy love. The epistle does not teach "sinless perfection," as 3:9 and 5:18 may appear to indicate, but, rather, whoever is born of God does not continually practice sin (compare 1:8–2:2).

Book Features and Structure

The only biblical references by name to the "antichrist" are found in his epistle (and its close companion, 2 John); see 1 John 2:18,22; 4:3; 2 John 7. What is striking in John's teaching is that not only will there come a future antichrist, but that there are already many antichrists present. The essence of the "antichrist spirit" is to deny the essential character of Jesus as God incarnate, the Messiah. Thus John was more concerned about his readers firmly identifying and rejecting the antichrist spirit active in their own day than in their identifying the future (end-time) antichrist.

The letter is noted for its rambling style, which is reflective of an old saint of God with much wisdom to pass along. This, however, makes it almost impossible to generate a clear outline for the letter. In general, chapters 1–2 focus on walking in the light, while chapters 3–5 focus on living in love.

Exterior of the Church of St. John in Ephesus

2 JOHN

THE SECOND EPISTLE OF JOHN

Titled according to its author, this is the second canonical letter by John, the apostle of Jesus.

○ KEY TEXT: VERSE 8

"Watch yourselves so you don't lose what we have worked for, but that you may receive a full reward."

○ KEY TERM: "FAITHFUL"

Although the word "faithful" does not appear, this letter is in essence an encouragement to remain faithful to the truth of the gospel in the face of deceivers.

○ ONE-SENTENCE SUMMARY

Those who "remain in Christ's teaching" know the Father and the Son and will one day be fully rewarded.

Terraced houses in Ephesus, dating to 100 B.C. These structures were discovered around 1960 and are still in the process of restoration. They provide a glimpse into the lifestyle of the wealthy. These houses were two stories with a courtyard, living rooms and dining rooms on the ground floor, and bedrooms upstairs. They were heated in the winter and had both hot and cold running water.

GOD'S MESSAGE IN THE BOOK

Purpose

Second John was written to combat the same false doctrines that were written about in 1 John. In the first letter, the teachings were to be applied to a congregational setting; in the second letter they were applied to a personal family setting.

Christian Worldview Elements

This book directs attention to the worldview categories of *discipleship* and *ethics and morality*. John rejoiced about the children of a Christian woman continuing in Christian discipleship ("walking in truth"), and he strongly urged living according to the love command.

> God
> Creation
> Sovereignty and Providence
> Faith and Reason
> Revelation and Authority
> Humanity
> Rebellion and Sin
> Covenant and Redemption
> Community and Church
> ○ **Discipleship**
> ○ **Ethics and Morality**
> Time and Eternity

Teachings about God

God is the Father of Jesus and is the one who has issued commands that his children are to live by. Jesus is the Messiah, the Son of the Father, who came "in the flesh" (v. 7). The Holy Spirit is not mentioned.

Teachings about Humanity

This book shows (negatively) that many deceivers and antichrists are out to oppose God's people. It also shows (positively) the great good that one Christian ("the elect lady") can accomplish. (See also *Teachings about Humanity* for *1 Timothy*.)

Teachings about Salvation

The only teaching directly related to salvation is the crucial importance of the incarnation of the Son of God. Those who deny this doctrine are cut off from salvation (vv. 7-11). Redeemed people "walk in" or "abide in" love and truth as a way of living.

 CHRIST IN 2 JOHN

John's key concern in this letter is to affirm that Christ has come in the flesh. John warns his readers not to go beyond this teaching about Christ and not to associate with people who modify this teaching.

GOD'S STORY

When the Events of This Book Happened:
Probably in the A.D. 80s
The only contemporary events the book mentions are the teachings of the heretics. These cannot be dated precisely, but the decade of the A.D. 80s seems to fit.

How 2 John Fits into God's "Story"
Second John is part of "chapter 5" of God's story: God spreads the kingdom through the church. The kingdom of God is not directly mentioned. However, Jesus is referred to as "Christ" (Messiah) three times, who is opposed by the "antichrist" (v. 7). This implies the concept of the "kingdom of God" set in opposition to all other kingdoms, developed elsewhere in Scripture.

ORIGINAL HISTORICAL SETTING

Author and Date of Writing:
John the apostle, possibly ca. A.D. 80–90
This letter claims to be written by "the elder," who is otherwise unnamed. Some have speculated that he was an unknown Christian leader, but the style and content are so much like 1 John that these letters are acknowledged to be written by the same person. Christian tradition has uniformly asserted that this author was John the apostle. (See *Author and Date of Writing* for *John* for more information.) Most scholars believe that this epistle was written some time after the Gospel, but it is impossible to be certain. The decade of the A.D. 80s is a good estimate for the composition of this letter.

First Audience and Destination:
An unnamed Christian lady, probably living somewhere in Roman Asia
The letter was written to "the elect lady and her children." She is otherwise unknown, but she had taught her children to follow the gospel. Since John seems to have known her well ("dear lady," v. 5), she was evidently someone he had met during his ministry, which was centered in Ephesus. Some have suggested that the congregation addressed generally in 1 John was meeting in the home of "the elect lady." While 2 John certainly fits this reconstruction, there is not enough data to confirm it.

Some scholars have proposed that "the elect lady" is a figurative expression to refer to a particular congregation. This does not seem likely, because this letter is so evidently parallel to 3 John, which was written to a named individual.

Occasion
John knew this lady well. He was prompted to write because he had recently become aware of the excellent Christian reputation of her children (v. 4). They

had apparently related to him facts about a heresy they had faced, identical to the false doctrine facing the recipients of his first epistle. (See *Occasion* for *1 John*.) He penned this letter as a personal note to advise his friend about the heresy and to urge her to continue in Christian love.

 ## LITERARY FEATURES

Genre and Literary Style:
A brief epistle written in Koinē *Greek*
Second John is the fifth of seven General Epistles in the New Testament, all of which are titled according to their author. One of the usual features of an epistle (thanksgiving) is missing. There is a salutation (vv. 1-3), body (vv. 4-11), and farewell (vv. 12-13). This is a pastoral letter, driven by the occasion and needs of the recipient, rather than a tractate (a formal treatise). The Greek style is identical to that of 1 John.

Themes:
The incarnation of Christ; living in truth
As is universal in Scripture, truth in doctrine and truth in living go hand in hand. This little note shows that those who deny Christ's incarnation cannot possibly live faithful lives.

Book Features and Structure
This is the second-shortest book in the New Testament, weighing in with only 244 words in the original and 13 verses. (The shortest is 3 John with 219 words and 13 verses.) The body of the letter has two sections. First is John's positive exhortation to walk in Christ's commandments (through v. 6). Second is John's warning about deceivers (from v. 7 to the end).

3 JOHN
THE THIRD EPISTLE OF JOHN

Titled according to its author, this is the third canonical letter by John, the apostle of Jesus.

○ KEY TEXT: VERSE 8

"Therefore, we ought to support such people so that we can be coworkers with the truth."

○ KEY TERM: "TRUTH"

The word "truth" (Greek, *alētheia*) is used five times. Christians are called on to be committed to "the truth"—and to show hospitality to Christian leaders involved in ministering the truth.

○ ONE-SENTENCE SUMMARY

Christians are to recognize and to work for the truth of the gospel, and one way they do this is to show hospitality to Christian ministers who are hard at work.

The tomb of St. John the Apostle in the Basilica of St. John, Ephesus, Turkey

GOD'S MESSAGE IN THE BOOK

Purpose

Third John was written mainly to advise Gaius about his responsibility to receive warmly a group of traveling ministers. Gaius was also warned to beware of a troublemaker (Diotrephes) and to welcome a newcomer (Demetrius).

Christian Worldview Elements

This book directs attention to the worldview categories of *community and church* and *discipleship*. It provides one of the last pictures in the epistles about congregational life and how believers ought to live.

God
Creation
Sovereignty and Providence
Faith and Reason
Revelation and Authority
Humanity
Rebellion and Sin
Covenant and Redemption
○ **Community and Church**
○ **Discipleship**
Ethics and Morality
Time and Eternity

Teachings about God

God is mentioned three times (vv. 6,11) as the source of good, not evil, who expects his people to live worthy of him. The essence of God's glory is summarized by calling him "the Name." He is not called Father (in contrast to the first two epistles of John). This is the only New Testament book that does not directly mention Jesus Christ or the Holy Spirit.

Teachings about Humanity

This letter is full of contrasts. On one hand, there are several shining examples of what people committed to the truth can accomplish (Gaius, Demetrius, John himself, the traveling ministers). On the other hand, Diotrephes is a negative example of someone who obstructs the truth. (See also *Teachings about Humanity* for *1 Timothy*.)

Teachings about Salvation

Teaching about salvation is found indirectly by John's constant use of "the truth" (vv. 1,3,4,8,12). "The truth" is evidently his paraphrase for "the gospel of Jesus Christ," thought of in broad terms. This truth is nowhere defined, but its importance is evident.

CHRIST IN 3 JOHN

John describes a man named Diotrephes who had to be first in everything. This man is the opposite of Christ who humbled himself, became a slave, and suffered an ignominious death. John then urges his readers not to imitate evil but imitate good. Christ is the supreme example of goodness.

GOD'S STORY

When the Events of This Book Happened:
Probably in the A.D. 80s

The contemporary events the book mentions are the travels of the Christian ministers and the activities of certain individuals. These cannot be dated precisely, but the decade of the A.D. 80s seems to fit.

How 3 John Fits into God's "Story"

Third John is part of "chapter 5" of God's story: God spreads the kingdom through the church. The kingdom of God is not directly mentioned. However, "church" (Greek, *ekklēsia*) appears three times (vv. 6,9,10), the only direct references to church in John's letters. Since in the present age local congregations of Christians are manifestations of God's kingdom, the health of churches is of direct concern to the growth of the kingdom.

ORIGINAL HISTORICAL SETTING

Author and Date of Writing:
John the apostle, possibly ca. A.D. 80–90

See *Author and Date of Writing* for *2 John*.

First Audience and Destination:
Gaius, a Christian living in Roman Asia

Gaius is known only through this letter. He was a fine Christian whom John loved and knew well ("dear friend," v. 5). He probably had leadership responsibility in the congregation that John mentioned in his letter. Where he lived is not known, but it was probably near Ephesus, the place where John lived during his last years.

Occasion

The occasion for this letter is entirely different from the occasion for 1 and 2 John. John had received a report from traveling Christian ministers, who had evidently gone out with his blessing (vv. 3,7). They had told him about Gaius's good ministry and his hospitality to them (v. 5). Yet they reported that Gaius had a question about whether giving such a warm welcome was actually the right thing to do.

Thus John wrote his friend a short note. In it he commended the practice of showing hospitality for the sake of the gospel. Along the way, he warned about the troublemaker Diotrephes, who had rejected the traveling ministers (vv. 9-10). He also endorsed Demetrius, who was perhaps the letter carrier (v. 12).

LITERARY FEATURES

Genre and Literary Style:
A brief epistle written in Koinē *Greek*

Third John is the sixth of seven General Epistles in the New Testament, all of which are titled according to their author. This letter has all four standard parts of a first-century epistle: salutation (v. 1); thanksgiving (in this letter, a brief petition, v. 2); main body (vv. 3-12); farewell (vv. 13-14). Third John is a pastoral letter, driven by the occasion and needs of the recipient, rather than a tractate (a formal treatise). The Greek style is identical to that of 1 John.

Themes:
Welcoming those with the truth, rejecting those without the truth

Since the definition of truth is assumed in this book, its themes are mainly practical. On one hand, ministers of truth are to be recognized and helped whenever possible. On the other hand, those who hinder the truth, especially in a local church, are to be noted and rejected.

Book Features and Structure

This is the shortest book in the New Testament with 219 words in Greek and 13 verses. It is important for the incidental way in which John gave information about his sense of responsibility as an apostle. After more than 50 years of ministry, he was still in the business of giving pastoral care (v. 5) and good advice (v. 12). Even more important was his deliberate awareness that any letter he wrote should be considered authoritative (vv. 9-10). This concept became significant in the second through the fourth centuries when the New Testament canon was being discussed and developed.

The body of the letter has two sections. First is John's positive exhortation to welcome those with the truth (through v. 8). Second is John's warning to those who hinder truth (from v. 9 to the end).

JUDE
THE EPISTLE OF JUDE

This letter is titled according to its author, Jude, who was probably the half brother of Jesus.

○ KEY TEXT: VERSE 3

"Dear friends, although I was eager to write you about the salvation we share, I found it necessary to write, appealing to you to contend for the faith that was delivered to the saints once for all."

○ KEY TERM: "CONTEND"

This letter is a reminder that Christians are soldiers in a spiritual warfare. They must "contend" or continue the fight to maintain the truth of the gospel.

○ ONE-SENTENCE SUMMARY

Christians must defend the faith against false teachings and false teachers, and at the same time they must build up their own faith in Christ.

Jude described the apostates as "wild waves of the sea, foaming up their shameful deeds" (Jude 13).

GOD'S MESSAGE IN THE BOOK

Purpose

Jude was written to condemn false teachers who were trying to persuade Christians that they were free to sin since they had been forgiven and were under God's grace. Jude wanted his readers to oppose this teaching with the truth about God's grace.

Christian Worldview Elements

This book focuses on the worldview categories of *revelation and authority* and *ethics and morality*. It especially emphasizes that God's revealed truth should not be meddled with or changed.

> God
> Creation
> Sovereignty and Providence
> Faith and Reason
> ○ **Revelation and Authority**
> Humanity
> Rebellion and Sin
> Covenant and Redemption
> Community and Church
> Discipleship
> ○ **Ethics and Morality**
> Time and Eternity

Teachings about God

God is referred to as Father, Savior, and Lord (vv. 1,9,25). Jesus (v. 5) saved a people out of Egypt. The grace of God is the attribute that comes to the fore in this book (v. 4). Jesus is also called Lord, and he is the one who keeps his people and brings them to eternal life (vv. 1,21,25). The Spirit, never given to those who reject the truth, enables the prayers of the saints (vv. 19-20).

Teachings about Humanity

Jude shows the great evil of those who are enslaved by falsehood: "wild waves of the sea, foaming up their shameful deeds; wandering stars for whom the blackness of darkness is reserved forever" (v. 13). On the other hand, redeemed humanity looks forward to everlasting joy: "Now to him who is able to protect you from stumbling and to make you stand in the presence of his glory, without blemish and with great joy" (v. 24).

Teachings about Salvation

Jude had intended to write about the "the salvation we share" as believers, but he wrote instead about false teachers (vv. 3-4). He refers to God as "Savior" (v. 25). Verse 24 makes it clear that salvation is God's doing from start to finish (see also v. 1).

 CHRIST IN JUDE

Jude looks to the day when Jesus will reward his followers. He looks from the present perspective, talking about believers being kept for Jesus (v. 1). He knows eternal life is based on Jesus's mercy (v. 21).

GOD'S STORY

When the Events of This Book Happened:
Probably in the A.D. 60s

The only contemporary events the book mentions are the coming of false teachers. These cannot be dated precisely, but the decade of the A.D. 60s seems to fit.

How Jude Fits into God's "Story"

Jude is part of "chapter 5" of God's story: God spreads the kingdom through the church. The kingdom of God is not directly mentioned. Yet Jude shows great awareness of the history of God's kingdom through time by mentioning a number of men (and angels) involved in God's kingdom activities from ancient times: Enoch, Moses, Michael. He also mentions those opposed to God's kingdom: Cain, Balaam, Korah, and the devil. These references show that there have been opposing camps, from the beginning until Jude's time, and on until God's glory is fully manifested.

ORIGINAL HISTORICAL SETTING

Author and Date of Writing:
Jude, perhaps in the A.D. 60s

The author was "Jude, a servant of Jesus Christ, and a brother of James" (v. 1). Jude is the English translation of the Hebrew name "Judah." (The name "Judas" is identical, *Ioudas* in Greek, but most English translators reserve "Judas" for Jesus's betrayer because of the negative connotations of that name.) There were several Judes in the New Testament, but the only one who was James's brother was also the brother of Jesus (Matt. 13:55). He was the son of Mary and Joseph, and, like all Jesus's brothers, had not believed in Jesus until after the resurrection (Acts 1:14). Little is known about him as a Christian leader beyond his authorship of this letter. The decade of the A.D. 60s fits because of the connection of this epistle with 2 Peter. (See *Occasion*, below.)

First Audience and Destination:
Believers living in an unknown location

This letter contains no specific information that permits identification of the first audience. They were Christians whom Jude knew well ("dear friends," v. 3) and wanted to warn. His quotation of Jewish sources suggests that the recipients were Jewish, but beyond that nothing can be determined.

Occasion

Jude had intended to write on one subject but changed his mind when he learned about dangerous false teachers. They had already infiltrated the congregation, and Jude heaped condemnation on them (v. 13). Their problem was that they were "turning the grace of our God into sensuality" (v. 4). This evidently referred to a libertine understanding that God's grace entitles believers to do whatever they want morally without reference to God's commandments. The false teachers were motivated by their own sensual lust and what they perceived as their own advantage (v. 16). Thus Jude wrote this letter of warning. Not only did he attack falsehood; he also encouraged these believers to stay true to the faith and to reach out compassionately to those who were tempted to compromise with the false teachers (vv. 20-22).

 LITERARY FEATURES

Genre and Literary Style:
An epistle written in **Koinē** *Greek*

Jude is the last of seven General Epistles in the New Testament, all of which are titled according to their author. One of the usual features of an epistle (thanksgiving) is missing, although there is a salutation (vv. 1-2), body (vv. 3-23), and a farewell (in this letter, a doxology, vv. 24-25). Jude is a pastoral letter, driven by the occasion and needs of the recipients, rather than a tractate (a formal treatise). The Greek style is awkward and is hard to read. (The repetition of the word "ungodly" in v. 15 is an example of the stylistic difficulty.)

Jude quoted noncanonical Jewish sources to back up his arguments, both The *Assumption of Moses* (v. 9) and *1 Enoch* (vv. 14-15). He did not call them Scripture or imply that they were inspired. Rather, he used them as sources of information. The apostle Paul sometimes used noncanonical sources as well (Acts 17:28; 1 Cor. 15:33; 2 Tim. 3:8; Titus 1:12).

Themes:
Contending for the faith, identifying and rejecting what is ungodly

The two themes are complementary. To do one is necessarily to do the other. Forms of the concept of ungodliness (Greek, *asebeia*) are used five times (vv. 15,18). This is the opposite of godliness (Greek, *eusebeia*), the *Key Term* for *1 Timothy*.

Book Features and Structure

There is a striking parallel between this letter and 2 Peter 2, both in content and order of presentation. The following may be cited:

- Sinning angels now held captive by God (2 Pet. 2:4; Jude 6)
- Divine destruction of Sodom and Gomorrah (2 Pet. 2:6; Jude 7)
- False teachers who slander heavenly beings (2 Pet. 2:10; Jude 8)
- Balaam as a false prophet (2 Pet. 2:15; Jude 11)
- False teachers destined for blackest darkness (2 Pet. 2:17; Jude 13)

It is impossible to determine whether Peter used Jude as a source, Jude borrowed from Peter, or whether both adapted a common (but now lost) source. Most scholars accept the first alternative, because it seems more likely that a longer letter (2 Peter) would incorporate much of a shorter letter (Jude). (The literary relationship between 2 Peter and Jude is parallel to the literary relationship between Matthew, Mark, and Luke.)

The body of this epistle has two sections. First is Jude's warning about false teachers (through v. 16). Second is Jude's encouragement to pursue the truth (from v. 17 to the end).

Panorama of Patmos, Greece. In the foreground are buildings of the Monastery of Saint John the Theologian. In the background: islands of Ikaria and Fourni.

REVELATION
THE APOCALYPSE

The first word in the Greek text of this book is *apokalypsis*, which means "revelation" or "unveiling." Although some English Bibles title it "The Revelation of John," the work is manifestly a revelation to John by Jesus Christ.

⊙ KEY TEXT: 1:7

"Look, he is coming with the clouds, and every eye will see him, even those who pierced him. And all the tribes of the earth will mourn over him. So it is to be. Amen."

⊙ KEY TERM: "PROPHECY"

This book self-consciously calls itself a prophecy at both its beginning and its end (1:3; 22:18-19). It is the only New Testament book that is essentially prophetic.

⊙ ONE-SENTENCE SUMMARY

Jesus, the Lord of history, will return to earth, destroy all evil and all opposition to him, and bring the kingdom of God to its glorious culmination.

GOD'S MESSAGE IN THE BOOK

Purpose

This prophetic book originally intended to teach that faithfulness to Jesus ultimately triumphs over all the evils of this world and that Jesus will return to earth as King and Lamb-Bridegroom. God's people who read and study Revelation today should view it with this original purpose in mind.

Christian Worldview Elements

Revelation deals particularly with the worldview categories of *rebellion and sin*; *ethics and morality*; and *time and eternity*. No Bible book more fully teaches how God is moving time, history, and all creation to the goal he has determined.

God
Creation
Sovereignty and Providence
Faith and Reason
Revelation and Authority
Humanity
⊙ **Rebellion and Sin**
Covenant and Redemption
Community and Church
Discipleship
⊙ **Ethics and Morality**
⊙ **Time and Eternity**

Teachings about God

Revelation teaches the supremacy and glory of God in all things. God is the primary mover who will bring about the return of Christ and the end of the world. The righteous wrath of a holy God is fully displayed in Revelation.

John the Theologian on the Island of Patmos by Andrei Mironov

The book teaches about the Trinity and contributes greatly to an understanding of the deity of Christ.

Teachings about Humanity

Revelation shows the sinfulness of humans in stark terms. There are only two kinds of people in Revelation: those who follow the Lamb (and bear his special mark) and those who follow the beast (and bear his mark). Those who follow the Lamb are given unimaginably great blessings, but they are a minority. The majority that follows evil is destined for eternal damnation.

Teachings about Salvation

Salvation from sin in Revelation is presented mainly in terms of something God purchased through the death of the Lamb (the first coming of Christ). Those who are saved oppose evil "by the blood of the Lamb and by the word of their testimony; for they did not love their lives to the point of death" (12:11). Final salvation after the resurrection is presented mainly in terms of "the holy city, the new Jerusalem" (21:2).

 CHRIST IN REVELATION

Christ is the Alpha and the Omega, the first and the last, the one who was coming, is coming, and will come. When he appeared to John on Patmos, the sight was so overwhelming, John fell at his feet like a dead man. Jesus told him not to be afraid but to write down the things he would show him, the things that will take place.

 GOD'S STORY

When the Events of This Book Happened:

From creation to consummation, but particularly the time of the consummation

Revelation zigzags through time. Although some chronological sequences seem reasonably clear, the visions of the book were not meant to form a seamless story. Revelation includes events from the the foundation of the earth (17:8) and the fall of Satan (12:4) to the first century A.D. (chaps. 2–3) to the new heavens and new earth (chaps. 21–22). In general, the events through chapter 6 focus on the period up to the "great tribulation," while the events described beginning with chapter 7 seem to belong to the end-time scenario. Those who have a premillennial perspective see the Great Tribulation as an end-time period, but amillennials see it as a time of suffering beginning with the cross and intensifying in the end-times.

John writes Revelation encouraging Christians to remain faithful.

**THE SEVEN CHURCHES
OF REVELATION**
- City
- Cities of the Seven Churches
— Major road

How Revelation Fits into God's "Story"

Revelation tells "chapter 6"—the last chapter—of God's story: God consummates redemption and confirms his eternal kingdom. The kingdom theme can hardly be missed. Christ is the victorious King wearing many diadems. He comes and judges the world's people at the end. One of the great announcements in Revelation, near the center of the book is, "The kingdom of the world has become the kingdom of our Lord and of his Christ, and he will reign forever and ever" (11:15). Revelation shows how the plan of God to bless all nations through the covenant he began with Abraham (Gen. 12) will reach final fulfillment. The kingdom of God inaugurated with Jesus's first coming will be consummated at his second coming.

 ORIGINAL HISTORICAL SETTING

Author and Date of Writing:
The apostle John, ca. A.D. 95

The book was written by John. He had great authority, even from his place of banishment, the tiny island of Patmos some 35 miles out in the Aegean Sea. Most (but not all) early Christian references to the authorship of Revelation affirmed that this was Jesus's apostle of that name. (See *Author and Date of Writing* for *John* for more information.) Tradition records that John had a long and successful ministry in and around the city of Ephesus during his later life. Some scholars believe the author of Revelation was some other (unknown) John. There is no good reason, however, to deny that the author was indeed the apostle—also the composer of the Fourth Gospel and three epistles.

Revelation originated during a time of Roman persecution of Christians. Some have suggested the last days of Emperor Nero (ruled A.D. 54–68) as the time of composition. The severity of the persecution (as well as the spiritual decline of the churches in Rev. 2–3) suggests a later date to most scholars. The last years of Domitian (ruled A.D. 81–96) are a more likely date for the origin of this book. If this is so, Revelation was the last book of the New Testament to be written.

First Audience and Destination:
Persecuted Christians living in seven cities in the Roman province of Asia

The recipients and destination of Revelation were not John's choice. He was following divine orders. This is explicit in 1:10-11: "I was in the Spirit on the Lord's day, and I heard a loud voice behind me like a trumpet saying, 'Write on a scroll what you see and send it to the seven churches: Ephesus, Smyrna, Pergamum, Thyatira, Sardis, Philadelphia, and Laodicea.'" The list follows the order the letter carrier traveled after arriving on the mainland from Patmos.

Occasion

John explained what prompted him to write. While he was exiled on Patmos, the exalted Lord appeared to him and gave him visions that he was instructed to write down. The recipients were Christians living through vicious persecution. All Bible books are inspired by God, but this one, more than any other, bears a sense of divine dictation.

LITERARY FEATURES

Genre and Literary Style:
A prophecy composed in Koinē *Greek*

Some students of Revelation have classed Revelation as apocalyptic literature. This kind of writing, then popular among Jews, had a number of features: (1) the claim to originate from God through a mediating being; (2) the use of symbolic creatures and actions; (3) conflict between this evil age and the coming age. However, Revelation lacks certain other apocalyptic features: (1) claim to be written by a famous Old Testament character; (2) extensive angelic interpretation; (3) belief that the Messiah was still future.

Revelation is better seen as a prophecy, a message to God's people exhorting them to remain faithful to him. Unlike the apocalyptic literature, Revelation contains serious calls for God's people to repent of sin. Like Isaiah and Jeremiah, it predicts both near and remote future events. The apocalyptic elements are secondary to the book's prophetic message.

The Greek style of Revelation is simple. It is more like the Greek of the Fourth Gospel and the three epistles of John than any other part of the New Testament. The book has a number of grammatical peculiarities that make its Greek unusual in places. This may be accounted for by either (1) the author's loss (or change) of a secretary or (2) the author's eagerness to write down his experiences, causing him to write in haste.

Themes:
Christ as slaughtered Lamb and conquering King, the second coming, God's sovereignty in history, God's wrath against sin, followers of Jesus overcoming

Revelation's portraits of Jesus show him as a slaughtered Lamb, yet occupying heaven's throne. Further, he is the conquering King who will judge all the world. Christ's return is portrayed in glorious but highly symbolic language. God is clearly in charge of everything that happens, even though he allows evil to have temporary triumphs. Ultimately his wrath against sin is fully poured out. In the face of this, followers of the Lamb are challenged to be faithful overcomers.

Book Features and Structure

Revelation is filled with references to the Old Testament, but John rarely if ever quoted it directly. Most of the book is a prophecy, but there are a number of other literary elements. The prologue and epilogue are similar to the New Testament Epistles. The seven short letters to individual churches (chaps. 2–3) are clearly epistle-like. Several of the chants or songs are poetry, sometimes like the great poetry of the Old Testament.

Revelation is organized into four great visions, of which the second is the longest. The beginning of each vision is announced with the words "in the Spirit" (1:10; 4:2; 17:3; 21:10), meaning, "I had a new vision brought about by the Spirit."

PHOTO AND ART CREDITS

B&H Publishing Group is grateful to the following persons and institutions for use of the graphics in the *Ultimate Bible Guide Handbook*. Where we have inadvertently failed to give proper credit for any graphic used in the *Handbook*, please contact us (*bhcustomerservice@lifeway.com*) and we will make the required correction on the next printing.

PHOTOGRAPHS
PHOTOGRAPHERS

Biblical Illustrator (Brent Bruce, photographer), Nashville, Tennessee: p. 250 (Israel Museum/Jerusalem).
Biblical Illustrator (Bob Schatz, photographer), Nashville, Tennessee: p. 45.
Biblical Illustrator (Ken Touchton, photographer), Nashville, Tennessee: p. 30.
Biblical Illustrator (Jerry Vardaman, photographer), Nashville, Tennessee: p. 49.
Illustrated World of the Bible Library: p. 200.
iStock: pp. 144 (digitalskillet), 183 (pawopa3336), 208 (traveler 1116), 221 (lekavicius), 307 (swissmediavision), 361 (Andy445).
Wikimedia Commons: pp. iii, middle (History/Carnegie), 8 (H. Grobe), 9 (Studio 31), 22 (walknboston), 25 (Yoav Dothan/ Samuel and Saidye Bronfman Archaeology Wing, Israel Museum, Jerusalem), 43 (Eli Zahavi), 55 (Wilson44691), 76 (David Castor), 91 (Mike Peel/British Museum, London), 93 (Institute for the Study of the Ancient World), 101 (Masoudkhalife), 111 (Bernard Gagnon), 115 (Lee Sakal/ Pikiwiki Israel) , 117 (I.o.Tangelini), 121 (Lewis Clarke), 131 (Ian Poellet), 135 (Fernando Espi), 136 (artemtation), 147 (Wilson44691), 149 (Piotrus), 157 (Shlomi Kakon), 160 (Jasmine N. Walthall, U.S. Army), 180 (Aleijadinho [1730/1738-1814]/ Luis Rizo, photographer), 191 (filmrausch.com), 196 (British Museum/ William Henry Goodyear, *A History of Art: For Classes, Art-Students, and Tourists in Europe*, A. S. Barnes & Company, New York, 1889, p. 133), 197 (Sargis Babayan), 202 (Neptuul), 209 (Austin Henry Layard [1817-1894], *The Nineveh Court in the Crystal Palace*), 214 (P. Lemeiro/The Cathedral of Santiago de Compostela, Galicia, Spain), 215 (Bridget 8149/Wirth Gallery of the Middle East at the Royal Ontario Museum, Toronto), 220 (*The Story of the Bible from Genesis to Revelation*), 223 (Iehava arad/PikiWiki Israel), 226 (ArionEstar), 227 (Diego Delso), 236 (Stefan Aßmann), 239 (Dina Melamed), 241 (Tjibbe), 245 (Itamar Grinberg/israeltourism), 257 (DrusMAX), 258 (WomEOS), 289 (Elie plus), 293 (Vancouverquadra), 295 (Jean Housen), 298 (Carole Raddato), 299 (NASA), 301 (©Frank van Mierlo), 305 (Adrian Farwell), 311 (Jordan Klein), 316 (Marsyas), 317 (Carole Raddato), 324 (European Southern Observatory/ Yuri Beletsky), 328 (Snowdog), 329 (JFKennedy), 334 (Colin W.), 336 (Hermann Hammer), 346 (Lalupa), 347 (Barbaking), 352 (Jerzy Strzelecki), 353 (Jebulon), 357 (Pascal Radigue), 367 (Marek Bednarz), 373 (Brocken

Inaglory), 385 (Bernard Gagnon), 390 (© José Luiz Bernardes Ribeiro), 391 (Ronan Reinhart), 395 (Bernard Gagnon), 399 (Archangel12), 404 (Tomisti).

ILLUSTRATIONS AND RECONSTRUCTIONS
ILLUSTRATORS

Biblical Illustrator, Linden Artists: p. 16.

Goolsby, Abe, Principal, Officina Abrahae, Nashville, TN: pp. 1, 23, 84, 86, 99, 146,165, 168, 217, 262, 284.

Latta, Bill, Latta Art Services, Mt. Juliet, TN: p. 246.

PAINTINGS
ARTISTS

Anonymous (http://www.neumeister.com), p. 71.

Bacot, Edmond (Christie's), p. iii, top left.

Berchem, Nicolaes Pieterszoon (Musée d'art et d'industrie de Saint-Étienne, Saint-Étienne, France), p. 342.

Blake, William (The Morgan Library and Museum, New York), p. 109.

Bloch, Carl Heinrich (Frederiksburg Palace, Copenhagen), p. 260.

Da Brescia, Il Moretto (Church of Saint John Evangelist, Brescia, Italy), p.173.

De Favray, Antoine (Wellcome Images), p. 366.

De Voss, Cornelis (Kunsthistorisches Museum, Vienna), p. 68.

Di Buoninsegna, Duccio (The National Gallery, London), p. 379.

Doré,Gustave (Doré's English Bible), pp. 98, 186.

Fugel, Gebhard, p. 161.

Ge, Nikolai (http://www.picture.art-catalog.ru), p.275.

Gebler, Otto (Hampel Auctions, Munich), p. 133.

Healy, George Peter Alexander (The White House Historical Association), p. iii, lower.

Kozenitzky, Lidia, p. 13.

Kramskoi, Ivan (Tretyakov Gallery, Moscow), p. 253.

Leroy, Paul Alexander (Odessa Museum of Western and Oriental Art, Odessa, Ukraine), p. 103.

Lievens, Jan (North Carolina Museum of Art, Raleigh, NC), 107.

Lievens, Jan (Nationalmuseum, Stockholm), p. 322.

Lilien, Ephraim Moses, p. 126.

Linnell, John (Cleveland Museum of Art/Wmpearl), p. 378.

Martin, John (Yale Center for British Art, New Haven), p. 267.

Mayno, Juan Bautista (Prado Museum, Madrid), p. 278.

Michelangelo (Sistine Chapel, Vatican City, Rome), pp. 140, 234.

Mironov, Andrei, pp. 256, 265, 272, 384, 406.

Pelz, George A. (*Home Talks out of the Wonderful Book*/Library of Congress, Washington D.C.), p. 114.

Platzer, Johann Georg (http://www.dorotheum.com), 269.

Rembrandt (Rijksmuseum, Amsterdam), p. 154.

Rembrandt (The National Gallery, London), p. 171.

Rembrandt (Hamburger Kunsthallen, Hamburg),p. 264.

Rembrandt (Widener Collection, National Gallery of Art, Washington, D.C.),
   p. 288.
Renoir, Pierre-Auguste (The Barnes Foundation, Philadelphia), p. 127
Roberts, David (Colored Lithograph by Louis Haghe), pp. 28,39,203.
Siberdt, Eugène (Mayfair Gallery Limited, London), p. 63.
Styka, Jan (Private Collection/MOtty), p. 291.
Thoma, Hans (The Städel Museum, Frankfurt), p. 118.
Von Carolsfeld, Julius Schnorr (National Gallery, Trafalgar Square, London),
   p. 51.
West, Benjamin (Art Gallery of New South Wales, Sydney), p. 36.
Wildens, Jan (The State Hermitage Museum, Saint Petersburg, Russia), p. 268.